PAST AND PRESENT

PAST AND PRESENT

THE CONTINUITY OF CLASSICAL MYTHS

MEYER REINHOLD

DRAWINGS BY ANNA HELD AUDETTE

HAKKERT   TORONTO 1972

Drawings by Anna Held Audette

Set in Aldine Roman
by A.M. Hakkert Ltd.

Printed in The United States of America

Standard Book Numbers
Cloth: 88866-508-3
Paper: 88866-509-1

Library of Congress Catalogue Card Number
72-78016

A.M. Hakkert Ltd.
554 Spadina Crescent
Toronto 179, Canada

Ye kindly gods! Poor is he who knows you not. In his coarse breast discord never rests, and his world is all darkness, and no joy, no song thrives for him.

Only you, with your eternal youth, nourish in hearts that love you a child's wonder, and amid cares and doubts never allow genius to despair.

From Friedrich Hölderlin's
poem "The Gods," 1800

O antique fables! beautiful and bright,
And joyous with the joyous youth of yore;
O antique fables! for a little light
Of that which shineth in you evermore,
To cleanse the dimness from our weary eyes,
And bathe our old world with a new surprise
Of golden dawn entrancing sea and shore.

From James Thomson's
poem "Proem," 1884

Myths have no life of themselves. They wait for us to give them body. Let but one person in the world respond to their call, they offer us their vitality unimpaired.

From Albert Camus' essay
"Prometheus in Hell," 1946

A NOTE ON THE PRONUNCIATION OF NAMES

Most of the names in the classical myths are Greek ones. To transliterate these names into our alphabet would impose an unprofitable burden on the student, for it has been traditional since the Renaissance to employ the spellings used by the Romans. It is therefore most practical to use the English forms of the Latinized equivalents of the Greek names. Even so, complete consistency is not attainable.

The simplest rule is to pronounce names of mythical personalities as if they were English words. There are, however, no silent letters in Greek or Latin; thus there are as many syllables in a word as vowels or diphthongs. E.g., the name Io has two syllables; Odysseus three; Antigone and Nausicaä four. The diphthongs ae and oe (or oi) are pronounced like ē (as in bee); ei as ī (as in ice). The combination ch is always to be pronounced as k (e.g., Achilles). The basic rules for accentuation are the following: the last syllable is never accented; the accent falls either on the next to the last syllable (penult) or the second from the last (antepenult). Thus the proper accent on words of three or more syllables is not obvious but must be learned. A complete alphabetical list of names in this text with their proper accents indicated will be found in the Index.

One caution is necessary. English rules of accentuation sometimes affect Greek and Latin names. For example, such famous names as Daedalus, Oedipus, and Aeschylus are pronounced either Dedalus or Dēdalus, Edipus or Ēdipus, Eschylus or Ēschylus.

PREFACE

The justification for making available the study of classical mythology to college students in our times lies in its utility for their lives. Judgments on the priorities in pertinence of the various fields of study will differ, but the continuous life and vitality of the Greek and Roman myths in the culture of the Western world are not debatable. Yet the study of mythology will be valued only to the extent that it enlarges students' appreciation of art and literature, and their understanding of their own culture and of themselves.

The general student, for whom this textbook has been written, will not profit by the mere narration of the mythic tales, however indispensable the learning of the stories may be in this study. Nor is there any place in such an approach to mythology for learned commentaries of interest to the specialist or students of classical literature and civilization. In the exploration of classical myths, illumination comes from the constant discovery that many of the aspirations and dilemmas of man today were already known thousands of years ago. In this connection the study of the nature and meaning of mythmaking and mythic thinking in early civilization will guide students to an understanding of man's early intellectual history and value systems. Moreover, for the last 600 years the heritage of classical myths in continental European, British, and American literature and art has been so massive that knowledge of these tales is well-nigh indispensable for their appreciation. Finally, the vitality of the classical myths in the Twentieth Century in many areas makes knowledge of them a tool for expansion of understanding of our own culture.

The varied approaches and emphases given to the study of mythology in this text are designed to allow the special interests of individual students freer rein. It should be pointed out that least attention has been devoted in this volume to artistic and musical representations of mythical subjects. In the cases of works of sculpture and painting, in particular, it is anticipated that teachers using this book will want to employ such visual aids in their classrooms and lecture halls. The problems of exposing students to operas, ballets, and oratorios inspired by classical myths are more formidable, though such experiences contribute to enlarging the student's knowledge and appreciation of mythology.

It will be helpful also to indicate what this textbook on classical mythology is not intended to accomplish. It is not designed as an introduction to Greek and Roman literature, though knowledge of the myths is indispensable for reading classical literature. Many students will undoubtedly be attracted to the reading of the Greco-Roman classics when equipped with a solid background in myths, which are the inspiration of so many of these works. Nor is this book designed as an introduction to Greek and Roman culture, nor as a systematic study of the ancient religions. Though some attention to Greek and Roman religion is unavoidable, since there were many myths of the Greek and Roman gods, and the gods were often involved in the myths of human heroes and heroines, this subject will be touched upon only to clarify myths. The reader should also not expect either a full-scale treatise on mythology nor an exhaustive encyclopedia on the subject. Every effort has been made to select from the vast body of ancient myths those stories that are most productive in stimulating thought, imagination, and creativity, as well as those that have been most influential in moulding later literature and art.

My thanks are due to several colleagues who have read portions of the first draft and made helpful suggestions: Charles F. Saylor, Theodore A. Tarkow, and Ronnie C. Barnes.

Columbia, Missouri   *Meyer Reinhold*
August 1971

CONTENTS

DRAWINGS

PAST AND PRESENT

I

THE CLASSICAL MYTHS AROUND US

Only about fifty centuries separate us from the origins of human civilization — some 150 generations, a minute fraction of the time mankind has inhabited the earth. Despite countless changes in human society, slow or cataclysmic and revolutionary, there is a bedrock of continuity made up of survivals from man's early civilization that, because of their utility and vitality, have come down to us in the Twentieth Century. Beginning with the first civilized communities established in the fertile river valleys of Mesopotamia and Egypt about 3000 B.C., and continuing with the diffusion of culture throughout the Near East and the lands around the Aegean Sea in the eastern part of the Mediterranean to the end of the Bronze Age, about 1000 B.C., an astonishing number of inventions and discoveries were made, and systems of thought, belief and values created that still affect our lives today.

The basic nature and durability of these innovations make this period one of the most remarkable in mankind's history. This innovative time produced such great advances as systems of writing (in particular, the alphabet), writing materials, the calendar, urbanization, navigation, irrigation, the wheel, number systems, creative literature, law codes, and the rules and procedures of international diplomacy. The continuity between mankind's culture in the first 2000 years or so of civilized life and ourselves is manifest also in another major contribution: a body of myths and folktales which incorporate much of the wisdom and values and many of the achievements, dilemmas and anxieties of early civilized man. Many of these imaginative stories still retain power to delight us, to charm our attention, illuminate our thinking, and inspire us to adapt them to our own aspirations and dilemmas. Of all these myths created in the Bronze Age, the most lasting, plastic, and influential have been those handed down to us by the ancient Greeks.

Every region, every community, every social group of the ancient world possessed its own peculiar local myths, folktales and legends. But from time immemorial a considerable number of these narratives were diffused over wide areas because they were relevant not only to a specific group but were structured upon fundamental and universal aspects of human nature and existence. Imaginative tales embodying basic situations, of brother and brother, brother and sister, son and father, son and mother, man and the gods, man and animals, man and natural phenomena, and achievements of remarkable men and women, were told, retold, handed on, instinctively borrowed, and adapted to new environments with necessary changes in names and details. These stories became the universal possession and the common heritage of the international culture of the eastern Mediterranean in the second millenium B.C., particularly in the area around the Aegean Sea.

When the people who were to become the Greeks of historic times (Hellenes as they called themselves) invaded this Aegean culture area from somewhere in mideastern Europe around 2000 B.C., they brought with them their own religious beliefs and practices, as well as their own mythic and folkloric traditions. The interplay of this immigrant body of belief and story with existing prehellenic practices and traditions, fired by the humanistic perspectives and the remarkable creative imagination of the Greek people, produced in time an outpouring of myths unparalleled in any other culture of mankind in their volume, diversity, charm, lucidity, and continuing appeal. These Greek myths were then gradually diffused and accepted throughout the ancient world wherever Hellenic influence penetrated, from as far east as India (and thence to China) to the ends of Europe in the West.

Eagerly absorbed by the Romans, who had relatively few myths of their own, the mythology of the Greeks lived on in literature and art for many centuries after the eclipse of Greek political importance. When the Roman Empire fell, the classical myths survived into the Middle Ages, for, despite their pagan character, they were not suppressed by the Christians but rather adapted by them to new purposes and interpretations in harmony with the Christian religion. Beginning with the rebirth of classical learning at the end of the Fourteenth Century, Renaissance humanists elevated classical mythology to a new heightened importance. For hundreds of years it was an indispensable part of the knowledge of all educated people in Europe and the Americas, and continues in the Twentieth Century as a pervasive influence in our culture. Matched in their universality and pertinence only by the Biblical narratives, the classical myths (both the Greek and the relatively small number of native Roman ones) continue to supply contemporary society with a large pool of powerful and evocative images, concepts, themes, and terms. In the sciences, the fine arts, music, literature, the theater, and the symbols and trade names of advertising — to single out the most significant areas of modern influence — the classical mythic tradition remains a vigorous, self-renewing vehicle of inspiration and imagery.

One need look no farther than one's own body: each of us has a number of parts named from classical mythology. The first cervical vertebra of the neck, which supports the head, is called the atlas, first so named by the famous Flemish anatomist Vesalius about 1540 A.D. Since the middle of the Seventeenth Century the delicate weblike membrane covering the spinal cord and brain has been called the arachnoid tissue. In 1593 the Dutch surgeon Verheyden first applied the term Achilles' tendon to the sinew above the heel, and this is the standard medical term now in use. Everyone knows that the colored disc of the eye surrounding the pupil is called the iris, a term derived from the name of the Greek goddess of the rainbow, Iris. The complex winding internal ear is known as the labyrinth, a term borrowed from a classical myth for this part of the body by the great Italian anatomist Fallopius about 1550 A.D.

Much earlier than the invention of these relatively modern terms, mythology gave names to the planets, stars and constellations. More important, the power to influence human life was attributed to these celestial bodies endowed with mythic names. Mesopotamian culture created these practices, but it was the Greeks who, borrowing this age-old usage from the Near East, gave to many heavenly bodies the mythical names they still bear today. On a clear starry night, of the approximately 2000 stars visible to the naked eye, many have mythical names and star myths attached to them. Many of these star myths will be found throughout this volume.

In the second half of the Twentieth Century, with the birth of space science, spacecraft and propulsion rockets took names from classical mythology in imitation of the traditional practice of naming celestial bodies. For instance, American space scientists and planners chose for the individually manned flights to obtain data on space travel the term "Project Mercury," after the messenger of the gods. The first such orbital flight, in 1962, carrying astronaut John H. Glenn, Jr., was in a Mercury capsule launched by an Atlas rocket. The subsequent two-manned flights were appropriately named "Project Gemini" (Twins). The official name of the space project to land astronauts on the moon was "Project Apollo" — a misnomer, since Apollo was not the Greek god of the moon.

In another science, Chemistry, discoverers of new elements often assigned mythical names to chemical elements in the periodic table. Actually, fourteen of the elements have nomenclature derived from classical mythology: tellurium, titanium, tantalum, cerium, iridium, mercury, palladium, selenium, niobium, uranium, helium, neptunium, plutonium, and promethium.

In like manner, with the modern systematization of the biological sciences in recent centuries, the adaptation of names derived from classical mythology became widespread, and this nomenclature has been retained by contemporary scientists. In the Eighteenth Century the great Swedish botanist Linnaeus assigned mythical names to many species of birds, fish, mollusks, and butterflies. Although Linnaeus' knowledge of classical mythology was, unfortunately, not very accurate, his sometimes faulty choice of names has been retained as standard. Moreover, when modern naturalists assign classical names to newly discovered species there is not always a direct, obvious connection between the myth and the modern name. Current scientific terminology in the biological sciences abounds in mythical names. Some large moths are known as Atlas moths or Polyphemus moths. The term Arachnids is used to designate the class spiders (as well as scorpions and other creatures with four pairs of legs), after the girl Arachne who was an outstanding weaver. Cyclops and Cyclopean, used to refer to tiny water fleas which appear to have a single eye and to insects with a single median eye, derive from the name of the mythical one-eyed giant Cyclops. Organisms which possess both male and female sexual characteristics are called hermaphrodites, from the child of the Greek divinities Hermes and Aphrodite. Nectar, derived from the drink of the Greek gods, is the name used for the sweet substance sought by bees from flowers and certain leaves. Proteus, the sea divinity who could change his shape at will, gives his name to the Proteidae, newts which have white skins that turn black on exposure to light. A mollusk whose shell and tentacles resemble a ship with oars bears the mythical name Argo.

Psychiatry and psychoanalysis have also reached back into classical mythology to find terms to characterize contemporary emotional syndromes. Freud was profoundly impressed by the similarities between the subconscious drives of his neurotic patients, particularly as expressed in their dreams, and the themes contained in Greek myths. Freud thought the myth of Oedipus, who unknowingly killed his father and married his mother, especially significant, and coined the term Oedipus Complex for what he considered the basic cause of mental illness. We also have the term oedipism, to signify intentional self-inflicted injury to one's own eyes. The myth of Narcissus, the handsome young Greek who fell in love with his own reflection, gave us the term narcissism to describe abnormal self-love as the basic emotional root of homosexuality. The Electra Complex, too, often called the female Oedipus Complex, has a central position in Freudian psychoanalysis. A similar term, Medea Complex, characterizes a mother's hatred or death-wish for her children, with accompanying unconscious desire for revenge against the father. In many other ways psychiatrists have explored and studied classical myths for clues to modern human behavior.

Modern industry and business, constantly in search of attractive, appropriate trade names and themes for marketing products and services, frequently turn to the classic myths. For example, American automobile manufacturers have, since 1900, many times adopted for their cars and trucks names derived from classical mythology. The roll call of models produced by the American automotive industry includes names like Ajax, Mercury, Olympian, Apollo, Argo, Electra, Titan — all but one now obsolete.

Similarly, trade names and symbols in many fields of industry are derived from figures of classical mythology. Among the most popular names are: Ajax (for varnishes, cleansers, tires); Atlas (chemicals, cables, tires, industrial tools); Hercules (explosives, bicycles, cargo airplanes, safes); Mercury (outboard motors, phonographs, shotguns, power supplies); Phoenix (clothing, ale and beer, hosiery); Titan (batteries, uniforms, paper products).

Besides these commercial uses, periodicals all over the world, both scholarly and general, bear names from appropriate mythological personages. For example, *Daedalus* is the name of the journal of the American Academy of Arts and Science, as well as a technical periodical published in Sweden. Two periodicals dealing with art, one published in London, another in Brussels, have the title *Apollo*. Many magazines are named *Prometheus* — science publications, and art, literary and cultural periodicals. The goddess Athena's name is popular for periodicals, in line with a long tradition of entitling learned societies and learned publications *Athenaeum*. And the messenger god of antiquity has lent his name to many publications, like the world famous newspaper *Mercure de France*. A Parisian journal devoted to aviation is appropriately called *Icare*, and the International Journal of the Solar System bears the title *Icarus*. Hygieia, daughter of the Greek god of medicine, lends her name to the journal of the American Medical Association.

More significant, in the field of the fine arts the Twentieth Century has vigorously continued the age-old practice of seeking inspiration and culling themes and motifs from classical mythology. For example, in 1950 Oskar Kokoschka painted his great work entitled the *Prometheus Legend*, portraying scenes of the punishment of Prometheus, the progress of mankind, and the regenerative powers of nature as symbolized by Hades and Persephone. In the same year an exhibit held in Hanover, Germany, displayed 150 works by surrealist artists in all media under the general theme of "Ancient Myth in the New Art." The Italian painter Giorgio de Chirico too was partial to scenes from classical mythology, with his *Departure of the Argonauts*, and his favorite subject *Hector and Andromache*, of which he painted a number of versions between 1916 and 1924. And Picasso has been deeply influenced by the classic myths, using them, for example, in his painting *Ulysses and the Sirens*, and in many ceramic pieces with Greek fauns and nymphs as subjects.

Among Twentieth Century sculptors, the American Paul Manship was especially famous for his mythological subjects and the perfection of his classical style. His long roster of sculptured mythological subjects includes the *Prometheus Fountain* seen by millions in Rockefeller Center in New York City, along with Lawrie's bronze *Atlas*, shown supporting the world on his shoulders. The bronzes of the great French sculptor Aristide Maillol include a *Leda*, a *Juno*, a *Flora*, and a *Venus*, and classical mythology had a profound influence upon Rodin, who worked into the first decade of the Twentieth Century to produce such masterpieces of sculpture as *Psyche Carried Off by a Chimaera*, and *Orpheus and the Maenads*.

Turning to music, we find for example, Igor Stravinsky's opera-oratorio *Oedipus Rex*, composed for a text by Jean Cocteau, which derived from the Greek tragedy of Sophocles. Stravinsky also composed a melodrama, *Persephone*, and a ballet, *Orpheus*. The German composer Carl Orff, well known for his popular *Carmina Burana*, frequently turned to classical myths for themes, for example, in his compositions *Lament for Ariadne*, *Orpheus*, *Triumph of Aphrodite*, *Prometheus*, and the French-American composer Darius Milhaud has often been attracted to subjects from classical mythology. Among his many compositions of classical inspiration are his choral works *Agamemnon*, *Choëphoroe*, and *Eumenides*, based on Nobel Prize winner Paul Claudel's version of the *Orestes Trilogy* of the Greek tragedian Aeschylus, the opera *The Sorrows of Orpheus*, a modernized adaptation of the myth, and three "mini-operas," *The Rape of Europa*, *The Abandonment of Ariadne*, and *The Liberation of Theseus*. These "mini-operas" of Milhaud transform the Greek myths into modern, witty, sophisticated satires on Greek tales. Many modern operas have been composed to classical mythological subjects. Some of the most famous are the so-called Hellenic operas of Richard Strauss: his *Elektra*, *Ariadne at Naxos*, *The Egyptian Helen*, *Daphne*, *Loves of Danaë*.

Many modern writers have staked their artistic lives on bold retelling of the Greek myths in various literary media, adapting and remodeling the classical stories to serve as commentaries on the human condition in the Twentieth Century. Several Nobel prize winners have devoted much of their creative energies to profound rethinking of classical myths — the Swiss poet Carl Spitteler, the German dramatist Gerhart Hauptmann, the French literary greats André Gide, Paul Claudel, and Jean-Paul Sartre. The great Twentieth Century dramatists have exploited the classical mythic tradition particularly effectively for plots, themes, and symbols. For example, in 1912 George Bernard Shaw adapted a theme from a minor Greek myth about a sculptor who fell in love with a statue he had created of a beautiful woman. This theme had been a very popular one in many literary and artistic works since the Seventeenth Century. Shaw's *Pygmalion* was one of his most successful plays, and had enormous acclaim also as a movie. The musical version by Lerner and Loewe, *My Fair Lady* — the direct descendant of a Greek myth told over 2500 years ago, but derived from a much older Near Eastern folktale — has been the most financially successful theatrical production of all time.

II

INTERPRETATIONS OF MYTHS

The endless stream of adaptations of Greek and Roman myths to contemporary purposes reveals dramatically the continuity of cultural tradition from the beginnings of civilization to our own day. At the same time the vitality of classical myths also demonstrates that many basic human problems and dilemmas confronted in antiquity are still with us today, though in somewhat altered form. The relevance of myths is still sensed today because in their tales the ancient mythmakers embodied in universal form fundamental aspects of human behavior, feeling and thought. This extraordinary malleability and pertinence of the classic myths has impelled modern man, especially since the middle of the Nineteenth Century, to try to discover the origins of myths and to interpret them as understood by the peoples who created and employed them for many centuries as living, functional mechanisms of their cultures.

Now it is certain that we do not actually know the origin of even one single classical myth. Most were first told in a relatively primitive age, long before there could be any record of how and why and by whom any specific myth was first invented. Moreover, the human imagination produced myths at a time when literature was oral, and tales which appealed to the needs of a specific community were handed down by word of mouth for many centuries, inevitably altered in the course of such oral transmission. Equally important, most ancient myths and folktales appear in the works of sophisticated authors like Homer, the Greek tragedians, Vergil, and Ovid, who altered the traditional myths to harmonize with the environment of their own times and with the artistic requirements of their works.

By the end of the Fifth Century B.C., among the Greeks themselves, because of basic cultural changes and of increasing rationalism and skepticism, many myths lost their special functional values to society and therefore their credibility as "true" stories. Once myths ceased to serve an active function in preserving the value system of Greek life, their original significances faded even for the Greeks. Hence Greek thinkers, as we shall see, developed various theories to interpret the now forgotten original meanings of myths. Their efforts to explain their traditional mythology were the standard explanations until the Nineteenth and Twentieth centuries, when new sources of information, the comparative study of many cultures and languages, and the discoveries of archeology, generated new interpretations.

The *Symbolical Theory* had very common acceptance in the early Nineteenth Century. According to this interpretation, ancient priests did not propound their religious views in formal theological doctrines, but rather employed myths as an array of symbols of their religious views. Thus interpretation of myths requires the unraveling of a symbolic code. This is a very speculative business at best, and assumes, moreover, that primitive peoples and their priests systematized their beliefs in such an advanced manner, or were indeed capable of the abstract thought required of them by this theory. Actually, the symbolist theory is merely a variant of the allegorical method invented long ago by the Greeks, and suffers from the same defects of arbitrary interpretation.

New thinking was promoted by comparative methods. Since adequate data were lacking for the satisfactory understanding of ancient mythology, students of myth compared the languages of many cultures and the myths of many primitive peoples, especially modern primitives, to unlock the secrets of ancient mythology. Thus the study of Sanskrit, the ancient classical language of the Hindus, and research in comparative linguistics led to the *Indo-European Theory*. According to this view, all known myths and folktales survive from an immense body of original myths of an Aryan (or Indo-European) parent people, the ancestors of the Greeks, Romans, Hindus, Germans, Celts. Though we know very little about the Indo-European people, who may have lived in prehistoric times in mideastern Europe between the Carpathian and Ural mountains, and who spoke a language which was the ancestor of many known languages, it is clear that the role of Indo-European myth was very limited. Very few genuine Indo-European myths survived, and Greek myths were not predominantly Indo-European in origin, but were borrowed in great measure from the prehellenic Aegean culture area, and from Near Eastern (especially Egyptian and Semitic) myths.

A different approach to myth based on comparative mythology attracted the so-called *Philological School*, which enjoyed great acclaim and influence until about 1900 but is now also discredited. By correlating the names of mythological figures from various languages, scholars traced patterns of borrowing of mythology to disclose interrelations among the myths of different cultures. For example, the Greek *Adonis* and the Semitic *Adon* are obviously related, as are Sanskrit *Dyaus-pitar*, Greek *Zeus pater*, and Latin *Jupiter*. Following this method of comparative analysis of mythological names, the philologists enunciated the theory that mythological tales arose out of a sort of "disease of language." For instance, since objects of nature had names with masculine and feminine genders in many languages, it was an easy step for primitive man to personify nature in male and female form. Then in time the original meanings of words came to be misinterpreted and were applied in new ways, producing stories. The philological method often degenerated into fanciful etymologies and arbitrary correlations and interpretations.

Max Müller propounded a very influential interpretation of mythology as an extension of the philological method. This is the *Nature Mythology Theory*, which argued that ancient gods were simply personified forces, and myths symbols of natural phenomena, in particular personified tales of heavenly bodies. Basically, according to this theory, all myths are but variations of stories about one universal deity, the sun. This theory, which also claims the solar myth as originally Aryan, cannot be supported by any evidence. In Greek mythology, for instance, nature symbolism does not play much of a part, and there are relatively few nature myths, particularly about heavenly bodies. Indeed, most mythologies of the world are more concerned with the human, social aspects of life, and historic events than with religious myths involving nature and vegetation rituals. The concept of personification inherent in the solar myth theory (e.g., that the Greek god Zeus is merely the personification of the sky) demands a blanket assumption that mythmakers always talked in metaphors. But many of the gods worshipped were unquestionably separate from the natural phenomena they were thought to control.

Undeterred by the criticisms of the solar myth theory, moon mythologists have set forth a competing nature myth theory. They claim that a moon cult in all cases preceded sun worship, and that therefore all myths contain disguised stories about the moon. Robert Graves, for instance, is an unreconstructed advocate of the lunar myth theory. Both sun and moon mythology suffer from two fundamental errors: they seek to organize all myths into one unified system, and they identify myth with religion. Of course, there are some myths about the sun and about the moon, but myths and religious ritual are not identical. It is true that at particular stages of man's development, myths, religious beliefs and ritual, and magical practices may be closely intertwined, but most of Greek mythology had nothing to do with religious ceremonies intended to influence or neutralize supernatural beings.

The search for a universal explanation of all myths is a basic mistake: there is no one single fountainhead. Such unitary interpretations are simplistic theories, whether they seek their monolithic interpretations in natural phenomena, or psychological behavior, or history. They are faulty because they close their eyes to the plurality of causes and influences that shape myths. The obsession with a unitary theory of myth, especially prevalent since the Nineteenth Century and still influential in some quarters today, has not only led to many fallacies and errors, but, more important, has diverted attention from the multifarious origins of myths and their evolution as they are handed down orally, or migrate from place to place.

The most fruitful of the Nineteenth Century interpretations of myth is that of the *Anthropological School*, still not obsolete today. This school was influenced by Darwin's theory of evolution, the idea of progress, the comparative procedures of the Nineteenth Century, and the belief in the survival of primitive ideology in myths. Since ancient myths contain so many elements which are baffling for lack of evidence, the Anthropological School sought to reconstruct and understand the original prehistoric myths of the Greeks by comparing them with the myths of contemporary primitive peoples. As a fundamental doctrine, this theory asserts that the myths of all peoples originate in the evolutionary stage of savagery. The Anthropological School thus finds evidence of primitive savagery, especially belief in vegetation demons and totems, in every myth, folktale, and legend. Since such stories often survive long after the original primitive meaning and purpose have decayed, all Greek myths must be considered as having evolved from them. Despite the extreme position, this approach and the research conducted into contemporary primitive societies have contributed many valuable insights into ancient mythology.

In fact, the Anthropological School made a remarkable discovery: patterns often recur among the mythologies of many peoples all over the world. The leading proponents of this method explain these parallels by arguing that the human mind everywhere responds in the same way at the same stage of development, and therefore invents the same types of mythic tales. Hence the irrational, grotesque myths invented by contemporary savages have their parallels in similar stories invented by ancient peoples when they were at the same stage of evolution. When such stories survive into later civilized ages, continuators of these myths reject and alter the original savage elements.

But for all its valuable contributions the Anthropological School went astray in its excessive reliance on its comparative method, and overemphasis on the myths of contemporary primitives. It failed to distinguish sufficiently between the myths of savage societies and those of civilized people, which are often new creations and not merely updated survivals of savagery. The basic assumption of the Anthropological School is questionable — that the human mind is a sort of machine that will react everywhere in identical patterns under like circumstances at the same levels of cultural development.

The comparative method concentrates on similarities and parallels, arguing that the many recurrent patterns of myth in unrelated cultures prove the theory that the human mind operates in fixed ways. Of course, fundamental common experiences of social life and of the natural environment, as the reproductive process, family relations, intertribal relations, earthquakes, floods, dangerous animals, the heavenly bodies, death, and the like, may evoke parallel stories in different cultures in response to such basic situations. Yet these commonplaces of the human imagination, many of them thousands of years old, exhibit resemblances that are actually accidental or minor, and in many of the cases cited by the Anthropological School the similarity of incidents is not very great. The most important characteristic of all myths is their infinite diversity; few myths are identical in different cultures.

Nevertheless, striking resemblances and parallels appear in the themes of myths of peoples in various geographical areas of the world and in various historical periods. The universal flood, the fire-bringer, the slaying of a dragon by a hero, primeval paradise, the wandering exile seeking to return home, the father slayer, the abandonment of the future hero at birth, the exploits of twins, the hero as civilizer and savior, sibling rivalry, incest recur very commonly. The widespread distribution of similar myths — for example, pre-Columbian America and primitive Australia possessed "the whole bag of tricks" of mythology — needs explanation. The *Diffusion Theory*, to meet this problem, proposes that myths and folktales similar in different areas of the world spread by diffusion from one geographical center which originated them, as Mesopotamia, Babylonia, India, or the Aryans. In this theory people borrowed myths originally invented in a parent center and adapted them to new environments. They merely changed the names and some of the details but retained the basic theme and structure of the myth. It is highly doubtful that this theory of a single center has any validity, even though diffusion and transmission of myths from one people to another did take place through seepage across borders, conquest, prisoners of war, slaves, hostages, marriage, migrations, fugitives, sailors, merchants, itinerant entertainers. The alternative theory, suggested above, and often called the *Polygenesis Theory*, maintains that such similarities and parallels have a spontaneous, independant origin in numerous places in the world as the result of the tendency of the human mind to react in the same way to similar conditions and experiences.

Another "one key" theory proposed to unlock the door to the interpretation of myths is the *Ritual Theory*, which takes the view that all myths are verbal accounts invented to accompany religious rituals. That is, primitive man during religious rituals accompanied the "things done" (ritual) by "things said" (myth), which were narratives recited as stories of the first occasion that gave rise to the given ritual. While there are undoubtedly some myths that have their origin and significance in religious rituals, particularly in some Near Eastern religions, the rite-myth hypothesis, like other unitary theories, is an oversimplified interpretation. We know, for example, that some myths originated independently of ritual, and that other existing myths later generated religious rituals. There is also evidence that one people often borrowed myths from another without the accompanying ritual, just as they have taken rituals without the associated myths. Indeed, only a very small percentage of all known myths are ritual texts, and Greek mythology is almost entirely independent of specific cult rituals. And it is interesting to note that the early Romans possessed an elaborate ritual structure but relatively few myths.

The Nineteenth Century's search for "one key" theories generated another view which continues to exert an extraordinary influence today all over the world, the *Psychoanalytical Theory*. Sigmund Freud was profoundly influenced by Nineteenth Century unitary views of myths as well as by the prevailing comparative method used in studying myths. Thus he applied his unitary concept of the origins and nature of contemporary neuroses to explain the origins and nature of ancient mythology, and, conversely, found support for his psychoanalytical theories in mythology. Rejecting the theory that all myths personify natural phenomena, Freud turned his attention to human nature for an explanation. Impressed by the universality of mythic story-telling both in ancient times and among modern primitives, he decided that contemporary civilization harbored analogous phenomena in another form, and thus made the daring analogy between dream symbols of modern man and symbols he believed were contained in myths.

Freud proclaimed that "when we dream we think like savages." There are, he maintained, "numerous points of correspondence" between the psychology of folktales and the psychology of the neurotic today. Thus myths and dreams are indistinguishable for the Freudians, since, like dreams today, all myths were the wish-fulfillments of ancient man — that is, symbolic sex fantasies. Primitive man lived, as it were, in the "childhood of humanity," and reacted like any modern child who passes through a "primitive" period when he represses into his subconscious many impulses which later reappear as survivals in his dreams. Freud therefore called dreams "psychical antiquities." All myths, declared Freud, are sex symbols, distorted expressions of the libido of primitive man which assumed the form of fantasies as a result of repressing anti-social impulses. Thus, primitive mythmakers reconstructed their childhood fantasies through narratives that were symbols of unconscious repressions of sex impulses. In this manner Freud transmuted the Nineteenth Century search for one single explanation of myth into a unitary psychological theory based on man's sexuality.

Like the other unitarian theorists of the Nineteenth Century, the Freudians and their followers assume that myths mean something other than appears on the surface, and they claim to be able to elucidate "the real thing" by interpreting all the myths by the all-embracing method of sexual symbolism. This theory of myth is unscientific, superficial and subjective, based on a specious analogy and on intuitive psychological analysis, not knowledge of the social and environmental conditions that produced specific ancient myths.

Out of Freud's theory grew another interpretation that is popular today, the *Jungian Theory* of myth. Carl Gustav Jung, an associate of Freud in the psychoanalytic school, observed that patients with emotional problems expressed in their dreams a limited number of recurring themes. Combining this knowledge with the Nineteenth Century discovery that there are many common themes in the mythologies of all peoples, and convinced that he had discovered striking resemblances between modern dream motifs and the themes found in the myths of antiquity, Jung asserted that there was an actual connection between myths and the dreams of modern man. From this theoretical position he concluded that all myths reflect something that actually happened in primitive times, and that the mythic narratives were the recounting of primitive dreams by the mythmakers. Jung asserted that these primordial basic human motifs imbedded in myths, called "archetypes," like mother and child, journey of the hero, suffering, rites of passage, the healer, are part of the inheritance of modern man from primitive times. They survive and reappear in modern man's dreams through a somewhat mysterious psychological mechanism called by the Jungians the "collective unconscious." Since these archetypal mythic tales of primitive people reappear in dreams today, Jungian psychotherapy correlates the mythic archetypes with the dreams of neurotic patients, and the Jungians devote a good deal of attention to psychoanalyzing ancient mythical characters. But there is no evidence to support the Jungian view that myths are the narrations of dreams reflecting actual events in primitive times changed and distorted through the repression of the subconscious, and the position is a purely arbitrary one. Robert Graves has said,* "A true science of myth should begin with a study of archaeology, history, and comparative religion, not in the psycho-therapist's consulting room." On the efforts of the psychoanalytic school in general an expert in classical mythology has concluded: "I have failed to find in its writings a single explanation of any myth, or any detail of any myth, which seemed even remotely possible or capable of accounting for the development of the story as we have it."**

The first new influential approach to mythology since the speculations introduced by the psychoanalytical school is the *Structural Theory* of Claude Lévi-Strauss. According to this view all myths in all cultures have a single function — to bridge contradictions between two polarized extremes of tensions. Thus every myth can be analyzed and understood as a coded structure that seeks to mediate such contradictions in society. In applying his "scientific" method, as he calls it, Lévi-Strauss ignores the historical setting of a myth, the evolutions it may experience, the possible accretions over the centuries, and the impact of literary adaptations. The Structural Theory is a new unitary view of mythology, and suffers from the same limitations and arbitrariness of all one-key theories. Lévi-Strauss' theory of myth has greater validity for tribal societies, out of whose experience he developed

---

*The Greek Myths (Baltimore: Penguin, 1955), Vol. I, p.22.
**H.J. Rose, A Handbook of Greek Mythology (New York: Dutton, 1959), p. 10.

his method; it has little applicability to classical mythology.

The contemporary approach to myth abandons all efforts to find a single exclusive formula, whether totems, the sun, the moon, or the libido, to explain the infinitely varied phenomena called myths, and recognizes that social needs generate and adapt a particular myth. This *Historical-Critical Method* tries to find as many of the multitude of factors that influenced the origin and evolution of a myth as possible. Starting with the concept that myths maintained the stability and continuity of a certain society, it seeks to discover a specific myth's purpose by relating it to relevant aspects of that society. The method is particularly effective for the study of Greek and Roman mythology, both of which developed mainly out of borrowings from other cultures.

In accepting a plurality of influences on myths, the Historical-Critical Method recognizes that an original simple myth may have various layers added at later times, that myths change with the development of other aspects of a society, and that there may be many local variants of the same myth. By isolating the most primitive elements of a myth we may possibly succeed in discovering the place of origin of this kernel, the people who invented it, and the approximate date, and in following the evolution of a myth we may be able to discover the various layers of accretion.

In this connection the transformations of myths in the hands of writers and artists interest the mythologist particularly since, with extensive use of mythic stories and themes by Greek creative writers and artists, the original functional purposes of myth changed. A time arrived in Greek culture when the Greeks themselves no longer understood these original functional purposes. By the end of the Fifth Century B.C., after about 1000 years of mythic development, the formative age of Greek mythology came to an end. Indeed, after about 700 B.C. almost no great new myths were created, and all the important myths and sagas were enjoying universal currency in the Greek world. Travel, wider horizons, greater interest in the present and increasing sophistication tended to put an end to mythmaking. Yet the myths survived both in the popular mind and in the creative hands of poets and artists. The tragic poets of the Fifth Century — the Golden Age of Greek tragedy — based their plots on the myths of the past, and in the process became, as it were, mythmakers of a sophisticated sort by altering the traditional myths to adapt them to contemporary purposes and their own artistic needs.

The mythic tradition was so ingrained that even in an age of widespread skepticism and rationalism this archaic form of thought retained a hold on the minds of most people. Almost every author, sculptor, painter, ceramic artist, illustrated his creations with mythological references and scenes. Greek national thought characteristically exploited mythology for examples of models of behavior, much as our culture once used Biblical references widely. Mythology also served as one of the fundamentals of the educational process in Greek schools, so that from childhood through maturity the Greek of the classical age encountered the cultural dynamism of the national mythology as one of the unifying forces in Greek life. Even when the basically altered societal conditions no longer benefited from the original social purposes of the mythic tales, literature preserved them and became the principal medium for their survival. Indeed, the Greeks were the first people to employ myths as the content of creative literature, and one of the unique characteristics of their mythology was its final absorption into the whole body of creative literature. In this manner many myths lost their original functional purposes but did not disappear from knowledge, saved from extinction by scholars, artists, and writers who were interested in them as sources of themes and as bygone learning.

Even before the Fifth Century B.C. a process of degradation and decay of myths had begun. As early as Homer's *Iliad* and *Odyssey* (written about 800-700 B.C.) many myths had been "cleaned up" and reinterpreted under the influence of the rationalistic tendencies of the Greeks. Gradually, the growth of rationalism dealt a serious blow to the authenticity and credibility of myths, and ultimately new branches of thought — philosophy, science, history — replaced myth. Yet it was not until the end of the Fifth Century B.C. that the Greeks definitely abandoned their age-old confidence in the truth and validity of their myths. In that century the development of history, the teaching of the Sophists — the Greek equivalent of college professors — and the realism of the tragic poet Euripides combined to deliver the final blow. Thus myths came to be regarded merely as poetic fictions, and for the first time in mankind's history the term "mythical" came to mean "unreal, legendary, untrue." Fifty years later, Plato could look at traditional Greek myths with nothing but scorn.

As myths became less functional to the Greeks and their significance ceased to be understood, the first attempts were made to explain their meaning, as sophisticated Greek thinkers sought to explain away the irrational, bizarre, grotesque and immoral elements in the mythical heritage of their people. First with *Rationalism* they assumed that their forefathers must have meant something other than meets the eye, explaining, for example, the myth of the princess Oreithyia, snatched away from Athens by the North Wind (Boreas) to become his bride, as the story of an actual princess who was blown off a hill by a gust of wind and killed. The myth of Queen Niobe, turned to stone when all her children were killed, was interpreted to mean that in her profound grief she lost all feeling. The rationalists were thus attempting to justify their ancestors' good sense and the intelligence of their own age in preserving myths. We shall never know why the Greeks did not succeed in eliminating all the grotesque and irrational elements from their myths.

A very influential aspect of rationalist method is the more elaborate *Allegorical Theory*, first developed by the Greeks at the end of the Sixth Century B.C. and in use ever since. Allegory is a Greek word which means "saying other things," and applied to mythology, the theory assumes, fantastically, that cunning early priests and rulers deliberately invented falsehoods and deceptions — myths — to attract listeners so that they could control the masses of the people, and inculcate obedience to law and custom through such hoaxes. For example, in order to indoctrinate belief in the Greek gods they personified natural phenomena, explaining them in human terms and giving them the names of gods. This theory would have us believe that what is irrational or crude in myth must have some deep meaning concealed beneath the simple story, and that some brilliant men systematized beliefs in this way.

From the Fifth Century B.C. interpreters of allegory commonly explained away any demeaning myth of a god or hero and searched for some edifying meaning and ethical concept of an elevated nature. Later, both the Jews and Christians in antiquity reinterpreted aspects of Greek mythology allegorically, and commentators on the Old Testament adopted the allegorical method to explain away puzzling and grotesque passages (such as the *Song of Songs*). Even later, the humanists of the Renaissance salvaged as allegory many pagan myths during the age of the revival of classical learning.

Of lesser significance was the *Etymological Method*, based on the belief that the name of a mythological character signifies some basic truth about him, and thus explains the specific stories associated with that mythic person. The name of Hermes, for example, the messenger of the gods, was thought to be derived from the word *hermeneus*, "interpreter," Electra from *A-lectra*, "unwed," Hades from "unseen." This effort to penetrate to the significance of mythological figures by determining the "true meaning" of their names is futile, for as ancient etymologies are notoriously false and arbitrary, few myths can be explained in this way.

The Greek writer Euhemerus (ca. 325-275 B.C.), devised another interesting rationalist theory to explain objectionable elements in Greek myths. In the theory of *Euhemerism* all mythical personages, including gods, were once actual historical individuals. Their great services to their people transformed them in the popular mind into gods. Myths were thus the glorified adventures of persons who once lived, and gods were originally the culture heroes of a primitive age, great men who aroused such admiration among their grateful contemporaries that they deified and worshiped them. Behind this theory lay growing disbelief in a religion of many gods, and the increasing tendency among the Greeks to bestow religious rites upon outstanding men after their death.

The method of Euhemerism was assailed in antiquity as atheistic, and Plutarch, for example, rebuked Euhemerus' "false and unfounded mythology, which disseminates all kinds of atheism over the world, and reduces all deities alike to the names of generals, admirals, and kings pretended to have flourished in olden times." Though not very influential among the Greeks and Romans, Euhemerism was taken up with alacrity by the early Christian writers in order to belittle the pagan gods. In the Middle Ages it was a favorite explanation of classical mythology, was much in vogue during the Renaissance, and has been popular in modern times. But mythology is not a form of distorted history, and reason cannot argue away the belief in and worship of many gods among the ancient peoples. Because it starts with the wrong premise Euhemerism is an unscientific method whose adherents have proposed nothing but arbitrary explanations of myths.

Many ingenious explanations of myths, from the time of the Greeks to modern times, have been faulty because they did not address themselves to the true nature of myths and the social functions they served. Today it is possible for us to understand with greater clarity the essence of myths and related types of narrative, their creation and transmission, and their great value to the civilizations of mankind. Exploration of the nature of myth must precede study of the myths themselves.

III

THE NATURE OF MYTH

The original nature of myth emerges more clearly as we project ourselves backward in man's history, to a time when such tales held a special kind of truth for their hearers, when they were invented in great numbers, and were consciously passed down from generation to generation for their social value. Myths were once esteemed as much as technical skills, and were indispensable for the proper functioning and continuity of early cultures. We may find it difficult to appreciate the functional significance of "true" myths, because our scientific, technological society rarely engages in conscious mythmaking or the preservation and transmission of myths that are alive and vital to cultural stability. Even the word *myth* and *mythical*, which are Greek in origin, have undergone radical changes in meaning and in popular definition. To us they signify variously "lie, fabricated story, fanciful, arbitrary invention, superstition, fictitious, unreal." By contrast, even as late as the Sixth and Fifth centuries B.C., most rational intellectual ancient Greeks still considered myth as central to their way of life.

In origin, every myth was the creation of an anonymous unsophisticated primitive man, a spontaneous imaginative response to some important phenomenon or event significant to his culture. The mythmaker in a myth-telling society may relate a dream (regarded in primitive and archaic societies as a revelation or vital message from a god), or narrate some waking fantasy about, for example, a god, ancestor, animal, natural phenomenon, or some extraordinary happening. These anonymous creations of fancy were the products of primitive imagination at work in a perplexing and precarious world. Since myths were interpretations of the world told with poetic imagination, they actually formed part of the oral literature of early societies. Like a perceptive modern story teller or poet, the mythmaker captured in a radiant, memorable tale the essence of some significant experience or social pattern. These stories were so striking that they at once became part of the collective property of the culture to which the mythmaker belonged.

The fact that these myths became the cultural inheritance of all the people should not delude us into believing that they were creations of the whole people in a "mythmaking age." The creations of such individual story tellers survived only when they became collective property, and they lived on and were transmitted to succeeding generations only when they served special needs of the community. In all probability, countless tales told in primitive times quickly disappeared because they did not have the basic quality of vital relevance to their society. The myths that remained alive became part of what we might call the ideology of a group. And the individual mythmakers were probably persons who possessed both extraordinary perceptiveness and the gift of creating striking narrative.

The theory that priests (or official poets) created myths does not hold up, and there is just as little truth in the view that early priests systematized myths into creeds or articles of religious faith. The societies with the most exuberant mythologies — Greece, Scandinavia, Polynesia — did not even have a professional clergy. Myths generally stood apart from the functions of priests, and few have any connection with actual religious rituals. Thus Greek myths were not dogmas, there were no "official" myths, but frequent variant versions of the same myth, and myths were frequently altered in detail and interpretation to suit new needs and purposes.

Because of the insecurity, perplexities, and anxieties of the life of early man, a number of mechanisms developed to reduce tensions and maintain the stability and continuity of a way of life. In all societies certain religious rituals, performed periodically in the same manner, were considered essential to survival. In the same way, myths, repeated over and over again, helped to produce social cohesiveness, and a sense of rapport and togetherness among the members of the group. Myths, therefore, were not just explanations to satisfy curiosity about natural phenomena, divine forces, and extraordinary events. Rather they served as a special form of repetitive activity needed to maintain the stability of society, and differed from the ritual and prayer which aimed specifically at winning over or neutralizing divine forces. Through the retelling in story form what the group considered to be past precedents for current beliefs and social organization, the validity of the culture was reaffirmed, its values, social order and traditional modes of behavior justified.

Such periodic justification and reaffirmation were necessary because every society confronts its members with perplexities. The two major sources of anxiety and insecurity in primitive societies — still operative today in great measure — were the threats from the natural environment (for instance, from floods, lightning, severe storms, earthquakes, volcanoes, wild animals, droughts, famines), and from various tensions springing from interpersonal relationships of a variety of sorts both familial and extra-familial. The daily hazards, frustrations and insecurity of primitive society, often beyond human understanding and control, were the generative forces that brought myths into being. Once created, myths survived because they quieted fears and sublimated antisocial tendencies. In this role they were a real force promoting solidarity and stability. In their unsophisticated way, myths frankly expressed the fears, wonder, anxieties, and aspirations of primitive man, constituting for him a sort of repertory of guiding patterns for all aspects of life. In this context, primitive man was not troubled by irrational and grotesque elements in his myths. Primitive man, in fact, is well known to be quite capable of rational and accurate observation. But it is precisely those more perplexing and inexplicable elements of his life with which he could not easily grapple that he commemorated in mythic form. For all these reasons myths, protecting and transmitting cultural values, are a precious key to the morality, value structure, and acceptable behavior patterns of a particular society. Frequently they tell us more about a people than their history.

Because of constant threats to their survival, primitive societies have an intense fear of change; stability at all costs is the ideal. In this yearning for stability, myths served an important function because they embodied the traditional values of the past. In this way they constitute timeless, exemplary models that serve as fixed points in a world of insecurity and change; their repetition made it easier to face the insecure future. Everything that happened was thus measured by a mythic prototype. Yet myths in time underwent basic changes themselves, indicating that, despite efforts to prevent change, many changes, both obvious and subtle, constantly impinged on primitive societies. People took note of this by abandoning obsolete myths, or altering them, or inventing new ones.

Myths thus do not arise as literary fictions merely to entertain, or from man's prescientific speculations about the origin and nature of the universe. When Aristotle said "the maker of myths is a sort of philosopher," he simply meant that a myth is not a story that reports an actual specific event; a myth survives because it has caught in its narrative some highly significant, *typical* aspect of life, applicable under many diverse situations. To the original mythmaker, however, the story is real, as it is to his society, even if it contains fantastic, irrational elements. The primitive myth-maker is thus neither a conscious philosopher, nor a priest, nor scientist, nor historian, nor does he seek to conceal symbols or allegories in his tales. He records in myth the extraordinary events and recurrent phenomena of basic significance for the continuity of his particular culture. In sum, myth is one of primitive man's practical responses to a precarious environment; each myth encapsulates values of a particular society. In a brilliant analogy Marshall McLuhan once compared myth to ". . . a single snapshot of a complex process."

When myths changed, in spite of the conservatism of primitive people who used them, the changes resulted partly from a sort of ad-libbing, and partly by a process of adaptation to changed conditions and to startling new events. Myths were also often expanded by coalescing two or more unconnected myths to form a continuous story, or by borrowings from alien cultures. Because of this putting "new wine in old bottles," and because of the accretions added by many retellers, it is often impossible now to extricate the original form of the myth and its most ancient purpose. The changes in myths were exceedingly varied, brought about by many factors: contacts with other societies, migrations, extraordinary changes in the natural environment, evolution of social, political and economic organization, the flux of religion and ethical thought and practice. Of special importance is the fact that, as civilization advanced, conscious efforts were made by rulers to use myths for political propaganda, and for poets to refine myths by recasting them and cleaning away the more primitive and coarser aspects to adapt them to higher cultural needs. The surviving version of a particular myth is often, therefore, a purified version of the myth, although in many cases aspects of primitive savagery, as well as obsolete forms of behavior, remain imbedded in the myths.

Despite these problems of interpretation, the very plasticity of mythic patterns and symbols, particularly in the Greek classical myths, endows them with that perennial freshness which, to quote Nathaniel Hawthorne in the preface to his *Wonder Book*, written in 1851, makes them "... marvelously independent of all temporary modes and circumstances," and assures that "so long as man exists, they can never perish; but, by their indestructibility itself, they are legitimate subjects for every age to clothe with its own garniture of manners and sentiment, and to imbue with its own morality."

The many influences upon and changes in these primitive tales make the term *myth* difficult to define. Efforts to limit the concept of myth to some specific type of primitive narrative are arbitrary and difficult to justify. For practical purposes a working definition would be: *A myth is a story about gods, other supernatural beings, or heroes of a long bygone time.* It was precisely because myths had their setting in the "brave days of old," "when men were ten feet tall and closer to the gods," that the irrational and unreal elements in them were readily believed by even more civilized people. Thus, since myths treated events, heroes, and phenomena as more grandiose than the ordinary, they possessed a special truth and a power to guide actions by serving as models for emulation or deterrence. Primitive and archaic men believed that the events in myths actually occurred in an earlier, more heroic age. Therefore, even if the events were outside the realm of verifiable experience, myths possessed a quality of grandeur that continued thereafter to lend them a special potency for evaluating the petty phenomena of the present. This is what

Homer, the greatest of the mythic poets, meant when he said he was telling about heroes greater than men "as they are now."

The *myth proper* is therefore a narrative of an event believed to have taken place in the remote past (involving divinities and/or heroes), or of a recurrent phenomenon, like the story of the chariot of the sun riding across the sky daily. The story of the murder of King Agamemnon by his wife Clytemnestra, which may in fact record an historical event, became a significant myth because it was told as a timeless story of the murder of a husband by his wife. Similarly, the murder of Clytemnestra by her son Orestes is a myth, whereas the death of Agrippina at the hands of her son the Roman Emperor Nero is an historical fact. Likewise, the cruelty of a king toward his children would be an historical event, whereas the cruelty of the Titan Cronus toward his six divine children is a myth.

Because myths often concern gods (these are called *divine myths*), there is a natural tendency to confuse religion and its rituals with myths. But religion and cult are concerned with belief in the existence of gods and with the ceremonies performed to befriend or appease them; these may be intertwined with but are basically different from the mythic tales themselves. Similarly, myth is different from history. It is quite possible, indeed quite likely, that many of the characters who appear in Greek mythology (e.g., Agamemnon, Nestor, Theseus) actually once existed. Yet it was not the intent of the mythmakers to preserve a record of them as historical information. Modern conviction that there was an historical kernel of truth in the mythic tales preserved in the *Iliad* and *Odyssey* of Homer eventually led to the discovery by the archeologists Heinrich Schliemann and Sir Arthur Evans of the existence of a previously unsuspected magnificent Bronze Age civilization in the Aegean area. Even though individual mythic heroes may bear the names of persons who once existed, no incident related in the myths can be regarded as an historical event unless confirmed by some other source.

Besides the frequent changes in original narratives as they were handed down orally for many centuries, so that the events became blurred beyond recognition, there is the strong tendency for the charismatic figure of the hero, whether once an actual living person or wholly imaginary, to attract to himself a great variety of stories of totally unrelated origin. For example, anonymous folktales frequently become attached to a specific hero. It is equally common for myths originally told of a hero (these are called *hero myths*) to be transferred to a god and become divine myths and *vice versa*. Many myths are recognizable as widespread folktales that have taken new form in association with a hero or a god. The reverse process has also taken place: many later folktales are survivals of decayed myths.

But primitive people were not systematic mythologists. They did not distinguish myths proper, as we have defined them, from other types of narratives that served other needs and also found eager listeners. It is helpful, however, to make such distinctions, because other types of stories are often intermingled with myths. For example, an important type of early popular story is the *folktale*. Like myths, folktales are the products of imaginative creation, but they are told of nameless people ("Once upon a time there was a poor peasant . . .") and they serve to amuse and provide information. Anonymous prose narratives embodying practical folk wisdom handed down through the ages are a universal phenomenon, and it is striking how closely the folktales of most peoples throughout the world resemble each other. And as folktales, repeated from time immemorial, are often attracted to the person of a hero or a god to become myths proper, the same folktale may be attracted to the figures of many heroes and gods, with the result that we find doublets, triplets, and frequent multiple adaptations of the same story in myths. The motifs of folktales constitute an important element in classical myths: it is often possible to isolate the folktale material imbedded in them.*

Another kind of early narrative, closely related to folktale and having as its purpose to amuse and entertain, is the *fairy tale* (or *märchen*). This is a story of considerable length, told of anonymous persons, containing many episodes and folktale motifs, and often employing the element of the marvelous together with characters like giants, dwarfs, fairy godmothers, etc. *Cinderella* and *Snow White* are such tales. Greek myths contain not only folktale but also *märchen* motifs, for these originally

*The term *folklore* is used to designate the body of traditional customs, beliefs and practices of a people preserved in oral form, constituting a nonliterary fictional folk record of the traditional values of the preliterate age of a people.

nameless stories were prone to attach themselves to specific mythical figures, even to historical persons. The stories of the Greek heroes Odysseus and Perseus, and the romance *Cupid and Psyche* contain many aspects from age-old *märchen*. An instructive example of this process in English myth is the story of Dick Whittington and his cat. Dick Whittington was in fact an historical person; he served three times as mayor of London. But the story of the cat associated with him in the myth is centuries older than the historical Whittington. The *märchen*, a popular tale of fictional narrative over 5000 years old, often concerns a hero or heroine in a distressful situation, who, after a series of adventures in which there is marked intervention of the supernatural, achieves his or her goal and lives happily ever after.

Many a myth originates as an *aetiological tale*, a narrative told in response to the eternal questions, "How did this happen?" "Why do we act in this way?" "What is the origin of this name?" Such stories, which have been called the "naive guesses" of unsophisticated primitive man, were intended originally as explanation (aetiology) of significant experiences, like recurrent natural phenomena, catastrophic natural events, animal behavior, star formations and movements, names of places, odd features of topography and geography, the origin of the world, gods, and man, aspects of religious rites and social customs, violations of the social code, and anything unique and marvelous. Aetiological tales often later became attached to a god or demigod, or were given settings in an "heroic age," and thus became myths.

Still another type of story is the *legend*, an imaginative narrative which originated in some actual extraordinary event involving a real person, such as a memorable hunt or journey or deed of valor. In time such a tale acquired so many embellishments and elements of the marvelous that it is virtually indistinguishable from myth proper.

Related to legend is the *saga*, originally used to designate a medieval Norwegian or Icelandic narrative about a leading Norse family or hero, and believed to be true. The saga is a complex of legends based on an interrelated series of important historical events. Saga material appears in the narrative of the Trojan War and of the Theban War in Greek mythology. Though sagas have an original historical basis, the events preserved in them have been magnified and made larger than the ordinary, embellished with elements of the marvelous and the supernatural. In mythology the term *saga* has come to be restricted to an extensive tale of the exploits of a hero or an epic story in literary form told to delight audiences by aesthetic beauty and insight into human personality and behavior. The *Iliad* of Homer is an outstanding example. In contemporary popular usage any narrative or event of some grandeur may be called a saga (as in "the saga of the West"), or the term may be used of a novel telling the story of a family over several generations (e.g., Galsworthy's *Forsyte Saga*).

Finally, the term *fable* is limited to tales which employ animals as characters who speak and behave as humans. Though fables often drew upon folktales, they are not the anonymous creations of primitive men, but sophisticated stories composed by known authors. The oldest preserved fables are Greek and Hindu creations, and the first known author is the Greek Aesop. Though originally conscious literary creations, fables may later end up as folktales. There are no animal fables in Greek mythology.

The overlapping and fusion of these various types of primitive narrative in developed mythology explains why it is difficult to define the term myth with precision. In Greek mythology the formative age spanned a period of at least 1000 years, and so Greek myths have come down to us often as complex clusters of stories of different origins. A myth may begin as a basic story about a hero or a god, and over the centuries may accumulate aetiological tales, folktales, *märchen*, even legendary and saga elements. As a result, there may be layers upon layers of later narratives added to a primitive basic story. The original kernel may still preserve savage notions and practices unintelligible to later ages. One reason that Greek myths present difficulties in interpretation is that we often cannot peel off these different layers. Even the Greeks themselves often did not understand some elements of their own myths. Moreover, originally short separate tales were often combined into unified elaborate stories. Just as in many other aspects of their culture the Greeks were systematizers of knowledge, so too were they in their mythology. Many Greek myths as we now have them are later artificial composites, fused artistically by poets into unified sequences of mythic clusters or cycles of myths. The traditional mythic material always remained in Greek hands a malleable heritage which was constantly remolded for new purposes. For instance, popular myths might be adapted to local circumstances or attached to the exploits of a local hero or god in response to local pride. This accounts for the similarities, for one example, between the myths of the hero Heracles and those of the hero Theseus.

Until the Sixth and Fifth centuries B.C. the Greeks thought their myths were true. It is quite likely that many Greek myths took form during the Mycenaean Age, to be treated in the next chapter. The Greek migrants who settled in Hellas from about 2000-1000 B.C. brought some narratives with them from their original homeland in central Europe; others they took over from the indigenous population with which they mingled in the Aegean area; still others were borrowed from the international folktales and myths current in the Near East. In the Greek tradition there was a time in history called the "Heroic Age," the time when the events preserved in the myths about heroes were thought to have taken place. This mythical period, from about 1500 to 1150 B.C., corresponded to the end of the Bronze Age in history. It was the first great period of Greek power and affluence, a time when Greece enjoyed a uniform, sophisticated culture comparable to the magnificence of contemporary Near Eastern civilizations. This powerful Mycenaean Civilization was shattered and destroyed by great migrations of peoples about 1200 B.C., and although the Greeks of later centuries actually knew little of the history of this remarkable period, national pride preserved a vivid mythic memory of that "Heroic Age." In later centuries, from about 1150 to 600 B.C., a lively oral tradition of an age of glory survived in myths, although there were probably few new original mythic creations. The Greeks of the archaic and classical ages adapted their ancestral myths to new conditions, and their poets and artists especially drew upon them constantly.

Like myths everywhere in the world, Greek myths developed in response to important social needs, and were for a long time universally accepted throughout the Hellenic world as a living cultural force. Their mythic narratives dealt with such basic themes as: the gods, birth, death, survival, slavery, crime and punishment, revenge, immortality, catastrophe, hardships, per-plexing interpersonal relationships, culture heroes, natural phenomena. Some of their myths are concerned with such unique events as great floods, the notion of a primitive paradise, important happenings including historical events. Others deal with recurrent phenomena, the origin of the world and the gods, the origin of man, the meaning of death, inventions and discoveries, demons and monsters, appearances of gods among men, transformations of many kinds.

Among the Greeks, as in all myth-telling societies, myths for a long time were valued and handed down to justify and validate institutions, customs, beliefs. Greeks listened to repetitions of these myths, and themselves repeated them as mechanisms contributing to the cohesiveness and welfare of the group. For the Greeks, as for other peoples, such narratives of archetypal events, supposed to have happened "once upon a time," were authoritative precedents reaffirming the validity of current practices and values.

In addition to borrowing myths and folktales from other peoples, the Greeks themselves actively disseminated their own myths. In the great periods of migration away from the Aegean area, both in the centuries from 750-500 B.C., when they established colonies on the shores of the Black Sea and throughout the western Mediterranean, and at the end of the Fourth Century B.C., when in the wake of Alexander's conquests they poured into Asia up to India, they took their myths with them. Under such new conditions and environments, some myths disappeared, while others were modified through contact with the native populations in whose lands the Greeks settled. When myths travel from area to area, they inevitably lost some of their original local character, and assumed greater universality. It was in part a result of the enormous geographical expansion of the Greeks throughout the world that their native mythology acquired that quality of universality we sense in it today.

This timeless quality of Greek myths derives from other factors as well. The Greeks brought to their mythic tales qualities of mind that not only facilitated the growth of myths in more exuberant quantity than at any other time in mankind's history, but also gave to myths a distinctive human quality. Greek religion was the most anthropomorphic religion, as well as the most polytheistic, in the world. The whole universe, from its cosmic aspects to the tiniest part of nature, was, for Greeks, filled with an enormous number of divinities in human form. Since these gods, greater and lesser, had human desires and frailties, it was natural to relate stories about them in concrete human form. The Greeks thus humanized myths, bestowing upon them a quality that affords instant recognition of typical human situations and concerns. The human quality of Greek myths is particularly prominent because the Greeks rationalized their traditional myths. They had an aversion to the fantastic and grotesque elements in primitive tales, both their own and those they borrowed from alien peoples, and they took pains to alter myths to bring them closer to real human experience by rejecting what the great Nineteenth Century student of myth Max Müller called "the silly, savage, and senseless element." Such humanization and rationalism, as well as the Greek love of systematization, are already strikingly evident in the earliest preserved Greek myths, the Homeric poems, the *Iliad* and *Odyssey*. Homer organized many age-old myths preserved by the oral tradition into grandiose literary masterpieces made up of mythic materials which had been cleansed of much of the crudities of primitive myths. The Greek dislike of anything in primitive tales which was irreconcilable with real experience endowed their myths with remarkable qualities of cheerfulness and reasonableness. This sets Greek mythology apart from all others, which often fill the world with fear and terror and with weird creatures. Greek myths have no magic, few witches, few taboo concepts, no ghosts. This special character of Greek myth — its human quality — is the principal reason later ages have valued Greek myths above all others. It is this humanism that has made them the inspiration of an almost endless stream of great artistic and literary creations from antiquity to today. It also explains why Greek mythology has survived the extinction of Greek religion for over 2000 years.

And this is, moreover, why we today use the Greek word "myth" in preference to others for such stories. Originally the Greek word *mythos* signified "word, thing said, speech." Eventually, under the influence of epic, lyric, and dramatic poets who used myths extensively, it came to mean "tale, fiction, plot of a play," and "myth." On the other hand, the Greek word *logos*, which also originally meant "word, thing said," came to mean, under the influence of Greek philosophers, "rational, systematized thought."

Mythology is thus properly today "the systematic study of tales."
As we turn to the study of the Greek myths themselves, we may appreciate why even such a realist as Aristotle said "the philosopher is also a friend of myth," and why in his old age he confessed, "the lonelier I am, the more of a recluse I become, the greater is my love for myths." Aristotle was thinking of their universality, as was Nathaniel Hawthorne when he wrote in the introduction to his *Wonder Book*: "No epoch of time can claim a copyright in these immortal fables. They seem never to have been made; and certainly, so long as man exists, they can never perish."

IV

GREEK CULTURE

However universal in content and appeal the myths of the Greeks were, there was a cultural milieu in which they were invented, underwent changes, and were systematized, and which influenced them and was served by them. That culture had as its center the Mediterranean Sea, one of the cradles of civilization. In its diffusion from Near Eastern lands westward civilized life came first in Europe to Hellas, as the Greeks called the large eastern peninsula of Europe that juts into the Mediterranean. Though Hellas is very mountainous and has few natural resources and limited land suitable for agriculture, it was settled by peoples who wanted to be close to the rich, high civilizations of the Near East. The debt of the Greeks to these earlier cultures is incalculable, for they borrowed massively from them in the fields of art, writing, literature, religion, technology, and mythology.

The indigenous population of Hellas was conquered about 2000-1500 B.C. by invaders who came from Central Europe, where a culture and a type of language now called Indo-European had long existed. The amalgamation of these migrants with the indigenous population produced the Greek people of history. Thus Greek culture from its beginning was a mixture of religious practices, ways of living, and value concepts. For instance, the Aegean people were more peace-loving and settled than the Indo-European migrants with their aggressive warrior culture; the indigenous population was engaged in agriculture and navigation, the invaders were accustomed to a more nomadic, pastoral life; the principal divinity of the earlier population was an earth divinity, a mother goddess as symbol of fertility, while the Indo-Europeans had a male sky god as the head of their pantheon.

The small, barren country of Greece was highly mountainous, had no navigable rivers, possessed numerous small secluded valleys, and was dotted with many islands off its coast. Under these conditions peculiar ways of living developed to constitute some of the distinctive characteristics of the Greek way of life. One of these was the fragmentation of the population into a great many independent communities, all of which defended their separate ways of life and fiercely sought to maintain local autonomy and political freedom. This separatism among many small states led to mutual antagonisms, rivalries, disputes, and interminable wars. Collective action among the Greeks, such as during the Trojan War and the Persian Wars, was rare and only for specific limited purposes.

Because of the barrenness of the land, life in Greece was hard, as compared with the luxury of the Near East. As a result the Greeks placed at the center of their way of life the virtues of simplicity, self-restraint, and moderation in all things. "Nothing too much" became one of the distinctive guidelines of the Greeks. Compensation for this lack of plenty was found in perfection on a small scale, especially in the human body and mind. We shall meet in Greek myths a special emphasis on the virtue of moderation, on perfection of the body, and on intelligence.

The Greeks were, however, fortunate in having ready access to the Mediterranean Sea, and eventually to the Black Sea region. Travel by sea was more natural than by land, so that Greeks became the leading merchants and travelers of antiquity. In this way they not only absorbed many influences of the Near East, but developed wider and more sophisticated horizons and perspectives than any previous people in history. Contacts overseas brought them first into touch with Crete. That large island, south of Hellas, center of a unique and remarkable civilization from about 2000-1400 B.C., had an enormous influence on early Greeks. Its culture, today called Minoan from the names of the mythical kings of the island, was distinctive for its thriving overseas commerce and its great royal palaces. The most famous of these palaces was the one at Cnossus, near the northcentral coast. This was the scene of the famous myths of Minos, Daedalus and Icarus, Theseus and the minotaur. In these myths of Crete there are vestiges of her one-time power in Hellas.

About 1500-1450 B.C. Crete was conquered by Greeks from the mainland. The conquerors, however, did not long enjoy their newly won power, for about 1400 B.C. a great disaster, whose exact nature we do not know, destroyed the civilization of Crete. As a result, Cretan culture rapidly declined, and was lost to human knowledge until it was rediscovered about 1900 by the early archaeologist Sir Arthur Evans. With the eclipse of Crete the Greeks in Hellas became the leading power of the Mediterranean. This earliest period of Greek civilization, from about 1600-1200 B.C., is today known as the Mycenaean Age because the kings of Mycenae were among the most powerful monarchs of Greece. The golden age of Mycenaean Greece saw remarkable architectural structures – huge walled palaces, and great tombs of members of the ruling warrior class. The leading centers were the kingdoms of Mycenae, Tiryns, Thebes, Argos, Elis, Orchomenos, Pylos, and regions of Thessaly in the north. Since most of the important heroic myths of the Greeks were associated with these very places, it would appear that here were developed the earliest versions of Greek myths as a mixture of Indo-European traditions, indigenous stories, and borrowings from the Near East. But we cannot be certain of this, for not a single certain mythical subject has been found in Mycenaean art, and the familiar names of heroes of Greek mythology (e.g., Theseus, Orestes, Ajax, Achilles, Castor, Deucalion) appear in the inscriptions of the Mycenaean period as the names of ordinary people, farmers and soldiers. As heirs to the commerce of the Cretans the Mycenaean ruling class of warrior nobility enjoyed a level of affluence never equalled in classical Greece. Such literature as the Mycenaeans had was oral in form, and probably consisted mostly of tales glorifying great heroes. These were then handed down by word of mouth from generation to generation.

In the small kingdoms all over Greece, the principal activities of the ruling warrior aristocracy consisted of war, taking of booty, hunting, banqueting. The highest form of personal recognition was the narration of one's deeds in tales glorifying heroes. Each kingdom had its royal family, palace, aristocracy, local tales of all kinds, and intermarriage between royal families was probably common. For a time all Greek kings seemed to recognize the king of Mycenae as a sort of overlord. This is the Greek "Heroic Age," from about 1500 to 1150 B.C., to which they assigned most of their myths of great heroes.

Collective exploits among these states were rare, and memories of some that did occur are preserved in such myths as the Calydonian Boar Hunt, the war against Thebes, the expedition of the Argonauts, and the Trojan War. Of these the siege of Troy was the greatest collective action of the Greeks of the Mycenaean Age, and consequently it attracted a host of myths and folktales as no other event in Greek history. The memory of this action inspired many works of art and literature, especially the two great epic poems of Homer, the *Iliad* and the *Odyssey*. Though we know little historical about the causes and the events of this war, we do know from the archeological evidence that the palace of Troy was destroyed about 1250 B.C. by human agency.

Soon after, between about 1200 and 1100 B.C., Mycenaean culture itself was destroyed by a great turmoil that overwhelmed and shook to their foundations all the great cultures of the Near East. For example, invaders destroyed the powerful Hittite Empire (in what is now Turkey), attacked Egypt but were repulsed, and burned and destroyed the Mycenaean palaces. Refugees from Hellas settled in Crete and on the coast of Asia Minor, brought with them their culture and myths, and came into direct contact with the influences of the Near East. And as refugees fled, from the north the Dorians — a branch of the Greeks speaking the Doric dialect — came into Greece to occupy mostly the Peloponnesus, the southern part of the peninsula. These Dorians were culturally more backward and more militaristic than other Greeks, so that Greece entered a Dark Age, which lasted from about 1100-750 B.C., a retrograde step in this area comparable to the fall of the Roman Empire 1500 years later.

In this Dark Age Greece reverted to a lower level of culture, deprived of its commerce and affluence. The Aegean world remained cut off from communication with the outside world for some time, and in the interim the commerce of the Mediterranean was taken over by the Phoenicians, a people living on the coast of what is now Lebanon. These people brought to the Greeks not only wares from the Near East but also a host of myths and folktales, many of which at this time became part of the Greek tradition. Monarchy continued as the form of government of the various small states that dotted Hellas, the islands of the Aegean, and the coast of Asia Minor, but the kings were no longer the powerful men who ruled in an earlier age. Agriculture and grazing were now the dominant sources of wealth and power, and the king's power was limited by a council of aristocrats and an assembly of the people.

Greeks continued to tell stories of the exploits of the Mycenaeans of the "Heroic Age," stories which must have seemed like "ancient history" to the new breed of petty kings and landowning nobles. In this period there developed great emphasis on the honor and glory of the individual aristocrat as exhibited through his physical prowess — in war, feats of strength, skill in athletic competitions, and hunting. It is natural that many changes were made in the pool of myths inherited from the Mycenaean Age, not only because of the oral nature of these narratives, but because new cultural needs resulted in additions to and alterations in the ancestral stories.

At the end of the Dark Age, on the threshold of the flowering of a new Hellenic culture about 800-700 B.C., two of the world's greatest literary masterpieces, the *Iliad* and *Odyssey* of Homer, emerged. Borrowing from the oral mythic traditions going back to the Mycenaean Age, "when men were greater than they are today," as he says, Homer wove them into two highly sophisticated poems. To make the stories meaningful to his audiences, Homer not only organized into a subtle literary unity numerous separate stories, but eliminated from the myths many elements that appeared crude, grotesque, and irrational. Living on the coast of Asia Minor, he also amalgamated with older Greek myths many details from the literature and tales of the Near East. While Homer based his stories on heroes and values of a bygone age, some of which were obsolete in his day, he highlighted contemporary national values. His focus was on men and women of high social status — kings, queens, nobility. In keeping with the prevailing cultural milieu, Homer made his heroes into individualists, striving to demonstrate their personal worth to win glory and be remembered in story after his death. In this way the nobles sought to win a kind of immortality through their bravery in war, their plundering, and their physical might.

Yet Homer's heroes lived in social communities and sensed their obligations to others — family, friends, the people they ruled. Thus the conflict between the pursuit of personal power and fame on the one hand, and concern for the welfare of the group on the other is one of the dominant themes of the Homeric poems. The changing times demanded the curbing of the personal ambitions exhibited by the great heroes of the past, whose excessive pride was destructive of the rights of others and the welfare of the community. In the *Iliad* and the *Odyssey* we can detect a questioning of the validity of the ambitions of the heroes of myth. A new type of mythic hero was coming, with glory not in physical prowess but in service to the community. And the *Odyssey* shows the vastly expanding geographical horizons of the Greeks throughout the Mediterranean, and their contacts with numerous non-Greek peoples..

New myths were being created, collected, and organized to emphasize these changes. New myths, or old myths modified, reflected the need to curb the violence and excesses of the individualistic hero frequently depicted in earlier myths. Greek artists (particularly in vase painting and sculpture) began to exploit the vast collection of Greek myths for illustrative themes, and artists chose the scenes that were artistically practical or thematically pertinent. Each period of Greek art reveals different favorites among the myths, and different emphases. For instance, in the early period sculpture and vase paintings emphasize the battles of the gods; later, in the archaic and classical ages, the emphasis changed to the birth of the gods, their loves, and meetings. But with all the changes, from the end of the Dark Age on, scenes from mythology remained the dominant motifs in Greek art.

The new way of life glimpsed in Homer, involving the priority of the community and cooperation of all for the common good, was the institution of the *polis*, or city-state. From about 750 B.C. on, the city-state was the most distinctive characteristic of Hellenic culture. All over Greece the regime of hereditary kings was abolished, replaced with the administration of each state by the entire body of the aristocracy. This involved election of officials holding office for limited terms (eventually one year), the publication of law codes, vigilance to prevent one man from acquiring excessive power or wealth, and expectation that each man would be committed to the common good. In the military sphere the traditional fighting of duels by leaders as champions of their people (typical of early myths) was replaced by warfare employing compact formations of massed troops. Majority votes bound the entire community, and eventually more and more citizens, not merely aristocrats, were involved in city affairs. Governed from an urban center, each city-state maintained its sovereign existence.

There were many hundreds of these city-states throughout the Greek world, and for the first time in world history the concept of the dignity and the worth of each individual citizen became a dominant value. To the plain citizen and to forward-looking intellectuals the concentration of the traditional myths on kings and heroes must have seemed unrelated to their lives and aspirations. But the old myths continued to be used for new purposes, sometimes introducing humble people in a dignified light, or scaling down the awesome heroes of the past. The existence of hundreds of freedom-loving independent city-states in such close proximity inevitably generated frequent wars, so that in almost all Greek myths, as in Greek life itself, there is the assumption that war is the natural state of affairs.

Between 750 and 550 B.C. the Greeks launched the first great colonization movement in the world. Over-population in such a barren region as Hellas demanded safety valves. One of these was infanticide through the exposure of children, a common theme in Greek mythology. But most important, excess population was siphoned off in the sending out of colonies, permanent overseas settlements. Greeks from a multitude of states founded colonies in many places on the shores of the Western Mediterranean (especially Sicily and South Italy), and on the shores of the Black Sea, in the first great planned population shift in world history. This population shift was permanent, because in the Greek system, colonies were founded as completely independent new city-states. This colonization movement renewed connections with the Near East and produced a new wave of cultural borrowings, which brought many new mythical themes and folktales, increased sophistication, and spread Greek culture, including its traditional myths, over an area of 3000 miles, extending from the Straits of

Gibraltar to the eastern end of the Black Sea. Greek myths were not only diffused all over the world, but in turn grew and changed in their new environments.

Greek religion differed from that of other people in the ancient world, and each Greek city-state had its own special religious institutions and rites for the welfare of the entire community. Since the gods were anthropomorphic, thought of as having the appearance and behavior of human beings, in dealing with such "human" gods prayers and sacrifices were required to influence them. A prayer was a request for a favor. A sacrifice was a payment to a god in return for a favor, and usually consisted of food of some kind. Gods were housed in temples (which served as their homes), and were portrayed as statues; sacrifices were offered on altars in front of the "home of the god."

A group of twelve gods constituted the chief divinities – the Olympian gods, who lived in palaces on top of Mt. Olympus in northern Greece. A king, Zeus, governed them, and he too lived on Olympus among these gods who were members of his family and other relatives. The gods not only required sacrifices, in return for which they did favors for humans, but they also controlled the behavior of humans with the threat of severe punishments. In particular, it was believed that the gods were jealous of humans, especially any who exceeded the bounds of moderation in any aspect of life. A person who acted immoderately was said to be guilty of *hybris*, the sin of excess, the only sin in Greek religion. Those guilty, whether voluntarily or involuntarily, were punished by the gods as object lessons to mortals. The Greek mottoes "know thyself" and "nothing too much" embody the Greek cautionary lesson that humans must know their limitations. The greatest Greek virtue – one of the principal themes of Greek mythology – was therefore moderation (*Sophrosyne*), the avoidance of all excess. This pattern of thought aimed to curb excessive individualism, to limit the possession of power and wealth, and to maintain a nice balance between the striving for personal distinction and the welfare of the community.

The religion of Greek city-states was not directed towards satisfaction of the spiritual yearnings of each individual, and few could earn personal immortality through heroic deeds or services to mankind or a community. Private needs found fulfilment in a number of mystery religions, membership in which held promise of a happy afterlife to initiates. The leading mystery religions of the Greeks were the Eleusinian Mysteries (centered on the divinities Demeter, Persephone, and Dionysus), and the Orphic Mysteries (based on myths of the god Dionysus and his prophet the musician Orpheus). Through initiation ceremonies, purifications, a communion meal, and participation in the knowledge of some carefully guarded secrets, initiates might gain a blessed life after death. In this connection myths have preserved many stories involving the notions of death and rebirth, as well as the possibility of happiness in the afterlife.

In the Classical Age of Greece there were also many special ceremonies for the purification (*catharsis,* "cleansing") of persons from the guilt of crimes actual or imagined. Particularly in involuntary homicide special ceremonies were devised at the great temple of Apollo in Delphi for this purpose. A murderer needed liberation from blood-guilt, so as to free him from the traditional inflexible rule of tribal law: an eye for an eye, a tooth for a tooth. Greek myths hold survivals of the notion of vengeance as a form of self-help in obtaining justice, as well as stories of atonement through purification and acts of penance, and of the more advanced concept of civic justice through trial by jury. These represent different layers of stories that emerged with the advance of civilization among the Greeks.

Another peculiar Greek institution that commonly appears in myth is the oracle. In the absence of sacred books and a strong priesthood, Greeks devised ways to discover the will of the gods directly. Many clues were studied, e.g., the flight of birds, thunder and lightning, unusual natural phenomena, dreams. Frequently they consulted prophets and prophetesses, supposed to have been inspired by a god, especially by Apollo, with inner sight and knowledge of the will of the gods and of the future. Especially important were oracles at famous temples, notably the oracle of Zeus at Dodona and that of Apollo at Delphi. The latter became a kind of national religious shrine, because Greeks traveled to this central spot in Greece to consult the famous oracle of Apollo, where, in an inner sanctum the priestess of Apollo, called the Pythia, answered questions put to the god. While the replies given were usually ambiguous, and sometimes the credibility of the oracle was placed in doubt, it held the confidence of Greeks and foreigners all over the world for about 1000 years. In a Greek myth the inclusion of consultation of an oracle is presumptive evidence that this aspect was incorporated in the myth sometime in the Classical Age.

Despite rivalry and separateness among Greek city-states, there was a strong panhellenic feeling among them, as similar customs, a belief in common ancestors, a common literature and language gave them all a feeling of oneness. Periodically they came together from all over the Hellenic world in the great panhellenic festivals, religious gatherings held at Olympia, Delphi, Nemea, and Corinth. The festival at Olympia was believed to have been initiated in the year 776 B.C. Besides the special religious ceremonies involved in each of these festivals, the greatest attractions were the athletic contests.

The Greeks loved to compete to determine individual excellence in a particular field — for example, music, singing, playwriting, acting, athletics, dancing, etc. Winning such competitions, as a sign of excellence, was much prized. Especially esteemed were the triumphs in athletic competition among the Greeks, the first people to develop organized sports. Among the most popular of their sports (all of which we find reflected in Greek myths) were boxing, wrestling, foot races, discus throw, javelin throw, chariot racing. Victory in one of the panhellenic games made the athlete world famous. Although intellectual excellence was not without honor among the Greeks, it took second place behind athletic ability. Thus we find in Greek myths, notably in those of the panhellenic hero Heracles, glorification of the hero mostly for his physical prowess, but also for his cunning. The ideal Greek mythical hero Odysseus represents a nice balance between physical strength and cleverness.

Beginning about 750 B.C., with the Greek Renaissance, a new form of literature, lyric poetry, developed, to displace epic as the dominant literary form. Like epic, lyric poetry constantly reached into the pool of Greek mythology for illustrations and themes. New Greek art forms also came into being: the classical Greek temple, and the carving of life-size sculpture. The principal subject of Greek sculpture was the human figure, with the favorite theme a scene from the traditional myths, which supplied artists with idealized gods and heroes, and with timeless paradigms from their stories.

Unprecedented breakthroughs by Greeks also occurred in other fields, as, about 600 B.C., philosophy and science, the first attempts in man's history to construct rational explanations for natural phenomena in place of the accepted mythical ones. By 650 B.C. the aristocratic governments throughout Greece proved incapable of keeping pace with rapid changes taking place. Ultimately revolutions led to the establishment of a new form of government among the Greeks — rule by a tyrant. To the Greeks tyranny simply meant one-man rule gained by unconstitutional seizure of power. It was a transitional form of government, responsive to a general crisis, and the tyrants were in general regarded as beneficent rulers who brought better conditions to their cities. Later the institution got a bad name, so that some Greek myths glorify tyrant-slayers as heroes. For instance, in Athens the tyrant Peisistratus (560-528 B.C.) proved to be one of the great men in Athenian history, and his rule was generally beneficial, but his son Hippias was of lesser stature, becoming arbitrary and despotic. His rule led to several revolutions, which finally brought in 508 B.C. a new form of government — democracy (Greek for "power to the citizens"), the first in world history. This new type of government was established to prevent a return of either aristocracy or tyranny to Athens. Greek democracy provided for equality of electoral rights, equality before the law, and equality of speech for all citizens.

About 600 B.C. the Greek city-states began to feel themselves menaced by great empires in the East; they had been spared foreign invasion since the end of the Mycenaean Age. One by one the Greek cities in Asia Minor were conquered by the kings of the Lydian Empire (in what is now Turkey), the first Greek cities to lose their much-prized freedom. But their traditional culture was left undisturbed by the Lydians. However, with the founding and rapid expansion both east and west of the Persian Empire (emerging from present-day Iran), the Greeks of the Asiatic cities fell under a more despotic rule. The colossus in the East loomed as a despotic force comparable in Greek imagination to the forces of evil portrayed in many Greek myths. Anti-Persian feeling was so intense that rebellion broke out in 499 B.C. among the Ionian

Greeks in Asia Minor. This brash challenge by a small number of Greek cities to the world's superpower ended in disaster, and the Ionian Revolt was ruthlessly crushed by the Persians in 494 B.C.

The involvement of several Greek cities in support of the Ionian Revolt led to the Persian invasions of Greece in 490 and 480 B.C. To their own amazement, first the city of Athens, then a coalition of Greek cities repelled the Persian invasions. The defeat of Persia was one of the great traditions of Greek history, and meant much to the Greeks and to the Athenians in particular: the preservation of Greek freedom and culture; the growth of Athens as a naval power; the establishment of the Athenian Empire, in which a democracy kept under its subjection about 150 Greek cities. This power of Athens made possible the Golden Age of Athens (about 460-430 B.C.), dominated by the greatness of Athens' political leader Pericles, who made Athens the cultural, political, and economic leader of Greece.

Under the democratic constitution of Athens, the entire body of citizens wielded the ultimate power, and citizens were guaranteed equal opportunities for public office and other civic responsibilities. The women of Athens, daughters and wives of citizens, had no legal personalities, and were denied full civic rights, as were, of course, slaves, aliens, and members of Athens' empire. Nor did Athenian women share in the social life of what was a man's society; they were, in general, secluded at home to look after the household and bear and rear children. Marriages were arranged by parents, with dowries always a consideration. While infidelity on the part of the wife was severely punished by law, Greek men easily carried on extramarital unions, not only with female slaves, but with attractive alien women who flocked to Athens to entertain men as prostitutes or more elegant "companions."

As a standard public service, the government of Athens provided public productions of tragedies and comedies as a ceremony of the state religion. Drama was the distinctive literary form of the Athenian democracy, and the plots of almost all Greek tragedies were drawn from Greek myths. Yet it was the intent of the authors of these plays to explore contemporary problems and conflicts. Thus they selected myths which lent themselves most readily to illuminating the contemporary issues being dramatized, and frequently changed the myths to adapt them to the conditions and problems of the Fifth Century. Thus many Greek myths are known to us only in the form adapted to the artistic requirements and views of the playwrights.

Athenian writers altered many offensive myths during the Fifth Century in an atmosphere where freedom of thought and speech prevailed. Teachers of higher education, Sophists, rational- ists who opposed traditional Greek values, religion, and morality fostered skepticism in all areas of life. They denied the existence of gods, assailed a morality based on religion and fear of divine punishment, and held that each man acts always in his own self-interest. Man therefore behaves, they taught, not in accord- ance with ideals or principles, but only through self-interest. Their teaching stimulated a drive for personal power, which had to be curbed if the city-state was to survive.

Mutual suspicions between Athens and its only other powerful rival among the Greek cities, Sparta, led to the growth of two powerful blocs of cities and the outbreak of the disastrous Peloponnesian War (431-404 B.C.). This conflict brutalized all the Greeks and sapped their manpower, economic strength, and moral fibre. Sparta won the war ultimately, with the aid of the Persians, hereditary enemies of the Greeks, and Athens was defeated and surrendered unconditionally. Greece never really recovered from this disaster. Impoverished, disillusioned, the Greeks began to lose faith in the ability of the city-state to provide them with a viable way of life.

The jealously guarded independence of the Greek cities had exacted a ruinous price from the Greeks. Yet in the next century (404-330 B.C.) inter-city warfare continued unabated, internal struggles between rich and poor mounted in fury, and civic spirit and acceptance of community responsibilities, like military service, declined. Attempts to solve the dilemmas, notably the establishment of leagues of cities with reduced autonomy, or efforts to achieve a general peace to preserve the autonomy of the Greek city-states, failed to change the situation. Sparta succeeded Athens into the position of hegemony over the Greeks, only to be followed in about thirty years by Thebes. The failure of Sparta and Thebes to maintain their power over the Greeks reduced both of them, as the result of military defeats, to second rate powers.

The weakness of the city-states led to outside intervention in the internal affairs of Greece. Philip II, king of Macedon, a region just to the north of Greece, with diplomacy, bribery, and military brilliance became master of Greece by 338 B.C.. Philip intended to solve the problems of the Greeks and to increase his own power and empire by uniting Macedon and Greece under his rule, and then to invade and conquer the rich Persian Empire, but he was assassinated before he left for Asia. In 336 his throne passed to his much more famous son, Alexander the Great, who also inherited his father's plans to invade Persia.

In a series of whirlwind campaigns, from 336 to 323 B.C., Alexander with the Macedonian-Greek armies crushed the Persians, annexed the whole Persian Empire, and made plans to continue eastward through India as far as he could go. He conquered and unified under his rule the largest empire man had seen thus far. His policies included the building of many new cities, all on Greek models, throughout his empire, and the creation of a new interracial ruling class of Macedonians, Greeks, and Persians. Although Alexander's conquests and policies brought to an end the independence of Greek city-states, his great achievement was the spread of Greek civilization throughout the East as far as India. Ultimately, the amalgam of Greek culture with others spread to the West, where it was eagerly adopted by the Romans, so that, in effect, Alexander's conquests hellenized the world.

Greeks swarmed into Asia in the wake of Alexander's conquests, bringing with them their language, cultural values, literature, and myths. In this third great contact of the Greeks with the East (the first was in the Mycenaean Age, the second in the Age of Colonization), Greek myths received another layer of eastern myths and folktales. The new culture brought into being by Alexander is called Hellenistic, to differentiate it from the previous Hellenic civilization. It had many varieties, Greco-Egyptian, Greco-Indian, Greco-Iranian, Greco-Roman, and involved a mixture of races and cultural values. It flourished especially in great cities away from Hellas proper, especially in Alexandria in Egypt, and in Rome, and, among the transformations brought in this period, myths were subjected to new changes. In Alexandria many myths turned into romantic love stories, and in Rome many were adapted to the patriotic needs of her ruling class.

After Alexander's death his successors and generals tore his empire apart. Frequent wars, intense economic crises, and revolutions continued in an atmosphere of permanent international tension among the great powers. Ultimately, about 200 B.C., the Romans, already masters of the West after their defeat of the great maritime power of Carthage, intervened in the East. Gradually Rome absorbed the entire Hellenistic East into her own empire. Finally in 30 B.C., with the death of the last ruler of independent Egypt, the Macedonian queen Cleopatra, Rome completed the unification of the entire Mediterranean, *mare nostrum* ("our sea") the Romans called it. By about 150 B.C. all Greek creativity in the arts and literature came to an end, as the new masters of the Mediterranean imported into Rome, the new capital of the world, famous Greek artists and writers to embellish their own culture. Among the legacies that the Greeks handed on to the Romans, who adopted so many aspects of their culture, was the body of myths the Greeks had created and used so creatively for over 1000 years.

* * *

SIGNIFICANT DATES IN GREEK CULTURE
(All dates are B.C.)

Migration of Indo-Europeans into Hellas	2000-1500
Minoan Civilization of Crete	2000-1400
Mycenaean Age in Hellas — the "Heroic Age"	1600-1200
Greek invasion of Crete	1500-1450
Trojan War — siege and destruction of Troy	1250
Destruction of Mycenaean Culture	1200-1100
Dorian Invasion	1100
Greek Dark Age	1100-750
Homeric Epics	800-700
Creation of Greek city-state	800-750
Traditional date of first Olympic Games	776
Age of Colonization	750-550
Tyranny as form of government in Greece	650-500

Birth of philosophy and science	600
Peisistratus, tyrant of Athens	560-528
Athens becomes a democracy	508
Annexation of Greek cities by Lydia	600-550
Annexation of Greek cities by Persia	545-535
Ionian revolt against Persia	499-494
Persian invasion of Greece	490-479
Golden Age of Athens — Periclean Age	460-430
Peloponnesian War	431-404
Decline of city-state	404-330
Philip of Macedon conquers the Greeks	338
Alexander the Great conquers Persian Empire	336-323
Hellenistic Age	330-30
Rome absorbs Hellenistic World	200-30

V

TOWARD AN ORDERED WORLD

When Greek society emerged from the Dark Age about 800
B.C., with a new type of culture based on a multitude of
autonomous, self-confident, creative, and aggressive city-states, at
the center of Greek religion and mythology stood the sky-and-
weather god Zeus, "father of gods and men." His divine kingship
over the vast number of gods and other superhuman powers that
held sway over all aspects of the universe gave comforting
assurance to the Greeks of a just, ordered world. But his power,
however great, was neither absolute nor eternal. Like mortal kings,
Zeus was born, grew to manhood, and did not attain supremacy
until he had proved his worth.

As migrants from mideastern Europe into the Aegean culture
area about 2000 B.C., the Greeks had brought with them belief in
the Indo-European male sky god as chief divinity. They had to
adapt his worship to a new homeland in which there were age-old
traditions of the primacy of a mother goddess. Coming as
conquerors into the glamorous Aegean civilization as relative
late-comers themselves, the Greeks conceived of Zeus too as a
late-comer in the evolution of cosmic history. Like Greeks on
earth, Zeus in the sky had to battle his way to rule. In adjusting
Zeus' supremacy to the traditions they found, the Greeks filled in
the earlier period with a narrative of the evolution of the universe
from the beginning to the triumph of Zeus. What emerged was an
amalgam of indigenous prehellenic traditions (in both Hellas and
Crete), Greek pride and imagination, and the internationally
diffused mythic and folktale traditions of the Near East. In brief,
the establishment of Zeus as ruler and orderer of the cosmos was

set forth as the culmination of a very long, turbulent evolution in which primordial divinities, often cruel and violent, had previously held sway. This cosmogony (an account of the creation and origins of the universe) was new, and called also for a new account of the origin (theogony) and family history (genealogy) of the gods.

There existed a wide range of Near Eastern creation myths long antedating our first sources of Greek mythology. But while the earliest Greeks borrowed for their cosmogony a great deal from the Near East, their own ethnic concepts are apparent at once. Unlike other ancient peoples, the Greeks had no belief in a creation "from nothing," nor did they have any view of gods as divine creators. The Greeks, with their humanistic bent of mind, created their gods in the image of man, and their myths without irrational happenings and grotesque creatures. Thus the gods by their very nature did not have the power to create the cosmos. In place of instant creation the Greeks substituted the concept of gradual evolution as a kind of automatic process. Inherent in this, the Greek concept of change, or flux, as a basic principle in the world, controlled their views of even the gods themselves, who were not viewed as static and unchangeable.

But for Greek cosmogonies as against others, all things developed from some pre-existing starting point which existed from all time. Whatever this starting point was – and there was no single authoritative doctrine as in other religions – the universe evolved through a series of stages in which order was slowly fashioned out of disorder before reaching completion and perfection under Zeus. These stages involved cycles of divine generations or families who displaced one another from the most ancient group of primordial nature gods to the "modern" Greek sky god. The rise and fall of divine families was set in an unstable, turbulent world, full of violence and cruelty, in which each takeover of power was accompanied by catastrophic transitions. All this turmoil was part of the process of the final reduction to order and harmony culminating in the just reign of Zeus.

Our earliest knowledge of the Greek view of the starting point of the evolution of things to be comes from the poetry of Homer, who wrote over 1000 years after the Greeks brought their Indo-European traditions into the Aegean. In Homer's view everything in the universe began and subsequently evolved from an eternal body of water called Oceanus. Had Homer written a theological work, he might have affirmed: "In the beginning there was water." This primal river of sweet water flowed in a circle around the earth, which floated on it like a flat disk. Without beginning or end, and self-renewing, Oceanus constituted a kind of definite border around the earth, guaranteeing its regularity and fertilizing it. The outer limits of Oceanus ended somewhere, but no one knew at what precise point. Thus Oceanus served as a reassuring boundary between man's knowable earth and the unknown Beyond, in a way lost to modern man. Originally a fabulous, awesome place, a cosmic principle in Near Eastern cosmogonies, Oceanus was transformed by the Greeks into a god with human traits. As primordial all-father, he was married to Tethys ("Nourisher"), who was a sort of primal mother figure. This pair had many offspring, including all the rivers of the world and many daughters called Oceanids, who were kindly nymphs, benevolent guardians scattered in many places both on land and in the depths of the sea. In keeping both with their antiquity and the importance of water for human life, animals, and agriculture, Oceanus and Tethys were an elderly, kindly, majestic couple, living peacefully in a palace in the far distant West.

In general, the venerable Oceanus remained neutral in all the upheavals of this early period of the world. If not completely removed from the center of action, he lent his services as mediator. For example, during one of the world-shaking combats of early times, the battle between the Titans and the gods, Zeus' sister Hera was evacuated from the combat area and received shelter in the palace of Oceanus and Tethys. And in a famous scene in the *Prometheus Bound* of Aeschylus, Oceanus tried unsuccessfully to mediate the dispute between Zeus and Prometheus. As a benevolent survivor from the "good old days" he was generally thought to have supported Zeus in his struggle for control of the universe.

When Greek philosophic-scientific thought began to displace traditional mythological explanations of phenomena, Thales, "father of philosophy," in the Sixth Century B.C. decided that water was the single substance that made up the universe. He arrived at this conclusion partly because water can be solid and gaseous as well as liquid. But, in fact he was also clinging to the traditional ancient Greek view of the original starting point of the universe — the river Oceanus.

A crisis in this belief that Oceanus flowed all about earth as a body of sweet water emerged when the Phoenicians and the Greeks first sailed outside the Straits of Gibraltar and explored the waters there. While they were prepared to believe that this was indeed part of the river Oceanus, the salt water there led to the invention of such names as "Sea Outside the Pillars of Heracles," "Outer Sea," and then "Atlantic Sea." The Greeks coined the name Atlantic from the name of the Titan Atlas, believed to be stationed in the far west of North Africa. They concluded that the river Oceanus proper flowed much farther beyond the part of the Atlantic then known. Belief in all-encircling Oceanus survived until the Fifteenth Century A.D., and Columbus and his fellow explorers knew that Greek geographers as early as the Third Century B.C. asserted that if one sailed west from Europe one would reach India by following the circular path of Oceanus.

Rivers were popular symbols of fertility among the ancient peoples. But it is strange that a standard Greek view of the origin of things should have been the primacy of a river of water, since there are no rivers of any consequence in Hellas except for the Acheloüs River in west central Greece. In fact, most Greek rivers dry up completely in the summertime. Geographical environments have a profound influence upon speculations about the beginning of things, and in arid regions and where river water was scarce, as in Greece, there was always anxious reliance on rain for agriculture. But in the East, great rivers were the major sources of fresh water, and it is likely that the conception of river water in the Homeric poems as the first beginning came into Greek thought as a borrowing from Near Eastern creation legends.

The very concept that the world had a beginning is a remarkable one, unknown to primitive man, to whom the world seemed always unchanging and without beginning or end. The notion probably arose from the analogy of the phenomenon of birth in humans and animals, so that the beginning of the cosmos found biological explanations, such as hatching from an egg spontaneously, or birth through sexual union. With the development of artistic creativity and technological skills, the notion of a "maker" or "creator" of the universe took shape. The earliest cosmogonic texts with emergence myths date from the middle of the Third Millenium B.C., and come from Mesopotamia and Egypt. In both of these regions — the birthplaces of civilization — great rivers (the Nile, the Tigris and the Euphrates) are fertilizing forces that make life possible there. It is therefore not surprising that for the Egyptians, the Sumerians and Babylonians water was the primordial beginning of things. In Sumerian-Babylonian mythology the world began when the male Apsu, an ocean of sweet water under the earth, mingled with Tiamat, the female salt sea. In Egypt the "first time" is Nun, the primeval waste of sweet water, a sort of watery chaos out of which land emerged in the form of a hill which then produced a divine creator. Such notions of beginnings may have reached the Greeks on the coast of Asia Minor, where Homer lived, possibly brought to them by the Phoenicians. It is noteworthy that in Hindu mythology, which similarly arose out of a river civilization the starting point was also primeval cosmic waters.

Hesiod, who lived in a farming region in central Greece (Boeotia) and wrote his theogony about 700-675 B.C., had a different conception of the origin of the world. Perhaps because he was closer to the soil Hesiod assigned priority and greater importance to Earth as mother of all. But his *Theogony*, the most systematic account of the origin of the world and gods in Greek literature, is just one man's attempt to systematize Greek beliefs about the gods, organized into a genealogically interconnected system. Though Hesiod borrowed from older literary sources and popular tradition, his own rationalist inclinations, poetic inspiration, and personal views played an important part in moulding his system.

Hesiod's cosmogony begins with Chaos as the earliest state of the universe. Chaos is not a god but a cosmic principle, which posits a state of disorder as the starting point, an abyss of vast empty space filled with the material of creation in a shapeless disordered mass (cp. Milton's "void and formless infinite"). This concept is original with Hesiod, so far as we know. By starting with Chaos, Hesiod was able to glorify all the more Zeus' final victory, his justice, and the stable order he brought to a turbulent universe. From Chaos in primordial time there came into being first Gaea (or Ge), Mother Earth, from whom all else in the universe evolved, including eventually both gods and men. Next after Gaea, Chaos produced Eros (Desire), Erebus (Darkness), and Nyx (Night).

Gaea (the Roman equivalent is Tellus, or Terra Mater) is for Hesiod the universal mother of all things, fertile renewer of all life. Such a great earth goddess had long been the supreme divinity in the ancient world, known to all peoples from the Mediterranean to India from remotest antiquity, especially wherever settled agriculture was the way of life. She was the principal object of worship in the Aegean world before the coming of the Greeks, venerated in many forms as the personification of fertility and maternity, and accompanied by a young male god subordinated to her as her consort-begetter. In antiquity Crete, before the coming of the Greeks, showed the fullest expression of the supreme Mother Goddess. In India today, every village still worships Maha Mata (Great Mother), and gau mata (mother cow) is still a sacred animal. From this archetypal feminine fertility symbol arose many myths about death and rebirth, especially in the vegetation cycle, and about immortality.

Hesiod tells us that out of her teeming fertility — she had almost countless offspring — Mother Earth produced spontaneously Uranus (Sky) as a cover for earth, then the mountains, and Pontus (Sea, probably a personification of the Mediterranean). But Hesiod also introduced a novel concept, the principle of Eros (Desire, or Love) as one of the oldest forces in the universe. For, in addition to what appeared to be spontaneous growth in nature, sexual desire brought male and female together and caused pairing and offspring. Thus Hesiod introduced into theogony a purely secular and rationalizing concept — Love that mitigates the disorder of Chaos by causing voluntary unions producing new growth. Thus through the force of Eros, Chaos' son Erebus, personification of the darkness inside Earth, and his daughter Nyx, personification of night on Earth, united to beget their opposites: Aether, personification of the upper sky above the clouds, and Hemera, personification of day upon Earth. This concept that through union otherwise terrifying forces can produce beneficent things is one of Hesiod's significant contributions to human thought.

By the force of Eros, Gaea herself paired with her son Pontus to produce the ancient sea god Nereus, "old man of the sea," wise and benevolent, reflecting the high valuation the Greeks placed on the Mediterranean. Nereus had the power to foretell the future, as well as the ability to transform himself into many different shapes, a power possessed by other sea divinities. This concept undoubtedly survived from a primitive practice of seeking prophecies of the future from some rituals connected with the sea. The Greeks after Hesiod told the myth that before Nereus would consent to prophesy he had to be seized and held while he sought to escape by changing his shape. Subsequently Nereus paired with the Oceanid Doris to beget the benevolent and beautiful daughters of Nereus, the Nereids (usually given as 50 in number), who lived in Nereus' palace at the bottom of the sea. Nereus and his daughters illustrate the role of the sea in Greek life and portray the existence of benevolent forces in the universe side by side with destructive and cruel ones. The best known of the Nereids were Amphitrite, Thetis, and Galatea.

Much more decisive for the evolution of the world, Gaea and her son Uranus united to become the parents of eighteen children of superhuman size and might. Their own fertility and the monstrous nature of some of their offspring reflects the lush productivity, disorder and violence of the youth of the world. This union of the primeval divine couple, Earth Mother and Sky Father — a basic myth all over the world — the primordial "Sacred Marriage," personifies the fertilization of the earth in climates where water from the sky, rather than from rivers, is the life-giving source. This "Sacred Marriage" recurs in many forms in Greek mythology, and appears in the ritual of Greek religion as a fertility ceremony to portray the renewal of life in nature. The myth depicts in macrocosm a grandiose unity of heaven and earth, the oneness of man with the universe and nature, just as each farmer and his family in microcosm depend for continuity on fertility and the reproductive process.

Gaea and Uranus had as offspring twelve Titans, three Cyclopes, and three Hecatonchires. These three Cyclopes (called "Uranian Cyclopes" to distinguish them from other types of Cyclopes) were gigantic nature forces of lightning, thunderstorms, and volcanic actions, named Brontes ("Thunderer"), Steropes ("Lightning"), and Arges ("Shiner"). Tradition sometimes pre-

sented them as early divine smiths. Similarly, the Hecatonchires
("Hundred-Handers") named Cottus, Gyes (or Gyges), and
Briareus (or Aegion), represented the roar and pounding of the
waves of the stormy sea, and perhaps volcanic eruptions. The birth
of these offspring from Earth and Sky in sacred marriage reveals a
significant reversal of an age-old concept of the Aegean. The
invading Hellenes found in the Aegean area a great female mother
goddess to whom was joined a subordinate young male god as
consort, who died when his fertilizing function was completed,
was then reborn or replaced by another male god. In the Greek
myth, however, the earth goddess is the passive feminine element,
while the sky god dominates. The Hellenes thus identified the
male with their sky god, and reversed the statuses of male and
female, to roles typical of a strongly patriarchal society like that
of early Hellenic culture.

After the banishment of Chaos beyond Oceanus, somewhere in
outer darkness, Uranus became the first "king in heaven" in Greek
mythology. Now Oceanus and Gaea had been benevolent divinities, but Uranus, the son and consort of Gaea, was the first to
introduce evil into the universe. His dominant characteristic was
his hatred of his children and his cruelty toward them. Though his
fertility produced an exuberant progeny, he sought to prevent
their birth from Earth into the daylight. Closely embracing Mother
Earth (originally Earth and Sky were not separate), he succeeded
in confining his children inside Gaea, promoting evil as he held
back further development and in a sense favored a return to
Chaos. Despite the existence of Eros, Uranus' suppressive act
introduced potential strife into the universe. It is noteworthy that
it was Mother Earth who, thinking of the future and posterity,
favored the younger generation against the cruel and self-indulgent
father. In order to punish Uranus and to permit continuity into
the future, Gaea produced metals and fashioned a weapon (called
harpe, the reaping tool of the Near East), with which she armed
Cronus, the youngest of the twelve Titans, and released him from
inside her body. Attacking his father as he lay on Mother Earth,
Cronus castrated him. Thus Heaven and Earth were separated, in a
famous myth widely diffused throughout the world. The separ-
ation of the Sky from Earth released new forces of fertility, and
Uranus, deposed as ruler of heaven, retired into obscurity, his

fertilizing power ended. It is interesting that in this myth, of Near Eastern origin, the son attains freedom by removing his father as sexual and political rival. This myth influenced Freud to declare fear of castration one of the dominant aspects of male psychology.

With the emasculation of Uranus, new life began in Mother Earth. The blood from Uranus' wound produced new creatures as the drops fell on Mother Earth: the Erinyes (Furies), the Giants, and the Melian Nymphs. Moreover, as his severed genitals fell into the sea Aphrodite, goddess of love and beauty, was born, the first creature in the universe that was not monstrous. And with this birth the unrestrained reproduction in the youth of the world came to an end.

Upon the removal of Uranus all his children were released from Mother Earth, and Cronus assumed the "kingship in heaven," with his sister the Titaness Rhea as his consort. The conflict between Cronus and Uranus was the first round in the struggle between successive generations of gods for the "kingship in heaven." One divine dynasty displaced another until Zeus triumphed as god of justice and order. At each succeeding stage a new sky god ruled with the support of his brothers, sisters, and relatives. This process eventually achieved complete victory over elemental disorder in the universe.

Cronus headed the new rulers of the universe, the Titans and Titanesses, twelve huge divinities of remote antiquity, representing primary forces of nature. The Greeks did not even know the meaning of the word "Titan." Of great beauty and power, these divinities were probably gods of the prehellenic population, some of them belonging to the heavens, others to the earth, some benevolent, others violent and destructive. It is surprising that Oceanus and his mate Tethys appear among the Titans, even as the eldest, since they had been so important in early cosmogonies, and they must have subsequently been demoted from their awesome starting point to passive members of the second divine dynasty. The developing Greek tradition organized these early gods into a dynasty of twelve Titans, in imitation of the twelve Olympians, with six Titans, Oceanus, Coeus, Crius, Hyperion ("Up Above"), Iapetus ("Hurler"), Cronus, and six Titanesses, Theia ("Divine One"), Rhea, Themis ("Steadfast"), Mnemosyne ("Memory"), Phoebe ("Bright One"), Tethys ("Nourisher").

The Titan generation, huge in size but human in form, begat many varied offspring. Iapetus married one of the Oceanids, Clymene ("Famed One"), by whom he had four children, Atlas, Moneotius, Prometheus, and Epimetheus, also Titans though not among the original twelve. Iapetus' name is reminiscent of Japheth, son of Noah in the Old Testament, and there seems to be some common source of both in the Near Eastern myths, since a descendant of the Titan Iapetus, Deucalion, was actually the Greek Noah. Hyperion, apparently a primitive sun god, and his sister Titaness Theia had three children, Helios, the Greek sun god, Selene, the moon goddess, and Eos, goddess of the dawn. Coeus married his sister Phoebe and engendered Leto, later famous as the mother of the gods Apollo and Artemis, and the Titanesses Themis and Mnemosyne, who long remained unmarried, eventually united with Zeus. Themis, goddess of law and justice, is unique among the Titanesses, for she was later admitted to Mt. Olympus and lived with the Olympian gods. Cronus and Rhea, a new sky-earth pair, were the parents of Hestia, Demeter, Hades, Poseidon, Hera, and Zeus, who formed the nucleus of the great Greek pantheon.

When Cronus, the youngest of the twelve Titans and the first great figure of Greek mythology became supreme ruler, he ushered in a new age of plenty and progress. The Greeks identified his rule with the Golden Age and later idealized his reign proverbially as "life in the time of Cronus." He may have been a prehellenic agricultural god before he was elevated by the Greeks to the position of sky god before Zeus, for in some parts of Greece there was celebrated annually a harvest festival called the Cronia. According to the Greeks, the "time of Cronus" at the beginning of history afforded a happy primitive existence, a sort of paradise on earth in which men did not work, lived forever, and were close to the gods. The Greeks placed this vision of an earthly paradise, a myth known all over the world, in the remote past, and never had the view, as did the Iranians, Jews and Christians at times, that such a period would return in the future. Nor did they have a myth of the coming catastrophic end of the world, like that in Scandinavian/Germanic mythology.

Paradoxically Cronus, the god of the Golden Age, the original benign agricultural god, ruled the universe in the sky violently and craftily, so much so that he was often called "crooked-counseling

Cronus." First he imprisoned again in Tartarus, deep inside Earth, the monstrous Cyclopes and Hecatonchires, whose awesome might he feared. Finally, when the aged Uranus and Gaea issued from retirement the terrifying prophecy that Cronus would be overthrown by one of his own children, he took drastic measures. He swallowed each of his children as soon as it was born from Rhea. After the disappearance of her fifth child Rhea plotted to save her next child, and became the instrument of the salvation of the gods, just as Gaea had earlier favored the younger generation against her husband Uranus. She bore Zeus on the island of Crete, hid him away there, and substituted a stone dressed in swaddling clothes for Cronus to swallow. Then, when Zeus grew up and was sufficiently strong, he seized his father Cronus and compelled him to disgorge his sisters and brothers.

The revolt of Zeus against Cronus unleashed a struggle for power between the older generation of Titans and the younger generation of Olympian gods. This battle, called Titantomachy, shook the earth in its fury and violence, and put the very existence of the world in jeopardy. In this first great battle of the immortals in Greek myths, comparable in Norse mythology to the world conflict that ended in the twilight of the gods, and to the battle between the good angels and the bad angels in the *Apocrypha*, repression of further progress or the establishment of a more humane and just order was at stake. Once more progress came only as the result of violent events. The participants in the struggle were males on either side (Hera, for example, as we have seen, was sent to take refuge in the palace of Oceanus and Tethys in the far West).

In Northern Greece, in the region of Thessaly, the Olympian gods Zeus, Hades, and Poseidon took their stand on Mt. Olympus, while the embattled Titans, greater in number and size than their opponents, used as their base of operations Mt. Othrys nearby. Oceanus remained neutral, while one son of Iapetus, Prometheus, actively supported Zeus during this ten year struggle, a convulsion which, according to the ancients, produced the indications of natural upheavals visible in the area in antiquity. Eventually it became apparent that Zeus and the Olympians, representing a new rational principle in the universe, could not prevail by intelligence alone, or without the use of force, so Zeus released the

three Cyclopes and the three Hecatonchires from Tartarus. Paradoxically again, in the evolution of the universe, although the end desired was a world of reason and justice, the means used were force and violence, and the primordial monstrous beings who represented original turmoil and disorder were now needed for order and civilization and the victory of Zeus. In gratitude for their liberation the Cyclopes created new weapons for Zeus, the thunderbolt and lightning, gave Poseidon the trident, Hades a helmet that made him invisible, and the Hecatonchires used their hundreds of arms to hurl a barrage of huge rocks upon the Titans on Mt. Othrys. After this combined attack overwhelmed the Titans, Zeus hurled most of them into Tartarus, and there set over them the Hecatonchires as eternal guards.

Although Cronus was not obviously much preferable to Uranus in his behavior, his struggle with Zeus involved the new issue of civilized behavior of individual to individual, of the failure of violence and selfishness as a way of governing. So another, better divine generation was required, and Cronus must be defeated by his son Zeus. It is striking that in this myth Cronus evolved from a young hero to older villain, from rebel to tyrant, from liberator to suppressor. Zeus only overthrew his oppressor as youth, Uranus only fell as parent, but Cronus, as the middle generation, had both experiences. In this myth of the child's development by repression, the parent drives the victim into violent rebellion, even against the father. Like all surviving myths, the Uranus-Cronus-Zeus story retains its validity because of its universality.

Cronus, the father of the victorious gods, was either eternally banished, or fled west to the Isles of the Blest or Italy. Since there had long been in Italy a humble agricultural god named Saturn who very early was identified by the Romans with the Greek god Cronus, it was believed that the benign Greek god had brought the lost innocence of the world with him there to reestablish the Golden Age – the Age of Saturn as the Romans called it. (Through a false etymology Cronus was associated with the Greek word *chronos*, "time," and became the symbol Father Time). Also in the West, Zeus stationed one member of the second generation of Titans, Atlas ("Enduring One" or "Carrier") in northwest Africa to support there the heavens on his shoulders as punishment. This sky-supporting Titan has given his name to the Atlas Mountains in North Africa, the mythical lost continent Atlantis, and the Atlantic Ocean. The use of the word atlas to designate a book of maps comes from the portrayal of Atlas holding a globe of the earth on his shoulders, a picture that used to appear on map collections.

After his victory over the Titans, Zeus faced a second earth-shaking revolt. In anger at the harsh treatment meted out to her children the Titans, Gaea stirred up against the Olympian gods the Giants, sons of Earth, born from the blood of mutilated Uranus. Monstrous in size, the Giants (Greek *Gigantes*) appear completely human in the earliest Greek artistic representations in existence as violent armed warriors, though larger than humans, but Hellenistic representations show the giants as savage monsters, with human bearded heads and serpents in place of lower extremities, wearing animal skins and fighting with huge rocks and trees.

The Gigantomachy, the second great struggle between the forces of order and disorder, occurred (depending on the tradition one follows) either in the peninsula of Pallene in Thrace or in Arcadia in the Peloponnesus. Unlike the Titans, the Giants were mortal, so Gaea sought to make them invulnerable by means of a magic herb. But Zeus discovered the existence of the herb first, forbidding Helios, Selene, and Eos to shine until he found it. Even so, it was revealed that the gods would not defeat the Titans in this cosmic battle for Olympus without the aid of a mortal, and Zeus, therefore, summoned his son Heracles to his aid. Among the gods, Athena especially fought by her father's side, though others among the gods, such as Apollo, Hera, Dionysus, Hecate, Hephaestus, Poseidon, Hermes, Artemis, Aphrodite, and even the Fates lent their aid. Attacking leaders of the Giants, Heracles and Athena killed Alcyoneus, Athena slew Pallas and Enceladus, and Zeus' thunderbolts and Heracles' arrows disposed of Porphyrion. Heracles' arrows finished off most of the other Giants after Zeus' thunderbolts struck them down. The survivors were imprisoned under volcanoes, and still continue to smoke from the thunderbolts; for example, the body of the Giant Enceladus was said to have been placed under the island of Sicily. The Giants remained throughout antiquity the principal adversaries of the Olympians, symbolical of the struggle between the forces of chaos and order, barbarism and civilization.

The greatest challenge to Zeus' rule was yet to come. Infuriated at the Olympian gods, Gaea united with the grim Tartarus and produced the largest of all her offspring, the worst of all monsters Typhon (or Typhöeus), an enormous winged dragon with 100 serpent heads, 100 hands and feet (or pairs), spewing flames from eyes and mouths. (Typhon was sometimes equated with the fiery whirlwind, hence the origin of the word typhoon). In violent earth-shaking battle the thunderbolts of Zeus and the roars of Typhon reached every part of the world, and the lightning and dragon fire caused vast conflagrations throughout the world. Most of the other gods fled before Typhon into Egypt, where, to protect themselves, they changed into shapes of animals. When thunderbolts thrown from Mt. Olympus could not defeat Typhon, Zeus descended to earth to fight directly with him on Mt. Casius in Cilicia in Asia Minor. First Typhon immobilized the immortal Zeus by severing the sinews of his arms and legs and hiding them, but the gods Hermes and Aegipan restored them so that he regained his strength. Zeus then pursued the fleeing Typhon and eventually overcame him with his thunderbolts, placing Mt. Etna in Sicily over his smoking body. As the result of this victory — a kind of David-Goliath combat — Gaea finally abandoned her hostility to her grandson and became reconciled to the rule of Zeus. While the problems of Zeus were not completely ended (there were other challenges to him later, e.g., from the Aloades, Prometheus, and his own fellow gods), the victory over Typhon, who had brought him to the brink of disaster, established his supremacy for eternity.

Zeus is the first of many dragon-slayers who figure in Greek mythology. The dragon, a concept of Sumerian-Babylonian origin in the Near East, originally personified the constant threat to civilization and order by catastrophic assaults of nature. The turbulent waters of the overflowing Tigris and Euphrates Rivers in Mesopotamia, insinuating their snake-like way as they flooded the plain between, called forth the image of a huge water serpent. The dragon combat story, an age-old myth with over 1000 versions all over the world, first appears in Babylonia as the victory of the god Marduk over the water divinity Tiamat, to symbolize the victory of man over the forces of disorder, destruction, and death. From there it spread eastward to India and China, westward to Egypt, Greece, and Western Europe, and the variants of the myth all present the same general pattern of personification of the evil forces of disorder in the form of a dragon which a god or hero destroys. The dragon of these myths is a composite monster with serpent characteristics dominant, often winged, sometimes fire-breathing, usually associated with water.

Although Greek mythology most frequently uses the dragon combat story (Zeus, Apollo, Heracles, Perseus, Cadmus, etc., fight dragons), there are famous battles in other traditions — Siegfried killing Fafnir, Beowulf killing Grendel, Tristan overcoming a dragon. The Christian myth of St. George and the dragon arose from the story of a Roman officer who suffered martyrdom in the Third Century A.D. In the Christian account the dragon is the incarnation of the devil or represents heresy, a reinterpreted version acceptable to the Church, and England adopted St. George as its patron saint during the crusades of the Middle Ages.

The dragon in the Typhon myth is not the only theme in the Greek theogony that originated in the Near East. Long before the Greeks, Near Eastern cosmogonies and theogonies worked out the whole formulation of divine dynasties in succession, each in turn struggling with the forces of disorder in theomachies, or battles of the gods, and each in turn falling when it abused its power. This theme has been discovered in Hittite texts written about 1400-1200 B.C., and these tales were adapted from still older Hurrian texts of about 1500 B.C. that contained motifs going back to Babylonian and even Sumerian myths. In the Hurrian-Hittite Kumarbi myth the starting point, Alalu, a divine nonentity, was dethroned by Anu, his son, god of heaven. In turn Anu's son Kumarbi, a vegetation god, castrated his father with a *harpe*, violently separating heaven and earth, and seized power in heaven. Like Cronus, Kumarbi also swallowed a stone, until finally, the weather god Teshub overthrew his father and seized the rule of the sky. While there are many differences between the Greek and the Hittite-Hurrian struggles between the generations of gods, the story is basically the same, an age-old cosmogonic heritage of the Mediterranean-Oriental culture area. The Greeks may have taken this story as early as the Mycenaean period and adapted it to their

needs, or may have received it from the Phoenicians as inter-
mediaries during the Dark Age.

Similarly, the Hurrian-Hittite myth of a primeval giant,
Upelluri, who carried heaven, earth, and the sea on his shoulders,
may be the Near Eastern source of the myth of Atlas. Still another
Hittite-Hurrian myth, the Song of Ullikummi, tells of a prodigious
serpent-footed monster which threatened the reign of the young
weather-god Teshub in battle — an obvious parallel to Typhon's
challenge to the rule of Zeus, and localized on Mt. Casius in
Cilicia, the very spot where Zeus battled Typhon. Other Near
Eastern texts, found at Ugarit (Ras Shamra) in Northern Syria,
dating from 1400-1200 B.C., recount the successions of four
generations of gods. Baal struggled with Yam, the sea god, for the
kingship in these myths, and the Canaanite sky-harvest god El is
specifically equated with Kumarbi in the Hittite-Hurrian myth.
The Phoenicians took over these dynastic succession myths, and
the Greeks themselves equated the god El with their Cronus.

All these close parallels indicate that Hesiod's version of the
divine succession, whatever its immediate source, was an adaptation to Greek myths of common traditions of the Near Eastern
cultural heritage. All this evidence tends to disprove the earlier
view that the Greek cosmogonic and theogonic stories record
survivals of folk memories of struggles between the invading
Greeks and the indigenous population, and the displacement by
Indo-European gods of local divinities. The original and significant
Greek contribution in Hesiod's narrative of the cycles of divinities
is the victory of a just god, Zeus, king of the Olympian gods.

VI

OLYMPIAN GODS:
Zeus, Hera, Poseidon, Hestia

The composite nature of Greek mythology as an amalgam of tales and concepts from many origins is the principal reason most Greek gods have multiple functions which are so diverse and unrelated that their association with one divinity seems incomprehensible. This composite quality also explains the duplication of functions in several divinities. But whatever the Greeks borrowed from other religions and mythologies they recast it to accord with their anthropomorphic conception of the supernatural, to make Greek religion the religion of anthropomorphism *par excellence*. As we have seen, anthropomorphism is a concept of the divine which portrays gods not only in human form, but also with human traits like love, sexual desire, jealousy, competitiveness, hate, etc. While other religions, like the Egyptian, were theriomorphic (characterized by gods in the form of animals), Greek religion had no animal or vegetable divinities, though vestiges of such earlier beliefs survived in their stories.

Greek myths of the immortal gods tell stories of birth, marriage, parenthood, sometimes even of their deaths. In most cases when divine children were born they behaved almost immediately like adults, although in a few instances they had true childhoods and were nursed and brought up like children. The myths of Zeus and Dionysus, for example, contain the classical birth and childhood stories of divine children. In keeping with the human qualities of the gods, some usurp the powers and domains of other gods who lose theirs, while yet others may rise to more important functions. Indeed, some mortal heroes and heroines in Greek mythology were in earlier times undoubtedly originally true gods (the so-called "faded gods") who had in the course of time been displaced as divinities but survived in story as mythical humans. In other cases mortal heroes and heroines were elevated to divinity because of their achievements or virtues.

Thus the line between the anthropomorphic gods and heroic mortals was very thin, although it was basic in Greek thought to maintain some such barrier between men and gods. The basic principle of proper behavior for men, as we have seen, was to avoid the sin the Greeks called *hybris*, on the assumption that the gods were jealous of humans. Therefore any human being who was in any way exceptional, whether involuntarily (such as possessing great beauty or intelligence) or knowingly (for example, holding great wealth, power, skill) ran the risk of arousing the jealousy of the gods and being punished by them. So the practice of moderation was considered the wisest course, mindful always of the principle of the limitations of man. The Greek gods, represented by statues and housed in temples, were thus comfortable to deal with on the human level, particularly since they varied as people do. Some of them, the heavenly or Olympian gods, were more jovial, while others, the chthonic gods, were more serious or grim, associated with the earth and regions under the earth.

The relationship between humans and gods was considered to be one of mutual advantage. The gods were thought to need gifts of food and drink, though they had their own special foods (ambrosia and nectar), and could be flattered by the offer of foods by humans. Hence ritual in Greek religion consisted not of inner faith and declarations of such faith to the gods, but of acts of friendship toward them. The gods, in general, did not volunteer favors to humans. If a Greek desired divine aid, he first prayed, expressing to a specific god's statue precisely what favor was desired, then he performed a sacrifice. Such sacrifices consisted mostly of food, such as animals, birds, wheat, cakes, wine. To assure that the food would reach the gods, wine was poured out as a libation to evaporate; other foods were burned, and the odors were thought to reach the nostrils of the Olympian gods. Sacrifices to chthonic gods, on the other hand, were often buried in the ground.

After the Olympian gods came to power as the result of the revolution against the Titans and the rule of Zeus was firmly established, the victors divided the world. Zeus assumed control over the sky, to Poseidon was assigned the sea, Hades obtained sovereignty over the underworld, and they agreed to hold the earth in common. In accordance with Indo-European patriarchal custom, only the three males among the original gods participated in sharing the power, while the females Demeter, Hestia, and Hera were assigned subordinate roles. In time Zeus and Poseidon and their three sisters were joined by seven children of Zeus, four male (Apollo, Hermes, Ares, Hephaestus), three female (Athena, Aphrodite, Artemis). This group constituted the famed twelve Olympian gods, so called because they dwelled in palaces on top of Mt. Olympus, the highest peak in Greece (about 10,000 ft. high), located in Thessaly in Northern Greece. (The word "olympus" was a pre-Greek word meaning "mountain;" there were at least fourteen mountains with that name in various parts of Greece and Asia Minor.) This inaccessible celestial city of the gods was idealized by the Greeks as a blessed place, but in actuality the top of Mt. Olympus is snow-covered and very cold.

Most of the gods who came to be called the children of Zeus were of foreign origin, known elsewhere before they were incorporated into the Greek pantheon. But Greek imagination early moulded the twelve gods into a single royal family on the model of the patriarchal royal houses and monarchies of the Mycenaean Age, and the concept of a family of gods gave an additional sense of order to the world.

The number twelve as a collective group first had both practical application and mystical meaning among the Babylonians. From them we have inherited the twelve months, the concept dozen, the twelve hour pattern, and the twelve signs of the zodiac in astrology. From such Near Eastern traditions Greeks living in Asia Minor adopted the notion of the special significance of twelve in their pantheon, although there were very strong ambitions among the lesser gods to be admitted to the exclusive twelve on Mt. Olympus. For a time the "thirteenth god" was Dionysus, and efforts to apotheosize famous mortals into the "thirteenth god" occurred from time to time.

The twelve Olympian gods lived in separate palaces but frequently met in council in Zeus' palace. Here, together with their entourage who ministered to their pleasure, they spent their

time banqueting, enjoying music and dancing, and carrying on
intrigues among themselves. Their food was ambrosia (meaning
"belonging to immortals"), their drink nectar (probably a kind of
honey drink). In general they preferred to remain on Mt. Olympus,
but often descended to mingle with mortals or to perform their
earthly or marine functions. Their blood was of a special divine
liquid called ichor. Though they were immortal, they were not
omnipotent, for they could be wounded, or have their power
temporarily curtailed, and they could be chained or imprisoned, or
limited in other ways. In keeping with Greek legal and social
practice, they were monogamous, although their married state did
not deter them from having affairs among themselves on Olympus
or with other divinities elsewhere, and especially with mortals,
from whom they had numerous illegitimate offspring. This is
especially true of the head of the Greek pantheon, Zeus.

Despite their special Hellenic anthropomorphic complexion,
the Olympians, as well as lesser Greek gods, retained vestiges of
earlier religious and folktale traditions. Thus they had the power
to transform themselves into various shapes, and such transformations or metamorphoses were especially common in Cretan
religion. There the mother goddess, as well as her male consort,
were capable of appearing on earth in many, varied forms. The
concept of an earthly manifestation of a god, epiphany, persisted
in Greek religion. Sometimes the Greek gods took animal forms
(bull, bear, swan, horse) – a vestige of more primitive therio-
morphism (belief in gods in shape of animals) – sometimes they
took on human disguises. Such magic power to change shape
belonged not only to Zeus, but also to such gods, for example, as
Proteus and other water divinities. Shape-shifting was especially
used in combat, when a god struggled to avoid an enemy. In this
connection, the gods had the power to transform humans into
other forms, both animal or plant, as punishment or reward.

At the head of the Olympians stood Zeus, the Greek version of
the chief Indo-European sky god. (The linguistic root of this
name, *div*, means "to shine," with reference to the bright sky). His
counterparts elsewhere are the Italian Jupiter, the Hindu Dyaus
pitar, and the German god Tiu. But in the developed myths, the
Greek god Zeus embodied in his figure not only the sky god of the
Indo-European warrior folk but also mythic aspects derived from

the young Cretan male consort of the prehellenic mother goddess, as well as from Near Eastern myths. His multiple origin accounts in part for his paradoxical nature: the highest god of the Greeks was majestic, awesome, well-nigh omnipotent, yet at the same time lecherous and petty, interfering in many insignificant affairs on earth.

Though the youngest son of Cronus, he is the father figure among the gods, the patriarch of the divine family. Called "father of gods and men," he was really neither, but rather simply "head of the family." Usually portrayed in art as a majestic king, with heavy beard, flowing hair, and a scepter, in his royal role he sat on a throne in his palace. But he was also father as procreator, for through his union as sky father with the earth mother (in the form of his sister-wife Hera) he participated in agricultural fertility. His principal function was that of weather god, for he controlled such atmospheric conditions as clouds (he is frequently called "cloud gatherer"), rain, hail, snow, storms — in short, whatever affects agricultural productivity. He hurled his weapon the thunderbolt from Olympus as sign of his wrath; lightning and thunder were its manifestations. The bull too is often associated with him. These symbols of power and fertility — thunderbolt and bull — were already current in the Near East as attributes of the sky and weather god, but the eagle, also associated with Zeus, appears to be a Greek innovation. As patriarchal protector he also was a civic god, thought to protect law, order, morality in the state and in family life. For this reason he was the god of hospitality, and oaths were sworn in his name. So, like the Mycenaean kings, he maintained order and justice in all spheres, enforcing the laws and striking the disobedient with his lightning. However, even though Zeus thus brought harmony to both nature and society, he was not omnipotent or all-wise. In particular, he was limited by the assigned powers of other gods and by Fate, which he could not change, even when it affected those dearest to him. Whatever else he may have been, Zeus, as we have seen, was not a divine creator.

In Greek myth, the union of Zeus with the Aegean mother goddess in the form of Hera brought him into association with the principal Cretan male god, a fertility god subordinated to the earth mother. This Cretan male god was born, united with the mother goddess, was worshipped with orgiastic ceremonies, often took the

form of a bull, died, and was reborn. Out of this complex originated the Greek myth of the birthplace of Zeus, usually located in a cave in Crete, sometimes in Arcadia in Greece, sometimes even in Asia Minor. When Zeus was rescued by his mother, Rhea, from his father Cronus, who sought to swallow him, he was brought to Crete, where he was secreted in a cave. There he was nursed by the goat Amaltheia (or a nymph by that name, which means "plenty"; other versions say he was fed by bees, or a pig, or doves). In gratitude to Amaltheia for nursing him, Zeus gave great honors to the goat, and when one of her horns later broke off, he made it the horn of plenty (the cornucopia), eternally overflowing with fruits of the earth. Her skin became Zeus' protective breastplate, the aegis, later fortified with the symbol of the head of the Gorgon Medusa. (Actually, the aegis was probably originally the storm cloud as symbol of Zeus, but through a false etymology from the Greek word for goat, it was associated with the skin of Amaltheia). Finally, it is said that Zeus elevated Amaltheia to the rank of a constellation called Capella.

The helpless baby son of Rhea was protected in Crete by the Curetes, warrior priests or primitive demons, worshippers of the Mother Goddess, who clashed their shields in an orgiastic rite to conceal from Cronus the crying of the baby Zeus. Some believed that Zeus died in Crete, and actually showed his tomb there, scandalizing those who believed in an immortal Zeus.

In another important function, prophecy, Zeus was the principal rival of his son Apollo. The great oracular shrine of Zeus, located at Dodona in Epirus in Northwestern Greece, instituted far earlier than the Delphic oracle, was of high antiquity, indeed originally an oracle of Gaea. At Dodona Zeus, when he assumed this function, manifested himself as a sacred oak, an object of great veneration among the Greeks, and spoke through the rustling of the leaves of the tree. Here Greeks consulted him and his consort Dione on a variety of problems, and the priests of the shrine, the Selloi, and a priestess, who sang a hymn which contained the line, "Zeus was, Zeus is, Zeus will be," interpreted the noises of the leaves. There were two other oracles of Zeus, one at Olympia (which specialized in inquiries about athletic competitions), the other, that of Zeus Ammon in the oasis of Siwah in

Egypt, in later times the principal rival of the Delphic oracle. In classical times, just as Dione was ousted by Hera as wife of Zeus, so Apollo at his shrine in Delphi usurped the role of center of prophetic activity, largely because Delphi, being centrally located, was more conveniently reached by most Greeks.

Zeus played an important part in a great number of specific myths. So many of these deal with his unions with all manner of women both divine and mortal that he has been called a "sexual athlete," and his unrestrained sexuality is unparalleled in world mythology. It has been estimated that, besides his legal wife Hera, Zeus had over 100 women, by whom he had an enormous number of children. It would be wrong to think that the Greeks were frivolous or irreverent in portraying their chief god in this way, as if to establish a divine prototype for their own sexual freedom, for in most cases the union of Zeus with a goddess or mortal woman represented originally an instance of the "sacred marriage" of an earth goddess with the fertilizing sky god. The Aegean mother goddess had many forms, which the Greeks concretized into separate divinities and united with their sky god. Furthermore, it was a great honor for cities and noble families to be able to trace themselves back to Zeus, so many myths report ancestry from the god through a semi-divine child born of a local heroine courted by Zeus.

The tradition reports that before Zeus married Hera he had as first wife (or lover) Dione, by whom in one version he was the father of Aphrodite. His second wife was said to be Metis ("Thought"), an Oceanid. A water creature, she at first resisted his attention by taking various shapes. When she was to have a child by him, Gaea uttered her second great prophecy, that a child of Zeus by Metis would overthrow and replace him as sovereign, so to prevent this he swallowed Metis, and eventually gave birth himself to his beloved daughter Athena. By producing her from his own body, he subordinated her to him, and thus put an end to the cycle of dynastic successions in the struggle for kingship in heaven. Another wife (or lover) of Zeus was the Titaness Themis ("Steadfast"), by whom he had the Moerae (Fates), the Horae (Hours, Seasons), and Dike (Justice). We shall meet many more of his lovers and children in the Greek myths.

Compared with the turbulent regimes of earlier sky gods, the reign of Zeus after his victory over Typhon was relatively peaceful. There were challenges to his sovereignty, none serious, for example by the giant twins Otus and Ephialtes, and once by a revolt of the gods. Hera, Athena, and Poseidon, in a plot against him, put Zeus into chains, but he was quickly rescued with the help of the Nereid Thetis, who, to avert civil war on Olympus, summoned the Hecatonchire Briareus to release him. We can gauge the major concerns of the Olympian gods by the uproar caused by Zeus' decision to replace his own daughter Hebe as cupbearer of the gods with a handsome young Trojan Ganymedes, with whom he had fallen in love and whom he had carried to Olympus.

The queen of the Olympian gods was Hera, sister and wife of Zeus. Although she was in origin the supreme prehellenic earth goddess, in her relationship with the chief male deity of the Greeks she was relegated to an inferior position. In the Greek pantheon Hera was the goddess of formal marriage, conceived as both a sacred and legal institution, and so she served as the divine protectress of marriage and the family, the divine model of married women, a personification of monogamy and marital fidelity.

When Zeus fell in love with her, she resisted his attentions and rejected him, but his yearning for her was so strong that he transformed himself into a cuckoo (harbinger of spring in the Mediterranean) and came to her in this guise. When Hera fondled the tiny cuckoo, there was consummated, in the form of the ancient fertility rite, the sacred marriage of Zeus and Hera. The formal wedding of the king and queen of the gods took place in the Garden of the Gods, situated in the far West. Here Gaea presented as a wedding gift for the bride a tree of apples, symbol of love and fertility, later known as the Apples of the Hesperides, from the nymphs stationed to tend and guard them. This tree is the Greek adaptation of the famed tree of life myth of the Near East. Hera and Zeus are usually said to have had three children, Hebe, Ares, and Hephaestus, who were in fact not really genuine offspring of Zeus and Hera. They were associated with Zeus and Hera to develop a family for the Greek goddess of marriage, who is herself derived from the unmarried ancient mother goddess. Hebe is simply an abstraction, symbol of the eternal youth of the gods, Ares was not originally a Greek god, and Hephaestus as a baby was said to have been produced by Hera without sexual union. Hera was portrayed in art as a dignified, self-assured matron, often with her own special symbols of fertility, the peacock, pomegranate, cow.

But the most distinctive aspects of the myths of Hera depict her conduct as an angry wife and her domestic strife with her unfaithful husband Zeus. As protectress of marriage, she was hostile to and jealous of the lovers of Zeus, whom she spied on and vindictively sought to persecute. In particular she persecuted many of her husband's illegitimate children, notably Heracles and Dionysus, and a late myth tells that her hostility to Heracles formed the Milky Way when Zeus secretly ordered that the baby Heracles be placed at the breast of sleeping Hera so that by drinking her milk his son might achieve immortality. But Hera awoke, and when she pushed the baby away, refusing her breast to Heracles, the milk spilled over the heavens, producing the Milky Way. Several incidents highlight the marital problems and tense relationship of Zeus and Hera. It was Hera who led a palace conspiracy to chain Zeus, and on one occasion Zeus was so angered with Hera that he hung her from Mt. Olympus with anvils tied to her ankles. And, as in Greek society itself, the double standard in the sexual sphere prevailed among the gods, so any advances made to Hera by males enraged Zeus and brought forth severe punishments from him.

Below the heavens, ruled by Zeus, was another domain, the sea, for the Greeks a central element in their lives, providing easy communication for travelers and merchants, as compared with the difficulties of travel in their highly mountainous country. It is natural that they possessed an important sea god, Poseidon. Yet for the earliest ancestors of the Greeks the land, not the sea, was the dominant aspect of their environment, and thus originally the earliest Greeks had no mythology of the sea. For this reason, Poseidon was originally an earth god, probably an Indo-European fertility god, and his name, in fact, means either "Husband of Earth" or "Possessor of Earth." In Northern Greece Poseidon was worshipped as a husband of Gaea, and in parts of Southern Greece the myth was told that Poseidon loved Demeter (that is "Mother Earth") who, in flight from him, transformed herself into a mare. Poseidon then took the form of a stallion, by whom Demeter had the miraculous horse Arion. This earthly origin and epiphany of Poseidon as a horse is in keeping with his role as god of horses among the Greeks. The horse, indeed, appears to have been first domesticated in central Europe, the original heartland of the Indo-Europeans, and then diffused from there by invading Indo-Europeans into the Near East and Greece in the Second Millenium B.C. The association of the thundering of wild horses across a plain may be the origin of one of Poseidon's titles "Earth Shaker," and in this sense he was also connected with volcanic activity and earthquakes. As fertility god he sometimes, like Zeus, appeared as a bull.

After the Greeks became dominant in the Aegean Sea, Poseidon changed from an earth god of fertility and horses into an anthropomorphic god, elder brother of Zeus and god of the sea. An older god of the Mediterranean, Pontus, faded into oblivion, remaining only a shadowy figure of waters. This evolution explains why Poseidon is a composite god, with both land and marine characteristics. As god of the sea, he had a palace in the Aegean, yet also maintained a mansion on Mt. Olympus. Just as Zeus' domain was the sky, so Poseidon regulated all aspects of marine phenomena and activity, such as storms on the sea, disappearance and rise of islands, marine animals. As sovereign of the sea he rode over it in a golden chariot pulled by winged horses, accompanied by an entourage of sea animals, especially dolphins, and other sea divinities, particularly his wife Amphitrite and his son Triton. He is portrayed, like Zeus, as a bearded, long-haired, mature man carrying his special weapon, the three-pronged trident. The trident itself as symbol of Poseidon and the sea had its origin in an unrelated Near Eastern symbol, and may originally have been the symbol of the thunderbolt.

When Poseidon became god of the sea, it was necessary to change his mate from an earth goddess to a sea divinity. Thus he consummated a sacred marriage with the ancient marine divinity Amphitrite, who became queen of the sea, just as Hera was queen of the sky. Amphitrite was a lovely Nereid, daughter of Nereus, old man of the sea, and her sole function was to serve as faithful wife of Poseidon. Like the wives of Zeus and Hades, Amphitrite at first rejected Poseidon's attentions, and when he tried to seize her near the island of Naxos in the Aegean and pressed his attentions upon her, she fled from him, escaping to Atlas and the Atlantic Ocean. After a long search, some dolphins found Amphitrite, convinced her to return, and escorted her through the Mediterranean to Poseidon to be his bride. Their marriage, another of the ritual sacred marriages, celebrated in myth with great splendor, produced two children, Triton and Rhode. Like Amphitrite herself, her son Triton would appear to be a pre-Greek god. Represented as a merman, man from waist up, the lower part fish, he carried a conch shell, which he blew to start and end storms. Originally there was only one Triton, but later mythology multiplied this figure, so that in the entourage of Poseidon and Amphitrite there were many Nereids and Tritons, in imitation of the nymphs and satyrs who accompanied the god Dionysus.

Like Zeus, therefore, Poseidon is a composite god, combining the violence and terrifying dangers of the sea, as well as its blessings to mankind. Like Zeus, too, he had many love affairs (some of which we shall observe in other myths) and produced numerous offspring, some of them giants and monsters, others horse-formed. It is not recorded that Amphitrite was jealous.

Poseidon sometimes became irked at his subordination to Zeus. When he joined the plot to chain Zeus, he was compelled as a punishment to serve Laomedon, king of Troy, for whom he performed menial labor in connection with the building of the walls of that famous city. Like Zeus, Poseidon was vindictive, wrathful, cruel, and his hostility to and persecution of Odysseus is famous. On occasions he sent sea monsters to plague those who offended him.

The myths that tell of Poseidon seeking to give his name to various places in Greece on or near the coast may be reminiscences of conflicts between sea-roving Greeks and indigenous Aegeans for possession of lands on the shore. For example, he competed with Hera for control of Argos, but lost the contest. In the most famous event of this kind, Poseidon vied with Athena for the privilege of becoming the patron divinity of Athens and giving it his name. In the formal contest Poseidon struck a rock on the Acropolis in Athens with his trident and caused a horse to spring up out of the earth (other versions say a spring of fresh water). There is a rock with three holes on the Acropolis in Athens which is pointed out today as the very rock Poseidon struck. Athena, on the other hand, caused an olive tree to spring up, and won the contest.

By contrast with the original male gods of Olympus, the sisters of Zeus and Poseidon were models of virtue. Hestia, the maiden sister of Zeus and Poseidon, was the Indo-European goddess of the hearth, protectress of the home and domestic life, and by extension the state. She was symbolized by fire kept eternally burning in each house and in a central place in each city, and just as fire, having been domesticated, as it were, has its eternal place in the sacred hearth, so Hestia is a "stay at home," never leaving Olympus, eternally virgin. She was venerated as a symbol of the continuity of life in the home and the state. It is obvious that Hestia was little anthropomorphized, not developing much beyond the mere idea of the hearth, for she has no mythology.

VII

OLYMPIAN GODS:
Demeter, Athena, Ares, Hephaestus, Aphrodite

Somewhat more venturesome than Hestia was her sister Demeter, originally an Aegean mother goddess who properly belongs on the earth. Her name means "Earth Mother," but unlike Gaea and Hera she became a specialized agricultural divinity whose realm was the cultivation of wheat instead of remaining a generalized cosmic force of fertility or symbol of fecundity in human marriage. To appreciate the veneration in which Demeter was held we must remember that long before the beginnings of civilization in the Near East and Europe, wheat had taken on the role of the staff of life, comparable to rice in the Far East and maize in the Americas. Apart from the myth of Poseidon's love for Demeter in the form of a horse, all her myths concern the fertility of the earth. She did not marry, but devoted herself wholly to concern for the earth's productivity of wheat. The story is told, in this connection, that a certain Iasion fell in love with her. In one version she repulsed his attempted violence to her and was rescued by Zeus, who destroyed Iasion with his thunderbolt, but in the usual version, Demeter returned his love "in a field that had lain fallow and was three times plowed." Their child was Plutus ("Riches"), originally a symbol of the abundance of the earth.

Demeter also had a love affair with her brother, the sky god Zeus, and had a daughter by him, Persephone, or Kore ("The Girl"). This beloved only daughter of Demeter was originally a prehellenic nature goddess whose name Kore characterized her as the "grain girl," and her relation to her mother is the central myth of the goddess Demeter. A joyful creature, attended by lovely nymphs, Persephone roamed the fields, but one day as she was picking flowers in Sicily (other versions say in Crete, or Arcadia in the Peloponnesus, or at Eleusis near Athens), the earth suddenly opened up, and her uncle Hades, god of the underworld, appeared, seized her forcibly, and took her to his palace under the earth. Demeter heard her cry of terror, but the rape of Persephone, which took place with Zeus' knowledge and consent, had few witnesses, and so Demeter did not know where to seek her daughter. Thus began the long search of the "sorrowful mother" for the lost child, one of the most famous themes in world thought. Holding a torch in each hand, Demeter frantically roamed the world, refusing to return to Olympus until she had found Persephone, and in the meantime withheld her divine aid from the earth. Wheat ceased to grow, famine came bringing suffering to mankind and distress to the gods, who required sacrifices from men now too troubled and poor to perform them. As long as Persephone remained under the earth, no grain would ever grow again.

In her wanderings Demeter, disguised as an old woman, reached the town of Eleusis, near Athens, where she received the hospitality of King Celeus and his wife Metaneira. In gratitude the childless Demeter undertook to serve as nurse for their son Demophon. In order to bestow immortality upon her nursling, Demeter in secret began to burn away the mortal parts of the child with fire, and when Metaneira accidentally discovered this, Demeter suddenly revealed her true nature and ordered a ritual in her honor to be established at Eleusis. To another son of the king and queen of Eleusis, Triptolemus, she gave the role of diffusing and teaching agriculture throughout the world. The mission of Triptolemus was a very popular theme among the Greeks, for it symbolized agriculture as the foundation of civilized life for the Greeks. Many cities later claimed that the hero Triptolemus had stopped there in his wanderings.

After a year of famine Zeus was compelled to compromise. He interceded with his brother Hades to release Persephone, on condition that she had eaten nothing while in the realm of Hades (there was a folktale that those who broke the taboo against eating in the underworld would have to remain there eternally). But Hades had anticipated this, and offered Persephone a pomegranate, from which she ate several seeds. Accordingly, she was

permitted to return to her mother most of the year, but obliged to stay with Hades as Queen of the Underworld several months each year (some versions say four months, some three).

This myth is one of the most famous of the ancient tales embodying the concept of the vegetation cycle. The kernel of the story is the death or disappearance of a young god, the yearning and search for the divinity, and the eventual rediscovery or rebirth of the god, assimilating the natural cycle of the "death" of vegetation in the winter, the survival of apparently dead seed, and the return of growth in the spring to the human feelings of sadness for a lost or dead dear one and hope for a return.

When Persephone rejoined her mother, she remained either on earth or returned with Demeter to Olympus, but during her months in the underworld she was a stern, inflexible matron, sharing with Hades the rule over the dead. Hades was the only one of the three original Olympian male gods who remained eternally faithful to his wife, even though she spent little time with him each year.

Out of this myth of Demeter developed a remarkable religious institution at Eleusis, about 14 miles northwest of Athens. Here a famous shrine became the center of the Eleusinian Mysteries, whose rites, based originally on primitive agricultural beliefs, inspired awe and respect for over 1000 years, and the initiates to the Mysteries were confident that as individuals they would attain a happy afterlife. The Eleusinian cult was secret, the rituals were never revealed in antiquity, and the secret was so well kept that we are not reliably informed about particular beliefs or the rituals themselves. They are called "mysteries" not because of this secrecy but because a formal initiation was required for admission, and the initiates were called *mystae*. A mystery religion – there were many in antiquity – is one in which individuals voluntarily agree to be initiated into the belief, as distinct from a religion which one followed because it was the religion of one's parents. Of course, initiates into such mystery religions (except much later in the case of Christianity) did not give up the traditional cults of their ancestors, but continued to practice them to ensure the welfare of the family or entire community. The Eleusinian Mysteries had only one concern – assurance of a more blessed afterlife.

Once a year those who desired to be initiated at Eleusis gathered in Athens, and heard a proclamation that only those who were ritually pure could be initiated (this excluded unpurified murderers and those guilty of other major crimes). The rites were open to all: men, women, children, even slaves. Then each initiate, carrying a small pig, was purified in the sea by a sort of baptism (a Greek word which means "dipping"), after which the pig was killed and sacrificed. Then a grand procession of all the initiates, bringing sacred objects of the cult from Athens to Eleusis, took the sacred road to Eleusis. During this 14 mile religious procession, the initiates shouted "Iacchus." At Eleusis the initiates gathered in the great Initiation Hall, where a sacred drama (perhaps the myth of Demeter and Persephone) was performed, and certain sacred objects were shown in an atmosphere of great solemnity. The initiates had been required to fast during some of the days of the initiation period, and now at the end there may have been a sacred meal for them, constituting a kind of communion meal.

The rites now completed, the initiates left, apparently filled with joy and confidence in a happy immortality. The ceremony for each initiate appears to have been a "one shot" experience. Initiates were not obliged to follow special rules of conduct, or to return periodically to the sanctuary at Eleusis, or even to worship the goddess Demeter regularly. Yet, whatever the actual secret rites were — this is one of the best kept secrets in the religious history of the world — the impact on the participants was extraordinary, so that Eleusis became one of the most renowned sites in the world. Starting as a local agricultural rite, the Eleusinian Mysteries became at first a panhellenic institution, attracting Greeks from all over, and eventually a worldwide one when it was adopted by the Romans.

Another of the Olympian goddesses had original connections with agriculture. The Cretan mother goddess, venerated in many forms as divinity of the earth producing sustenance and affluence for man, was transformed by the Mycenaean warrior chieftains into an armed protector of their royal palaces under the name Athena. In this way the goddess Athena took on warrior traits in the Greek pantheon, emerging as Zeus' favorite child in his capacity of king and father. Her composite nature, partly political-military, partly economic, is reflected in her dual name —

Pallas Athena.

The birth of Athena is one of the famous miraculous births of mythology, a stock folktale motif the world over. The child that Metis (Zeus' early wife) was carrying when Zeus swallowed her to prevent the birth that would eventually overthrow him was Athena. After some time this daughter sprang out of Zeus' own head, fully grown and fully armed, with a thunderous shout. This earliest version portrays the motherless birth of Athena as a kind of divine epiphany, perhaps preserving the vestiges of a primitive belief in the emergence of a god from a mountain top, the domain of the sky god. In a later, more fully anthropomorphic period, when it was popular to portray advances in civilization as due to great culture heroes, we find a more complex version. Zeus is said to have had severe head pains, whereupon the god Hephaestus, craftsman of the gods, was summoned (sometimes it is Hermes or Prometheus). Equipped with an axe, he split open the head of Zeus to permit the release of Athena. Whether Zeus produced Athena unaided or by the mediation of Hephaestus, the result was the subordination of Athena to her father Zeus, and in this way Zeus escaped the fate of Uranus and Cronus.

Like the Minoan mother goddess Athena remained unmarried, having as one of her cult names Parthenos ("Maiden"). Her chastity and modesty were constantly extolled. Once, when a Theban Tiresias inadvertently beheld her bathing in the nude, she struck him blind (though she compensated him with the gift of wisdom). Another story is told about the god Hephaestus, who, before he was married to Aphrodite, was overcome with passion for Athena. She successfully fought off his violent attentions to her, and in the struggle his seed was spilled on the ground of Attica, fertilizing Mother Earth to bear the Attic hero Erichthonius. Moved by latent mother instincts, Athena became the child's foster mother.

At first the protector of Mycenaean royal palaces, Athena took on the functions of goddess of war, particularly in defensive measures, and so, appearing as an armed maiden warrior goddess, like Zeus she wore the protective breastplate, the *aegis*. Then with the development of the Greek city-state as a political form, she became the protector of cities, known as Athena Polias (guardian of the city). In this capacity of protector of cities her divine power

was thought to be concentrated in the form of a statuette of the goddess called after her the *palladium*. Believed originally to have fallen from the sky, this protective talisman was especially associated with the city of Troy and its myths.

As protector Athena befriended many famous mythical heroes. In particular she was the protecting divinity of the city of Athens, to which she gave her name after winning the formal competition with Poseidon. The olive tree, with which Athena won, or olive branch, became one of her standard emblems, symbol of prosperity and peace. As goddess of civic peace, she was also patron goddess of other important aspects of the economy, the technical arts and crafts, especially such important ancient "woman's work" as spinning and weaving, and is said to have invented such advances as the ship, the plow, and the double flute. This musical instrument Athena attempted to play herself, but when her puffed cheeks distorted her maidenly features, she threw it away. The flute was promptly picked up by the satyr Marsyas, who became an expert on this plebeian instrument.

It was a natural development that, as patroness of the technically advanced city of Athens, she became also goddess of wisdom, an appropriate patron of the city which was for centuries the intellectual capital of the civilized world. Her favorite bird, the owl, became the symbol not only of the goddess but also of her favorite city Athens. From the Fifth Century B.C. the owl began to appear on Athens' coinage as the standard symbol of the city, and these world-famous coins themselves came to be known popularly as "owls." The Athenians maintained the cult of Athena intensely and lavishly, and built on the acropolis, the religious center of the city (originally the site of a royal palace), her famous temple the Parthenon (Temple of the Maiden), the greatest masterpiece of Greek temple architecture. (It was preserved intact for over a thousand years after the early Christians ended the cult and transformed the temple into a church of the Virgin Mary). Every four years in antiquity the Athenians celebrated a festival of Athena known as the Panathenaea, which lasted four days and included athletic contests, and competitions involving the recitation of the poems of Homer. The Panathenaea concluded with a solemn religious procession of the entire Athenian population ending on the acropolis, where a new robe was placed on the great statue of the goddess in the Parthenon.

As patron divinity of Athens the goddess was originally represented as a young maiden, but in the middle of the Fifth Century B.C., when Athens was head of a powerful empire, she began to appear in artistic representations as a powerful, authoritative woman, with helmet, spear and shield in her hands, and aegis on her breast. She thus served as the first female symbol of a state in man's history, establishing a tradition which later produced such well known symbolic national figures as Roma, Britannia, and Columbia.

A society in which war between cities was so common is likely to have a full-fledged war god, and for the Greeks this was Ares. Though incorporated into the Olympian family as son of Zeus and Hera, Ares was probably an alien god whose worship penetrated the Greek world from Thrace, northeast of Greece, and he never was wholly adapted to Greek religion, as might have been the case in a society that placed military values above all others. In fact Ares was an unpopular god among the Greeks; Zeus once called him "the most hated of the immortals who dwell on Olympus." It would appear that he was originally a vegetation god, with the power both to fertilize nature and to protect the fields of his worshippers by killing their enemies. The transition from a vegetation god to a god of war is understandable in a society which already had a number of nature and fertility gods, and similar developments are to be found in connection with Mars in Roman religion and Wotan in Germanic beliefs.

Ares' principal trait was his violent nature (his very name may mean "Destruction"), both in war and in his personal relations as anthropomorphic god. Accordingly, the dog and vulture were his emblematic animals, symbolic of violence and wanton destruction. It is curious that, though he was an Olympian god, he did not possess any weapon like Zeus' thunderbolt or Poseidon's trident, but used such human weapons as the sword, spear, and shield. Most myths of Ares illustrate his proverbial violence. He was said to have been the first defendant in a murder trial, held when he killed the youth Halirrhotius, a son of Poseidon, who tried to violate Ares' daughter Alcippe, and Poseidon prosecuted him before a jury consisting of the Olympian gods. The trial, which resulted in Ares' acquittal, took place in Athens on a hill

thereafter known as the Areopagus ("Hill of Ares"). The turbulence Ares caused led to retaliation and efforts to control him. The Greek hero Heracles defeated him in combat by twice wounding him, as did Athena and Diomedes in the battles before Troy, and once two human giants, Otus and Ephialtes, succeeded in imprisoning him for over a year, stopping all war for a time.

Even as a lover Ares was violent, and had many illegitimate children, many of whom were themselves violent and warlike. Though in some sources he is said to have been the husband of the goddess of love Aphrodite, and to have had a daughter by her named, significantly, Harmonia, the usual myth of the relations of Ares and Aphrodite involved an illicit love affair. To conceal his clandestine meetings with Aphrodite, Ares posted a sentinel named Alectryon (Rooster) to signal the coming of the dawn. Once Alectryon fell asleep, and Helios (the Sun) detected the lovers and reported the intrigue to Aphrodite's husband Hephaestus.

It is often said that Ares was the ancestor of the Amazons, a female warrior people. At the Greek city of Thebes, where his cult was especially important, he was worshipped in his composite form as nature god and war god, and as god of a spring protected by a son of his in the form of a dragon.

Also of alien and composite origin was the Olympian god Hephaestus, a strange amalgam of Indo-European fire god, Near Eastern god of metallurgy, and magician god. The ambivalent image of Hephaestus as both divine technician-artist and ludicrous figure reflects the original high esteem of the artisan in the prehellenic world, contrasted with the Greeks' own depreciation of manual skills. Hephaestus is remarkable in being the only Greek god with a deformity — he was lame. There are several possible explanations for this strange appearance of a god. In primitive societies, men with physical defects that prevented them from being warriors were assigned to work as artisans, and there was also a widespread folktale motif that persons with physical defects were compensated with heightened gifts of hand and mind, or that persons with such gifts paid for them with a physical deformity.

The cause of Hephaestus' lameness is told in two versions, and there was even uncertainty about how he was born. One version made him son of Hera and Zeus, another told that Hera once, in

anger at Zeus' infidelities, decided to produce a child of her own
without sexual union, and thus bore Hephaestus as Zeus had
produced Athena by himself. When he was born deformed, Hera
decided to expose the baby, just as the average Greek treated
unwanted children. The child was thrown from Olympus and fell
into the Aegean Sea, where he was taken in by two Nereids, Thetis
and Eurynome, who brought him up in a grotto in the sea, and
taught him metallurgy, forging, and the creation of finely wrought
things. The other version of Hephaestus' lameness holds that he
was born and grew to maturity without deformity, but that
because he intervened on behalf of his mother Hera during a
quarrel with Zeus, his father threw him out of Olympus. After a
long fall, he struck the island of Lemnos and became lame. Here
he was cared for and taught by the Sintians of Lemnos, who were
skilled metallurgists.

On Olympus Hephaestus was the divine artisan, smith, and
architect. As well as the workshop on Mt. Olympus, he had
workshops under volcanoes, where he was assisted by Cyclopes. As
an artisan he frequently appears in art with a workman's apron
and a round pointed laborer's cap. Hephaestus built the gods'
palaces, made Zeus' scepter, fashioned the famous necklace of
Harmonia, and created many works of beauty and art, especially
those made of metal. At the request of their divine mothers he
forged the armor of the great epic heroes Achilles and Aeneas, and
even created tripods that moved automatically and robots of gold
in the form of automated maidens who assisted him in his work.
Among his creations were also Pandora, the first woman, and
Talos, the great bronze giant that guarded Crete. And because of
his skill as an artisan it was he who was summoned to open Zeus'
head for the birth of Athena.

As a magician god he had the power to cause immobile things
to move, as well as to immobilize moving things (symbolical of his
power over metals in the forge). His magic worked particularly by
binding or chaining, and it was he who bound Prometheus to a
rock in the Caucasus Mountains by order of Zeus. In his most
famous myth he sent a magic throne to his mother Hera as a gift
when he was in the care of the Nereids, and when Hera sat on the
throne she was bound to it immovably by invisible chains. Threats
failed to induce Hephaestus to return to Olympus to release Hera,

but finally Dionysus made him drunk and escorted him in an
ungodlike procession on a donkey back to Olympus, where he
released her. On another occasion when Zeus chained Hera for
persecuting Heracles, Hephaestus released his mother.

Partly because of his deformity, partly because of his
crudeness, Hephaestus was by way of compensation paired with
beauty, in a sort of allegorical representation of the union of
craftsmanship with beauty. His attempt to rape Athena contrasts
with other accounts of his married life. In some versions he had as
his wife Charis or Aglaea, one of the beautiful Graces, but usually
he is said to have been married to Aphrodite, goddess of beauty,
whose hold over her deformed and usually work-begrimed
husband was strong, while she was unfaithful to him with Ares.
The Greeks liked to tell the story that the cuckolded Hephaestus,
learning of the clandestine meetings of his wife with Ares,
constructed a skillfully woven net which he hung invisibly over the
pair's bed. Here it fell upon them in their lovemaking and
entrapped them. Hephaestus then summoned all the other gods to
see and laugh at the helpless pair.

Aphrodite, a latecomer in Greek religion, had been a Near
Eastern Semitic goddess, a vegetation divinity often known as
Ishtar or Astarte. Like other mother goddesses in the ancient
world, the Semitic goddess was a divinity of fertility and fecundity
in nature, with emphasis on the generative forces that cause
fertility. The Greeks, in borrowing this cult, first combined it with
the Aegean vegetation fertility rituals, then Hellenized the divinity
by converting her into a goddess of sex and beauty in humans.
Aphrodite thus became principally the goddess of the sexual
instinct and the reproductive drive. As goddess of heterosexual
love she shed beauty on lovers and aided their amorous acts, and
was herself portrayed in art as an exquisitely beautiful young
woman, usually in the nude. Worshipped in this form by the
Greeks, her representations were among the greatest artistic
creations of Greek artists, the most famous being the Cnidian
Aphrodite of Praxiteles. The dove and the myrtle were her
symbols, and she was usually attended by such lovely female
creatures as nymphs, Graces, and Hours.

The birth of Aphrodite was a famous myth. The oldest version
is that she was "foam born" (an erroneous attempt to etymologize

the word Aphrodite), from the severed genitals of Uranus as they fell into the sea after his castration by Cronus. Born in the sea, she was then brought up by sea nymphs, and eventually rose, completely formed in a divine epiphany, out of the sea near the Greek island of Cythera, and proceeded to her famous ancient cult center on the island of Cyprus. Hence she is sometimes called Cytherea, more often the Cyprian. Partly because Greeks borrowed elements of her cult from the seafaring Phoenicians, partly because she was believed to have been born from the sea, Aphrodite also became the protector of sailors, a concept having nothing to do with her original functions. Seafaring in the Aegean in antiquity was suspended during the winter months and resumed in the spring, so that Aphrodite's birth from the sea symbolizes another form of the ubiquitous death/rebirth pattern usually associated with vegetation goddesses.

In Hesiod's version Aphrodite belongs to the first generation of gods, miraculously born as an offspring of Uranus after his emasculation. But this version appeared to many Greeks later as grotesque and repulsive, so it was abandoned, and in its place Aphrodite was made the daughter of Zeus by an early consort Dione.

Though married to Hephaestus, Aphrodite preferred Ares as a lover. In some sources she was called Ares' wife, and often was herself considered a goddess of war through her frequent association with Ares. For the Greeks this injected a rather confusing note (Zeus is quoted in Homer's *Iliad* as saying to his lovely daughter who vigorously sided with the Trojans: "Not to thee, dear child, are deeds of war allotted"). By Ares she had a daughter Harmonia, and a son Eros (god of love), considered a violent force instilling sexual desire in both gods and mortals and originally depicted as a young handsome man. Eventually in the Hellenistic Age Eros was transformed into a playful boy, often with wings, and still later equipped with a bow and arrows, whose unerring shots injected love. A still later development showed little winged figures (Erotes or Amores) surrounding and attending Aphrodite.

Aphrodite had other lovers besides Ares. By Hermes she had the boy Hermaphrodite, named after both his mother and father. The story is told that Hermaphrodite, a lad of exquisite beauty, was brought up by nymphs in Phrygia, and travelling came once to a lake in Asia Minor where the nymph of the waters, Salmacis, fell in love with him. He repulsed her attentions, but when he entered the lake to bathe, she clung to him, praying that the gods join their bodies eternally. So arose the double nature of the bisexual divinity Hermaphrodite, frequently represented in ancient art with the bodily characteristics of both male and female. The Greek legends of bisexual figures, as well as stories of transformations from one sex to another, may have their origins in folk beliefs in the power inherent in the unity of both sexual characteristics. For instance, in some marriage ceremonies in the ancient world the bride and bridegroom exchanged clothing.

Aphrodite was also the lover of the Trojan prince Anchises, by whom she had the famous hero Aeneas, the focal point of the most important Roman myth. Her most famous lover was Adonis, who died and was reborn, in the familiar vegetation cycle. Like many other divinities Aphrodite had a cruel streak. Her vengeance on those who rejected her power is well known, the most famous being the stories of the women of Lemnos and the tragedy of Hippolytus. We shall meet these stories later.

In the Near East the Semitic goddess from whom Aphrodite sprang was worshipped with licentious rites in which sexuality played a prominent part, especially in the sacred prostitution practiced at temples of the goddess. This sacred prostitution, in which the women serving the goddess gave their favors to men as a form of worship, came to Greece in the wake of the worship of the goddess from the Near East. Particularly famous throughout Greece were the prostitutes at the temple of Aphrodite at Corinth, whose loveliness and devotion to the goddess moved even the severe Greek poet Pindar to praise.

VIII

OLYMPIAN GODS:
Apollo, Artemis, Hermes

According to early Greek theogonies, the Titan Coeus and the Titaness Phoebe had a daughter Leto, who became the mother of the Olympian gods Apollo and Artemis. Actually in origin Leto was a prehellenic Near Eastern mother goddess, symbol of fecundity, the Lycian goddess named Lada ("Lady"), and we do not know how or when she came to be in Greek mythology the mother of Apollo and Artemis. Curiously, though she was once a powerful divinity, by being associated with Apollo and Artemis in Greece her worship declined. For instance, Apollo ousted her from her earliest sanctuary on the famed Greek island of Delos in the Aegean by the Fifth Century B.C.

In the Greek myth the mother goddess Leto united with the sky god Zeus in a "sacred marriage." Driven by the jealousy of Hera, Leto, pregnant with twins by Zeus, wandered seeking a place to give birth to her children. But Hera had forbidden all lands to give asylum to Leto. Finally, the floating island of Delos (or Ortygia; this was identified with Delos, and may be an earlier name), consented to give her refuge, and as a reward ceased to float and was solidly anchored in the sea. But Leto's woes were not over, for although all the goddesses had pity on the expectant mother, Hera ordered her daughter Eileithyia, the goddess of childbirth, to remain on Mt. Olympus. Thus birth was delayed nine days and nights, but finally, Eileithyia, bribed with the gift of a beautiful necklace, came to Leto's assistance. Thus at length Apollo and Artemis were born. In actuality, in origin neither one was associated with Leto, nor were they twins. How Greek mythology assembled them into a family we shall never know.

The relationship between mother and children in this myth was very close. This was apparent shortly after the birth of the twins. Some time before, Zeus had made love to Elare, and when she was to have a child by him, in fear of Hera he buried her in the earth, where she produced a huge giant named Tityus. Hera now instigated this giant to violate Leto, but the twins, still infants, repelled him with their bows and arrows and rescued their mother. Tityus was eternally consigned to Tartarus as a punishment. There his body occupied many acres, and his liver was perpetually eaten by two huge vultures.

The concept of three divinities forming a group was very common among the Greeks. For instance, there were three Gorgons, three Graces, three Fates, etc., and triple-formed creatures like Cerberus, the Chimaera, and Geryon. The number three in ancient folk beliefs had mystic qualities as a sort of completed number containing beginning, middle, and end. The universality of three could be grasped in the evolution of man from child to adult to old man, and in the triads heaven-earth-underworld, past-present-future. It is thus a symbol of unity for gods to associate with each other in triads, as Zeus-Poseidon-Hades, although in the case of Leto and her children, the "holy family" of mother-son-daughter is a rare combination in antiquity. In the Eleusinian Mysteries we find a close relationship in the triad Demeter-Persephone-Triptolemus, and among the Romans in the especially important cult of the Capitoline Triad, consisting of Jupiter, his wife Juno, and his daughter Minerva, a rare case of the triad of father-mother-child. Concepts of the divine triad had firm roots in the religious thought of antiquity.

We have seen that Apollo, although originally unrelated to either Leto or Artemis, became in Greek mythology both son of Leto and twin brother of Artemis. He was indeed in origin a foreigner to the Greek world, originally an Anatolian god whose worship was centered in Lycia. In time he acquired not only a family, but Aegean as well as Indo-European characteristics, and eventually the composite Apollo became the very epitome of the Hellenic spirit. The Greeks of the classical age would have been astonished to learn that the god who embodied the most characteristic values of their culture was a prehellenic Near Eastern god in origin.

Shortly after his birth on the island of Delos and rescue of Leto from the giant Tityus, Apollo grew to adulthood instantaneously and went to the land of the Hyperboreans. This mythical people, usually associated with Apollo, lived in the far North (their name means "Beyond the North Wind"), either in Northern Europe or Northern Asia. They were Apollo's favorite people, and he visited them periodically, especially during the winter months. In the classical period the Greeks conceived of the land of the Hyperboreans as a sort of utopia, with ideal climate and great longevity of the people (it was said that old people among the Hyperboreans, when they had had enough of life, threw themselves voluntarily from a cliff into the sea). At the time of Apollo's birth two Hyperborean virgins brought offerings to Delos to propitiate the safe delivery of Leto, and two others were said to have brought the cult objects of Apollo to Delos. Tombs of these four Hyperborean maidens were venerated at Delos in antiquity, and modern excavators have actually found these tombs. At any rate, in historic times gifts (ears of wheat) were said to have been sent annually to Delos by the Hyperboreans along a fixed route. It is said that Apollo kept his weapons among the Hyperboreans, and the story is told that once a Hyperborean named Abasis flew around the entire world without once eating by holding on to an arrow of Apollo.

From the land of the Hyperboreans Apollo went directly to Delphi, which he conquered a short time after his birth. Here he had to destroy the dragon Python, a monstrous creature that guarded the oracle of Delphi belonging to the earth goddess Gaea. Next to Zeus' struggle with Typhon, Apollo's combat with Python was the most momentous dragon combat in Greek mythology. As a result of Apollo's victory, Delphi became the second great sanctuary of Apollo, and the young god succeeded Gaea as the god of prophecy. His control of the oracle did not go unchallenged, for once the hero Heracles, dissatisfied with his treatment at the oracle, tried to seize the sacred tripod from Apollo, but Zeus intervened to put a stop to possible violent combat between his two sons.

In time Delphi became the principal oracular shrine of the Greeks, "the most truthful oracle." An oracle was a sacred shrine at which a god was thought to communicate with men when they

wanted to know the future. The competition of Apollo's shrine at
Delphi put into the shade older oracular gods, such as Gaea,
Themis, Zeus. As a result, Delphi became the most sacred place of
the Greeks, a sort of Jerusalem or Mecca, the nearest to a
panhellenic religious center the Greeks had. Here too was the
omphalos ("navel"), the sacred stone said to indicate the very
center of the earth. Sacred stones were treasured in many places in
antiquity as symbols of fertility and power, and the *omphalos* at
Delphi stood in a spot in the temple said to have been indicated by
Zeus. To determine the "navel of the earth" he sent two eagles
from the ends of the earth to fly toward each other, and they met
at this spot in Delphi.

One of the reasons for the importance of oracles among the
Greeks is their lack of a sacred book of the sort that provides
many peoples with relief from the anxieties of the insecurity of
life. In their attempt to understand the enigmas of the world and
society, the Greeks employed many methods to try to divine the
will of the gods, making interpretations of omens, dreams, and
oracular utterances from the gods in an effort to win divine
guidance in making decisions. The procedure of the Delphic oracle
is well known. Inquirers first made sacrifices to Apollo and paid
substantial fees. Questions were given in writing or orally to the
priests of the temple who then took the questions to an inner
shrine where the priestess of Apollo, the Pythia, sat on a tripod.
The Pythia was in a sort of ecstatic trance induced by religious
fervor, some say by drinking from a sacred spring at Delphi called
Castalia, others say by chewing laurel leaves. The chaotic
utterances of the priestess, supposed to be the medium through
which Apollo spoke, were given coherence, interpreted, and put
into verse by the priests. When the pressure of inquiries was
unusually heavy, a faster and cheaper method of providing answers
was used — the lot oracle. In this method questions had to be
posed in a form making possible a "yes" or "no" answer, and the
Pythia picked one of two colored beans at random, one color
signifying "yes", the other "no." Extended answers were, however, usually ambiguous, giving rise to the proverbial phrase
"Delphic response" for an ambiguous reply.

Despite our modern skepticism, the Delphic oracle was held in
high esteem among the ancient peoples for about 1000 years. So

many people visited Delphi every year that it became an informed international center, a kind of clearing house of information from everywhere in the world, the first important place of this kind in man's history. The priests received odds and ends of information from so many places that they appeared extraordinarily wise, and often they gave answers that were simply commonplace folk advice, or the most merciful answers, so that inquirers felt kindly towards the oracle. Its trustworthiness remained high also because frequently the oracle was asked to choose between possible alternatives that had previously already been narrowed down by governments or individuals. Hence often the oracle simply expressed a preference for one of two sides on critical issues in Greek cities. From the Eighth Century B.C. on, Greek cities always consulted Delphi before sending out colonies to various parts of the Mediterranean and Black Sea, for advice on the proposed colony, its location, and similar vital matters. For this reason Apollo has been called "the colonizing god." We may gauge its prestige by the respect that the Athenian philosopher Socrates paid the oracle of Delphi. When a friend of his asked the question, "Is anyone wiser than Socrates," the negative answer given posed a religious and political problem for Socrates which, he affirmed, imposed upon him the obligation of questioning his fellow citizens to test the true meaning of the oracle. He finally concluded that what the oracle meant was that he is truly wise who, like Socrates, admits his ignorance.

The credibility of the Delphic oracle was seriously shaken in the Sixth and Fifth Centuries B.C. because of major errors which affected the very fate of the civilized world. For instance, the king of Lydia, Croesus, in his conflict with the rising Persian Empire under Cyrus the Great, consulted the oracle on the advisability of engaging in war with the Persians. It appeared that the oracle's reply was encouraging, but when Croesus attacked he was utterly defeated and his empire annexed by Persia. When criticism of the oracle followed, the defense given by the priests was that the oracle had really said, "If you attack, a great empire will be destroyed," and that this was a reserved not an affirmative answer. Furthermore, in the attacks by the Persians on the Greek cities, at a time when the very independence of all Greece was at stake, the oracle took a defeatist position, urging surrender to Persia. It is said that when the Athenians, in response to their inquiry about the coming Persian attack, were advised to submit to Persia, their envoys to Delphi returned for a second response, saying "O lord Apollo, utter some better oracle about our native land." After the unexpected victory of the Greeks under the leadership of Athens and Sparta, the oracle switched its position opportunistically in 480/479 B.C.

Despite such errors, its authority remained strong until the end of the Fifth Century B.C., when conservative forces in Greece captured the oracle. Their use of it as an overt political tool, together with a sharp rise in rationalism and skepticism in the course of the Greek Enlightenment spearheaded by the Sophists, brought a sharp decline in respect for the Delphic oracle. This was aided by a decrease in the traditional forms of ancestral cults. But the oracle continued until its pagan rites were suppressed by the Christians in the Fourth Century A.D. When the Emperor Julian, who sought to restore paganism in that century, including the Delphic oracle, consulted the oracle, he received from its priests a gloomy response about the disrepair of the shrine and the drying up of the prophetic sources of Apollo.

Greek mythmakers localized the sources of divine prophecy at Delphi with great frequency, and crises in myths led to consultation of the oracle to resolve questions about famines, pestilences, foreign invasions, bloodshed, childlessness, anxiety about the future of children and grandchildren, killing of a kinsman. The orders for human sacrifice in responses of Apollo are undoubtedly vestiges of primitive rituals. Often the god advised purification to atone for bloodshed.

The god Apollo himself twice had to do penance for a fault in order to purify himself. For his part in the palace revolt of the gods against Zeus, he was ordered to serve as workman for a king of Troy, Laomedon, for whom he helped build the walls of Troy. Later, when Zeus killed his son Asclepius with thunderbolts, Apollo in retaliation killed the Cyclopes who manufactured these weapons for Zeus. As part of his punishment to achieve ritual purification from this blood guilt, Apollo was subjected to Admetus, king of Thessaly, whom he loyally served as herdsman for a year. In time this humbling of the great god Apollo and his contrite acceptance of punishment were converted into some of the highest religious ideals of the Greeks. We have seen that the priests of Delphi institutionalized the concept of purification (*catharsis*) for sin, especially the shedding of blood, in place of the primitive concept of revenge by relatives in accordance with the rules of inflexible tribal justice. Apollo's priests supported the development of a higher form of justice involving ritual cleansing of involuntary or justifiable homicide, together with a year's exile from the native city of the murderer. At Delphi a new moral ideal was associated with Apollo in the famous mottoes said to be inscribed on the god's temple, "Know thyself," and "Nothing too much."

Thus Apollo's functions multiplied, and he was known as Apollo, or Phoebus ("Radiant One"), or Phoebus Apollo, or the Pythian god. His functions were indeed very complex. In addition to prophecy and purification, he retained his earliest function (of Near Eastern origin) as herdsman god, protector of flocks and herds, but on higher levels he became a benefactor of man, affecting the welfare of his body and soul. He was one of the gods of healing, though it was his son Asclepius who ultimately replaced him as the Greek god of medicine. This contrasts with his dreaded role as the god of pestilence. Particularly in August, the Dog Days, the hottest and most unhealthy time in Greece, widespread sickness was attributed to his anger, supposedly symbolized by the rays of the sun, which were thought of as arrows shot by Apollo.

As benefactor of the soul, through prophetic, poetic, and musical inspiration, Apollo achieved great prominence among the Greeks. The god of music, he carried and played the lyre, and, often accompanied by the Muses, was called Musagetes ("Leader of the Muses"). The seven-stringed lyre invented in the Near East became among the Greeks the most venerated instrument, particularly among the upper classes and aristocracy, while the flute remained a more humble instrument. Thus Apollo was represented in art as holding a lyre, as well as the bow and arrows which probably symbolize his more primitive functions of protection. Because of his handsomeness, he became the Greek ideal of physical perfection in the male and therefore the patron god of athletes. In the Sixth and Fifth Centuries B.C., a rationalizing age which explained the dragon Python allegorically as a force of darkness, his conqueror was erroneously elevated to the god of the sun, and it is curious that in modern times Apollo is mostly remembered as the radiant god of poetry and the sun. For the Greeks he was the god who summed up in his person those aspects of their culture that marked them off from the rest of the world: music, poetry, athletics, moderation, restraint, respect for the individual.

Apollo remained unmarried, but had many female loves in which he was the aggressor and seducer, and in which he displayed a streak of violence. He has been called an anti-feminist god, but in fact he displayed bisexuality. As symbol of male beauty, he also had lovers who were boys, the most famous being Hyacinth. Another primitive aspect of the god Apollo is his swiftness to take brutal vengeance when provoked.

Equally ambivalent — both cruel and gentle — was Apollo's twin sister Artemis, in origin a prehellenic Aegean-Near Eastern nature divinity, particularly of wild life and animals, a manifestation of the mother goddess. From her original function of "mistress of animals," associated with forests and mountains, she was absorbed in a specialized form into the Greek pantheon and became the protector of wild animals, especially the young, and at the same time goddess of hunting. In this latter capacity she was, like her brother Apollo, equipped with bow and arrow. This apparent paradox of Artemis being both huntress and protector of animals is in keeping with her function as one of the supporters of human life. This required not only killing of dangerous animals, but also protection of meat as part of food supply, and domestication and reproduction of animals for this purpose.

Thus Artemis became a goddess of fertility, retaining her affinity to the ancient mother goddess. For example, the famous temple of Artemis at Ephesus in Asia Minor, one of the Seven Wonders of the World, held an image of her as a many-breasted matron. Yet in Greek mythology Artemis remained unmarried, preeminently the goddess of chastity in women, as husbandless as the prehellenic mother goddess who had male partners but no husband, and acted as protectress of young women. Her association with the myth of a Minoan predecessor whom she supplanted, Britomartis ("Sweet Maid"), also often called the Cretan Artemis or Dictynna, epitomizes her virgin purity. Britomartis as goddess of wild life avoided humans, determined to remain eternally virgin, and when she was attacked by the Cretan King Minos she jumped into the Aegean Sea, to be rescued by fishermen with their nets. Artemis was the favorite goddess of virgin nymphs, who formed a company of attendants for her, and she punished any violations of chastity on their part severely. Her swiftness to anger and cruelty also showed in her treatment of males who sought to affront her own chastity.

After Apollo and Artemis were joined, their twin nature resulted in mutual influences. For example, she was represented as a typical beautiful young Greek maiden, and became the ideal of Greek womanhood, just as Apollo was the ideal of young men. They both carried bow and arrows. When Apollo was transformed into a sun god, Artemis was assimilated to the moon, though she has no legitimate claim to being a moon goddess. Finally, because of her identification with the moon and wild animals, Artemis came to be associated with a goddess of the underworld, the grim witch goddess Hecate.

Another highly complex god was Hermes, puckish, practical, nonmoral. He was basically a Greek god, with some prehellenic vestiges, born of Zeus and Maia ("Little Mother"), daughter of the Titan Atlas, one of the Pleiades, in mountainous Arcadia in a cave on Mt. Cyllene. It is noteworthy that in this case Hera did not persecute either the mother or the child. The divine child was precocious, acting like a young god on the very day of his birth, when with bright and inventive genius he created the lyre. This he did when he caught a tortoise, scooped out the body, and used the shell as a sounding board for strings. On the evening of his first day he revealed other characteristics, his guile, inclination to thievery, and humor. He stole fifty cattle from a flock belonging to his half-brother Apollo, and concealed their hiding place in a cave by driving them backward so it would be difficult to track them down. Apollo, suspecting Hermes, hauled him before their father Zeus. During the questioning Hermes stole Apollo's quiver of arrows, which made even Apollo laugh. On Zeus' urging the brothers were reconciled, Hermes returned the cattle, and they exchanged gifts. Hermes gave Apollo the lyre, while Apollo bestowed upon Hermes the wand known as the *caduceus*.

From time immemorial the *caduceus* had been a fertility

symbol in the Aegean and Near East, as well as a magicians' wand.
It is a staff with two snakes, male and female, symbolic of fertility
and well-being, intertwined about it. In the hands of Hermes, it
was his distinctive symbol.

In his varied functions, Hermes was the helper *par excellence*
of gods, both Olympian and chthonic, heroes, and ordinary men
and women. For example, he helped Zeus conquer Typhon. On
another occasion when Hera created a 100-eyed monster, Argus,
to spy on one of Zeus' sweethearts, the young Argive princess Io,
Hermes found a way to lull the monster to sleep and kill it. Hence
he was often called Argeiphontes ("Slayer of Argos"). In general
he carried out the will of Zeus, acting as his messenger (the Greek
word for messenger is *angelos*) and running errands for him, but
with the dignity of a king's herald. He was also useful to Hades
because he guided the souls of the dead on their proper journey to
the underworld, using his *caduceus* to escort them. Speed was his
greatest asset, and he was especially the guide for both gods and
men. For instance, it is he who brought Pandora to Epimetheus,
the three Olympian goddesses to Paris for his judgment on their
beauty, the infant Dionysus to his nurses, King Priam of Troy to
the tent of Achilles. As traveler, always busy despite his great
speed, Hermes wore the typical broad-brimmed hat of Greek
travelers, the *petasos*, but his *petasos* had wings on them, as did his
sandals, called his *talaria*.

Hermes was also the Greek trickster god, cunning, guileful, full
of knavery, the patron divinity of thieves because they thrive on
speed and cunning. Since in early times brigandage and commerce
were not separated, Hermes became the patron god not only of
travelers, but also of merchants and trade in general. By extension
he later became god of eloquence and orators, in whom a degree
of cunning was conceded, and because of his youth, handsomeness
and swiftness, he was also one of the patron gods of athletes.

Two very primitive functions of the god Hermes survived in
the classical period. His original Arcadian role as a pastoral god,
primarily a god of shepherds, persisted later, as did an early
fertility function. In prehellenic times in the Aegean area stone
heaps or single stones, as landmarks or memorials at waysides or to
mark off fields, had a sacred character as protective symbols and
symbols of fertility. In classical Greece such stones, called *herms*,

were placed before every house and public building as symbols of good luck and affluence, and eventually they took the form of a block of stone with a head of Hermes and an erect phallus.

Hermes remained a bachelor god. Considering his busy activities, it is understandable that his recorded love affairs are relatively few.

IX

OLYMPIAN GODS:
Dionysus

In the case of the god Dionysus, a late addition to the Greek pantheon, we can actually see some of the processes by which the god was assimilated into Greek religion and mythology. He eventually became the thirteenth Olympian. The worship of this foreign god was spreading as early as the Mycenaean Age, not without strong opposition, as we find reflected in myths. A great new invasion of the cult began about 800 B.C., sweeping like wildfire over Greece, spread by ecstatic bands of worshippers acting as missionaries of the "god who liberates," leaving both wild enthusiasm and terror in their wake.

In Greek mythology the birth of Dionysus constitutes the classical childhood story of a god, comparable only to that of Zeus. In Phrygia in Asia Minor there was an earth goddess Zemelo, the Phrygian mother goddess. When we meet her in Greek myth she had "faded" into a mortal named Semele, one of the famous daughters of Cadmus and Harmonia, king and queen of Thebes in Greece. Zeus and the young princess Semele became lovers, but she did not know his identity, for he visited her only in the dark of night. Zeus' jealous wife Hera learned of their clandestine meetings, and, as usual, sought to harm his lover. She visited Semele in the shape of her nurse and persuaded her to try to discover the true nature of her mysterious lover, so one night Semele tricked Zeus into making a promise that he would fulfil whatever she asked of him. He swore an irrevocable oath by the River Styx in Hades, the most sacred oath in the universe, and thereupon she asked to see him in his true form. Appalled but helpless to undo his promise, Zeus appeared as the dazzling god of lightning and thunder, and Semele was instantly burned to death. Zeus quickly rescued the embryo of his future son from her body, and sewed it into his own thigh, and in due time Dionysus (his name may mean "son of Zeus") was born from his father's thigh. The manner of his birth was appropriate for the god whose cult and myths emphasized the physical nature of man. Equally important, this myth symbolized that Dionysus was "twice born," indicative of the self-regenerating powers of the god.

The story of Semele and the birth of Dionysus may preserve vestiges of primitive folklore, for example, that lightning fertilizes the earth. Even among the Greeks places struck by lightning were regarded as sacred; persons struck by lightning were considered to be "holy," and were therefore never cremated. In primitive folklore also the thigh is a symbol of male sexual power.

Although Zeus often neglected his children by mortal women, he exhibited unusual concern for Dionysus. He ordered Hermes to take the holy child to Semele's sister Ino and her husband Athamas, who brought up Dionysus with their own children, dressing him as a girl to conceal him from Hera. But when the vindictive Hera drove Ino and Athamas insane, Zeus himself caught up the child and brought the boy to the mythical land of Nysa, the legendary place where wine was discovered, to be nursed by the nymphs there. Hera was unrelenting, however, and continued to persecute Dionysus at every turn. So great was Dionysus' suffering that he was thought to die annually, yet each time was inevitably reborn, appearing suddenly in the springtime, just as the vine seems suddenly reinvigorated, almost overnight. This death and rebirth of the god of wine is another form of the mythical representation of the vegetation cycle.

When Dionysus was a young man Hera drove him insane, and the mad, intoxicated god wandered over the entire world as far as India. Wherever he went he triumphantly introduced the cultivation of the vine and established worship of his godhood. In his wanderings he was accompanied by swarms of ecstatic worshippers and attendants, mostly women. This male god attracted them because he represented in dramatic form the procreative forces in nature and man. These bands of female followers of Dionysus, aroused to ecstatic frenzy, were called Bacchantes ("Followers of Bacchus"), or Maenads ("Frenzied Ones"), or Thyiads ("Possessed

Ones"), or Bassarids ("Wearers of the Fox-Skin"). His male followers were mostly primitive demons of fertility, somewhat anthropomorphized by the Greeks into half-human, half-animal form. One group were the Satyrs, two-legged half-man, half-goat creatures, depicted as mostly human with animal horns and ears, hoofs and tails, lusty and sensual, bestial in nature and possessed of animal passions, fond of drinking and sexual pursuit of reluctant nymphs. Another group, the Sileni, often not completely distinguished from Satyrs and often thought to be merely older Satyrs, also represented uncontrolled natural desires. They were part animal like the Satyrs but had horse characteristics, including horse tails. One of them, Silenus, the private tutor and favorite companion of Dionysus, was incorrigeably fond of wine and usually tipsy. The entire retinue of Dionysus was called a *thiasos* ("revel band").

When Dionysus decided to return to Greece after his victories in Asia, opposition to the god of ecstasy was vigorous and widespread in the land of his birth. There are various myths of the hostility to the introduction of his cult into Greece, survivals of historical events attending the westward spread of this alien cult. The rituals of this god were repugnant to many in Greece because of their orgiastic, violent and barbarous character, and because the unrestrained drinking and sexual orgies placed an extreme emphasis upon individual physical self-indulgence. To many in Greece these tendencies represented a danger to society. The traditional Greek religion was a civic religion, with the principal aim of assuring the continuity and security of the whole community. The Dionysiac cult was not in essence a social one, having as its goal ecstatic union of the individual worshipper with the god Dionysus, and the excesses, the rural character of the cult, and its individualistic perspectives seemed to many in Greece at the time of its spread to constitute a socially disruptive backward step. Hence the opposition to the cult and the persecution of Dionysus and his followers.

As the Dionysiac *thiasos* approached the borders of Greece, King Lycurgus of Thrace sought to oppose the new god. In the earliest version of the myth he drove the baby Dionysus and his nurses, the nymphs of Nysa, out of his kingdom. In fear Dionysus leaped into the sea, where he was rescued by the Nereid Thetis. As punishment for this cruelty Lycurgus was blinded by Zeus. In another version, Lycurgus refused permission to the grown Dionysus and his army of followers to cross his country. When Lycurgus captured the Bacchantes and Satyrs, Dionysus sought refuge with Thetis in the sea. But when Lycurgus ordered all vines in his kingdom to be cut down, he was driven insane, and as a result killed his own son. When he regained his reason, sterility fell upon the land, and the people of Thrace, blaming Lycurgus for the famine, had him torn to pieces by tying his limbs to four wild horses. In still another version Lycurgus was punished by being caught among vines which crushed him to death, and in the underworld was eternally punished in death by having to pour water into a broken pitcher.

Another myth of the opposition to Dionysus concerned the three daughters of King Minyas of the famed Mycenaean city of Orchomenus in Boeotia, named Leucippe, Arsippe, and Alcithoë. They refused to participate in a festival of the new god, remaining discreetly at home rather than joining the reveling Bacchantes. In punishment they were driven insane, and in this state they seized the son of one of them (the boy Hypasus) and tore him apart with their hands. Then they joined the Bacchantes in the hills, and were finally transformed into bats. Similarly, the daughters of Proetus, king of Tiryns in the Argolid in the northeastern Peloponnesus, were said to have mocked the followers of Dionysus, and as a result were driven insane. The early hostility in the Peloponnesus to the orgiastic cult survived in one of the myths of the Greek hero Perseus. In the earliest version Perseus, though himself a son of Zeus, opposed the introduction of the cult. He met the god in single combat, defeated and killed him, and threw his body into the sea, together with that of his wife Ariadne. In a later version Perseus was indeed victorious in the combat, but the two hostile sons of Zeus were reconciled by still another of his sons, Hermes.

The most famous of the opponents of Dionysus was Pentheus, king of Thebes, the legendary birthplace of Dionysus. When Dionysus and his *thiasos* arrived at Thebes, the women of the city gladly joined the revel in the mountains nearby. However, King Pentheus regarded the cult as bestial, improper for women, uncivilized, destructive of law and order, and therefore ordered the arrest of the Bacchantes as well as their leader, who was none other than the god Dionysus himself disguised as a missionary of the god. The stranger miraculously released himself from prison, and suddenly the royal palace went up in flames. Pentheus, however, passionately devoted to reason and order, ignored the visible signs of the presence of an awesome divine power, so Dionysus resolved to punish Pentheus, and slowly drove him insane. In this state Pentheus revealed an interest in viewing the orgiastic rites being performed by the women. Dionysus conducted him to the place where the women were reveling, and suggested to him that he hide in a tree top to observe them. But the Bacchantes caught sight of him, and mistaking him for a wild animal, dragged him from the tree and tore him limb from limb. Pentheus' mother Agave led the procession back triumphantly to the city, bearing the head of her son on a pole, and only when she regained her senses did she become aware of the tragic fate of her son Pentheus and her own part in it. The Athenian tragedian Euripides told this story in his haunting play the *Bacchae.*

The victories of Dionysus were climaxed by a final triumph, revealing his awesome power. Having conquered the mainland of Greece, Dionysus was crossing the Aegean Sea to the island of Naxos on an Etruscan ship. The sailors, turning to piracy, tried to seize the elegant passenger, but at once vines began to grow on the mast and held the ship fast in the sea, and wild animals appeared about the god. The Etruscan pirates in terror leaped overboard into the sea, and were transformed into dolphins, who were thenceforth the benevolent fish of the Mediterranean.

When Dionysus arrived at Naxos, he discovered a beautiful woman lying asleep, fell in love with her at first sight, and woke her with a kiss. The girl was Ariadne, daughter of King Minos of Crete, whom Theseus, after slaying the Minotaur, had abandoned on the island. In another sacred marriage of an earth goddess and her male consort, Dionysus made her his wife, giving her as a marriage gift a wondrous crown, which was later placed in the sky as the constellation Corona Borealis (Northern Crown).

Having completed his work of spreading the vine and the worship of his divinity all over the world, Dionysus attained apotheosis, becoming an immortal god, though born of a mortal woman. So favored was he that he joined the exclusive group of great gods on Mt. Olympus as the thirteenth Olympian god. (The number thirteen was most commonly regarded as a lucky number in antiquity, e.g., by the Greeks, Romans, Jews. Because there were thirteen at the Last Supper and one of these betrayed Christ, beginning with early Christian tradition the number came to be regarded as unlucky.) Having acquired immortality and having taken up residence on Olympus together with his wife Ariadne, Dionysus decided to make his mother Semele also an immortal. Accordingly, he descended to the underworld, restored Semele to life, and brought her back with him to Olympus, where she joined the immortals as a kind of retired concubine of Zeus.

Known by many names, among them Bacchus, Dionysus, whom Keats called "god of breathless cup and chirping mirth," was a god of vegetation, especially of the vine, and of the power of fertility in animals and humans. He had a dual quality, representing both the blessings and the destructive forces of nature, and these contradictory elements of his worship evoked exaltation, joy, and sacrament, but also barbaric rites, horror, and cruelty. Dionysus gave to man sexual desire and fertility, and release from the anxieties of life through the intoxicating power of wine, but at the same time his worship symbolized the violence and destructive forces of unrestrained nature. This latter materialized in the orgies which were part of the cult, wild orgiastic dancing, unrestrained licence, sexual excitation and fulfilment, involving both men and women. In the rites the worshippers shouted the magic words "Evoe! Evoe!"

These demonic orgiastic rites aimed to achieve a communion of the worshipper and the god through ecstasy and enthusiasm. By wild dancing, frenzied abandon, and drinking of wine the worshipper achieved *ecstasis* ("standing outside oneself") and *enthusiasmos* ("the state of having a god inside oneself"). As an important aspect of the cult, worshippers tried to acquire within themselves the potency and reproductive power of nature, which they envisioned as inherent in Dionysus. One way to achieve this total involvement with the god was to drink the god (that is, wine), while another was to eat the god (raw animal meat). To practice the latter the Greeks tore apart wild animals (especially the goat and bull) and ate the flesh raw, as a sacred meal which transmitted the potent forces of the god to his followers. (The Greeks did not invent the drinking of wine as a sacrament, nor did they invent the ritual of theophagy, "eating of a god." Both of these were practices of the Near East). The tearing apart of the sacred animal explains why we hear so much of human beings torn apart in connection with this cult, as well as the close connection of the goat and the bull with Dionysus. Wine and goat meat were such common staples in ancient Greece that even the poorest could worship Dionysus readily. He was "the poor man's god," the "liberator," the "savior" god.

Besides these animals and the vine associated with Dionysus, his attributes were the fawn skin and the *thyrsos*, a staff entwined with ivy and vine shoots and topped by a pine cone, carried by Dionysus and his followers. The ivy and pine, hardy winter plants, were thus sacred to Dionysus as god of eternal regeneration. His worshippers often wore masks in their efforts to impersonate the god and thus acquire his potency.

The tremendous expansion and appeal of the cult of Dionysus introduced special problems into the rational and civic-centered civilization of the Greeks. Aside from its gross sensuality the cult placed special stress on the happiness of the individual and his freedom. The faithful who worshipped independently of civic and family ties in their self-abandonment and exaltation through mystic union with Dionysus crossed the borders supposed to exist between men and gods, and their wild shouting, dancing, music, orgies shattered the traditional order imposed on social relations and individual behavior. Ultimately, however, at the beginning of the Sixth Century B.C., the conflict of the Dionysiac concept of unrestrained freedom and present ecstasy with the emphasis on control, reflection, moderation, and self-discipline in the cult of Apollo was resolved. In a remarkable compromise the priests of Delphi officially assimilated the Dionysiac cult of the savior god with that of the prophetic god, and henceforth Dionysus shared Delphi with Apollo, even if in a secondary role. This alliance made a compromise between the demands of social order and the yearning for ecstasy and individual fulfilment, so that the frenzy of the Dionysiac cult was tamed and channeled into socially useful purposes.

Athens too in the Sixth Century B.C. absorbed the Dionysiac cult into the state cult. Festivals of Dionysus, as god of the lower classes, were established and attained a prominence second only to that of the goddess Athena. And Athens made a major literary innovation with the hymns to Dionysus, called dithyrambs, which had originally been sung and danced by choruses of men disguised as Satyrs, wearing masks and goat skins. These hymns had been performed in a circular area called *orchestra* (literally "dancing place"), and in about 535 B.C. a dramatic aspect was added to this choral performance by an Athenian named Thespis, the "father of the drama," and theater was born out of the cult of Dionysus.

This literary form became one of the greatest achievements of the Greeks and of the human spirit. The Greek theater was in fact a shrine of Dionysus, and plays were performed as religious ceremonies of the state religion, for example at the festival called the Great Dionysia in Athens celebrated at the beginning of spring. From Athens the construction of theaters and the performance of plays spread all over the Greek world, and then to the Romans and the rest of the Western world. The very names of dramatic forms are derived from the cult of Dionysus. Tragedy in Greek means "goat song," though we cannot be certain whether this originated in a popular word for the performances of the dithyramb, or from the prize of a goat given to the best performances. Comedy means "song of revelry," and has its origin in the ribald processions and unrestrained language and behavior attending some aspects of the worship of Dionysus.

The Dionysiac cult, which justified "letting oneself go" and "being oneself" through ecstatic enjoyment of the present in physical terms, was a satisfactory experience for many Greeks, but for others, who were of a more mystical temperament, life on earth was too short to be man's principal concern. Hence they sought some means of assuring themselves a happy afterlife. It is true that their myths and religious tradition taught that great human heroes, like Heracles and Asclepius, could achieve apotheosis and immortality through extraordinary services to mankind, but for most people a less demanding, less heroic shortcut to immortality was necessary. In the Sixth Century B.C. a new religious movement held forth for all the possibility of a happy life after death. By an ingenious amalgamation and systematization of a variety of Greek and non-Greek myths, a remarkable system of belief and practice was assembled.

Orphism, as this religion is called today, developed its own

cosmogony through a revision of Greek traditions. In the most
common Orphic version the starting point of the universe was not
Oceanus or Chaos but Chronos (Time), who existed everlastingly.
This divinity generated Aether, Chaos, and Erebus, and the climax
of Chronos' productivity was a cosmic egg, out of which emerged
the god Phanes ("Shining One"), the first king of the gods, a
bisexual figure who created out of himself all that followed. In
turn Phanes had a daughter called Nyx (Night), and in union with
her were born Uranus and Gaea. From this point the Orphic
cosmogonic evolution paralleled Hesiod's: the Titans were born;
Cronus castrated and supplanted Uranus; Cronus in turn, after
swallowing his children the gods, was overthrown by his son Zeus.
For the Orphics Zeus was the supreme god, "the beginning, middle
and end of all," and to solve the problem of Phanes, who was also
the creator and author of all, the Orphics had Zeus swallow
Phanes, assuming all his power and making a fresh creative start.

By his sister Demeter Zeus produced Persephone-Kore, and
finally by his daughter Persephone fathered the sixth and last ruler
of the universe, Dionysus. As Zeus' favorite child Dionysus was
heir apparent, destined to succeed him as king of the gods, but
jealous Hera stirred up the violent Titans against Dionysus, and
they tore the divine child to pieces and ate his limbs. Athena
succeeded in rescuing the heart of Dionysus, which Zeus promptly
ate. From this seed, as the result of Zeus' subsequent union with
the Theban princess Semele, Dionysus was reborn, thus literally
the "twice-born god." The evil Titans were destroyed by Zeus'
thunderbolts, and out of their smoldering ashes man was created.

Thus mankind was thought to have a twofold nature. From
the body of Dionysus came a divine element, the soul, and from
the Titanic inheritance came man's innate evil. Tainted by such
original evil makeup, man was doomed to eternal punishments in
the afterlife unless he succeeded in purifying himself of his
"Titanic" nature. The body of man was thus impure, a sort of
prison of the divine soul. In their concept of the soul the Orphics
adopted from the Orient the belief in reincarnation and trans-
migration of souls. Since human life was a punishment, and return
of the soul to the body renewed man's suffering, Orphism tried to
teach man how to escape from the chain of rebirths, the eternal
wheel of reincarnation, and recommended a special Orphic way of

life to achieve this. This involved an initiation ceremony which included the sacrament of eating raw flesh of animals to attain communion with Dionysus, ascetic practices to mortify the flesh, purification rituals, and the following of various taboos. Through such rites of purification the Orphic could achieve salvation from rebirth and finally enter into an eternally blessed afterlife in Elysium.

In this system of thought the central myth is the suffering of the god Dionysus, who dies and is resurrected. Strikingly, Orphism substituted asceticism and self-discipline for the unrestrained licence and orgies of the standard Dionysiac cult. The mythic hero Orpheus himself fits into Orphism as the gentle, suffering musician whose knowledge of the underworld and whose martyrdom (he was torn apart by the women of Thrace) won for him the function of founder and prophet of the cult. The sacred writings of Orphism (the only Greek religion with sacred texts) were thought to have been written by Orpheus himself.

X

OTHER GODS:
of Olympus, the Sky, the Sea

Besides the twelve (later thirteen) Olympians other divinities lived in the celestial city of the gods, either intimately associated with Zeus as his helpers, or considered indispensable for assuring the blessed life of the gods. Zeus and Hera, besides their sons, the Olympian gods Hephaestus and Ares, had a daughter who lived on Olympus, Hebe, the goddess who symbolized the eternal youth of the gods. She served as cupbearer of the gods, a divine servant whose principal duty was to pour nectar for her parents and relatives, but her services proved to be neither indispensable nor eternal. Once Zeus, looking down from Olympus, caught sight of a shepherd boy of Troy, Ganymedes, who was of an extraordinary beauty, indeed the handsomest boy in the world. So smitten was Zeus with love for the boy that he decided he must have the boy with him forever on Olympus.

Thus began the famous seduction and seizure of Ganymedes, proverbial in antiquity for boy-love. Such elevations of a boy to heaven had Near Eastern antecedents, but in Greek mythology this became, beginning with the Sixth Century B.C., the story of the passion of an older man for a boy, replete with erotic elements, and involving the king of the gods and an insignificant mortal. In the earliest form of the Greek myth Zeus himself descended from Olympus, going to Mt. Ida in Troy, where he pursued the frightened lad, and carried off his beloved to Olympus. There Ganymedes became the pretty-boy of Zeus, was made immortal and supplanted Hebe as cupbearer of the gods. Zeus compensated Ganymedes' father, King Laomedon of Troy, with the gift of a wonderful breed of immortal horses, or a golden vine. As for

Hebe, she later married Heracles when he was elevated to godhood on Olympus. The usual story is that when Zeus was enamored of Ganymedes he simply sent his eagle to carry the boy up to Olympus, but this was a deliberate alteration of the original myth in which Zeus personally descended. In the Fourth Century B.C. a new concept of Zeus as an august and austere god had crystallized, and contemporary Greeks considered the ancient myth too undignified. At an even later time, the Romans and the early Christians transformed the rape of Ganymedes into an allegory of the soul being elevated to heaven, and Zeus' beloved boy became a symbol of immortality.

On Olympus also dwelt Iris ("Bow"), daughter of Thaumas, a primeval sea god. She represented the rainbow as a kind of bridge between heaven and earth, and was herself primarily the winged goddess of the rainbow. Accordingly, she was the earliest messenger of the Olympian gods, and when she was eventually supplanted in this function by Hermes, she continued to serve as special messenger of Hera, queen of the gods.

Also on Olympus were a group of daughters of Zeus called the Charites, the three Graces, goddesses of the gaiety and charm that attend all festive occasions, spreading pleasure and joy among gods and humans. Originally there was but one Grace, Charis ("Joy"), but usually, in keeping with the popularity among the Greeks of triads of divinities, three Graces were standard, Aglaea ("Radiance"), Euphrosyne ("Gaiety"), and Thalia ("Bloom"). They are often portrayed in art as three beautiful nude maidens with their arms about each others' shoulders.

Though basically an earth goddess, the Titaness Themis was associated with Zeus on Olympus. In her original capacity Themis succeeded Gaea as divinity of the oracle of Delphi, and eventually lost this function to her sister Titan Phoebe when she rose to join Zeus as his consort. On Olympus she became goddess of law and order, and had by Zeus the following children: the Moerae (Fates), the Horae (Hours), and the goddess Astraea (or Dike), goddess of justice.

Contributing greatly to the charm of life on Olympus were the Muses, patron goddesses of music, literature, singing and dancing. At first there was only one Muse, inspirer of reciters of epic poems, but later this concept too expanded to three, the so called

Muses of Helicon, named Melete ("Practice"), Mneme ("Memory"), and Aeöde ("Song"). In the most usual version of the myth of the Muses Zeus loved the Titaness Mnemosyne ("Memory"), and after nine nights of love in Thessaly at a place called Pieria she gave birth to nine daughters, the Nine Muses. They were: Erato, patroness of lyric poetry, especially love songs; Euterpe, other types of lyric poetry; Calliope, epic poetry; Clio, history; Melpomene, tragedy; Polyhymnia, serious songs, such as hymns; Terpsichore, dancing; Thalia, comedy; Urania, astronomy. The last one seems the least appropriate, but her presence among the nine indicates that originally for the Greeks astronomy was less a science than one of the arts. The Muses lived mostly on Mt. Olympus, where, as a sort of chorus for Apollo Musagetes ("Leader of the Muses"), they entertained the Olympians with singing and dancing. They were said to have favorite abodes in such other places as Pieria, Mt. Helicon in Boeotia, and on the slopes of Parnassus near Delphi. Two springs of water in particular were regarded as sacred to the Muses, Aganippe and Hippocrene.

The Muses were also helpers of mankind in the composition and performance of the various arts they represented, so it was customary to pray, in an "Invocation to the Muse," for assistance at the beginning of an artistic performance. Schools and even such learned institutions as Plato's Academy and Aristotle's Lyceum were placed under their protection. Our word museum is, of course, derived from the Greek belief in the Muses, a word first used for an important building in Hellenistic Egypt. This Museum was a research institute established about 280 B.C., attached to the great royal library in Alexandria, which housed many scholars who studied the literature of the bygone ages of Greek culture. Modern museums are an extension of this original association with the activities fostered by the Greek Muses.

With regard to gods of the sky, it was not until late in the Hellenistic Age, that a host of star myths became part of Greek mythology, under the influence of Near Eastern precedents. This tendency produced the great vogue of astrology among both the Greeks and the Romans, peopling the heavens with numerous figures from Greek mythology, and assigning planets, stars and constellations power over the destinies of humans.

The Greeks had few original sky myths of their own. Indeed,

their great gods, even Zeus who controlled phenomena in the sky, lived on earth and were mostly concerned with affairs of the earth. It was almost exclusively in connection with the sun and the moon that formal myths existed. The classical Greek sun god, replacing Hyperion, one of the original Titans, was Helios, portrayed as a young handsome god equipped with a chariot pulled by four winged horses. Each morning Helios began a journey across the sky. Starting in the waters of the great river Oceanus in the Far East, he drove his fiery chariot upward, appeared overhead at midday, and then descended toward the West to conclude his daily trip in the waters of Oceanus there. Here, after "splashdown," a boat picked up Helios and his chariot and transported them along the waters of Oceanus around the earth to the customary starting point in the East, where the daily journey began again the next day. It is said that Helios possessed herds of cattle in Sicily, sacred white animals with golden horns, taboo for mortals.

In general, the Greeks of the classical age thought worship of heavenly bodies barbaric. Yet on the island of Rhodes there was a popular cult of Helios, and in the harbor, which became a famous shipping center, there was a great bronze statue of the god about 100 feet high, the famous Colossus of Rhodes, which was one of the "Seven Wonders of the World." In the Fifth Century B.C. the sun god Helios was erroneously identified with Apollo, and thereafter Apollo was called god of the sun.

Helios' control of the course of the sun was unerring. It is said that if he ever strayed from his course the Erinyes (Furies) would quickly bring him back to his proper route but on one occasion there was a solar catastrophe that affected the whole world. Helios had an illegitimate son by Clymene named Phaëthon. For long the boy did not know who his father was, and when he discovered that it was Helios, Phaëthon tested his father's affection by asking him to grant him one wish. The indulgent father swore an irrevocable oath by the River Styx to grant him any wish he asked for, so when Phaëthon asked permission to drive the chariot of the sun for a day, Helios was helpless to forbid it. Phaëthon proved to be a reckless, inexperienced driver, and caused untold damage to the world by his erratic control of the solar vehicle. Deserts were created where he drove his chariot too close to earth, the skin of some humans was scorched into permanent dark colors, and bleak ice fields appeared in the North where the chariot veered too far away from the earth. Since there was grave danger of a universal conflagration, Zeus intervened, killed Phaëthon with a thunderbolt, and restored order to the climatic conditions of the world. But, of course, some irrevocable damage had already been done.

Phaëthon's body fell from the chariot into the Po River in Northern Italy. Here his sisters, the nymphs called Heliades ("Daughters of the Sun") took up the body of their brother and mourned so inconsolably for him that they changed into poplar trees, while their tears became drops of amber. Modern scientists have sought to discover in the myth of Phaëthon vestiges of folk memories of a great natural catastrophe. One of the theories proposed is based on our modern knowledge that at one time the Sahara desert in North Africa was a prosperous, cultivated region with a multitude of inhabitants. At some time in the Palaeolithic Age (say about 8000 B.C.) extraordinary changes in world climatic conditions, involving great shifts in wind and rainfall patterns, gradually transformed this region into a desert, and some hold that the myth of Phaëthon recalls this process. Another recent theory proposes that the myth of Phaëthon arose about 1400 B.C. as the result of great devastation in the Aegean area caused by a catastrophic eruption of the island of Santorin (ancient Thera), a volcanic island in the Aegean north of Crete.

The chariot of Helios in its normal course across the sky was always preceded by a kind of herald in the form of the goddess Eos, the dawn, riding in a chariot in the sky for a brief journey at the start of each day. In Homer's poetry she is often called "rosy-fingered Dawn." Strangely, Eos was said to be very amorous, with many lovers, particularly young hunters, and one may explain this by the fact that hunters often arose at night and began to hunt at dawn. There are many myths of Eos' erotic adventures with young hunters, such as those with Orion and Cephalus. The most famous of her lovers was Tithonus, a young Trojan of great beauty, by whom she bore the famed Memnon, king of the Ethiopians, who was to be slain by Achilles in a duel at Troy. Eos' love for Tithonus was so great that she obtained for him from Zeus the gift of immortality, but forgot to ask for eternal youth as well. As a result, the immortal Tithonus grew constantly older, and also shrank so in size that Eos kept her lover in a baby's crib. Finally he was transformed into a chirping cricket. It was said that the morning dew was caused by the tears Eos constantly shed for Tithonus, while other versions say that the tears of the Dawn were for her beloved son Memnon.

Myths of Selene, the moon goddess, twin of Helios, are scarce. The most famous one, concerning the boy Endymion whom she loved, we shall meet later. She too rode across the sky in a chariot, but at night, paralleling the daily journey of Helios. Because of her association with darkness, she was often said to be the protectress of magicians, thus readily identified with the witch goddess Hecate.

As compared with the relatively orderly conditions on Olympus, myths of the many inhabitants of the sea were not carefully systematized. The confusions and duplications we find in Greek marine mythology have their source in the fact that in their origins the Greeks were an inland people, with no experience of the sea. Indeed, the usual word used by the Greeks for sea, *thalassa* (or *thalatta*), is of prehellenic origin, just as the sea gods and sea myths which were in time assimilated by the Greeks had been developed by early inhabitants of the Aegean area long before the Greeks arrived. The Aegean and the entire Mediterranean became for the Greeks the great highway connecting most areas inhabited by them, and was a fundamental factor in their economic life and cultural unity. They were early led across the sea by the spirit of adventure, the lure of commercial profits, the need to import food and export products and surplus population, and next to the Phoenicians they were the most famous sea-faring people of the world until modern times. But the bountiful sea, with its dangers, unpredictability, and strange animals, was a mixed blessing, and the Greeks feared as well as loved it.

While Poseidon was the "Zeus of the Sea" in the thought of classical Greeks, he had predecessors. The primordial sea god of the Mediterranean was Pontus ("The Path"), son and mate of Gaea, the conception of the sea in its early cosmic form, as useless, infertile, chaotic. One could not till it, live on it, or control it as easily as the earth. Then, just as Helios supplanted Hyperion, Poseidon replaced Pontus. It is in keeping with the establishment of a Hellenic pantheon that Pontus' descendants were often considered hostile to the Olympian gods, and that Greek heroes, such as Heracles, Bellerophon, and Perseus in their famous exploits were champions of order against descendants of Pontus.

Pontus' children by Gaea were all sea gods of the prehellenic religion, and the most important were Phorcys, Thaumas, Ceto, and Nereus. Ceto was a female marine monster, representing the weird character of some sea animals and the dangers of the sea. Her brother Phorcys, another strange sea divinity, represented the terrors of the sea and was the father (by his sister Ceto) of sea monsters such as Scylla and Echidna, and of other monstrous creatures like the dragon Ladon, the Gorgons and the Graeae. Thaumas ("Marvel") represented the wonders of the sea.

Phorcys was one of a number of ancient sea gods who acquired the title "Old Man of the Sea." These were apparently prehellenic sea divinities, all of them thought capable of transforming themselves into many shapes. The third brother of Ceto, Nereus, another primordial sea god who had the title "Old Man of the Sea," was especially symbolical of nautical wisdom. He was most famous as father of the 50 sea nymphs called the Nereids, whom he had by the nymph Doris. Only three of the Nereids — Amphitrite, Thetis, and Galatea — were individual personalities, but all are generally represented as lovable, friendly sea creatures who live in palaces in the sea but delight to rise to the surface to sun themselves, sit on the rocks, comb their hair, or ride on dolphins. Generally the Nereids were reluctant to marry. Originally they may have been primitive inland spirits of waters and springs but became sea nymphs when the Greeks settled on the shores of the Mediterranean, and today in Greece nature demons are still known as Neraids.

Another "Old Man of the Sea" was Proteus, in Greek mythology demoted to the position of guardian of Poseidon's seals. Though sometimes even further humanized into the figure of an Egyptian king, Proteus kept the animals at the island of Pharos off the coast of Egypt. The seal, once fairly common in the Mediterranean, was a favorite of European folklore, and was believed capable of changing shape, even into that of humans. Proteus was especially famed for his ability to foretell the future, but would not give a prophecy unless he was first caught, a possibility that was exceedingly unlikely because of Proteus' ability to change his shape rapidly (into a lion, serpent, panther, boar, etc.). Some heroes, such as Menelaüs and Aristaeus, succeeded in holding on to him throughout his swift transformations and obtaining prophecies from him.

A similar amalgam of the good and evil in the sea, as the Greeks viewed it, appears in the characters of the sea demons called Sirens. In their earliest form these were two maidens, completely human in form, who lived on an island in the Mediterranean from which they bewitched sailors, luring them to certain death by singing their beautiful songs, so that the men leaped into the waters to reach the island and died. These temptresses were not all evil. In their bewitching songs they offered both erotic temptations and all knowledge, and they too possessed the gift of prophecy. Phoenician sailors may have spread the tale of such a magic island inhabited by dangerous female temptresses (the Semitic word *shir* means "song"). In the Eighth and Seventh centuries B.C. the Greeks imported from the Near East a new artistic motif of female winged figures, and not long after encountered and adopted from Egypt the concept of depicting souls of the dead on tombstones as "soul birds," that is, winged demons of the dead. All these concepts were somehow amalgamated into a new mythic personality, the classical Sirens, conceived as harmful tempting creatures signifying death, now three or four in number. The standard ancient representation of Sirens soon became formalized as a hybrid of half-woman, half-bird. The concept of fish Sirens is not an ancient one, for the portrayals of such beautiful fish-tailed temptresses, like the Lorelei of the Rhine in Germany, were first invented in the Middle Ages.

Another malevolent female sea creature was Scylla, a monster living in a cave at the Straits of Messina between Sicily and Italy. The upper part was that of a woman, the lower part was surrounded by six ferocious dogs who seized and devoured passing sailors from their ships. There are various tales of how such a female monster originated. One version tells that Poseidon fell in love with a girl named Scylla, and therefore jealous Amphitrite caused her to be transformed into a monster. In the straits opposite Scylla was yet another monster, Charybdis, a voracious whirlpool which three times daily sucked everything in the waters down to the depths of the sea, and three times surged back. Sailors who sought to avoid Scylla by sailing out from one side of the straits were then trapped by Charybdis. The peculiarity of the story of Charybdis is that the Mediterranean has no whirlpools and is tideless. It is therefore likely that such stories of a great whirlpool in the Mediterranean were sailors' tales of phenomena observed outside the straits of Gibraltar in the Atlantic.

There is another sea god, a minor one, said to have been a human being originally, the fisherman Glaucus, who one day by chance tasted an herb which made him immortal. Then he leaped into the sea, became a marine god, and acquired the gift of prophecy. The story of such a magic sea leap appears also in the tale of the sea goddess Leucothea ("White Goddess"), originally the mortal Ino, princess of Thebes, who, because she tried to bring up the child Dionysus, was driven insane by Hera. As a result of her suffering, in her madness she leaped into the sea together with her son Melicertes. Ino, transformed into the sea goddess Leucothea, and Melicertes, into the sea god Palaemon, were both regarded as benevolent to sailors.

XI

OTHER GODS:
of the Earth and the Underworld

The absence of any large bodies of water within Greece led to special veneration of rivers, especially the bigger ones. This explains why the river Acheloüs in west central Greece (the modern name of the river is Aspropotamo), the largest in Greece, had exceptional prestige. In its waters lived the river god Acheloüs, honored as one of the oldest sons of Oceanus and Tethys. A symbol of water in general Acheloüs was often represented either as a bull (to symbolize its size and fertilizing powers), or as a bearded human head with the horns of a bull. In keeping with older traditions about water gods, Acheloüs too had the gift of prophecy and the power to transform himself into many shapes. Like Zeus, another prime fertilizing force, Acheloüs was said to have had many loves, giving rise to tales which traced back many local heroes and aristocratic clans to a divinity whose lineage stemmed from the very beginnings of the universe. The most famous myth of Acheloüs was his combat with the hero Heracles, which we shall meet later.

A smaller river, in the southern part of Greece, was the Alphaeus, the largest river of the Peloponnesus. As a river god Alphaeus, like Acheloüs, was also a son of Oceanus and Tethys, and like Acheloüs he was said to have had love affairs. In particular, he tried to seduce even the chaste Artemis and her faithful nymphs. Once the nymph named Arethusa was bathing in the river Alphaeus, and when the god became amorous she resisted his attentions and fled, leaping into the sea off the coast of Greece. She swam until she reached the city of Syracuse in Sicily, and there was transformed into a spring. The god Alphaeus, loving

Arethusa, pursued her with his waters through the sea, the sweet water of the river remaining miraculously pure despite its contact with salt water. Finally he found Arethusa in Syracuse, where he mingled his waters with hers in the spring, a story perhaps in origin a traditional folktale theme of "distant lovers" who are eventually united. Arethusa became famous as the symbol of the city of Syracuse, her head portrayed on the money of the city, which are among the most beautiful of all Greek coins.

Among the divine inhabitants of the earth there was a vast number of minor female nature divinities called nymphs ("maidens"), represented as beautiful young women, each associated with some limited aspect of nature, in the fields, woods, hills, and waters. The nymphs were generally happy, sprightly creatures who spent their time in natural surroundings playing, dancing, and singing. Some formed the entourage of Artemis, some were attracted by the merriment attending the followers of the god Dionysus, and most were in constant dread of such semi-bestial creatures as the bawdy Satyrs, Sileni, and Pan, from whose amorous advances they frequently fled. In general nymphs, like the major goddesses, did not like to be seen by mortals. Men who came close to nymphs were in grave danger. A person "seized" by a nymph was said to be *nympholeptos*, bewitched by a divine madness and emotional frenzy called nympholepsy.

Every tree was said to have its own guardian nymph, called a Dryad. Since they were immortal they could move from one tree to another, and when a nymph abandoned a tree it died. Some nymphs called Hamadryads, each associated always with one specific tree, lost their lives when their own trees died. The Naiads ("Swimmers") were nymphs of springs and small streams, in reality fertility divinities in the role of guardians of fresh water, which was so precious in Greece. The Oreads were nymphs who guarded specific mountains, and the oldest of all the nymphs were the Oceanids, daughters of Oceanus and Tethys. The Meliads ("Ash Nymphs"), associated with ash trees, were said to have been born from the blood of Uranus, and were thought to be one of the sources of the origin of the first men. Also venerated for their antiquity were the Nereids, daughters of Nereus, one of the old men of the sea. There were also other types of nymphs, and their multiplication in Greek thought tended to crowd the world with untold numbers of guardian deities.

Some nymphs formed special groups. Among the most famous of these were the Pleiades, seven daughters of the Titan Atlas by one of the Oceanids, Pleione, whose names are usually given as Electra, Alcyone, Celaeno, Maia, Asterope, Taygete, Merope. All the Pleiades married divinities except Merope, who was the wife of Sisyphus, a famed Greek king who turned out to be the most unscrupulous character in Greek mythology. These sweet nymphs were very close to each other. Once when they were together they were overtaken by the famous giant hunter Orion, from whom they fled, and when Orion brazenly pursued them, Zeus came to the rescue, sweeping them up and placing them in the sky as the constellation Pleiades. One of the seven stars in this constellation appears very faint, and the Greeks called it the lost Pleiad, telling the story that Merope's star faded because she was ashamed of her marriage with a mortal. Actually, when the constellation Pleiades is viewed through a telescope rather than with the naked eye hundreds of stars are visible.

Another famous group of nymphs, also daughters of Atlas, were the Hesperides ("Evening Nymphs"), usually said to be three in number, Aegle, Eurythie, Hesperarethusa. They tended the Garden of the Gods situated in the far West, at the foot of the Atlas Mountains, a divine paradise reserved for the Olympian gods which held a remarkable tree bearing the famed golden apples of the Hesperides, a Greek adaptation of the very ancient concept of the Tree of Life. The tree with the apples of the Hesperides was guarded by a hundred headed dragon named Ladon, reminiscent of the name Lotan for a dragon in the Near East.

The Tree of Life was a basic Near Eastern symbol, and appeared first in that part of the world. It became a recurrent theme diffused into the religions and folklore of many peoples throughout the world, and in origin was a sacred symbol of the creativity, fertility, and rebirth of nature. The basis of this symbol is the belief that there was some sort of divine life inherent in each tree, comparable to the Greek belief in Dryads. The veneration of a sacred tree was part of the vegetation cult of the mother goddess in Crete, and from the Cretans the concept spread to the Greeks, who located the tree in some mythical divine garden in the West. For the Greeks the fruit of this tree came to symbolize not only fertility of the earth but also love and immortality. Everywhere the Tree of Life tended to be rooted in a paradise, in some cases a human abode as the Garden of Eden of the ancient Hebrews, while for both the Mesopotamians and the Greeks it was a garden of gods. The transference of the original fertility aspect of the Tree of Life to the theme of rejuvenation and even of immortality was a natural one, for the renewal of vegetation in the springtime, an annual resurrection of nature as it were, was associated with man's yearning for immortality.

It is noteworthy that in the Garden of Eden story in the Old Testament there are two trees — a Tree of Knowledge (a concept unknown to the Greeks), guarded by a serpent, and a Tree of Life. Adam and Eve were tricked by the serpent into exclusive interest in the Tree of Knowledge, and by eating the apple they acquired wisdom but lost immortality, which was reserved for the divine, as it was in the Greek myth of the Apples of the Hesperides. The concept of the Tree of Life survives today both in the Christmas tree and the May-pole ceremonies, and the symbol has been in existence for as long as 5000 years.

A minor god of fertility on earth was the god Pan, divinity of woods, fields, particularly flocks, who caused fertility in such animals as the goat. Pan, a hybrid god of nature, mostly human but retaining animal characteristics of a hairy body, horns, feet, ears and tail of a goat, was said to have been born to Hermes and the nymph Cyllene in Arcadia. His birth caused consternation because he was so ugly, but his proud father Hermes brought him to Olympus to show off his progeny. As a nature god and stimulator of fertility in animals, Pan roamed the hills and woods, and was thought to instill panic in men and animals by his sudden movements in the woods or among flocks, especially at midday. In keeping with his own semi-bestial nature and his function of stimulating fertility, Pan was himself an erotic god, a joyful companion at the revels of Dionysus, and an amorous pursuer of both nymphs and young boys. The story was told that once he loved the nymph Syrinx, but she rejected his attentions and eluded him, leaping into a nearby stream. When he tried to catch her as she fled, he grasped instead reeds growing on the bank, and from these reeds, by way of consoling himself, he created the shepherd's pipes, or Pan's pipes. From this we get the biological

term syrinx for the windpipe of songbirds and the word syringe.

Although in Greek mythology animals do not talk and there are no animal fables in their tales, the Greek imagination assigned voices and musical skills to Pan and other hybrid creatures such as Silenus, the Satyr Marsyas, and the Sphinx, because of their basically human characteristics. In the case of Pan, as the result of his skill with his wind instrument he challenged Apollo, who was skilled on the lyre. In the contest between the plebeian syrinx and the aristocratic lyre the judge was King Midas of Phrygia. Being a non-Greek king he chose Pan as the winner, a piece of bad judgment, as we shall see, for which he endured the humiliating punishment of having his ears turned into donkey's ears.

Because of an erroneous correlation between the name of the god Pan and the Greek word *pan* meaning "all," the god Pan was later elevated to a greater significance than his cult and myths merited. Milton, for example, calls him "Universal Pan," and a famous story is told about the god Pan by the Greek author Plutarch. One day – the time was during the life of Christ in the reign of the Roman Emperor Tiberius – a ship was passing an island in the Aegean, when suddenly a voice was heard saying "The great god Pan is dead." When this report was relayed from the ship to another island, a great sound of lamentation arose from the island. We may assume that some form of local vegetation rite symbolizing the cycle of the seasons was involved, but the early Christians who knew the story emphasized this event as a harbinger of the beginning of the decline of paganism.

Another fertility god of the Greeks, Priapus, was a late entrant into the Greek cults, becoming popular in the Hellenistic period. Priapus, the illegitimate son of Dionysus and Aphrodite, had his origin in Asia Minor, from which his worship spread all over the Mediterranean. He was a rustic god of the generative forces in nature, especially in garden cultivation, had the phallus as his symbol, and often appeared in the retinue of Dionysus. His best known myth typifies the unsophisticated rural god. One night he sought to take by surprise while she slept a nymph Lotis who constantly fled his amorous attentions, but a donkey brayed and woke up everyone, causing uproarious laughter at his discomfiture.

A group of minor vegetation goddesses who symbolize the blessings given by the rhythmical orderly patterns of nature have the name Horae (Hours), and are usually depicted as three young women whose names were Eunomia ("Good Rule"), Eirene ("Peace"), and Dike ("Justice"). Originally nature powers who caused the maturing of vegetation at the proper season of each year, later they were associated with the seasons themselves, eventually with a fourth added producing the concept of the four seasons. Since they represented law and order in nature, as it were, it was not an unnatural step for them to be thought of as guardians of law and order in society, and they were sometimes said to be the guardians of the gates of Olympus. The concept of Hours as parts of the day did not develop until quite later.

We have seen that there were Greek mystery religions, the Eleusinian Mysteries and Orphism, that claimed to prepare people for a happy afterlife. The standard Greek view of the afterlife, however, was an utterly cheerless one. While the Greeks believed that the individual soul continued to exist eternally after death, they thought of this as a gloomy uneventful existence somewhere under the earth, in the realm of Hades and his queen Persephone. Hades represented a king, or Zeus, of the nether world (his name may signify "The Unseen"). Hades did not have an entourage like that of Zeus on Mt. Olympus, and though he possessed a horse-driven chariot, the only time he ever left Hades was to seize Persephone to make her his wife. He was a stern, pitiless, forbidding divinity, whose principal function was defense of the Underworld and rule over the souls as King of the Dead. He was not a Satan or devil, a concept alien to the Greeks, and in fact, under another name, Pluto ("Riches"), he had the characteristics of a god of fertility, thus an underworld force for good as well as death. As king he sat on a throne holding a scepter; the helmet presented to him by the Cyclopes, when they gave his brothers Zeus the thunderbolt and Poseidon the trident, was said to render him invisible. Originally the name of this god, the term Hades eventually designated the place of habitation of dead souls, located somewhere under the earth in the far West, and associated vaguely with the far distant stream Oceanus at the ends of the earth.

Since there are no dogmas in Greek religion, many contradictory versions of the afterlife existed side by side. The popular Greek view of an afterlife of unrelieved gloom and boredom was closest to widespread Near Eastern ideas of a "land of no return," like the gloomy Sheol of the Jews before the Babylonian Captivity, and the later Teutonic Hel. The Greek belief that souls simply continued to exist as shadowless ghosts flitting aimlessly about in the Underworld contrasts with the millenia-old highly optimistic Egyptian view of the afterlife, that with proper ceremonies the soul could attain a blessed afterlife. The Minoans, too, appear to have developed a notion of eternal happiness, at least for the few, in a faraway place which the Greeks were later to call the Isles of the Blest.

In the normal Greek view, the soul, in order to reach its final resting place, had to go on a long journey, crossing various bodies of water. Guided by Hermes, the soul reached the entrance to Hades at the shores of a river, and awaited transportation. To assure that the soul would reach its final abode in the Underworld it was necessary for the person's closest relatives to perform proper funeral rites for the dead. Whether cremation or inhumation of the body was practiced, the basic ceremonies consisted of the scattering of a few handfuls of earth over the body and the burial of a small coin with the remains. This duty of relatives was so fundamental that the Greeks considered it a barbaric practice not to permit the enemy in war to bury their dead. Two famous myths show the power of this tradition: Priam's risking his life to obtain the body of his son Hector for burial, and Antigone's sacrifice of her life to give decent burial to her brother Polynices.

Once the soul reached the actual terrain of Hades it faced obstacles in the form of a number of rivers: Styx ("Hateful"), Acheron ("Woe"), Cocytus ("Wailing"), Pyriphlegethon ("Burning"), and Lethe ("Forgetfulness"). Although most of these were swamp-like streams, fearful but fordable, the outermost was very large. (It is not clear whether this was the Styx or Acheron). In either case, there was a ferry for souls operated by a minor divinity called Charon, who was depicted as a bearded, unkempt old man, obviously weary, bored, and ill-tempered because of his eternal task. Charon accepted only those souls who had transportation money in the form of the small Greek coin called an *obol* placed with the dead, hence the term "Charon's obol" for the coin buried with the body at funerals.

The notion of a ferryman of the boat of the dead has its origin in pre-Greek cultures that go back to time immemorial. Originally many articles of food, clothing, and equipment — sometimes all of a person's valuables — were placed in the tomb to furnish the soul with the necessities of a long sea voyage and of life in the other world. Eventually, after coinage was invented, a single small coin was substituted as a token symbolizing provision for all expenses of the soul. In the end, the practice was rationalized, so that the coin was considered a fee for the ferryman of the dead. This concept of placing a coin with the dead has survived until today, and is found widely diffused among many different cultures all over the world. The Christians, for example, continued the pagan practice of "corpse coins," but assigned new motives to explain the custom. The myth of Charon still survives most vividly today in Greece, where the peasant will frequently express his hostility to the demon of death, whom he calls Charos.

The River Styx, the oldest of the children of Oceanus and Tethys, was the principal and most famous of the mythical rivers of the Underworld. It is said that because Styx aided Zeus in the Gigantomachy, the Olympian gods accorded the river special status by swearing their mightiest oaths in its name, oaths that were then utterly irrevocable.

When the soul, after traversing the rivers of Hades, reached the great palace of Hades, it found the entrance guarded by a huge watchdog called Cerberus. An offspring of the monsters Typhon and Echidna, the hound of Hades was usually said to be three-headed, although it was originally viewed as a huge monster with 50 or 100 heads. Cerberus' three heads ensured his eternal watchfulness, so that he could prevent unauthorized souls from entering or leaving the realm of Hades and guard against living persons seeking illicit admittance. The ferocity of Cerberus could, however, be appeased by throwing him a special honey-cake, the so-called "sop to Cerberus."

Once past Cerberus, the soul came before a tribunal of judges, Minos, Rhadamanthus, and Aeacus, all men of the highest integrity when they were alive, and who now assigned punishments to great sinners. The most famous of these sinners were Tityus, Tantalus, Sisyphus, Ixion, and the Danaïds. (Their myths will appear elsewhere in this book.) Those souls that received serious punishments were consigned to a lower depth of Hades known as Tartarus, located, with the Greek love of symmetry, as far below the surface of the earth as Olympus was above it. In general all other souls, whether of minor sinners or the virtuous, simply wandered aimlessly in Hades. The name Tartarus (or variants therefor, such as Erebus and Orcus) was then given to the entire realm of dead souls.

In one of the unusual aspects of the Greek concept of the kingdom of Hades, living people frequently tried to descend there for various purposes. The most famous of these in classical mythology are Odysseus, Heracles, Theseus, Pirithoüs, and Aeneas, and their adventures parallel descents to the underworld in the mythologies of other peoples like the well-known Near Eastern myth of Gilgamesh. Involved in such voluntary descents to the Underworld is the striving of remarkable human beings to overcome and defy death by contact with and return from it.

Among the early Greek aristocrats, a drab posthumous existence in Hades was thought to be the penalty one paid for an uneventful life on this earth. Hence as part of their heroic code they lived by the belief that by their glorious deeds, especially in war, they could achieve a kind of immortality by being remembered after their death. Thus the hero Achilles in his search for glory was willing to give up his life at an early age so as to be remembered by posterity and be immortalized in the songs of men, even if his soul simply vegetated in Hades.

But out of this code there developed in time a widespread belief among the Greeks that some men, because of their extraordinary services to mankind, merited real immortality. Some, like Asclepius and Heracles, were actually thought to have become gods, while others were treated as semidivine, their tombs becoming places of worship. Such men were called heroes, a category half-way between gods and men. In a parallel view belief grew that there was a place called Isles of the Blest, or Elysium, first thought of as a place on earth, somewhere in the far West near Oceanus, reserved exclusively for favorites of the gods. In this ideal place the privileged elite lived in a kind of earthly paradise, retaining their bodies yet immortal. In time, however, the location of Elysium as the place of the blessed was transferred to the Underworld, a portion of which was called the Elysian Fields. Thus, although all souls were thought to go to Hades, the place now had two distinct divisions, Elysium for the souls of the blessed, Tartarus a kind of hell and place of punishment for sinners. The notion of a blessed afterlife in heaven is alien to the Greeks, for whom the pleasures of a heavenly abode were reserved for the Olympian gods and their entourage. It is from later Near Eastern mystery cults that the notion of a celestial afterlife developed.

In Hades there was also an old Greek goddess, one of the generation of Titanesses, Hecate, goddess of sorcery, black magic, witches, associated with the world of ghosts. She was in reality originally an ancient earth goddess, both benevolent and harmful, with a composite character that identified her with such better known good-bad goddesses as Persephone, Artemis, and Selene. Since crossroads were considered haunted by travelling ghosts, Hecate was often worshipped there, represented as a three-bodied, three-faced goddess. Her attendant was a black dog.

Often considered divinities of the Underworld were the Erinyes (Furies), avenging demons who punished crimes. Their antiquity was embodied in the myth that they were among the creatures born from the blood of Uranus. These malevolent divinities, named Tisiphone ("Avenger of Murder"), Allecto ("Unwearied"), and Megaera ("Grim"), were terrifying in appearance, with snakes in their hair, and they punished relentlessly any violations of asylum, hospitality, and oaths. Especially did they avenge murders of close kin, above all matricide and patricide, and they are best remembered for their retribution on Orestes, who was driven insane by them. While we may rationalize the Erinyes into the force of conscience, the Greeks believed in the external existence of such immortal avenging deities who preserved the social and family order. By a characteristic twist of the Greek mind, which often substituted a euphemism to give a pleasant word or expression to an unpleasant concept, the Erinyes were also called Eumenides, "Benevolent Ones."

XII

VARIOUS OTHER GODS

There were a number of Greek divinities who had no relationship to nature but were important in the domain of social relations and the great moments of an individual's life. Among these were the goddesses Atë and Nemesis, the principal divine agents for the enforcement of moderation in all things, which, as we have seen, was one of the basic values of Greek culture. When the sin of *hybris*, or excess in anything, was committed, the jealousy of the gods was aroused and the goddess Atë ("Infatuation") was dispatched to attack the sinner. She made him lose his grip on reality, so that he became unbalanced, affected by mental and/or moral blindness, and with his now limited vision sank deeper into sin, committing graver acts of *hybris*. We would say "It went to his head;" the Greek proverb was, "Whom the gods would destroy they first make mad." Once the victim was blinded by Atë, a second goddess Nemesis ("Retribution") inflicted the specific punishment ordained by the gods. In this way the gods restored order and balance to the cosmos, which had been disturbed by the act of *hybris*. The frequency of this theme in Greek myths reveals how deeply the Greeks felt the need to inculcate the virtues of moderation and self-control.

In many areas of life man had the freedom of choice to determine the course of his life, and by proper dealings with the gods, however vast in number they were, one could obtain blessings or avert evils. Of course, freedom of choice is not unlimited, as we cannot, for example, choose not to die, so the Greeks, while not fatalists, believed that some aspects of man's life were inevitable and predestined. This belief was concretized in the figuresⅠof the Moerae, the three Fates, daughters of Zeus and the Titaness Themis, who belonged to remote antiquity. They were represented as three ugly old women: Clotho ("Spinner"), who spun a thread as symbol of each human's life; Lachesis ("Apportioner"), who drew out the thread to a specific length; and Atropos ("Inevitable"), who with a scissors cut the thread wherever she determined. Thus each man's fate was allotted to him by the Moerae at the time of birth, and not even the might of Zeus could alter the decisions of the Fates, whose great power represented the supreme order of the universe, superior to all the gods. The view that "it wasn't fated" gave comfort in time of failure, particularly when worshippers were confident that they had done everything proper to influence the gods.

Marriage was the province of the god Hymen (or Hymenaeus). The Greeks believed that he was present during the ceremony as the particular divinity of the wedding procession and the wedding song. Depicted by the Greeks as a very handsome young man, the god Hymen was an anthropomorphic representation of the very ancient cry *hymen, hymen!* shouted at Greek marriage ceremonies, its very meaning no longer known.

When someone died, it was believed, the god Thanatos appeared to claim him, and shortly after the soul left the body to be conducted by Hermes to Hades. A son of the primordial Nyx ("Night"), Thanatos personified death as a malevolent mysterious power in human form. A similar personification was Hypnos ("Sleep"), said to be a brother of Thanatos, depicted as a winged youth who brought sleep by pouring a mysterious liquid from a horn into one's eyes. Related to these two was the god Morpheus, god of dreams, a son of Hypnos.

For a people like the Greeks, who glorified athletics and the athlete, the maintenance of health was of high importance, and by the end of the Fifth Century B.C. they had founded scientific medicine. But for centuries before this, and parallel with it throughout the rest of antiquity, there existed the worship of the beloved god of medicine, Asclepius. Beginning as a local healing demon in Thessaly — the region of Greece long famous for magic practices and medical lore — Asclepius suddenly in the Fifth Century B.C. rose to extraordinary popularity and celebrity as the great god of medicine.

There had been an earlier Greek deity specializing in healing, Paean, perhaps prehellenic but with his origin lost in the mists of prehistory. When Delphi emerged as the greatest religious center of the Greeks, perhaps sometime in the Sixth Century B.C., Paean was assimilated with Apollo, to add healing to the complexity of that god. Although the healing function remained a minor aspect of Apollo's functions for a long time, in Thessaly, the cradle of Greek healing lore, very strong traditions of medical knowledge came into conflict with this new development in the cult of Apollo. The Thessalians appear to have made an effort to rescue their local healing demon Asclepius from being entirely supplanted by Apollo in this sphere, and Asclepius not only succeeded in holding his own in Thessaly but became the panhellenic god of medicine.

In the myth of the birth of Asclepius we find him associated with Apollo, who, we are told, loved a princess of Thessaly, Coronis, sister of King Ixion of the Lapiths. While Coronis was carrying Apollo's child, it was discovered that she had been unfaithful to the god with a mortal named Ischys. The news of this betrayal was brought to Apollo by a raven, and in anger Apollo, with the aid of his sister Artemis, goddess of chastity in women, killed Coronis with arrows. The body of the unfortunate girl was already being cremated on the funeral pyre when Apollo, remembering the child in Coronis' womb, quickly rescued the child about to be born, and thus Asclepius, like Dionysus, was "twice-born," risen to life from the dead, a good omen for a future physician. It is said that because of its part in this tragic event, the feathers of the raven were turned permanently black. The child Asclepius was taken to Chiron, the famed centaur in Thessaly, who brought him up and taught him the art of medicine.

Despite his status as a minor healing deity of Thessaly in early times, most Greeks regarded Asclepius as a human who had lived in the Heroic Age, but was later worshipped as a semidivine hero because of his services to mankind. They remembered him as a great physician of Thessaly, a craftsman in an age of warriors and adventurers, a man of peace — the ideal physician. His two sons, Machaon and Podilarius, were said to have been physician-warriors in the Greek army attacking the city of Troy. Asclepius' skill as a healer achieved its greatest triumph by restoring a number of dead heroes to life, most notably Hippolytus, but, since Asclepius had by his medical skill discovered how to make man immortal, Hades complained to Zeus. The king of the gods agreed to stop such medical miracles in order to preserve the established order, killed Asclepius with a thunderbolt, and ended his activity for a while.

During the latter part of the Fifth Century B.C., disillusionment with civic life and the community-oriented state religion of the polis intensified the yearnings of the Greeks for personal happiness. Thus Asclepius, restorer of health to the individual, suddenly became popular, and, long honored as a hero and a great benefactor of man, he was elevated to divinity. Greek myths related that though he had been slain by Zeus he had been restored to life as one of the immortals. A savior god, the most human and beloved of all the gods, Asclepius supplanted other healing gods and demons including his father Apollo. So revered was he that among all the Greek gods there was never any scandal told of him. He was surrounded by a loving wife Epione and a divine family, two sons Machaon and Podilarius, and three daughters, Hygieia ("Health"), Panacea ("Cure-All"), and Iaso ("Healing"). Unlike the family of the Olympian gods, Asclepius' family was a loving one, and all members aided him in carrying out his function. He became the patron saint of Greek physicians, who called themselves in his honor Asclepiades ("Sons of Asclepius"), thus linked together in their respect for the "father of physicians." The most famous Asclepiad was Hippocrates of Cos, the father of scientific medicine.

Asclepius' importance as a great divinity appears to have been established first in the city of Epidaurus in the northeastern Peloponnesus. There a great temple of the god of medicine grew up and expanded into a kind of sanatorium for the sick, to which people flocked from all over the world, confidently expecting to be cured of their illnesses by individual communion with the god. This was facilitated by the rite of incubation: the ill first drank from sacred waters in Epidaurus, were put on special diets, and then went to sleep in a great hall attached to the temple; the god appeared to them in dreams, and in the morning they were improved or miraculously cured. Many such miraculous cures were reported by worshippers of Asclepius. In gratitude to the god, those helped usually had a sculptured or painted plaque made indicating the part of the body cured (such as eyes, leg, arm, etc.), and attached this to the walls of the sanctuary. From a similar Roman practice, such offerings were known as *ex voto* dedications, because they were set up as the result of vows made before entering the incubation hall. Since persons with illness often wanted to have a prognosis of their maladies, the god Asclepius was given prophetic powers, and in the field of medicine he became a competitor of Apollo at Delphi. Asclepius was especially beloved by the common man, since the absence of any fees (or at most very minimal ones, as compared with the costs of consulting the Delphic oracle) made the services of Asclepius readily available to all. The temple of Asclepius at Epidaurus is one of the origins of the concept of philanthropy in the western world, and the earliest forerunner of the institution of the hospital. From Epidaurus the worship of Asclepius and his miraculous cures spread everywhere and similar sanctuaries were established in many places, including the city of Rome.

As a healing god and benefactor of man, Asclepius was revered to the end of the ancient world. As a healer and savior of the individual, he came into competition later with Christ, and indeed remained the most vigorous competitor of Christianity in the struggle for the hearts of men, for his shrines were maintained as late as the Sixth Century A.D., long after paganism had been generally wiped out.

More primitive was a triad of pre-Olympian goddesses, the Graeae ("Old Women"), who lived somewhere in the far West. Said to be the daughters of Phorcys and Ceto, primitive sea gods, the Graeae were born old women, and possessed among them one common eye and one common tooth. In mythology their principal function appears to have been to guard the way to the dwelling place of their three sisters the Gorgons.

As special physical characteristics the Gorgons had large grotesque heads, snakes in their hair, and large protruding teeth and tongues. The Gorgons ("Fearful Ones") symbolized man's fear of the terrors of nature, particularly of wild animals. The three Gorgons were Medusa ("Cunning One"), Sthenno ("Mighty"), and Euryale ("Wide Leaping"), and the sight of them was thought to transform humans into stone. Of the three Gorgons only Medusa was mortal, but even her severed head had the power to turn men to stone. Masks depicting the Gorgon's head (called *gorgoneion*) were often used by Greeks as protective amulets (e.g., on the aegis of Zeus and Athena, on temples, and on shields of soldiers). The belief in the apotropaic power of the Gorgon's head may have developed from primitive times, when priests wearing such masks proceeded to the borders of an inhabited area and roared through the mouth of the Gorgon head to frighten away wild animals. After the danger of wild animals disappeared from urbanized centers in Greece, the continued use of the Gorgon mask required the transformation of the meaning of the symbol, so that the Gorgon's head became a generalized symbol of protection, mostly against dangerous humans. Even the original grotesque appearance of the Gorgon was humanized. In the Greek myth originally Medusa had been a beautiful girl whose hair was so lovely that in her pride she committed *hybris* by comparing herself to Athena. In punishment her hair was turned into snakes, and the sight of her thereafter could turn humans into stone. Another version had her punished in this way because the god Poseidon had violated her in a temple of Athena. The killing of Medusa was the great exploit of the Greek hero Perseus, whose story will be told later. From Medusa's dying body is said to have sprung the magic winged horse Pegasus and the giant Chrysaor.

Pegasus can be related partly to the original horse nature of Poseidon as a sky and earth god, partly to the Near Eastern winged steeds who may have represented thunder gods. In Near Eastern myths there were many winged horses of supernatural speed, but in Greek mythology only one such existed. After his birth as son of Poseidon from the Gorgon Medusa, Pegasus was said to have created by the stamp of his hoof such sacred springs as Hippocrene on Mt. Helicon in Boeotia and Pirene near Corinth. Pegasus sometimes carried Zeus' thunderbolts, sometimes heroes, such as Bellerophon. Among the Romans Pegasus was transformed into a symbol of immortality, but the concept of Pegasus as a poetic steed symbolizing flights of the imagination is entirely modern.

Three other pre-Olympian divinities called Harpies ("Snatchers"), named Aëllo, Ocypete, and Celaeno, supposedly children of the sea god Thaumas, were probably originally storm demons who swept up everything in their path. Eventually the Greeks transformed the Harpies into three ugly women equipped

with wings and huge bird claws. They were malevolent creatures who flew over people as they ate, defiled their food, and snatched it away like vultures.

The winds, too, were thought of as gods, with a home on a mythical island called Aeolia, supposedly north of Sicily. It is not clear whether Aeolus, who ruled over them as king, himself was believed to be mortal or divine, but he dwelt there with his twelve children, six sons and six daughters, married to each other in pairs and spending all their time making merry in banquets and dancing. A cave on Aeolia held the winds themselves, nature forces said to have been originally of the generation of the Titans. Greek myth told of four principal wind gods, all brothers, represented as winged humans or in horse form to symbolize speed. Their names were: Boreas, the North Wind; Zephyrus, the West Wind; Notus, the South Wind; Eurus, the East Wind. When instructed by Zeus or Poseidon, Aeolus let out the proper winds, which afterward dutifully returned to their cave after their services were no longer required.

The demon known as the Sphinx, one of the most distinctive mythical figures in Greek mythology, is connected with the tragedy of Oedipus. An enigmatic figure with the head of a woman and a winged lion's body, in origin the Sphinx was an Egyptian symbol — a lion's body without wings, with a male head portraying the Pharaoh in all his power as protector of Egypt. In this form the Sphinx is found throughout ancient Egypt, the most famous that of the Pharaoh Kephren at Giza near Cairo, at the site of the great pyramids. This famous Egyptian motif was borrowed by other Near Eastern peoples, transformed into a protecting demon with winged lion body and head of a female, and in this form it was diffused into the Aegean area as an art motif in Crete and the Mycenaean states originally without religious or mythical connotation. In the Eighth Century B.C. the Sphinx became a functional figure among the Greeks — a guardian demon on tombstones, and in time the Sphinx was anthropomorphized and became increasingly human. Thus the Sphinx came to have a human voice and human reason, and in the city of Thebes in Greece obtained a new meaning, based on the interpretation of her name in Greek as "The Strangler," she became a destructive force, but also a sort of intellectual monster, a characteristic symbolized

by the famous riddle connected with the myth of Oedipus. Those who could not answer her riddle she destroyed.

Among the few certain survivals of Indo-European mythology in Greek thought was a pair of divine twins, sons of the sky god, who came to serve as helpers of humans in distress. Such "heavenly twins" were known among other Indo-European peoples like the Hindus and the early Italians. The Greek counterpart of this primitive pair of "two gods," developed into the famous Dioscouri ("Sons of Zeus"), Castor and Polydeuces. In the Greek myths these twin "Sons of Zeus" (the Romans called Polydeuces by the name Pollux, and referred to them as the Gemini, "Twins") were in their anthropomorphized form somewhat diminished in divine stature. Their mother was Leda, queen of Sparta and wife of Tyndareus, whom Zeus visited in the shape of a swan. In the best known version Leda then gave birth to quadruplets, Polydeuces and Helen by Zeus (these two were thus immortal), and by her husband Tyndareus Castor and Clytemnestra (these two were mortal).

Both Castor and Polydeuces were frequently depicted as horsemen riding on white steeds, although Castor was more often the horseman, while Polydeuces became a skilled boxer. Both became celebrated culture heroes whose great popularity and services to mankind transformed them into gods. In keeping with their functions as helpers of men, they were called the "savior gods," bringing safety to men, especially in cavalry battles and on shipboard, and the constellation Gemini was one of the sure guides used by sailors. Static electricity seen on the tops of masts was thought by ancient sailors to be the Twins guiding their ships. The belief continued among the early Christians, transformed into "St. Elmo's fire."

The beloved twin sons of Zeus were participants in many famous Greek adventures, like the Calydonian Boar Hunt and the voyage of the Argonauts. Their final exploit involved a fatal struggle with another set of twins, either as the result of a dispute about some cattle or because Castor and Polydeuces tried to seize as their brides the twin daughters of Leucippus, named Phoebe and Hilaera, who were already the fiancées of Idas and Lyncaeus. In the battle that followed Castor was killed. Polydeuces was so attached to his twin brother that he begged his father Zeus to grant immortality to Castor also, so that they might always be together. Since Zeus could not annul the decrees of the Moerae, a compromise was worked out that enabled the devoted twins to share immortality. On alternate days Castor was restored to the upper world, while Polydeuces acted as substitute for his brother in Hades.

XIII

MAN'S BEGINNINGS

In Greek mythology there was no single pair to which all humans traced their origins, like Adam and Eve in the Judaeo-Christian tradition. Explanations of the origins of man in various cultures throughout the world differ, but the most important views are that man was made by a divine creator, or came from the body of a creator, or sprang from lower animals, or fell from heaven to earth. Greek mythology had no single orthodox view about man's beginnings, but rather a variety of explanations, of which there were two principal beliefs, one that men were first born spontaneously out of Mother Earth in the manner of the earliest divinities, the other that they were first moulded out of earth or clay and water by a beneficent creator who was a lesser divinity.

In some regions of Greece men were thought to have sprung from trees (particularly ash trees, with whom were associated the primordial Meliad nymphs), or from rivers as sources of fertility, or directly out of Mother Earth. The particular concept of origin usually depended on the natural features characteristic of each region. Various parts of Greece had local tales that the first humans who lived there were autochthonous, that is, born out of the earth there, a view which gave the local inhabitants a sense of national pride of origin. In this way they assured themselves, often unhistorically, that their earliest ancestors were not immigrants.

Such legends of autochthonous people were found all over Greece. We hear of Pelasgus of Arcadia, the mountainous area of north central Peloponnesus, as the first man who lived in that region and progenitor of the Pelasgians, said to be the earliest inhabitants of Greece, having been there even "before the moon." Similarly, the Dryopes claimed to be a prehellenic people in Greece from time immemorial, descended from a first ancestor named Dryops (connected with the Greek word meaning "oak tree"). In the myth of Thebes, among the first inhabitants were the Spartoi, armed men who sprang from dragon's teeth planted by Cadmus. The Athenians too believed themselves to be autochthonous, tracing themselves back to the earth-born Erichthonius, who sprang from Mother Earth out of the seed of the craftsman god Hephaestus. The tale was told that even the first king of Athens, Cecrops, was born directly out of the earth.

These original men, whatever their origin, from trees, rivers, or the earth, lived in an ideal time, the Golden Age of Cronus, before the coming of Zeus, when the earth was a paradise for all men, of unlimited abundance and of simple living. There was perpetual spring, everlasting youth for all, no illness, no evil, no war, and no need to labor, since Mother Earth poured forth spontaneously an abundance of food for her "earth-born" sons. Completely virtuous and happy, men were closer to the gods than ever after, and ended their extremely long lives simply by falling asleep. The contradiction of placing the Golden Age under the reign of the cruel and scheming Cronus, and later, poorer ages under the rule of Zeus, god of justice, was partly induced by the Greeks borrowing their concept of a primeval happy age of man from the Near East. Peoples in that region had long believed in four ages of man, Golden Age, Silver Age, Bronze Age, Iron Age, a cycle based on the pessimistic view that man's lot had progressively degenerated – the more technology advanced, the greater was man's moral decline and suffering. Such views start with the notion that the present is the worst of times, idealizing the past as the "good old days" when men were happier and more virtuous.

To this traditional sequence of ages characterized by metals the Greeks added an Heroic Age, thus establishing their own five ages of man. They placed this added period just before the beginning of the Iron Age, the harsh time in which they themselves were living, and assigned to this Heroic Age the great heroes of their mythology, from remembrance of the culminating achievement of their early culture, the Mycenaean Age, which lingered in the folk memory as an age of glory.

The golden race of men living in the age of Cronus retreated with him to the far West when he was deposed and exiled by Zeus. Then, with the establishment of Zeus as divine ruler, when the world was reconstructed as the Silver Age after the Titantomachy, a new race of men was created. The Titan Prometheus, aided by his brother Epimetheus moulded new humans out of earth or clay and water, in the image of the gods, a belief widely current in the Near East. The Silver Age in which these new men lived was a harsher time, for once the abundance of the Golden Age vanished, man was forced to strenuous labor in tilling the soil, winter and the other seasons made their appearance, and man's life span sharply declined. Subjected to a hard life, man began to develop evil traits, and for the first time violence and excessive pride made their appearance.

To lighten man's toil Zeus had granted him the use of fire, previously the exclusive prerogative of the gods, but men's evil grew, so that he considered the advisability of destroying all existing humans and making a fresh start. Dissuaded by Prometheus from such a drastic measure, he determined to increase the suffering and toil of mankind, and accordingly instructed the god Hephaestus to create the first woman as punishment to men. In the standard Greek myth this first woman was Pandora (her name means "All Gifts"), moulded by Hephaestus out of earth and water, and adorned with gifts from all the Olympian gods and goddesses. Thus this "beautiful evil" received, for example, beauty from Aphrodite, skill in handicrafts from Athena, guile from Hermes.

Actually Pandora was a form of Mother Earth, or the Aegean vegetation goddess, the source of all gifts to man. Early Greek art actually depicted her emerging directly out of the earth, extricated by Prometheus, Epimetheus, and Hephaestus using hammers and axes to free the goddess, thus symbolizing the toughness of the soil in Greece. It was Hesiod, an embittered Greek farmer-poet and woman hater, who boldly altered Pandora into a mortal woman, a trouble maker like the Hebrew Eve, the cause of original suffering for man. The original Aegean mother goddess had a dual character before Hesiod redesigned her. She both loved her male consort and caused his destruction, since his life ended after he united with her. Besides, there was an age-old Indo-European myth of a sacred substance jealously held by the gods, usually a food that produced immortality. When this food was stolen by evil demons, they created a beautiful female to seduce the thieves and thus retrieve the sacred divine substance. Out of this myth Hesiod created the story of the first woman whom he called Pandora because she resembled Mother Earth as the source of both fertility and of hard labor for man, to associate the two as prime sources of man's suffering. Such an attitude reflects not only the poverty of the soil in Greece but the decline in the status of women in Greek patriarchal culture from the higher position she occupied, for example, in Egyptian, Minoan, and Mycenaean civilizations.

While the first woman was being created, Prometheus warned Epimetheus to accept no gifts from the gods, but despite the warning, when the lovely Pandora was offered to him as his bride Epimetheus promptly accepted. Pandora brought with her as her dowry a very large jar, called a *pithos* by the Greeks, a standard storage receptacle for food. (This container is today often erroneously called "Pandora's box," an error introduced into the Greek myth by no less a scholar than the great Renaissance humanist Erasmus). Pandora was cautioned by the gods never to open the jar, but her curiosity prevailed, and when she opened the lid, a host of evils for man swiftly flew out. By the time she succeeded in putting the lid back on, she shut into the jar only one of its contents – hope. The embittered Hesiod thus transformed "All Gifts" into all evils, except the promise of hope.

This is not characteristic of traditional beliefs about Mother Earth, who was everywhere venerated as the source of all blessings. Hesiod's exception of hope symbolizes for him man's striving for a better future and his regret for a lost Golden Age. Unlike the Hebraic Eve, Pandora was not morally guilty of bringing evil to mankind, for she was merely the instrument of the vengeance of Zeus against men and Prometheus their benefactor, although both Hebrew and Greek imaginations strove in similar ways to explain the same dilemma of the origin of evil.

One of the elements of the Pandora story is the looking taboo. Her wrong in opening the jar is an example of a widespread folk concept that it is forbidden to look at certain persons (in Greek mythology, especially goddesses) and at certain objects. The punishment for such forbidden looking was death or serious injury like blindness, and there are many examples of this looking taboo in myths. In the Old Testament Lot's wife was turned into a pillar of salt because she looked back as the city of Sodom was being destroyed, while English legend tells the story of Peeping Tom of Coventry, who was blinded for looking at Lady Godiva as she rode naked through the streets on a horse.

Central to the myth of man's origin and progress is the Titan Prometheus, son of the original Titan Iapetus. After he and his brother Epimetheus created man, Prometheus (his name means "Forethought") remained the protector and benefactor of mankind, while his brother Epimetheus (his name means "After-thought") by his acceptance of Pandora as his wife undid some of the advantages brought to man by Prometheus. This is a typical folktale theme of the contrasts between brothers — the one intelligent and kind, the other stupid and evil. Perhaps the Greek myth transformed this theme by depicting Epimetheus as the dull-witted brother seduced by Pandora, the creation of the gods sent to spoil the blessings brought by his wise brother. Mythology and folktales delight in such paradoxes.

In his enduring love for mankind Prometheus had the courage and daring to engage in a dangerous struggle with the gods in order to improve the lot of man, although that friend of man was both a trickster and a thief, however meritorious his aim may have been. He first increased man's food supply and gave him opportunities to eat meat by a deception of the gods. When the ritual of sacrifice to the gods by man was being established for the first time, Prometheus tricked the gods out of the best parts of the sacrificial animals. He killed a bull, put the entrails and carcass to one side, then took the bones of the animal wrapped with layers of fat and burned them, so that when Zeus was asked to choose for the gods parts of the animal for future sacrifices, he chose the burnt offering because the odor of the burning meat delighted him. Thenceforth in making sacrifices the Greeks offered the gods token parts of the animals and kept the remainder for men. This is one reason why holidays delighted most Greeks, because they generally did not eat meat except on days important sacrifices were made to the gods.

Prometheus' deception is said to have angered Zeus so much that he withdrew the use of fire from mankind. In retaliation

Prometheus secretly stole fire (either directly from Hephaestus' forge on Olympus, or hidden in some *narthex*, a stalk of giant fennel), and brought it back to mankind. The stealing of fire or some other privileged possession of the gods for mankind is a world-wide myth, and, since the "domestication" of fire is the first of the great discoveries and inventions of primitive man, and among the most significant in man's history, it symbolized the great technological progress of man which the Greeks associated with the benefactions of Prometheus.

Zeus' punishment of Prometheus for his theft of forbidden fire was isolation and physical torture. He was seized, taken to a lonely cliff in the Caucasus Mountains, and, at the orders of stern Zeus, bound to the rock by the reluctant fire god Hephaestus. In his suffering Prometheus revealed that he had the skill of prophecy and knew a secret that concerned the very destiny of Zeus: if he fell in love with a particular (unnamed) female, and consummated a union with her, the woman would have a son who would subsequently overthrow Zeus as Zeus himself had previously overthrown his father Cronus. Through his herald Hermes, Zeus demanded the name of the woman, but Prometheus adamantly refused to aid the now tyrannical Zeus until he released him from his chains. Infuriated and frustrated, Zeus hurled thunderbolts at Prometheus, but the Titan was, of course, immortal, and so to increase his suffering Zeus sent his eagle to eat Prometheus' liver like a vulture. Every night the liver grew whole, and every day the eagle returned to gnaw at it. The impasse between the ruler of mankind and its benefactor continued for endless centuries — some sources say 30,000 years — through which Prometheus, though a god, suffered physical torture, comforted only by the foreknowledge that a savior would eventually come for him. Zeus, king of the gods, in his turn was tortured by his anxiety about the possible loss of his power, a fear enormously magnified by Zeus' uncontrollable amorousness. Eventually Zeus and Prometheus, both guilty of the sin of *hybris* through their excesses, relented after ages of suffering. Prometheus was ready to reveal the secret name at about the same time Zeus decided to unbind him. The name of the woman turned out to be the Nereid Thetis, and Zeus hastened to marry the reluctant nymph off to the noble mortal Peleus, by whom she had the great hero Achilles. Shortly after,

Prometheus' savior arrived, none other than Zeus' mighty son
Heracles, who killed the eagle. But the final release of Prometheus
had a further complication; it was necessary for some immortal to
give up eternal life and go to Hades as a substitute for Prometheus.
This sacrifice was made, as we shall see later, by the noble centaur
Chiron.

In this way Prometheus was victorious in his championing of
mankind. But the race of man was imperfect, infected with a sort
of curse that caused it to degenerate further, and a lower stage of
mankind known as the Bronze Age followed the Silver Age. In this
time of great troubles men became very warlike, and spent their
energies, lives and treasure in conquering and destroying each
other, and the unchecked and mounting evil in mankind determined Zeus to wipe out the human race and make a fresh start. To
achieve this Zeus decided not to employ his thunderbolts, but to
avoid burning up the whole world in a universal conflagration he
sent a great flood to rid the world of men, unleashing a worldwide
rain storm for nine days and nights. The universal flood destroyed
all humans except two, Deucalion and Pyrrha, who survived in a
wooden boat they had constructed before the flood began, due to
their preeminent virtue among the men and women of the world.
(In some versions Deucalion was said to be the son of Prometheus
by the nymph Celaeno, Pyrrha the daughter of Epimetheus and
Pandora.) The boat of the Greek Noah and his wife, without
animals or children, landed on Mt. Parnassus in central Greece.
The surviving two were very old, and were therefore concerned
about the future of the human race, so that when the waters
subsided, they consulted an oracle which was conveniently nearby,
some say at Delphi, others at Dodona. The oracular response
instructed them to cast the bones of their mother over their heads.
They were perplexed by this until Deucalion interpreted the
enigmatic prophecy to mean that their mother was Mother Earth.
When Deucalion cast stones over his shoulder men sprang up; from
the stones cast by Pyrrha women appeared out of the earth. Thus
the new race of man was, like the Titans, earth-born, as many
Greeks believed their local progenitors to have been. Deucalion
and Pyrrha were said by some to have had a son in their old age
named Hellen, the first Hellene, from whom descended two sons
Aeolus and Dorus, and two grandsons Ion and Achaeus, the

mythical ancestors of the Greek peoples known in historic times as Achaeans, Aeolians, Dorians, and Ionians.

The mythologies of almost all peoples ancient and modern (with the major exceptions of the Japanese and the African peoples) report a universal flood in the remote past. For a long time it was believed that there had actually been a universal flood like that in the Old Testament story of Noah and the ark, and anthropologists and mythologists today are inclined to believe that the flood myth incorporated the memory of an historical event, an unprecedented flood in Mesopotamia about 4000 or 3300 B.C. In Sumerian and Babylonian epics, which record the first versions of a universal flood, the cataclysm was provoked by the anger of the gods, either because man's progress and affluence had made him arrogant and brazen, or because he rebelled against the hard lot imposed on him by the gods. From Mesopotamia, according to many scholars, the flood myth spread East and West all over the world.

It is interesting to note that in no mythology did the deluge involve total annihilation of the human race, but it served rather as a sort of watery cleansing in the hope of producing a regenerated mankind. In a sense, too, the flood symbolizes a return to the waters and chaos of the first time of the universe. Looked at in this light, the waters of the deluge may be thought to absorb all the evil of the world, and purify and regenerate the little remnant to create a new race of men. The Greeks believed that the new race created by Deucalion and Pyrrha ushered in their Heroic Age, a glorious and relatively short period (usually no more than three generations) which ended with the victory of the sons of Heracles, an event which the Greeks equated with the coming of the Dorians into Greece, about 1100 B.C. This started the Iron Age, the fifth and last age in the Greek cycle of man's evolution.

The Iron Age was the world in which the Greeks lived, a time of the greatest decline of mankind, a period of woes, diseases, hard labor. So degenerate had man become that even the goddess Astraea, divinity of innocence and purity left the earth. Daughter of Themis and Zeus, she had lived with early mankind during the Golden Age and had not joined Cronus in his flight, but remained with man through the Silver, Bronze, and Heroic Ages. With the onset of the Iron Age she finally abandoned the earth in disgust, the last of the gods to remain on earth. Yet there was a belief that one day Astraea might return to earth, together with the other Olympians, and usher in the return of the Golden Age.

XIV

MYTHS OF CRETE

About sixty miles southeast of the mainland of Greece lies the large island of Crete, forming as it were the southern boundary of the Aegean Sea. Though Crete is equidistant from Africa, Asia, and Europe, the island has been "European" in culture, and developed its own unique civilization as the most significant prehellenic culture of the Aegean. From about 2000-1500 B.C. it dominated the area and exerted far-flung political and cultural influences, particularly upon the Greek mainland, which was being settled at this time by invading Indo-European tribes who were to become the Greeks. From Minos, the name of the most famous mythical kings of Crete, the culture is today called Minoan. The most affluent place in Minoan Crete was Cnossus, three miles from the sea on the northcentral coast, and the ruins of its great royal palace are still today among the most spectacular remains of the ancient world. Minos, ruler of a commercial state, is said to have established the first sea power in world history, governing from Cnossus, and this site is the setting of the famous myths of Crete.

While the Minoans were non-Greek physically and culturally, they were to influence the Mycenaeans profoundly, especially in that the Greeks adopted aspects of Cretan religion and mythology. The mother goddess and her young consort were Cretan, as were the cult of a sacred tree, the snake as symbol of immortality, and the belief that the dead were transported by water to a blessed afterlife. Crete was *par excellence* the land of transformation of divine powers as humans, birds, snakes, and various other animals, for there the borders between the animal, vegetable, human, and divine spheres were indeed thin. It is largely from the Minoans that the Greeks adopted the concept of metamorphoses of both gods and humans, seen in many of their myths, particularly the shape-shifting of sea divinities.

The myths about Crete — whether invented by themselves, or by the Phoenicians, or by the Greeks — assume a connection between Crete and Phoenicia on the Asiatic coast, through a king of Phoenicia named Agenor ("Valiant"), whose two most famous children were Europa and Cadmus. One day the princess Europa went down with her handmaidens to the shore to pick flowers in a beautiful meadow. When Zeus caught sight of the lovely maiden, he was smitten with desire, and so hastened to the place, having transformed himself into a handsome bull of such extraordinary mildness that the girls put garlands of flowers on his horns and petted him. When Europa sat on the bull's back, Zeus leaped into the Aegean and swam to Crete, followed by a joyous procession of sea divinities singing a marriage song. In Crete Zeus and Europa consummated a sacred marriage in a cave on Mt. Dicte, and had their children, Minos, Rhadamanthus, and Sarpedon. All these are pre-Greek names, as are those of Europa and Cadmus themselves. While Europa's name seems to mean "wide-faced" in Greek, it is more likely to be of Phoenician origin, from a root meaning "darkness" or "sunset." Similarly, Cadmus' name appears to be derived from a Semitic root meaning "sunrise." In any case, the story of the seduction and abduction of a Near Eastern mother goddess by the Indo-European sky god in bull form, and their "sacred marriage" in a Cretan setting reveal the amalgamation of many cultural strains. (The name of the continent Europe originally had no connection with the myth of Europa.)

It was the physical prowess of the bull, both as work animal in the fields and in reproduction, that made this animal a symbol of fertility and power and a significant theme in many myths. Almost from the beginnings of civilization the bull has been equated with kingly power, both in Egypt and Mesopotamia. In Egypt, for example, the pharaoh was identified with the bull, to symbolize his royal power and the fertility his rule brought to the land of Egypt. In Asia Minor and Syria the weather god, a divinity of brute force, sudden rage, and fertilizing power, was depicted as a bull.

For the Minoans the bull as religious symbol was ubiquitous.

The Cretans used "horns of consecration," that is, bulls' horns as symbols, in rituals and as a decorative motif, and also engaged in a bull sport, in which it seems that there was special efficacy in touching the horns of a bull to acquire its virility and might. It is possible that human beings were sacrificed in Crete to a bull god, and the kings of Crete may have impersonated bulls, even wearing a mask representing a bull. It is also possible that in fertility rites the king of Crete was equated with the bull and the queen with a cow. The Greeks adopted this reverence for the divine power inherent in the bull in the worship of such fertility gods as Zeus, Poseidon, and Dionysus. For this reason some water gods, such as Oceanus and Acheloüs, were depicted with bulls' horns to symbolize their fertilizing power. The continuity of this prestige of the bull – which we can trace back as much as 5000 years – still appears today in Spain and the Latin American countries, where contact with and killing of the bull is believed to transfer strength and virility to men.

After fathering three sons upon Europa, Zeus arranged for her to marry the Cretan king Asterius (or Asterion, "Starred One"), who brought up the boys as though they were his own sons. Minos appears to be either a title or the name of a dynasty, so that the myths of several Cretan kings by this name are difficult to disentangle. Sarpedon, said to have migrated from Crete to the region of Lycia in Asia, bears the same name as a later, more famous king of that region. Both Minos and Rhadamanthus, esteemed in their lifetimes as lawgivers renowned for their wisdom and justice, became judges of the Underworld, together with the righteous Greek hero Aeacus, another son of Zeus. There is a story that King Minos succeeded his father to the throne of Crete after a dispute with his brother Sarpedon. Both men were in love with a boy called Miletus, a very handsome son of Apollo, and when Miletus fled to Asia Minor and Sarpedon to Lycia, Minos became sole ruler of Crete. In another myth Minos is said to have invented boy love, though this cultural phenomenon is more characteristic of later Greek aristocratic society.

Minos' grandson, also named Minos, was the greatest of the kings of Crete, an outstanding statesman, city builder, legislator, conqueror, and founder of the Cretan sea empire. If we have here a memory of an historic figure, Minos was the first famous

European statesman. Some myths coupled with his name diminish his stature, but may be of early Greek origin, the product of hostility of the mainlanders to the Cretans. Once in a crisis Minos asked Poseidon for a favorable sign in the form of an animal, which he promised to sacrifice to the sea god. A beautiful white bull promptly emerged from the sea, but Minos admired the animal so much that he did not sacrifice it and substituted another in its place. As the result of this perfidy Poseidon made the bull become mad, and then had Minos' wife Pasiphaë, daughter of the sun god Helios, fall in love with it. Her unnatural passion for the bull was so great that she confided in the Athenian exile Daedalus, a famous craftsman and inventor resident at the court of Cnossus, who then helped Pasiphaë consummate her love for the bull by constructing a wooden cow, into which she secreted herself. The resulting offspring of Pasiphaë and the bull of Poseidon was a hybrid monster named Minotaur ("Bull of Minos") — a half-bull, half-human creature who fed upon human flesh. To confine the dangerous Minotaur King Minos built a complex, maze-like structure, the famous labyrinth.

The labyrinth was also designed by Daedalus, the archetypal artist and inventor of Greek mythology, who may actually have been a real person, a genius whose fame later gave rise to myths. Among other creations he is said to have invented animated statues that seemed to move their limbs and walk. Assigning inventions to Daedalus is characteristic of Greek thought, for when the Greeks sought to associate names of famous individuals with specific discoveries, they always found mythical personages for them. Daedalus, Demeter for agriculture, Triptolemus or Athena for the plow, Palamedes for coinage and weights and measures, Cadmus or Palamedes for the alphabet, all as heroes or gods gave significance and timelessness to their discoveries.

The presence of Daedalus in Crete, and the stay of one of Minos' sons, Androgeus, in Athens, indicates that the myths preserved a memory of cultural relations between the island kingdom and the mainland. In the myth we are told that Daedalus, a member of the ruling family of Attica, a relative of Erechtheus, was already famous as an artistic and inventive genius when he murdered his nephew, whose name is variously given as Perdix, or Calus, or Talus. This young man was so brilliant that Daedalus

accepted him as his disciple, but when the boy began to make great discoveries himself, Daedalus became so jealous that he killed him. As a result he fled his native land and took refuge with King Minos in Crete.

The word labyrinth is a pre-Greek word, and the knowledge of an intricate maze pattern was probably much earlier than the myth of the enclosure built to house the Minotaur. The labyrinth pattern was undoubtedly invented by someone in remote times (the earliest known drawing of it is on a clay tablet from the Mycenaean Age), and was rapidly diffused as a fascinating, tricky design, a sort of riddling folk symbol kept secret by those who had succeeded in learning how to make it. Actually the most famous labyrinthine building in the ancient world was the funerary temple of the Pharaoh Amenemhet III (about 1800 B.C.), but we do not know when and how the term came to be associated with the legendary labyrinth of Crete. The structure built by Daedalus has remained the classical example of the type. Excavation of the palace of the kings of Cnossus has revealed that it was a vast intricate maze-like structure, so that the Greeks may have associated memories of the palace itself with a labyrinth, and in fact the palace was decorated with a recurrent pattern of a double axe called in Greek *labrys*. The labyrinth was a very popular symbol in antiquity, and came to be associated in antiquity with complicated dance patterns and intricate horse riding maneuvers. In modern times the term labyrinth has been used for the inner ear, to describe the walls of Troy, and intricate patterns in landscape gardening as well.

The Minotaur was killed by the Athenian hero Theseus with the aid of Minos' daughter Ariadne. Though she has been humanized in Greek myth as a princess, Ariadne was in origin a variation of the vegetation goddess of Crete (her name means "Very Holy Maid"). When the handsome charismatic Greek youth came to Cnossus, with six other youths and seven girls, to be fed to the Minotaur as part of the tribute exacted by Minos from Athens, Ariadne fell in love with Theseus. Advised by Daedalus, she gave Theseus a sword and a ball of thread, which he was to unravel as he went into the labyrinth. He thus found his way out of the maze after killing the Minotaur, and then fled from Crete taking Ariadne with him.

When Minos discovered the killing of the Minotaur, the escape of the Athenians, and the elopement of his daughter, he arrested Daedalus. The great inventor and his young son Icarus were imprisoned on the island, not only as punishment for the assistance Daedalus had given to Pasiphaë and Theseus, but also to prevent him from disclosing the secrets of the labyrinth. But the inventive genius Daedalus, to escape from prison, constructed two large pairs of wings, by sticking the wings of birds with wax to long boards. He carefully briefed Icarus on how to operate the wings, cautioning him not to fly too high. Unfortunately, in his youthful excitement the boy flew too near the sun, the wax melted, the feathers dropped off, and Icarus fell into the sea north of Crete, where he was drowned. Ever since, the myth tells us, the body of water has been named Icarian Sea.

The story of Icarus has counterparts outside the Greek area. Winged demons, both male and female, were fairly common in the Near East, and there is a Semitic myth of the insolent, unsuccessful attempt of a certain Helel to fly to heaven. Some Greek mythmaker invented an entirely new concept of temporary, detachable wings for flying. It is possible that Icarus may have been a winged demon of the Minoans later joined to the myth as the young son of the Athenian inventor Daedalus, and further humanized by the Greeks as a tragic figure of youthful excess.

Daedalus, however, managed to fly to the island of Sicily, where he was granted asylum by King Cocalus of the city of Camicus (later the classical Agrigentum). Here the great genius lived incognito, a refugee for a second time, while Minos hunted for him all over the world, and finally trapped him by appealing to his pride in his inventive skill. Minos offered a reward to anyone who could put a thread completely through a snail's inner passages (this is reminiscent of the labyrinth motif), and when the snail was brought to King Cocalus, he referred it to Daedalus, who promptly solved the problem by tying a thread to an ant and letting it find its way through the snail's passageways. Thus Minos discovered Daedalus' hiding place, and invaded the island with a mighty expedition. Cocalus offered to negotiate with Minos and invited him to his palace, but the daughters of Cocalus, who admired Daedalus very much, killed Minos as they were bathing him − a proper duty of women of the household when guests were entertained in the Minoan-Mycenaean Age. They scalded him to death with boiling water or with pitch.

A number of myths are also told about Minos' amorous adventures, for example with Britomartis and Procris, and it is said that even the errant Pasiphaë was indignant at his behavior. Minos also invaded Attica in revenge for the murder of his son Androgeus there, and during this attack, conquered Megara and killed its king, Nisus, helped by the treachery of Nisus' own daughter Scylla, who had fallen in love with Minos. Now Nisus was invulnerable so long as he possessed a certain magic hair on his head (its color was red, or gold, or purple), which out of love for Minos, Scylla cut off, thus betraying both her father and country. This story is, of course, a version of the widespread folktale, best known in the story of the Herbrew hero Samson, of a person's strength being localized in his hair. Because of her treachery, however, instead of taking her with him to Cnossus, Minos had Scylla tied to the prow of a ship, and thus she was drowned.

Another famous myth associated with Crete is that of the great bronze giant Talus, a sort of personification of the technological advances of the Bronze Age. It is said that Hephaestus, the artisan god, invented this enormous robot and gave it to Minos as a gift to serve as guardian of the island. Three times a day Talus circled the island, driving off unauthorized ships and invaders, and when he seized strangers in his arms, he became red hot and destroyed them. Talus had but one, life-giving vein, from the neck to the ankle, filled with the blood of the gods, ichor. The Argonauts, with the aid of the witch heroine Medea, finally destroyed the bronze man, when they found the secret of opening up this vein and drained the life fluid out. It is noteworthy that, in addition to being able to become red hot, Talus threw stones at enemies, and so his name was sometimes associated with places where there were large amounts of boulders lying on the ground. It is possible that the myth of Talus is an anthropomorphic representation of volcanic activity in the Aegean, perhaps of the island of Santorin, the only active volcano in the eastern Mediterranean, where there was a great eruption about 1400 B.C.

Besides Ariadne, Minos had another daughter, Phaedra, who later married Theseus and came to a tragic end when she became amorously involved with Theseus' son Hippolytus by another woman. Of Minos' other sons, there is a remarkable story of the death and rebirth of the boy Glaucus. After Glaucus, while chasing a mouse, fell into a jar of honey and died, the Greek diviner Polyïdus ("Knows Much") of Argos was invited to try to find him. He successfully located the body of Glaucus in the jar of honey, but instead of being rewarded, he was locked up with the corpse and ordered to restore it to life. While pondering on this problem, which seemed hopeless, Polyïdus killed a snake, and then observed another snake bring an herb to the dead snake and restore it to life. With the same herb he brought Glaucus back to life, and Minos was so amazed at this miracle that he compelled Polyïdus to teach Glaucus the art of divination. This he did, but as he was finally to leave for his home in Greece, he told Glaucus to spit into his mouth; as a result the boy at once lost the art of divination.

The Near Eastern origins of the Glaucus story are obvious. The magic qualities of honey — the only substance for sweetening available to the ancient peoples — is an old theme of folklore. Babylonians sometimes buried the dead in jars filled with honey, as it was used in antiquity as a preservative, and the Babylonians also had the belief that saliva is synonymous with magic and sorcery, a notion that is still current today. With, however, the theme of death and rebirth, common in Minoan religion, as well as the snake symbol of rebirth and immortality, the Glaucus story constitutes another version of the seasonal cycle.

Another son of Minos, Catreus, succeeded him as king of Cnossus. A myth told about him appears to be a duplicate of other Greek myths. It is said that an oracle predicted Catreus would be killed by one of his children, and when his son Althaemenes and his daughter Apemosyne learned of this fate, they fled to the island of Rhodes, where the god Hermes ambushed Apemosyne and raped her. Not realizing that the assailant of his sister was a god, Althaemenes put his sister to death, and shortly after, catastrophe struck again when Catreus, having decided to bequeath his kingdom to his son, went to Rhodes to find him. In a dispute during which father and son did not recognize each other, Althaemenes killed Catreus. When he discovered what had happened, the miserable Althaemenes, in answer to his own fervent prayer, disappeared in a chasm in the earth that opened up before him.

XV

MYTHS OF ATHENS

Destined to become the political center of the large city-state embracing the entire peninsula of Attica, Athens was a small kingdom of second-rate importance during the Heroic Age. A strong Athenian folk memory emphasized the indigenous character of the population, with their earliest kings as being earth-born. The most popular tradition was that Cecrops was the first king of Athens, and had sprung out of Mother Earth — a hybrid creature, with upper part of a man and lower part of a snake. The latter detail signifies his close association with the native soil. Cecrops was a peaceful king in whose reign took place the famous contest between Athena and Poseidon for the prestige of being patron divinity of Athens. Was this a memory of an early religious struggle in which the Aegean vegetation goddess in the form of a warrior maiden protecting the royal palace of the king was preferred to the Indo-European earth god?

The successor of Cecrops was another earth-born hybrid figure, half-man, half-snake, Erichthonius or Erechtheus. This nature of Erichthonius may have symbolized the power of fertility embodied in the king, comparable to the half-man, half-bull Minotaur in Crete. After Erichthonius was born, miraculously out of earth as a result of Hephaestus' spilling his seed on the ground during his futile but passionate struggle with the chaste maiden goddess Athena, the patroness of Athens took up the child and cared for it. Eventually she decided to turn him over to the care of the daughters of Cecrops, named Aglaurus, Herse, and Pandrosus, and gave them a basket containing the baby, with strict instructions that they were not to look into the basket. But the curious

girls defied the "looking taboo," and what they saw in the basket
— probably a snake — so terrified them that they jumped off the
hill in Athens called the acropolis, and were killed.

Erichthonius (or Erechtheus), second king of Athens, became
the first savior of the city. In a war that was a continuation on the
human level of the conflict between Athena and Poseidon for the
possession of Athens, an army led by a son of Poseidon, King
Eumolpus of Thrace, attacked the city. When Erichthonius learned
from an oracle that the city would be saved only if he offered one
of his daughters to the goddess Persephone, he sacrificed his
daughter Chthonia. This led to the suicide of his two other
daughters, for the three devoted girls had made a vow not to
survive each other. Erichthonius was victorious and killed
Eumolpus, but Poseidon, intensely angered, appealed to Zeus, who
killed Erichthonius with a thunderbolt. The second king of Athens
was later honored as a god in Athens, where on the acropolis still
stands the lovely temple called Erechtheum in his honor.

Among the surviving daughters of Erichthonius were
Oreithyia, Creusa, and Procris, all of whom have their distinctive
myths. Oreithyia one day was standing on the acropolis (or at the
bank of a river in Attica) when the violent Boreas, god of the
North Wind, with a blast swept her away and made her his wife.
By him Oreithyia had two sons, Calaïs and Zetes, winged wind
demons. Creusa (her name means "princess") was violated by the
god Apollo and secretly gave birth to a boy named Ion — a story
related to justify the Athenian claim to be the ancestors of all the
Ionian Greeks. The illegitimate baby, exposed in a cave in Athens,
was whisked away by Apollo and made a temple attendant at the
shrine of Apollo at Delphi, while Creusa later married Xuthus.
When their union remained sterile, they journeyed to Delphi to
consult the oracle about their childlessness, and were told to
accept as their own child the first person they met as they left
the shrine. This turned out to be Ion, whom Creusa soon
recognized as her own child.

In Erichthonius' daughter Procris we meet a mythic figure to
whom many folktale themes adhered, together with some mythologized history. The principal folk theme associated with her is
the intense jealousy exhibited by a married couple who really love
each other very much. Procris was married to Cephalus, a famous

hunter, who had once been abducted by Eos (the dawn) who loved him. Because of his fidelity to Procris Eos released him but decided to undermine his marriage. Cephalus became fiercely suspicious and jealous of Procris, and to test her, once left home ostensibly on a journey, but soon returned disguised as a handsome stranger. When he sought to seduce her, she remained faithful to her husband. According to another version, she yielded to the stranger, but when he revealed his true self she fled in anger and shame to the court of King Minos of Crete, where she became the lover of Minos, receiving as gifts from him a hunting dog that never failed to catch its prey and a magic spear that never missed its mark. But in Crete, Procris now had to contend with the jealousy of Minos' wife Pasiphaë, so she soon returned to Athens, and, reconciled with Cephalus, presented him with the infallible dog and spear given her by Minos. But Procris' suspicious nature was her downfall. She began to suspect Cephalus of having a love affair with another woman, because he frequently left her in the middle of the night on hunting trips. One night she followed him. When Cephalus sensed some movement in the nearby bushes, thinking that a wild animal was lurking there he hurled the magic spear, killing her outright.

The successor of Erichthonius is said to have been King Pandion, father of Aegeus and two daughters, Procne and Philomela, to whom many folktale motifs were attracted. The princess Procne married King Tereus of Thrace, and they had a son named Itys. On a previous visit to Athens, Tereus had taken a fancy to Procne's sister Philomela, so that, consumed by uncontrollable lust, he journeyed to Athens alone, falsely informed his father-in-law Pandion that Procne had died, and asked for the hand of Philomela. This Pandion agreed to, and en route home Tereus raped Philomela. Because of her hatred of him and his fear that she would inform her sister Procne of what had happened, Tereus cut out Philomela's tongue and locked her up in a secret prison, but the unfortunate girl succeeded in weaving into a tapestry the story of Tereus' crime, and sent the tapestry to Procne. The horrified wife of Tereus then released her sister Philomela, and the two secretly plotted a dreadful revenge. Without revealing her knowledge to Tereus, Procne killed her own son Itys and served his flesh to her husband, then revealed to

Tereus that she knew the whole truth and fled with Philomela. When Tereus pursued the two sisters, the merciful gods intervened, transforming Philomela into a swallow, and Procne, still mourning her dead son, into a nightingale, whose song appeared to the Greeks to be a lament. Tereus was metamorphosed into a hoopoe bird. (Later the Romans succeeded in spoiling the story by reversing the roles: they made Procne the swallow and Philomela the nightingale.)

The tragedy of Procne-Philomela-Tereus-Itys, which was associated with the royal house of Athens, is based on a widespread popular folk theme told of many mythic characters, the motif of "the other woman." Sometimes she is a mistress, or a concubine, sometimes the wife's sister, or a second wife who turns out to be a cruel stepmother to the children by her husband's first wife. In mythology the "other woman" spells trouble, either because adultery is involved, or because of the jealousy of the man's wife, or because she is a cruel stepmother. Of the many such tales in Greek mythology, the most famous is the story of Jason and Medea. In these stories the jealous wife usually kills her own children in a fit of rage against her errant husband, although sometimes she intends to kill the other woman's children by her husband but mistakes her own children for them.

The first great king of Athens was Aegeus, son of Pandion, originally a local form of the Aegean sea god, but transformed by Athenian mythmakers into the hero Aegeus, king of Athens. After two marriages Aegeus was still childless, and travelling to the oracle at Delphi for advice he passed through Corinth where he met the famous Medea, whom he promised asylum in Athens if she desired it. At Delphi the oracle gave him an enigmatic answer which he could not decipher, but which actually warned him not to mate with any woman until he returned to Athens. On the way home he stopped in the town of Troezen, southwest of Athens, to consult the shrewd King Pittheus, who understood at once the oracle's response as a prediction that a famous child would be born to Aegeus. Accordingly he entertained Aegeus, made him drunk, and put his daughter Aethra into bed with him, so that she conceived. One story frequently told about this event was that the god Poseidon also visited Aethra that same night, thus leaving doubt whether Aegeus or Poseidon was the real father of Aethra's son Theseus. Before Aegeus left for Athens he placed his sword and sandals under a huge rock at Troezen, instructing Aethra that if a son was born he was to come to his father in Athens as soon as he was able to move the rock and obtain the sword and sandals.

When Theseus reached the age of sixteen he moved away the rock and secured the sword and sandals of his father, and so took the first significant step on the road to becoming a hero. The myth of Theseus, illegitimate son of Aegeus, in its original form depicted him as a typical early hero of the Heroic Age — a selfish, violent warrior, and abductor of women. Long without honor, Theseus was transformed in the Sixth and Fifth centuries B.C. into the national hero of Athens, an ideal statesman, humanitarian, and pious king.

The first effort by the Athenians to "clean up" Theseus involved his transformation into a hero of the Ionian Greeks as competition for the Dorian hero Heracles. This did not succeed, for while Heracles became the national hero of all the Greeks, Theseus remained little more than a local Attic hero. Like Heracles, he performed labors, six of them on the road to Athens to see his father. The boy had been advised to take the safer route by sea, but chose instead the dangerous land route, blocked by bandits and ruffians. First he met the giant Periphetes, a lame brigand with a bronze crutch or club which he used to bludgeon travelers to death, killed him and confiscated his bronze weapon. Next he fought with the brigand Sinis, a giant who seized all passersby, pulled down two huge pine trees and tied their limbs to these, then let the trees spring back, tearing his victims apart. Theseus used the same method to destroy Sinis. Though every great hero should have his dragon to slay, the closest Theseus ever came to this type of glorious combat was his encounter with the Crommynian Sow, a ferocious animal said to be the child of Typhon and Echidna. Theseus slew the sow with his sword, a scene far different from those involving the famous heroic dragon slayers. Next Theseus encountered the giant robber Sciron, an unpleasant individual who forced travelers to wash his feet, and while they did so kicked them off a cliff, at the foot of which was an enormous turtle that tore them apart. Then followed his encounter with Cercyon, a huge wrestler who compelled travelers to fight in hopeless combat with him. Theseus, young as he was, killed him by picking him up and dashing him to the ground. Finally, he destroyed the giant Procrustes ("He Who Hammers Out"). In his cruel treatment of travelers Procrustes compelled them to lie on a bed, which most people did not, of course, fit exactly, so if they were too short, he stretched them, and if their limbs stuck out, he cut them off. Theseus applied this same treatment to Procrustes, killing him.

These six labours of Theseus, devised at a late date in imitation of the labors of Heracles, glorified Theseus as champion of law and order. But he is far different from the more primitive Heracles and his primitive weapons — his club and bow and arrows. In keeping with the more civilized conditions of the Athenians when these myths were organized, Theseus emerged as a more genteel hero, a graceful athlete and sportsman, completing his labors with bare hands and a sword. Instead of the wild beasts Heracles had to face, Theseus' adversaries were mostly human waylayers of peaceful travelers.

When Theseus arrived in Athens he found his father Aegeus married again, this time to the infamous Medea, who had obtained asylum in Athens after killing her own children and several other people. Medea immediately knew who Theseus was, and determined to kill him to secure the throne of Athens to her own children by Aegeus. At a banquet she put poison in Theseus' wine, but when he drew his sword to cut some meat, Aegeus recognized it as the very one he had left under the rock at Troezen, and quickly overturned the cup of wine before Theseus could touch it. Medea fled with her children to the East.

Reunited with his father, Theseus assumed the role of heir to the throne of Athens. Since Aegeus' power was being threatened by the rebellious plotting of the Pallantids, the fifty sons of his brother, Theseus promptly fought and destroyed all his cousins. While on this military expedition in Attica, the young prince added a seventh labor to his record, the encounter with the Bull of Marathon, a wild beast who was ravaging the countryside. On the way to this deadly struggle, the hero was given hospitality by a poor woman named Hecale, who offered up sacrifices and prayers for his safety. After capturing the bull, in the manner of Heracles, Theseus returned to find aged Hecale dead, and promptly decreed special honors to commemorate her kindliness and patriotism.

This story was an adaptation of a widespread folktale of the hospitality of a poor, pious person to a god in disguise.

In the reign of Aegeus Athens faced a great political crisis. Androgeus, son of King Minos of Crete, and a famous athlete, on a visit to Athens won first prize in the athletic competitions and aroused fierce jealousy as a foreigner. Some versions tell that Aegeus himself had Androgeus treacherously slain, while others say that Athenian athletes ambushed and killed him. The sequel to this crime was a war of revenge against Athens by King Minos, who captured nearby Megara and began to menace Athens. The operation was a prolonged one, so that Minos prayed for vengeance to Zeus, who sent famine and pestilence upon the land. An oracle declared that maidens must be sacrificed for the deliverance of Athens, so a group of sisters, the Hyacinthides, patriotically volunteered, offering several lives to atone for the one killed, and they were sacrificed to Zeus. Unfortunately this act of self-sacrifice brought no results, and another oracle advised the Athenians to surrender to Minos. Then the Cretan king imposed upon the Athenians a tribute of seven boys and seven girls (either annually or every eighth year), to be sent to Crete and put into the labyrinth as food for the Minotaur.

As an aspect of the influence of Cretan power in the Aegean the myths of the tributary relationship of Athens to Crete may have developed to explain the presence of such Attic heroes as Daedalus and Theseus at the court of the kings of Crete. Can the killing of the Minotaur by Theseus be a vestige of a memory of the subsequent rule of Cnossus by the Mycenaeans about 1400 B.C.? But Greek occupation, though verified by archeological and inscriptional evidence, did not impress itself as a significant event in early Greek history, for there never developed a myth about the conquest of this great center of early Aegean civilization.

Theseus volunteered to be one of the 14 young Athenians sent as tribute to the Minotaur. Before he left Aegeus ordered that the ship which carried them should fly black sails of mourning, but that if Theseus somehow returned alive the sails were to be changed to white ones. En route to Crete Minos tried to molest one of the Athenian maidens. When Theseus rebuked him Minos boasted he was a son of Zeus, and promptly a clap of thunder was heard. Theseus then asserted that he was a son of Poseidon.

Thereupon Minos threw a ring into the sea and ordered Theseus to retrieve it, to prove his divine origin. Theseus dived overboard, was hospitably welcomed in the palace of Poseidon and Amphitrite, and to the amazement of all on board returned with the ring.

The famous story of the slaying of the Minotaur was the favorite Greek tale about the hero Theseus. He not only rescued the Athenian boys and girls sent as tribute to the Minotaur, but took with him Minos' daughter Ariadne, who had fallen in love with him and aided him in killing the Minotaur. Yet when they stopped on the island of Naxos, Theseus abandoned Ariadne as she slept and sailed off without her, and at the same time the god Dionysus landed at Naxos, fell in love with the sleeping beauty, kissed and awakened her. In some versions Ariadne is said to have died and been resurrected by Dionysus — an unusual variation of the vegetation cycle myth, in which the death and rebirth of a young male god is very common, while the death and rebirth of a fertility goddess is exceedingly rare, well-nigh unique. In this famous "sacred marriage" of Dionysus and Ariadne the god gave her as a wedding gift a crown, which later became the constellation Corona Borealis (Northern Crown). When Dionysus was elevated to the rank of an Olympian god he made his wife, like his mother Semele, immortal, and she too joined him in the celestial life on Olympus. The abandonment of his benefactress Ariadne by Theseus remained an embarassing event in the myths of the great Athenian hero, and many efforts were made to palliate the betrayal. In later versions, when Theseus' purity as a national hero was emphasized, the god Dionysus was assigned priority over Ariadne, and accordingly the pious Theseus was said to have obligingly bowed out of the picture in favor of the god.

When the returning Theseus neared the shores of Attica he forgot to change the sails of his ship to white ones, either because of his sadness over Ariadne, or his joy at seeing his home again. Aegeus, observing the black sails, concluded that Theseus was dead, and in grief over his beloved son and heir, leaped to his death into the sea, which thereafter was called the Aegean. Thus Theseus became king of Athens.

Theseus was credited with bringing about the political union of all Attica into one city-state. With the growing power and prominence of Athens, beginning in the Sixth Century B.C., he was elevated to the position of founder and national hero of the city, attracting stories of his dedication to law and order, defense of Athens against foreign invaders, and of various virtues. More and more the primitive aspects of the ancient hero were minimized, and he took on the characteristics of a profoundly religious king, a great statesman, a kindly and benevolent person — in short, the perfect man and ruler. The idealization of Theseus as folk hero was summed up in the Athenian proverb, "Nothing without Theseus," and Plutarch wrote a full-scale biography of him, comparing him to Romulus, founder of Rome. Incidents added to his myth depicted him as friend of the weak and champion of justice and the right. He granted asylum in Athens to the blind Oedipus who had been driven away from all other places, he attacked Thebes to compel the Thebans to give decent burial to the warriors who died in the famed war of the "Seven Against Thebes," and he interceded with Heracles to dissuade him from committing suicide after he had killed his wife and children in a fit of madness. He thus emerged as a man of grace, charm, beauty, intelligence — a civic hero who displaced the obsolete violent, physically powerful and self-interested heroes of the Heroic Age. It was pointed out that whereas Heracles performed his labors in obedience to King Eurystheus, a tyrant, Theseus fought for the freedom of his city. Even when Athens became a democracy, King Theseus remained a popular hero, as the mythic precedent for democracy.

Yet some of the adventures attributed to him during his ideal kingship surely belonged to a more primitive stratum of the myths of Theseus, and his friendship with Heracles, whom he tried to emulate, was established late in his myths. Theseus is said to have joined Heracles in one of his famous Twelve Labors, the attack on the capital of the Amazons, Themiscyra, to seize the girdle of the Amazonian queen, the symbol of her royal power. But Theseus' part in this adventure concerned his relations with one particular Amazon, Antiope, and in the original version this affair probably had nothing to do with the labors of Heracles. The story involved the love of the Amazon Antiope for Theseus. She had a son by him named Hippolytus, and, like Ariadne, voluntarily followed him to Athens, an account which appears to have been the accepted myth until the early Fifth Century B.C. Then when the story of Theseus and the Amazon Antiope was joined to Heracles' attack on the Amazon city, Theseus was made to seize Antiope by force, even to kill her. This theme of the forcible abduction of an Amazon queen from her homeland by Theseus then became a favorite one among the Athenians, since such a version was more palatable than his liaison with a foreign woman. Once having made Theseus hostile to the Amazons, the Athenians added a new tale, an invasion of Attic territory by the Amazons, either to retrieve their queen or to take revenge. Led by Theseus, the Athenians decisively defeated the Amazons in a battle on Attic soil. This struggle, known as an Amazonomachy, became a mythic model of a righteous war, and henceforth the myth of Theseus defeating the Amazons took its place as one of the favorite illustrations of the theme of the victory of civilization over barbarism, comparable to the Titantomachy, Gigantomachy, and Centauromachy.

The Amazons were a warrior society of about 200,000, exclusively composed of women, named perhaps from an Iranian word for warrior, *hamozan*. The ancient Greek etymology "breastless" is false, and originated in the belief that Amazons cut off their right breasts to facilitate use of the bow in war. Their capital was the mythical city of Themiscyra, located in the valley of the Thermodon River. The Amazons, who hated and shunned men, considered them useful only for breeding new Amazons, so that once a year they crossed the river to mingle with and make raids to capture men, whom they promptly killed after mating with them. They reared only female babies, and killed any boys that were born. Their principal activities were fighting and hunting, they always rode on horseback, and their favorite divinity was, suitably, Artemis, the virgin huntress. The Greeks believed that the Amazons were an actual barbarous Asiatic people who lived somewhere in northern Asia Minor. As their own geographical knowledge expanded to regions supposedly inhabited by the Amazons, the Greek myths moved them each time still farther East, at first into the interior of the Caucasus Mts., then to the north, always on the borders of the known world, until they lost all track of them. The notion of the existence of a nation of Amazons was very ancient and widespread, and belief in such a faraway female society survived throughout the Middle Ages. Marco Polo knew the story of a female island, and Columbus believed that in the Atlantic Ocean there was an island called "Island of Women." In the Fifteenth Century, when the Spanish explorer Orellana, about 1541, heard of a tribe of women in South America living near a great river, he believed that he had discovered the country to which the ancient Amazons had retreated, and so named the river the Amazon River.

Many theories have been proposed for the origins of a myth of such a female society. It may have had its basis in ancient knowledge of horse-riding nomadic tribes to the north and east of the Greek world, among whom women also rode on horseback. Little trust should be given to theories that the Amazons were a vestige of a matriarchal period of early human society, or that the Amazons shunned men because they were practicing a form of population control on account of limited food supply in the area.

Years after the birth of his illegitimate son Hippolytus Theseus married Ariadne's sister Phaedra, who had two sons by him and was a devoted, faithful wife to her much older husband. Her stepson Hippolytus, about her own age, grew up into a young man with an aversion for women, preferring the company of other young men, especially hunters. Phaedra fell madly in love with the chaste Hippolytus, and the secret of her love was discovered by Phaedra's serving woman, who promptly revealed it to Hippolytus, hoping to gratify her mistress' passion. But Hippolytus was horrified at the proposal, and Phaedra, fearing that Hippolytus would tell Theseus, was torn between love for Hippolytus and fear of social disgrace. She decided to protect her honor and the honor of her children, so she wrote a note falsely accusing Hippolytus of violating her, and committed suicide. When Theseus discovered the suicide note, he impulsively cursed his blameless son, and prayed to Poseidon to destroy him. Theseus only learned the truth after Hippolytus left in his chariot, and was killed by a tidal wave which came out of the sea and overturned the speeding chariot. It is said that the chaste and honorable Hippolytus was one of the mortals restored to life by Asclepius.

Theseus' best friend was Pirithoüs, and this attachment between the Thessalian king of the Lapiths, son of Ixion, and the king of Athens is one of the great mythological friendships. When Theseus set out to retaliate, after Pirithoüs raided Attica and drove off some cattle, they met for the first time and became inseparable friends at once. Pirithoüs invited Theseus to his impending wedding with Hippodamia, a magnificent occasion to which were also invited some strange relatives of the family of Ixion and Pirithoüs, the half-man, half-horse creatures known as centaurs. The bestial characteristics of the centaurs manifested themselves when they drank excessive wine at the wedding, and when one of them tried to seize the bride and others began to carry off women, a great battle ensued. This struggle of the centaurs against the Lapiths led by Pirithoüs and aided by Theseus and the Athenians became another of the famous mythical symbols of the victory of civilization over barbarism. The centaurs were routed by the Lapiths and Athenians, many of them were killed, and some were driven as far away from their homeland in Thessaly as the Peloponnesus.

The most famous Lapith who lost his life in the Centauromachy was the giant Caeneus. His story contains a number of folktale motifs, the most important of which is the theme of change of sex, since Caeneus was originally a girl with whom Poseidon had fallen in love. In exchange for her favors the god, as requested, changed her into a man whom he made invulnerable. When this happened Caeneus became so proud of his virility and military prowess that he committed the sin of *hybris*, and demanded that his javelin be an object of worship among the Lapiths. In the Centauromachy, the centaurs attacked Caeneus with sharpened logs because he was invulnerable to iron and bronze weapons, and finally killed him by hammering him into the ground and burying him under masses of tree trunks and huge rocks. A late version tells that after his death he was transformed again into a woman.

The home of the centaurs was originally Thessaly, especially the region of Mt. Pelion. The half-animal offspring of Ixion, king of Thessaly, and of Nephele ("Cloud"), wild and full of animal desires that were easily aroused, were lustful and especially partial to wine. Standardly represented as hybrid figures with four horses legs and the upper part of a man, the centaurs were not divinities or demons, but mortal, and not surprisingly, were localized in Thessaly, the region *par excellence* of horse breeding in Greece. Not all the centaurs were disposed to violence, and in particular two, Pholus and Chiron were noble, friendly and benevolent to men. Pholus, the son of Silenus and a nymph, was a very friendly type, and once even entertained Heracles. He opened a cask of wine for the hero, but it happened to be the common property of all the centaurs, who smelled the wine and attacked Heracles. The hero beat them off in a great battle in which the good Pholus was accidentally killed by one of Heracles' poisoned arrows.

The "most just of the centaurs" was Chiron, son of Cronus (or Poseidon) and Philyra, an Oceanid, conceived when Cronus, to elude his wife Rhea, transformed himself into a horse, so that Philyra's offspring was half-man, half-horse. About Chiron the Greek poet Pindar wrote: "If this poet's tongue might voice the prayer that is on the lips of all, I would pray that Chiron, son of Philyra, who is dead and gone, were now alive again." He had friendly relations with many Thessalians, and became the tutor of such heroes as Achilles, Jason, Asclepius, and Phoenix. Probably originally a Thessalian healing god, Chiron was noted for his wisdom and gentleness, conducted a school for doctors and warriors, and taught medicine, music, hunting, warfare, and good morals to his famous pupils. The beloved Chiron was unique among the centaurs because he was immortal. His great crisis came when he was accidentally struck by a poisoned arrow of Heracles which wounded him so painfully he wanted to die, but could not. When, coincidentally, it was decreed that Prometheus could not be released from bondage unless an immortal gave up his immortality as a gift to him, Chiron gladly seized the chance to die and became, as a reward, the constellation Sagittarius (or Centaur). The name Chiron is today associated with medicinal herbs, chironium and centaurion. So famous was his medical knowledge in the Middle Ages that a very popular work called *Herbarius* was actually thought to have been written by Chiron the centaur.

The two friends Theseus and Pirithoüs were determined to marry daughters of Zeus, and settled upon Persephone for Pirithoüs and Helen for Theseus, even though Helen was then a child of no more than twelve and Theseus was about fifty. The inseparable friends first abducted Helen and hid her away in Attica with Theseus' mother Aethra, then descended to the Underworld to seize Persephone, but were promptly captured. Though they had not died it was decided to keep them in Hades forever. They were chained to seats in such a manner that they would be immovable. Eventually Heracles, in his journey to Hades to bring back Cerberus, was allowed to release Theseus and restore him to the upper world, but Theseus was so firmly glued to the seat that he was removed with difficulty. The national hero of Athens left half of his posterior there. Pirithoüs, on the other hand, remained in Hades as an eternal prisoner.

Meanwhile the brothers of Helen, Castor and Polydeuces, invaded Attica, sacked Athens, and liberated their sister Helen, taking Theseus' mother Aethra as hostage. Worse, during Theseus' absence in Hades there was a rebellion in Athens, in which his throne was seized by a relative named Menestheus, so that when Theseus finally returned to Athens he found himself condemned to exile despite all his past services. Disillusioned, he uttered a curse upon the Athenians as he left, and retired to the island of Scyros, where he was given asylum by King Lycomedes, who, to curry favor with the new government in Athens, treacherously had Theseus assassinated. So ended the career of the national hero of Athens.

In the Fifth Century B.C. the Athenian government, in response to an oracle, requested and received from Scyros some bones believed to be relics of the body of Theseus. For these a shrine was built in Athens, where he received divine worship. The Athenians continued to idealize Theseus as the founder and savior of Athens, and especially during the Persian Wars venerated him as the personification of Athenian patriotism. He is said to have appeared at the Battle of Marathon to help the Athenians against the Persians.

The tradition of patriotism among the Athenian kings continued with the last king of Athens, Codrus, at the very end of the Heroic Age. Once when Athens was under attack an oracle revealed that the side which lost its leader first would win the war, so Codrus disguised himself as a farmer, entered the enemy's camp, picked a fight and allowed himself to be killed, thus saving Athens.

XVI

MYTHS OF THESSALY:
the Argonauts

The northernmost region of ancient Hellas, bounded on the north by Mt. Olympus, retained a more primitive cultural content and was less affected by outside influences. Location and geographical barriers cut it off from the main lines of influences of the more advanced cultures of Egypt, Crete, and the Near East. For example, in place of Zeus as sky god, the Thessalians long gave special prominence to an ancient earth god Poseidon (later the sea god of the Greeks) as consort of Mother Earth, and as a god with epiphanies as horse or bull, and Thessaly was for the Greeks and Romans the region of magic, witchcraft, and medicinal knowledge.

The Thessalians believed that they had been in the region from time immemorial, and claimed to be descended from Aeolus, a grandson of the Greek Noah, Deucalion. Aeolus was said to have had four sons, all famous kings: Sisyphus, the founder of Corinth; Salmoneus, who emigrated to Elis in the Peloponnesus; Athamas, a king in Boeotia; and Cretheus, founder and first king of Iolcus in Thessaly. By his niece Tyro, a daughter of Salmoneus, Cretheus had two sons, Aeson and Pheres, and in addition adopted two illegitimate sons of Tyro, the twins Pelias and Neleus, who had been fathered by the god Poseidon. When Cretheus died, the throne of Iolcus passed to his son Aeson, but his stepbrother Pelias deposed Aeson and usurped the royal power. Aeson's young son Jason, the crown prince, was promptly spirited away to protect his life, and handed over to be reared by the centaur Chiron. He remained with the kindly and learned centaur until he was twenty years of age, when he returned to Iolcus to claim his inheritance.

Meanwhile Pelias had been informed by an oracle that he

would lose his power to a man wearing one sandal. When Jason
was about to cross a river in Thessaly an old woman begged to be
carried across, and in the course of carrying her he lost one of his
sandals. The woman turned out to be the goddess Hera, who
thereafter showed him special favor. As Jason entered Iolcus,
Pelias caught sight of him and realized that this was the man
destined to displace him, so when Jason identified himself and
demanded the throne, Pelias agreed on condition that Jason prove
his fitness by trial of heroism. He assigned the task of securing and
bringing back a golden fleece kept in a far distant country called
Colchis, at the eastern end of the Black Sea (today Georgia in
South Russia).

This fleece had belonged to a sacred ram that had miraculously
rescued Phrixus and Helle, the two children of Athamas, who
happened to be first cousins of Jason's father Aeson. Phrixus, who
married the daughter of King Aeëtes of Colchis, had given the
precious golden fleece to his father-in-law, who placed it under the
jealous guard of a serpent. This apparently insignificant object led
to the mobilization of a great undertaking to secure it. This myth,
and other Greek stories about fleeces, suggests that in the
Mycenaean Age ritual fleeces (whether white, gold, or purple)
were precious talismans with magic properties, in effect symbols
of authority and of the fertility powers of the king. It is
noteworthy that the ram in the zodiac is the symbol of royal
power in astrology.

Jason agreed to seek the golden fleece of Phrixus, and
promptly sent messengers throughout Greece to summon great
heroes to accompany him on this glorious adventure. Meanwhile
Argus, a son of Phrixus, with the aid of Athena invented a new
type of ship, a fifty-oared vessel named Argo, suitable for long
voyages, and added a piece of wood from the sacred talking oak at
Dodona so that the ship had the power of prophesying. The
gathering of the Argonauts ("Sailors on the Argo"), the classical
symbol of the spirit of daring and adventure, attracted about fifty
famous heroes, most of the generation before the Trojan War, the
fathers of the heroes who fought in that last great collective effort
of the Greek heroes. The most famous of the Argonauts were
Jason, Zetes, Calaïs, Castor, Polydeuces, Telamon, Peleus, Idas,
Lyncaeus, Amphiaraüs, Caeneus, Mopsus, Argus, Tiphys, Meleager.

Some sources say that the Argonauts included a famous woman, Atalanta, and most belonged to the people called Minyans, from Thessaly and Boeotia. The original nucleus in the legend probably was only twenty-eight, but in time this increased to the round number of fifty as the various regions of Greece added their local heroes to all the major collective exploits of the Greeks. In this way such heroes as Heracles, Theseus, and even the Thracian musician-poet Orpheus found their way into the Argonauts.

Fully equipped, the Argonauts set out from the only harbor in Thessaly, Pagasae. It is not surprising that an important seafaring people like the Greeks should have given prominence to a myth about a daring long voyage of exploration and adventure. The Argonautic expedition is indeed the earliest record in mankind's history of such a long sea voyage, although the story as we know it is largely an amalgamation of myths and folktales. It has been asserted that there was an actual early voyage of this kind in the Mycenaean Age, a unique accomplishment involving technological feats comparable to the space voyages of the first astronauts of our times.

Some believe that Minyans of Thessaly made such a daring voyage to the end of the Black Sea in the late Fourteenth and early Thirteenth Century B.C., and that subsequently the memory of this feat in story received accretions of folktales and mythic elements originally unconnected with such a great sea voyage. The folktale framework is the well-known tale of a young man confronted by a hostile king or demon, forced to undergo difficult trials, and aided by the villain's daughter. The two finally escape by throwing in the path of their pursuers various objects which magically impede them. In addition, many stories of dangerous sea voyages were widespread among Egyptians and Phoenicians, so it is quite possible that the kernel of the myth of the Argonauts was a group of stories about a rich faraway land in the East, usually, however, reached from time immemorial by overland caravan routes. Actually, in the earliest known versions the destination of the Argonauts, and the locale of the golden fleece, was a place called Aia ("The Land"), ruled by a king named Aeëtes, a wonderland in the Far East on the borders of the primeval stream Oceanus, where the sun god Helios had his palace.

Leaving the Bay of Pagasae behind them, Jason and his fellow

Argonauts made their first stop at the island of Lemnos. Considering how close Lemnos was to Thessaly and what massive efforts were made to assemble an élite group of heroes, it is a surprise to learn that the Argonauts settled down for a year in Lemnos, particularly since their reception when they arrived far exceeded their accomplishments so far. It happened that the women of Lemnos were the only inhabitants of the island, for they had previously killed all their own men. Once when the Lemnian women had offended the goddess Aphrodite by neglecting to worship her, she punished them with a repulsive odor which caused their men to flee from them, so when they went to war against the Thracians the Lemnian men took foreign women as their mates. When they returned, the women of Lemnos fell upon their men in revenge and massacred them, and then chose as their ruler a woman, Hypsipyle, daughter of their king Thoas. In the year the Argonauts remained on Lemnos Jason and Hypsipyle became lovers and the parents of twins, while the other Argonauts helped to create a new race of heroes on Lemnos.

After the departure of the Argonauts the women of Lemnos discovered that Hypsipyle had saved the life of her father King Thoas and had been concealing him all this time. Because she was in danger of being put to death for treason, she fled, was captured by pirates and sold into slavery to King Lycurgus of Nemea in Greece, who appointed her nurse of the crown prince Opheltes. Shortly after, as the seven chiefs were en route to their famous attack against Thebes, they met Hypsipyle and asked her to lead them to a spring of water. When she relaxed her care of Opheltes, the child was killed by a serpent. Lycurgus wished to have Hypsipyle put to death, but spared her and allowed her to return to Lemnos, and in honor of the dead boy Opheltes instituted athletic contests called in classical times the Nemean Games.

It is obvious that the incident with the Lemnian women was not a dangerous adventure. Indeed, most of the heroes on the Argo, despite their famous lineage and personal reputations and gifts were inactive throughout the journey, and even Jason appears as a largely ineffectual, feeble hero. He achieved little personally during the voyage, had no shining heroic qualities, and the very success of his mission, not to say his very life, depended on a woman – Medea. Most of the heroes appear to be mere window dressing for a collective exploit.

The Argonauts then sped through the Hellespont (Dardanelles), making their next stop the land of the Doliones on the Asiatic side of the Propontis (Sea of Azov), where they were hospitably received by King Cyzicus. When they left, a storm drove them back to the land of the Doliones, who mistook them for pirates. In the ensuing battle Jason killed King Cyzicus. In his honor the Argonauts celebrated great funeral games, and set up a monument to mark his grave, which was still revered in historical times.

Next the Argonauts landed in Mysia, on the southern coast of the Propontis. Heracles with his enormous strength had broken an oar, and accompanied by his squire Hylas, a young boy of great beauty whom Heracles loved, went ashore to find a new one. When Hylas went to obtain water from a spring, the nymph in the spring, smitten by his beauty, dragged him under the waters. Inconsolably lamenting his lost companion, Heracles wandered about searching for Hylas, and when he refused to go on with the Argonauts without Hylas, they abandoned him. This story and a number of other adventures of Heracles with the Argonauts are found in late versions of the myth. On the whole, the presence of Heracles among the Argonauts, as well as Orpheus and Theseus, were late intrusions to satisfy local pride.

The next landfall of the Argonauts was the land of the Bebryces in Bithynia, whose king, Amycus, was a great boxer who challenged all visitors to a boxing match, usually killing them in the combat. The champion of the Argonauts was none other than Polydeuces, famed as a boxer, who killed Amycus. The theme of the evil king is prominent through the myth of Jason and the Golden Fleece. From the Bebryces the Argonauts came to Salmydessus in Thrace, where the blind seer Phineus was king. From him they learned the route to Colchis, especially how to pass through the dangerous Symplegades ("Clashing Rocks").

It is interesting to note that there are an unusually large number of blind people in Greek mythology, perhaps a reflection of blinding as a penalty for crimes in the Mycenaean Age. The Greeks thought of blindness as a divine punishment for various infractions. It might be imposed for sex crimes, or seeing what was forbidden, as a goddess or one's mother in the nude. In compensation for such blindness the sinner sometimes received an inner sight and became a prophet, musician, or poet.

Phineus' blindness came as the result of his unthinking cruelty toward his sons, Plexippus and Pandion, children by his first wife Cleopatra. When she died Phineus married Idaia, a typical cruel stepmother, who plotted to give her own children priority in the royal succession by falsely accusing her stepsons of trying to rape her. In consequence the two boys were unjustly punished by being blinded. For his part in this Phineus was himself punished by blindness and eternal hunger. Later Cleopatra's brothers, Calaïs and Zetes, the sons of the North Wind Boreas and of Oreithyia, freed their nephews and blinded Idaia in turn. The problems of Phineus were aggravated by the presence of the Harpies ("Snatchers"), winged demons with birds' bodies and women's heads, who flew over Phineus whenever he tried to eat, defiling his food and snatching it away. When the Argonauts asked him how to pass through the Symplegades, Phineus promised to reveal to them the way to Colchis if they would rid him of the Harpies. Accordingly, the winged Calaïs and Zetes attacked the Harpies, defeated them and drove them away as far west as the Strophades Islands off the southern coast of Greece.

On the advice of King Phineus the Argonauts first observed the rhythmical pattern of the opening and closing of the Symplegades, undoubtedly the cliffs on both sides of the Straits of the Bosporus. Belief in the existence of such phenomena (there was another set of clashing rocks near Sicily called Planctae) probably came from sailors' yarns. As soon as the Symplegades separated, the Argonauts sent ahead a dove, which got through before they clashed again, but lost its tail as the rocks closed. Imitating the dove, the Argonauts timed their rowing between the rocks and got through, though the ship lost part of its stern. Thereafter, it was said, the Symplegades remained fixed forever.

Without further significant incident (for example, they passed the River Thermodon in the land of the Amazons without stopping) the Argonauts reached the eastern end of the Black Sea. There they landed in the kingdom of Colchis, where Jason sought out King Aeëtes, and explained the purpose of his mission, but Aeëtes, represented in the myth as the typical "evil king," had no intention of relinquishing the precious fleece given him by his son-in-law Phrixus. He had hung it in the Field of Ares on a tree guarded by a serpent. Trusting he could get rid of Jason, he imposed on him as a first task the yoking of bronze-footed fire-breathing bulls, and sowing the Field of Ares with dragon's teeth. These teeth were some of those left over from the dragon killed by Cadmus, founder of Thebes in Greece, which Aeëtes had somehow obtained. The fearful Jason was in despair for his life. Fortunately the king's daughter Medea ("Cunning One") had fallen in love with him, and now secretly gave him a magic ointment which protected him from the fire of the bulls, so that he could yoke them and plant the dragon's teeth. At once armed men sprang up from the teeth and began to attack him. On Medea's advice he threw a stone into their midst, and they turned upon themselves and killed each other.

The figure of Medea in Greek myth is a complex one. We know her today mostly for her evil deeds, particularly as portrayed in Euripides' magnificent play about her, but she was originally a benevolent divinity, worshipped for example in Corinth, and probably in Thessaly for her knowledge of medical cures. The Greeks gradually reduced her to a female sorceress, then to a rejected woman and murderess. There came to be attached to her not only the magical powers of a witch (she is the greatest sorceress and witch in Greek mythology) but also the typical folktale motif of the lovely daughter of an evil king who loves and aids a young man in danger. As a benevolent magician Medea was associated with a magic caldron of regeneration. It is noteworthy that she specialized in using the children of her enemies to take revenge, and that, although criminals in Greek mythology were assigned punishments to serve as deterrents, Medea was unique in escaping all punishment for her crimes.

Confronted with his most dangerous task, getting the fleece away from the serpent, Jason would have failed had not Medea come to his aid again. She drugged the serpent and seized the fleece for him, and the two rejoined the Argonauts and fled, taking with them as hostage Medea's brother Apsyrtus. When Aeëtes pursued the Argo with his navy, Medea killed her brother and cast his limbs one by one into the sea. Aeëtes stopped to retrieve his son's limbs for burial, and so Jason and Medea escaped.

The return of the Argonauts to Iolcus with the golden fleece

set the pattern for and influenced many later famous stories of the returns of heroes from a great venture, the most notable the return of Odysseus from Troy. In its original form the return voyage of the Argonauts was uncomplicated, involving passage through the Black Sea, the now stationary Symplegades, the Propontis, Hellespont, and Aegean Sea. Eventually many additions were made to the story, and it was in turn influenced by the tale of Odysseus' adventures. Three other versions of the route taken by the Argonauts on their return journey grew up. In two versions they circumnavigated parts of the earth by reaching Oceanus, either sailing up the Phasis River near Colchis until, reaching Oceanus in the East, they went southward to the Nile and from there into the Mediterranean, or they took the Don River in Russia to the Baltic Sea, sailing around Europe westward and southward until they reached Gibraltar. The fourth route was up the Danube River into the Po River, and from there into the Rhone River and the Mediterranean.

The versions that brought the Argonauts into the western Mediterranean took them, among other places, to the island of Circe, Medea's aunt, who, herself a magician, purified Jason and Medea of the murder of Apsyrtus. Then they passed, like the ship of Odysseus, the island of the Sirens. Orpheus, one of the Argonauts, competed with them in song, and his music was so enchanting that the Sirens admitted defeat, although Boutes, one of the Argonauts, leaped overboard to the island of the Sirens and was drowned. They also passed the Planctae ("Wandering Rocks"), and were hospitably received on the island of the Phaeacians. There ambassadors from Colchis on orders of King Aeëtes demanded the surrender of his daughter Medea — provided she was still a virgin. She still was, but the good King Alcinoüs promptly married Jason and Medea, and their union was speedily consummated to save her. The last important stop of the Argonauts was in Crete, where they were harassed by the bronze giant Talus. Either through the bravery of some of the Argonauts or the magic of Medea the nail that closed the one vein of Talus was removed, so that his life blood flowed out and he was destroyed. Having eluded this final danger, Jason and Medea arrived in Iolcus after four months of wandering. Jason dedicated the ship Argo to the god Poseidon, setting it up as a memorial to the first sea voyage into the unknown, and eventually the Argo was elevated to the sky as one of the constellations.

Jason delivered the golden fleece to King Pelias, but he reneged on his promise to relinquish the throne to Jason. Medea was determined, however, to secure the royal power for Jason and herself, so she contrived a horrible revenge. Using her magic caldron to show the daughters of Pelias how to perform the miracle of rejuvenation, she took an old ram, killed it, cut it apart, put it into her caldron, performed the proper magic spells, and a young ram leaped forth. Thereupon the daughters of Pelias dragged their aging father to the caldron, killed him and put him into it. But Medea withheld her sorcery and Pelias did not rise again. The most beautiful of the daughters of Pelias, the only one of them not duped into participating in the killing of Pelias was Alcestis, who later sacrificed her life for her husband Admetus. For Medea's crime Jason and Medea were driven from Iolcus, and found asylum in Corinth.

Despite the reputation of Pelias as an "evil king" in his dealings with Jason, his death was the occasion of one of the most famous funerals in Greek mythology. Arranged by his son Acastus, it was attended by famous people from all over the Greek world, and these funeral games became a favorite theme of Greek artists. Especially singled out in these games was the contest between the noble hero Peleus and the famed Greek woman athlete Atalanta, who defeated him in a wrestling match.

Medea and Jason lived in Corinth with their two young sons. The king of the city, having no sons of his own, sought a distinguished son-in-law, so he offered the hand of the princess Glauce (or Creusa) to Jason, with the promise that he and his sons by Glauce would succeed to the throne. Jason opportunistically accepted. The news that Medea was to be discarded and exiled with her sons from Corinth for the political ambitions of the king and Jason infuriated her. For love she had given up family and native land, had committed heinous crimes, and as a woman of Asiatic origin was now living in a strange western land. When all appeals to Jason fell on deaf ears, she decided on a terrible vengeance. Pretending to be reconciled to the marriage, she sent Jason's bride a poisoned robe and crown which consumed the flesh of the unsuspecting Glauce when she put them on, and also destroyed King Creon, who tried to tear the poisoned gifts from his daughter. Finally Medea killed her own young children as scapegoats for their faithless father Jason, fled to asylum in Athens where she married Aegeus, and had by him a son named Medus. After she failed in her attempt to poison Aegeus' son Theseus and fled with her son into the heart of Asia, Medus became the ancestor of the Medes.

Jason was a broken man after the massacre perpetrated by Medea. In one account he committed suicide, but in the more common one, when he went to visit the ship Argo and took shelter under it, part of it collapsed and killed him. In such an inglorious way ended the career of the most famous hero of Thessaly.

The successor of Pelias was his son Acastus, brother of Alcestis, husband of Astydamia. To his court came Peleus, a famous prince exiled from the island of Aegina, son of the pious King Aeacus, known for his strict administration of justice (Aeacus became one of the judges of the Underworld). Peleus and his brother Telamon had been jealous of their brother Phocus, a famed athlete, contrived to cause his death, and for this crime were exiled by their father Aeacus. Telamon went to Salamis, and Peleus to Phthia in Thessaly, where he was purified of blood-guilt by King Eurytion, who not only married him to his daughter named Antigone but designated him successor to the throne of Phthia. An essentially upright man, Peleus had a career that was marked by one disaster after another. At the Calydonian Boar Hunt he accidentally killed his father-in-law Eurytion, so he was compelled to go into exile again, this time to the court of Acastus in Iolcus in Thessaly. There he was purified of blood-guilt by Acastus.

Then a new blow fell upon the righteous Peleus. Queen Astydamia fell in love with him, her husband's friend, and offered her love to him. When Peleus indignantly rejected her overtures, she took vengeance upon him by informing Peleus' wife Antigone that Peleus intended to divorce her and marry a daughter of Acastus, whereupon Antigone committed suicide. Then she informed Acastus that Peleus had tried to seduce her, so Acastus secretly tried to do away with him. On a hunting expedition, as the unsuspecting Peleus slept on Mt. Pelion, Acastus removed the

wondrous sword given Peleus by the gods as a reward for his chastity, and when centaurs came upon the disarmed Peleus they would have killed him had not the kindly, wise centaur Chiron rescued him by returning his sword. Eventually the truth was revealed, Peleus punished Astydamia, and returned to his kingdom in Phthia.

Then, when Zeus feared that his love for the Nereid Thetis would result in a child greater than himself, he decided to give her in marriage to the noble Peleus, the model of the virtuous man in Greek mythology. The marriage of willing Peleus, now a widower, and the reluctant Thetis was one of the most celebrated events of mythology, attended by gods and mortals alike, but the relationship between Peleus and Thetis was tainted from the beginning. Thetis was averse to the union, and when Peleus approached her she transformed herself into many shapes to avoid him, serpent, lion, dragon, fish, tree, fire, water, but he was persistent and continued to wrestle with her until she relented. This incompatible union between the best of mortals and the lovely sea nymph ended in disaster, and at the very marriage of Peleus and Thetis the seeds of the great Trojan War were sown, as well as further woe for Peleus. Eventually Peleus lost his wife, his great son Achilles, and his famous grandson Neoptolemus.

The theme of the adulterous wife and the chaste young man is a widespread motif of world mythology. In the Old Testament the most famous instance is the story of Joseph and Potiphar's wife, and in Greek mythology it is basic to the stories of Hippolytus, Bellerophon, and Peleus, among others. In this common folk motif an older woman, usually married, tries to seduce a younger man, who rejects her. The woman then accuses the man of attempted rape, her story is believed, and as a result the man suffers unjustly. In some cases the woman's deception is discovered and she is punished, while the youth's reputation is rehabilitated.

Another famous Thessalian center productive of myths was the land of the Lapiths, the most famous of whom was the best friend of Theseus, Pirithoüs. His father Ixion, the notorious king of the Lapiths, became one of the greatest sinners of antiquity, and the first to kill a relative. When he wanted to get rid of his father-in-law Deioneus rather than repay a debt to him, Ixion killed him by contriving to have him fall into a pit at the bottom of which were burning logs. Since Ixion was a favorite of the gods he was pardoned for this crime, and even invited to Olympus to be purified of blood-guilt, living on Olympus and partaking of the hospitality of the gods and eating at their table. But Ixion was as incorrigibly corrupt as Peleus was honorable. While on Olympus he tried to seduce Hera, queen of the gods, and when Zeus discovered this he sent a cloud (Nephele) to him in the shape of Hera. The union of Ixion with Nephele produced the centaurs. As punishment the great criminal — murderer, ingrate, and mocker of the gods — was tied to a fiery wheel and whirled forever in the air. In a later version Ixion was said to have been hurled into Tartarus and punished there on the whirling wheel.

XVII

CALYDONIAN BOAR HUNT

The region of Aetolia in central Greece, north of the Peloponnesus across the Gulf of Corinth, was an even more backwoods area than Thessaly, producing as its principal myth only the great Calydonian Boar Hunt, hardly a sophisticated story. The task involved resembles some of the early labors of Heracles, except that the great Dorian hero accomplished his feats virtually singlehandedly, while the Calydonian Boar Hunt assembled a great many of the leading heroes of Greece. There may have been some memorable historical clearing away of wild animals in Aetolia when the region was first settled, but the myths of the Calydonian hunt are heavily incrusted with folktale elements.

Oeneus ("Wine Man") and Althaea ("Healer") were king and queen of Calydon. It is said that Oeneus was the first person in Greece on whom Dionysus bestowed the vine. Their most famous children were Dejanira, the woman who later married Heracles, and Meleager, whose life span, by a chance occurrence, was in his mother's hands. He was seven days old when his mother Althaea saw the Moerae engaged in determining his fate. She asked them how long he would live, and they informed her that his life would last as long as the life of a log which was then burning in the fireplace, so she promptly snatched the firebrand from the flames, put out the burning wood, and hid it safely away. This tale is the classical example in Greek myth of the folk motif of the "external soul" or "life token," some object the possession of which makes it possible to control a person's life.

When Meleager was a young man, Oeneus in his sacrifices to the gods neglected to make proper offerings to Artemis, and in punishment the goddess sent a huge wild boar which ravaged the area of Calydon, terrorizing everyone. In despair Oeneus summoned all the heroes of Greece to help hunt and destroy the dangerous beast. They gathered from all parts to join one of the most famous collective ventures of the early Greeks, comparable to the Argonautic expedition and the Trojan War. The myth was popular also among the Etruscans and Romans, for whom the overtones of the concept of immortality in the story were especially attractive. Among the best known heroes who participated in this event were: Meleager himself; from Arcadia, Ancaeus (uncle of Atalanta and famous for his weapon which was a huge double axe); from Athens, Theseus; from Thessaly, Pirithoüs, Peleus, Acastus, Admetus, Jason; from the Peloponnesus, Nestor, Castor and Polydeuces, Idas and Lyncaeus; from Salamis, Telamon; also from Arcadia, the famed huntress Atalanta.

Though Ancaeus strenuously objected to Atalanta's participation in the hunt, Meleager permitted it, for he had fallen in love with this remarkable woman, the daughter of Iasus and Clymene of Arcadia. As a baby she had been exposed by her father, soon found and nursed by a she-bear, and then brought up by hunters of Arcadia. In this environment she developed into an expert huntress, skilled with the bow and a very swift runner. Atalanta, who decided to remain chaste and never marry, faithful to her favorite goddess Artemis, was once attacked by two centaurs who sought to violate her, but she not only outran these swift creatures but killed them with her bow and arrows. Her fame was so great that she was invited, as we have seen, to participate in the funeral games in honor of King Pelias of Iolcus.

Before the great Calydonian Boar Hunt began, it was decided that the one who actually killed the boar would be awarded the head and skin of the animal as a trophy. Several heroes died in the hunt. Atalanta was the first to draw blood from the beast with a well-aimed arrow, but Meleager killed the animal in combat, and because of his affection for Atalanta, decided to bestow the boar trophies on her. When Meleager's uncles, Plexippus and Toxeus, his mother Althaea's brothers, who wished the trophy to remain in the clan, objected strongly, a dispute ensued and Meleager killed one or both of his uncles. When Althaea heard what had happened, she was torn between mother love and the obligation to avenge her brothers' deaths, but ultimately she threw the log into the fire, and at once Meleager was stricken and died as the log disintegrated. Althaea's decision to kill her son represents the priorities of a primitive code of justice, in which the claims of father, mother, and siblings were dominant.

There is another version of the tragedy of Meleager probably based on an epic current before the composition of Homer's *Iliad*. Either because of the dispute over the trophy, or for some other reason, war broke out between the Calydonians and a neighboring people. As principal champion of Calydon, a sort of Aetolian Achilles, Meleager led his troops out to certain victory, but in the battle killed one of Althaea's brothers, for which Althaea cursed her son. His feelings deeply hurt, he withdrew from battle and obstinately refused to return, and in consequence the Calydonians were driven back and found themselves in dire straits. Without Meleager the Calydonian cause was hopeless. The entreaties of his father, friends, finally even Althaea herself, failed to sway the proud, petulant hero, but at length, when his wife Cleopatra urged him to return, he complied. The social values inherent in this new situation put emphasis on priority of love for wife over tie to mother, an advance from the primitive code of the tribe. Meleager was victorious but was mortally wounded in battle and died. As a result Althaea killed herself, followed in suicide by Meleager's wife Cleopatra.

As for Atalanta, her father consented to her design to remain unmarried, on condition that she defeat all suitors in a footrace. Those beaten by her were put to death. Not discouraged by the danger, a certain Hippomenes (or Milanion) prayed for assistance to the goddess of love and beauty Aphrodite, who provided him with three golden apples from the garden of the Hesperides. The apple was as an erotic symbol, and token of fertility often brought to weddings. In the race with Hippomenes, as Atalanta caught up with him he dropped one golden apple. When Atalanta in wonderment stopped to pick it up he darted ahead. When she caught up again, he dropped a second apple, and finally a third, just barely by this ruse defeating the swift Atalanta. Their marriage was a happy one, and they had a famous son, Parthenopaeus, one of the seven chieftains who marched against Thebes. Because of a religious sin Atalanta and Hippomenes were eventually transformed into lions.

XVIII

MYTHS OF THEBES

Another culturally conservative region of Greece was Boeotia. In Mycenaean times its two most powerful kingdoms were Orchomenus and Thebes. Of these Orchomenus is little known, for, although its historical importance was considerable, almost all its traditions have vanished into the mists of the past. The Greeks of later times believed the people of Orchomenus to have belonged to a tribal group known as the Minyans (from whom also stem the inhabitants of Iolcus in Thessaly), and that the founder of Orchomenus was a king named Minyas.

A later king of Orchomenus, Athamas, one of the sons of Aeolus, king of Thessaly, married Nephele, and had by her a son and daughter, Phrixus and Helle. Later he divorced her and took as his second wife Ino, daughter of the founder of Thebes, Cadmus, by whom he had two sons Learchus and Melicertes. Ino, another example of the cruel stepmother, conceived a plan to rid herself of Phrixus and Helle. Secretly she ordered the women of the region to parch their seeds so that a famine resulted, and when the oracle of Delphi was consulted about the problem, she bribed the messengers to report that Apollo ordered Phrixus (or both Phrixus and Helle) to be sacrificed to Zeus to avert the famine. When Athamas was about to perform this human sacrifice, Nephele (or Zeus himself) sent a ram with a golden fleece to rescue them. With Phrixus and Helle on its back the ram swam far into Asia across the Aegean and Black Seas, but en route Helle fell off and was drowned in the straits between Asia and Europe, which were thereafter named Hellespont ("Helle's Path"). In the original story the ram was depicted as swimming, but later versions of the myth had the ram fly.

The ram brought Phrixus to Colchis, where King Aeëtes received him hospitably, and gave him his daughter Chalciope as his wife. In gratitude Phrixus sacrificed the ram and gave the precious golden fleece to Aeëtes, for it to become the object of search by Jason and the Argonauts.

The story of Phrixus and Helle was a very popular theme in ancient artistic representations. It may have a vestige of the memory of human sacrifice practiced by the early Greeks or their predecessors in the region, and the escape from sacrifice is not unlike the substitution of an animal in similar ancient stories (for example, Abraham and Isaac in the Old Testament; Iphigenia at Aulis) which symbolizes one of the momentous advances in human civilization. To the Greeks of the classical age, as to the Hebrews, human sacrifice was a barbarous practice, still current among contemporary peoples elsewhere in the world, although the Greeks themselves in their early period may not have been very far removed in time from human sacrifice, for they did not quite succeed in eliminating this rite entirely from their myths. In the *Iliad,* Achilles, a Thessalian king, is depicted as resorting to human sacrifice at Troy.

Some versions of the story of Athamas' family troubles give him a third wife, Themisto, by whom he had four children. Themisto in turn also became a jealous stepmother, and planned to kill her stepchildren, the sons of Ino, during the night, but in the dark she mistook her own children for Ino's and killed her own. When she discovered what she had done she committed suicide.

Another Minyan king of Orchomenus was Erginus. When a Theban killed his father at a Boeotian festival, Erginus marched against Thebes to avenge his father, and, victorious, imposed an annual tribute of 100 cattle for a period of twenty years. It happened once that Heracles, returning from one of his minor exploits, met the envoys of Erginus coming to collect the annual tribute, cut off their noses and ears in Near Eastern fashion and sent them back scornfully to Erginus. In the ensuing war Heracles led the Thebans, killed Erginus, and imposed upon Orchomenus double the tribute which had been imposed upon Thebes, a service to his adoptive country for which he received in marriage Megara, daughter of the king. Such tales of wars between Thebes and Orchomenus probably recall historical events of the Mycenaean Age.

Erginus had twin sons, Trophonius and Agamedes. One of them is sometimes said to have been a son of Apollo, in accordance with the primitive belief that each of twins has his own father, and that one father is divine. In antiquity twins, often regarded as highly abnormal and therefore potentially harmful, were frequently exposed, and sometimes, as in the case of Leto, the mother too was persecuted. Hence twin-towns were founded as places of refuge, to which naturally flocked other outlaws. The classical example is the Roman story of Romulus and Remus.

Like some other famous twins (for example, Romulus and Remus, Amphion and Zethus, the Egyptian gods Horus and Set), Trophonius and Agamedes were master builders. Once, in building the treasury of a king, they inserted one movable block of stone, and in this way they were able to plunder the treasury at will. When the robberies were discovered, the king set a trap which caught one of the twins, and held him fast, so to avoid detection the other twin entered the tomb, cut off his brother's head and removed it. The historian Herodotus tells the same story about two Egyptian brothers, and the Greek story of Trophonius and Agamedes may have been the adaptation of the Egyptian myth, or an independent version of a well-known folktale. It should be noted that in Egyptian myths the twin gods Set and Horus built the temples at Luxor and Thebes in Egypt, and that the walls of Thebes in Boeotia were said to have been built by the twins Amphion and Zethus (is this name a Greek version of Set?).

The fates of Athamas and Ino were usually said to have been associated with the persecution of Dionysus by Hera. Ino, after the death of her sister Semele, at first brought up the young Dionysus, and, in anger, Hera caused Athamas and Ino to become mad. In this state Athamas killed his son Learchus outright and then put his son Melicertes into a caldron of boiling water, while Ino, to escape the frenzy of Athamas, who insanely pursued her, seized the corpse of Melicertes and leaped with it to suicide into the sea. The gods mercifully transformed both Ino and her son into benevolent sea divinities, Leucothea ("White Goddess") and Palaemon. This is another famous Greek example of the "sea leap" from a cliff, which was apparently a fertility or purification rite among the Greeks and other peoples of the Mediterranean.

Early Boeotia, especially Thebes, appears to have been considerably influenced by the Near East in Mycenaean times, and it is perhaps not without significance that Thebes in Boeotia, the great rival of Mycenae, has the same name as one of the great cities of ancient Egypt. Archeological discoveries in Thebes prove some connection of the Mycenaean kingdom with the Near East even before 1300 B.C., before the royal palace of Thebes was destroyed by fire sometime in the second half of the Thirteenth Century.

We find Boeotian myths claiming that the founder of Thebes was the Phoenician prince Cadmus. The legend of the founding of Thebes, perhaps the oldest of the foundation tales of Greek cities, appears to have become the archetype of such foundation stories, which generally follow a standard form. A hero searches for a place to found a new city; he is guided by a divinely sent animal; at the site of the new city the hero engages in combat with a dragon; the founding of the city is accompanied by other difficulties; it is sometimes followed by a sacred marriage; finally the founder is heroized. The association of Cadmus with Phoenicia, a firmly established tradition among the Greeks, appears to have originated quite late, in the Fifth Century B.C. in Ionia, and there is no evidence that the early Thebans were Phoenicians. The association may have been made because Thebes was traditionally the birthplace of the god Dionysus, whose career is intimately connected with the Near East. The theme of the slaying of a dragon at the time of the foundation of a city has its origin in the concept of the dragon as a primeval force of chaos, and by his victory over this hostile force the city founder was thought to bring order to the region. Special religious significance was attached to this event, for it was associated with Zeus' victory over Typhon, which saved the universe from chaos in remotest antiquity.

Cadmus, whose name appears to be of Semitic origin and to mean "East," or "Rising Sun," was the son of Agenor, king of Tyre (or Sidon) in Phoenicia. When his sister Europa disappeared, his father sent Cadmus and his brothers to search for her, with instructions not to return without her, and Cadmus wandered far and wide in his search, without success. When he came to Greece he consulted the oracle at Delphi, which instructed him to abandon the quest for Europa, follow a cow, and build a city where it came to rest and lay down. In preparation for sacrificing the cow at the site of the future Thebes, Cadmus looked for water, and when he found it guarded by a dragon, he fought and slew the monster, which turned out to be sacred to Ares, god of war. Cadmus later had to atone for the slaying of the sacred dragon by serving Ares as a slave for eight years. After killing the dragon, Cadmus was advised by the goddess Athena to pull out the dragon's teeth and sow them. From the teeth armed warriors sprang up out of the soil. When they seemed dangerous, on Athena's advice Cadmus threw a stone among them and this caused the warriors to turn upon themselves and massacre each other until only five survived. These were the earth-born *Spartoi* ("Sown Men"), who became co-founders of the city and helped Cadmus build the fortified citadel of Thebes, called the Cadmea. The *Spartoi* in historical times were the five aristocratic military families of the city of Thebes.

After his eight years of servitude to Ares, Cadmus was rewarded with the hand of Ares' daughter Harmonia in another memorable wedding of ancient myth. As wedding gifts Harmonia received from Aphrodite an extraordinary necklace, and from Cadmus a splendid robe, which remained an inheritance of "deadly gifts" in the royal family of Thebes.

The motif of "magic gifts" is a common one in the folklore of many peoples. Sometimes such gifts are given with benevolent intent, but circumstances or a twist of fortune transform them into evil, as in the case of the magic spear given by Procris to Cephalus. On the other hand, "magic gifts" are sometimes given with deadly intent, as, for example, Pandora the first woman, the Trojan Horse, and Medea's gifts to the princess Creusa.

Besides the founding of Thebes, Cadmus was credited with the introduction of writing to the Greeks in the form of what the Greek historian Herodotus called "Phoenician letters," that is, the alphabet. Although writing was known in Mycenaean times, the earliest records of the Greek language were written not in an alphabet but a complex syllabary today called Linear B script, deciphered in 1952 by the English architect Michael Ventris. With the destruction of the Mycenaean palaces about 1200 B.C., this

form of writing disappeared among the Greeks, who remained illiterate for hundreds of years after. About 750 B.C. the Greek alphabet, derived from the Semitic alphabet of the North Syrians, began to be used. The mythical attribution of the introduction of the alphabet by the Phoenicians under Cadmus in the Mycenaean period is an anachronism, first made in the Fifth Century B.C., when other Greeks were attributing the introduction of writing to the Greeks from Egypt by Danaüs, and Cretan writers claimed Crete as the place of the invention of letters.

In their old age Cadmus and Harmonia went westwards to the region of Illyria, and there they were transformed into benevolent serpents. They had had five children: four daughters, Ino, Semele, Autonoë, and Agave; one son, Polydorus. Ino married Athamas, king of Orchomenus, Semele became the mother of Dionysus and eventually a divinity on Olympus, and Agave married one of the Spartoi, Echion, by whom she had a son Pentheus, usually said to have been the successor of Cadmus as king of Thebes, and famous as opponent of Dionysus who came to a horrible end.

After the death of Cadmus' son Polydorus, two Boeotians, Nycteus and Lycus, related to the royal family of Thebes, became regents of the kingdom. Nycteus had a daughter, Antiope, a girl of extraordinary beauty whom Zeus visited in the form of a satyr. Soon Antiope found herself with child, and fearful of disgrace, she fled and later gave birth to twins, Amphion and Zethus, who were promptly exposed. After Antiope's uncle Lycus, exercising the royal power of Thebes, had her brought back to Thebes and locked in a dungeon, Lycus' wife Dirce, jealous of Antiope's beauty, was especially vicious in persecuting the unfortunate girl.

Meanwhile Amphion and Zethus were found by a shepherd, who brought them up. The Theban Dioscouri, as we might call them, were, like Castor and Polydeuces, a sharp contrast. Amphion had musical talent, while Zethus excelled as an athlete and herdsman. When the twins were grown young men, their mother escaped from Lycus, and the three met, recognized each other and were reunited. Then Amphion and Zethus put Lycus and Dirce to death for the harm they had done to their mother, killing Dirce in a particularly gruesome manner by tying her limbs to a wild bull so that she was quickly torn apart.

Amphion and Zethus then proceeded to build the walls of

Thebes. In keeping with their special abilities, Zethus carried the
huge blocks on his back, while Amphion, not having the physical
strength, merely played on his lyre. Yet the stone blocks moved
into the appropriate places of their own accord in response to his
music, a story recalling the widespread folkloric motif of the
"magic song." Such association of magic music with building may
arise out of the work songs so common both in the Near East and
the Mediterranean.

Amphion married Niobe, daughter of the Lydian king
Tantalus, whose famous son was Pelops. They had seven sons and
seven daughters called the Niobids (in some sources there were six
of each sex, in others ten of each), and Niobe was so proud of her
children that she boasted she was superior to the goddess Leto,
who had only one son and one daughter, Apollo and Artemis. For
this *hybris* on Niobe's part, Leto called upon her children to
punish Niobe, so Apollo and Artemis killed all the Niobids with
their arrows. Niobe's grief was so great that she changed into
stone, but still continued to weep. Amphion then committed
suicide. In Lydia, at Mt. Sipylus in Asia Minor, there was a rock in
the form of a woman's head which continually dripped water, and
this natural formation was probably the origin of the Niobe myth.

Zethus married Aëdon, by whom he had one son and one
daughter. Jealous of the numerous children of her sister-in-law
Niobe, Aëdon tried to kill Niobe's eldest son while he slept, but in
the dark by error she killed her own son Itylus who was sleeping in
the same room. Aëdon was turned into a nightingale, and
continued lamenting her loss.

After this the royal power in Thebes descended to Laïus,
whose marriage to Jocasta was childless for a long time. When
Laïus was a young man, during political disorders in Thebes he had
fled to the court of Pelops in the Peloponnesus, where he fell in
love with the boy Chrysippus, young son of Pelops. Laïus is thus
said to have been one of the inventors of pederasty. In his passion
for Chrysippus, Laïus carried him off, and as a result of this
abduction Pelops cursed Laïus and his descendants, the beginning
of the many disasters of the house of Laïus. When the childless
King Laïus and Queen Jocasta consulted the oracle of Delphi, they
received the terrifying answer that they would indeed have a son
but would find no joy in him, for the son was destined to kill his

father and marry his own mother. Therefore, when the child was
born they decided to expose the baby.

The theme of the abandonment of a newborn child through
exposure is especially characteristic of myths of heroes. The
classical Greeks would not have felt repelled by such stories, for
exposure of unwanted infants was not only legal but frequently
practiced in lieu of infanticide, motivated either by the poverty of
the family (especially if there were more than a few girl children,
all of whom would have to be supplied with dowries), or by social
reasons: illegitimacy, an incestuous relationship, or deformity.
Any deviation from normal was likely to cause anxiety, and the
community particularly feared deformed children as omens of
divine danger. The exposure took place either on a mountainside
or in a floating chest placed in a body of water, and any survival of
an exposed child was a sign of divine protection.

Exposure was especially connected with gods and culture
heroes in the mythologies of many peoples in Asia and Europe,
and can be found in the myths, for example, of Gilgamesh, Moses,
Sargon, Krishna, Zeus, Paris, Perseus, Dionysus, Romulus and
Remus, and many others. There are over 100 such myths of the
exposure of the king-child from all parts of the world. Often the
exposed god or hero was suckled by an animal, then reared by
shepherds. When the hero grew up he often fought a dragon or
overcame some other danger, returned to avenge himself on those
who had exposed him, and assumed his rightful place. This mythic
pattern of the birth and homecoming of the hero heralds a new
charismatic personality, often connected with the coming to
power of a new royal dynasty supported by the god who gave his
assistance to the hero in distress. The culture hero's arrival on the
scene introduces a "dangerous child" who causes the previous
balance and harmony to be disturbed, but his return, ultimate
victory, and restoration to power bring a new level of harmony.

Oedipus fits into this mythic pattern of "dangerous child."
Before exposing the child Laïus had its feet mutilated, to deter
anyone who found the child from wanting to bring it up (Oedipus
appears to mean "Swollen Foot" in Greek). The baby was then
given to a herdsman of the royal flocks with orders to expose and
abandon it on a nearby mountain, Cithaeron. (In another version
Oedipus, like Perseus, was put into a box placed in the sea). But

the shepherd took pity on the baby and gave it to another shepherd, the slave of the king and queen of Corinth, Polybus and Merope, who because they were childless decided to bring up the foundling as their own child. Many years later, Oedipus, heir to the throne of Corinth, heard rumors that he was not the true son of Polybus and Merope, and traveled to the oracle of Delphi to ask about his identity. He learned from the oracle that he would one day kill his father and marry his mother, and, deeply troubled, resolved never to return to Polybus and Merope, but to start life anew. Leaving Delphi he came to a three-forked road where he met a distinguished man and his entourage, and killed the man and all but one of his retinue in an argument about the right of way. The dead man was Oedipus' own father, Laïus, who was en route to Delphi to consult the oracle about a disaster that had befallen Thebes.

The murder of a father was, in the eyes of the Greeks, one of the most heinous crimes, second only in gravity to matricide, and in light of this the frequency of patricide in Greek myths is strange. Perhaps the myths were residues of very primitive tales of the conflict of generations in royal families for power. These conflicts between father and son in Greek myths should not be associated with sexual competition or the unconscious libido, so often the analysis of these myths by Freudians and Jungians, but rather have their origin in the struggle for power, which in many primitive tribes involved the rite of conquest of power by the younger generation. The successor to power often eliminated the preceding king by murder when the older man was no longer considered capable of exercising the royal functions properly.

Laïus had gone to consult the oracle of Delphi because the Sphinx had recently come to Thebes and was plaguing the city. It was in the Theban myths that this monster, originally an Egyptian figure as we have seen, became a central figure in myth. The Greeks, of course, tended to humanize not only the gods but also monstrous creatures derived from Near Eastern sources. What is, however, unique in this case, is that the Theban Sphinx was transformed into an intellectual monster, whose power over humans lay in her superior wisdom, a superiority symbolized by the riddle she asked. She crushed to death those who could not answer it. The riddle of the Sphinx took the following form in

Greek myths (it is preserved in verse form): "There is on earth a two-footed, three-footed, four-footed creature with one voice. It alone of all animals changes its nature on land, in the air, and in the sea. But when it walks supporting itself on most feet, then does it move most feebly on its limbs." The usual form of this very widely known folk riddle differed from the canonic Greek version, and referred to the animal as walking on four feet in the morning, two in the afternoon, and three in the evening.

When Oedipus came to Thebes he faced the Sphinx and answered her riddle, whereupon the Sphinx disappeared. The answer he gave was "Man." The significance of the riddle is that to survive man must know himself, his strength and limitations, and in that sense the answer might properly have been "Oedipus," for it applied equally to the enigma of his birth and the coming discovery of his origins. In the original version of the myth, Oedipus destroyed the Sphinx in physical combat, making her his equivalent of the mythical dragon. The remarkable characteristic of the developed myth is that Oedipus overcame the Sphinx not by force but by his superior intelligence, a typical late Greek change in a myth. Indeed, it is likely that the Sphinx and the riddle originally had no connection, but that some mythmaker in Thebes associated the two.

The riddle (the Greek word is *aenigma*) is as widespread a phenomenon as myths and folktales, containing a kind of compressed bit of folk knowledge. Riddles not only contained nuggets of wisdom, but were thought to have a sort of magic quality. Riddle solving was practiced among ancient peoples at critical moments, as if a crisis is resolved by sympathetic magic of solving riddles.

As in the typical folktale the hero is rewarded for slaying his dragon by marrying the princess, so Oedipus was married to Jocasta. In some instances of this theme, the suitor fights the girl, or, in extreme cases, the girl's father, as in the classic race between Pelops and Oenomaüs. But in Oedipus' story, since Oedipus won his own mother, the hero's victory produces the unknowing incestuous relationship between mother and son. The incest taboo is a very primitive one, most strictly avoided in the son-mother relationship. There are not a few instances of incest in Greek myth involving father and daughter, or brother and sister, but the case of Oedipus and Jocasta is unique. It is, of course from this myth that Freud characterized by the term Oedipus Complex the relationship he regarded as the root of all neuroses and the cornerstone of Freudian psychoanalysis. For Freud, all males as children desire sexual union with their mothers, and out of this unconscious love for the mother stems rivalry with the father and unconscious or overt hatred of the father. The suppression of this socially taboo libidinous desire causes conflicts, often revealed as wish-fulfillments in dreams. Freud's concept of sexual rivalry between father and son has been rejected by many who regard the father-son hostility in myths and in modern man as simply the rebellion of the son against the authority of the father in patriarchal societies.

In the earliest version of the myth Oedipus was married to his mother, a woman called Epicaste, by whom he had no children. The relationship was soon discovered, Epicaste committed suicide, Oedipus continued to rule in Thebes, and subsequently married again, this time to Euryganie, by whom he had four children, Antigone, Chrysothemis, Polynices, and Eteocles. It is even related that Oedipus had a third marriage, with a certain Astimedusa.

In the canonical version of the myth of Oedipus, which took form in the Fifth Century B.C., and is best known from Sophocles' famous tragedy *Oedipus Tyrannus*, the four children usually associated with him were born from his wife Jocasta. Many years later, when the children were already in their teens, a plague descended upon the city of Thebes, bringing sterility to the soil, animals, and humans. This could only mean that the anger of the gods was being directed against the entire people because of some defilement in the city, and when the oracle of Apollo at Delphi was consulted, the response came forth that the plague would not end until the murderer of Laïus was discovered. Oedipus himself issued a proclamation that if the murderer was a foreigner he would be killed, if a Theban by birth he would be exiled.

Because of his concern for the welfare of the city Oedipus summoned the blind prophet Tiresias, official seer of Thebes, to reveal the identity of the criminal. Tiresias, knowing Oedipus to be the guilty person, but not wanting to hurt the beloved ruler of Thebes, refused to talk, but when Oedipus, proud of his services to the city, browbeat and insulted the kindly old seer, Tiresias blurted out the truth that Oedipus was the murderer of Laïus and hinted at some worse offence. But Oedipus, suspecting a plot, accused Jocasta's brother Creon and the prophet Tiresias of conspiring to overthrow him. Jocasta defended the loyalty of her brother Creon, and proceeded to cast doubt upon the validity of the oracle, offering as proof that an oracle once warned that her husband Laïus would be killed by his own son, and that that son would marry her. But, she assured Oedipus, this prophecy was false because her first husband was killed not by one single man but by a group of robbers as was reported at the time, at a spot where three roads met. This revelation triggered a vivid remembrance in Oedipus of the murder he had committed many years before, and he now feared that he might indeed have killed Laïus, the former king.

Just then a messenger arrived from Corinth to announce that King Polybus had just died. Oedipus expressed sadness at the death of the man he had known as father, but relief that the prophecy given him by the oracle, that he would one day kill his father and marry his mother, could not now be fulfilled. As the skepticism of both Oedipus and Jocasta mounted, the messenger from Corinth then revealed that Oedipus was not the son of King Polybus and Queen Merope of Corinth, but rather a Theban, and that he himself when a young shepherd had received Oedipus as an abandoned baby from a Theban shepherd, a retainer of the royal household. When Oedipus summoned the Theban shepherd, who was by a remarkable coincidence the only survivor of the retinue of King Laïus when he was murdered, Jocasta realized the truth. She rushed inside the palace to hang herself. But Oedipus persistently questioned the old shepherd until he learned the truth with his own ears, then rushed into the palace to kill Jocasta, but found her already dead. With the brooches from her dress he stabbed out his own eyes, then sadly went into exile, leaving the kingdom to Creon.

The myth of Oedipus spread all over the world, even as far East as India, Indonesia, and Sumatra, where in each case it was adapted to local heroes. A bold attempt has been made by Immanuel Velikovsky to trace Oedipus back to the Egyptian Pharaoh Ikhnaton. Velikovsky noted that Thebes, the capital city of the 18th Dynasty, was famous for its 100 gates, and Thebes in

Boeotia for its seven. The Sphinx was an important Egyptian as well as Theban symbol. Oedipus had deformed feet, and portraits of Ikhnaton indicate some malformation of his legs. Ikhnaton and his mother Tiy had an incestuous relationship. Finally there was a famous seer at the court of Ikhnaton, Amenhotep, who was later revered as a deified hero, patron of the blind. Hence, Velikovsky concluded, the Greek myth of Oedipus had its origins in the historic Ikhnaton and was adapted to Greek conditions.

The myth of Oedipus was more probably simply an amalgamation of a number of folktales and myths, combined into a meaningful unity by a Boeotian mythmaker. Indeed, all the themes, the exposure of a newborn infant posing a threat to parents, the saving and good fortune of an abandoned baby, the combat of the hero with a dangerous monster, the hero's marriage with a princess whom he has rescued, a power struggle between father and son, unintentional incest, the riddle of the meaning of man, the mutual recognition of long separated persons, can be found in other Greek myths.

The mythic explanation of blindness as divine punishment arose from actual ancient practice of imposing blinding as a penalty, especially upon war captives and for sex crimes, such as seduction, rape, and incest. The classical example of the blind prophet is the great seer of Thebes, Tiresias. Of the different accounts of how he became blind, one famous version involved the goddess Athena, who was a close friend of his mother Chariklo. One day when Athena was visiting Chariklo, Tiresias happened to come upon the two women bathing in the nude. For this sin he was blinded, but in compensation was given the gift of prophecy and the power to understand birds.

In another explanation of the blindness of Tiresias, we are told that one day he saw two snakes copulating. To look upon snakes at such a time was an age-old folk taboo, and in India it is still considered bad luck to see snakes mating. Tiresias disturbed the snakes, killing the female, and for this act was promptly transformed into a woman. Seven years later Tiresias again saw two snakes copulating, and this time he killed the male and as a result was turned back into a man. Shortly afterward, Zeus and Hera were disputing whether males or females received the greatest pleasure from sex, and summoned Tiresias to settle the matter because he had experienced life both as man and woman. Tiresias answered that women enjoyed sex many times more than men, and Hera was so outraged by this that she blinded Tiresias, but compensated him with the gift of prophecy and old age. Possessing this inner sight, he became the prophet of the god Apollo. His daughter Manto and his grandson Mopsus both became famous seers, and Homer tells that Tiresias retained his prophetic powers even in Hades after his death.

After Oedipus' departure from Thebes, his uncle Creon, brother of Jocasta, acted as regent until Oedipus' sons Eteocles and Polynices came of age. According to one version, when they were old enough to assume the royal power Oedipus, who had been wandering about in beggary and blindness accompanied only by his loyal daughter Antigone, requested that his sons permit him to return to his homeland, and when they rejected his plea Oedipus cursed them, predicting that they would one day kill each other. Eteocles and Polynices ruled jointly, each possessing full power in alternate years, but when it came Polynices' turn to rule, Eteocles seized complete power for himself and expelled his brother. The exiled Polynices was given asylum in Argos, where he married King Adrastus' daughter Argeia, determined nevertheless to avenge himself on his brother and regain his power. With the aid of his father-in-law Adrastus, he organized one of the great collective expeditions in Greek myth, the Seven Against Thebes — seven famous heroes, each of whom was to lead an army against one of the seven gates of Thebes. Besides Polynices and Adrastus, the seven included Amphiaraüs, Parthenopeus, Tydeus, Capaneus, and Hippomedon (or Mecisteus).

Among the Seven the figure of Amphiaraüs is a striking one. A prophet, married to Adrastus' sister Eriphyle, he had a son, Alcmaeon, who was to become famous. Eriphyle had somehow obtained the power to make all decisions for her husband Amphiaraüs, and made him the classical example of a pious, honest and brave man whose destruction was brought about by a greedy, ambitious wife. Because he knew that if he participated in the war against Thebes he would lose his life in battle, he concealed himself in a place known only to his wife, but Polynices bribed Eriphyle to produce Amphiaraüs with a precious object he had taken with him when he left Thebes — the famed necklace of

Harmonia. Thus she betrayed Amphiaraüs' hiding place, and he became one of the Seven. Another outstanding member of the Seven was Tydeus, a refugee from Calydon. Polynices and Tydeus at first disliked each other and fought a duel, but Adrastus reconciled them, and Tydeus married another daughter of Adrastus, Deipyle.

Before the famous battle for Thebes began, Polynices sought the blessing of Oedipus. Attended only by Antigone, classical exemplar of filial devotion, Oedipus was then in a place of asylum in Athens, in the district called Colonus. He had been driven from place to place, and could find no rest because of the taint of patricide and incest until he reached Athens, where the pious and kindly King Theseus received him. A new oracle had declared that whoever had Oedipus would win the royal power of Thebes, the reason why Polynices now solicited the aid of his father. But the old man angrily rejected his son's pleas, cursing him and Eteocles anew.

Before the actual attack on Thebes, an effort was made to decide the issue by a single combat of champions. To arrange this Tydeus risked his life on an embassy to Thebes, offered to act as champion for the Seven, won the duel, but was betrayed and almost killed. After this breach of proprieties the siege of Thebes began in earnest, next to the Trojan War the most celebrated in Greek mythology, based probably on an historical event. So desperate were the straits of Thebes that Tiresias declared the city could not be saved unless a Theban aristocrat, one of the unmarried Spartoi, gave up his life voluntarily to save all, a sacrifice of "one for many" frequently found as a theme in ancient myth. The gesture was made by Creon's son Menoecus, who killed himself before the walls to save Thebes.

But this did not come about at once. In the great final battle outside the gates of the city Eteocles and Polynices met in a duel and killed each other, fulfilling Oedipus' prophecy. Amphiaraüs also lost his life, as did all the other Seven except Adrastus, along with many of their followers. One of them, Capaneus, revealed his own arrogance by boasting as he tried to climb over the walls of Thebes, "No one can touch me, not even Zeus." For this *hybris* he was struck down by Zeus' thunderbolt, and later his wife Evadne threw herself to her death into his funeral pyre in a sacrifice for love. Tydeus was mortally wounded by the Theban Melanippus, but managed to kill Melanippus in a final effort. Before he died the head of Melanippus was brought to him, and he opened the skull and ate the brains. Such eating of human flesh (anthropophagy) was believed in some ancient cultures to transfer the power and qualities of the victim to his enemy, but brains were taboo in classical antiquity – they were not eaten and not even sacrificed to the gods – so Tydeus' act was a gruesome cannibalistic ritual alien to the Greeks. Argos and the Seven suffered an overwhelming defeat.

After the death of Eteocles and Polynices and the retreat of the enemy, Creon again became king. His first decree ordered that all who had fought against Thebes be denied burial, their corpses to lie uncared for, prey to dogs and vultures. In so doing Creon acted in the name of "law and order" and the need for discipline in the crisis of the city, but he was in fact violating age-old religious law, which ordained that all dead be given proper burial.

After the death of Oedipus, at Colonus, Antigone had returned to Thebes, where she was living when her two brothers Eteocles and Polynices died in battle. The edict of Creon forbidding burial to Polynices as a traitor fell like a thunderbolt on her. Just as her allegiance to her father had taken precedence over her personal happiness and love for her brothers, so now did her loyalty to Polynices take priority to her allegiance to the state. Despite the efforts of her sister Ismene to dissuade her, she was determined to perform the proper funeral rites for the body of her brother, in defiance of Creon's proclamation imposing the death penalty for burying the bodies of the Argive aggressors. Challenging Creon's right to issue such an order, she evaded the guard and succeeded in giving ceremonial burial to Polynices, and when she was arrested and brought before her uncle King Creon, she defiantly admitted her act, glorying in the righteousness of her decision. The conscience of the individual, claiming allegiance to a "higher law," here came into conflict with laws of the state for the defense of its security. The confrontation of Antigone and Creon is the classic portrayal of this age-old dilemma. Despite the family ties involved, Creon pitilessly ordered Antigone put to death, determined to establish respect for authority in a time of political chaos, and at the same time proud of his prerogatives as head of the state. But he did change the method of execution to burial alive in a chamber tomb, and moreover he took this extreme action against Antigone though his own son Haemon was engaged to marry her.

The young Haemon came to his father and in an impassioned plea urged him to rescind the order, declaring that the people were opposed to it. But Creon was inflexible, Haemon fled in fury from his father, and at this crisis the blind prophet of Thebes Tiresias arrived to warn Creon that the gods were opposed to his barbaric decree. Though at first angered at the prophet's advice, Creon finally relented. First he hastened to give proper burial to the corpse of Polynices, then rushed to the tomb to release Antigone. When he arrived he found that Antigone had hung herself in the tomb, and that Haemon was there holding her body in his arms. In a wild frenzy Haemon lunged at his father with his sword, but missed, then committed suicide to join his beloved in death. Creon's woes were not yet over, because his wife Eurydice also killed herself when she learned of the death of her son. All this happened on the first day of Creon's reign.

There is a later version of this myth which told that instead of entombing Antigone, Creon handed her over to her fiancé Haemon to be killed. But the lovers fled and had a child. Later, when Creon recognized the child and found the hiding place of Haemon and Antigone, he ordered them both put to death, but Dionysus interceded, and the lovers lived happily ever after. It is also told that when the Argive dead were left unburied at Creon's orders, the sole important survivor fled to Athens, and asked Theseus to intercede with regard to the burial of the dead. But despite diplomatic negotiations Creon was adamant, so Theseus went to war with Thebes and succeeded in having the Argive dead returned to their relatives for decent burial.

The Seven had left a legacy to their sons – renewal of war against Thebes – by imposing upon them the obligation to avenge their deaths. Amphiaraüs, in particular, forseeing his own death, had made his son Alcmaeon vow to take vengeance on all who caused his death. Thus ten years after the war of the Seven Against Thebes the sons of the Seven mobilized for war against their paternal enemy. Collectively the sons were called the *Epigoni* ("Afterborn"), and their names are usually given as: Alcmaeon and Amphilochus, sons of Amphiaraüs, Aegialeus, son of Adrastus;

Diomedes, son of Tydeus; Promachus, son of Parthenopaeus; Sthenelus, son of Capaneus; Thersander, son of Polynices; Euryalus, son of Mecisteus.

Though bound to avenge his father's death, Alcmaeon was reluctant to participate. Again it was Eriphyle who made the decision, urging her son to join the war. She had been bribed again, this time with the cloak of Harmonia, given her by Polynices' son Thersander. The part played by Eriphyle in the death of his father Amphiaraüs still rankled in Alcmaeon's mind, and after the *Epigoni* were victorious over Thebes Alcmaeon consulted the oracle of Apollo at Delphi, which ordered him to kill his mother in revenge for having sent her husband to his death. Alcmaeon's murder of his mother is the only matricide in Greek myth besides the famous slaying of Clytemnestra by Orestes, and like Orestes, Alcmaeon became insane, pursued by the Erinyes of his mother as he wandered about seeking purification for the murder of Eriphyle.

He was finally purified in Arcadia at the court of King Phegeus at Psophis, and received Phegeus' daughter Arsinoë in marriage. As a wedding present Alcmaeon gave Arsinoë the necklace and robe of Harmonia. The Erinyes were still not appeased, and the land of Psophis became sterile, so Alcmaeon fled. Then the oracle ordered him to seek purification once more, this time at the hands of the great river Acheloüs. After a second purification, Alcmaeon married Acheloüs' daughter Callirhoë, who, as a condition for the continuation of the marriage, demanded the necklace and robe of Harmonia. And so Alcmaeon returned to Psophis to try to obtain the deadly gifts. King Phegeus agreed to this when Alcmaeon declared it was necessary to dedicate them to Apollo at Delphi, but when the deceit was discovered, Phegeus ordered his sons to waylay and kill Alcmaeon. The fatal necklace was then dedicated to Apollo at Delphi. In historic times the necklace of Harmonia was shown by priests not only at Delphi but also in temples at Amathus and Delos.

The fall of Thebes and its sack at the hands of the victorious *Epigoni* was one of the most memorable events in the Greek folk memory, as the most important conflict between Greeks in the Heroic Age, eliminating the principal rival of Mycenae for hegemony over the Greeks in Hellas. One of the famous events during the flight of the Thebans was the death of the prophet Tiresias, who died after drinking from the spring Telphousa. His daughter Manto became a famous prophetess at Delphi, and her son Mopsus migrated to Asia Minor where he became a great seer and political leader.

XIX

MYTHS OF ARGOS:
Perseus

The northeastern part of the Peloponnesus was a focal point of early Greek culture, with the important centers of Mycenae, Tiryns, Corinth, and Argos, all of which produced famous cycles of myths. Argos, a center of worship of Hera, traced itself back to primeval times, claiming as its earliest overlord the local river god Inachus, son of the original waters Oceanus and Tethys. When the Olympian god Poseidon challenged Hera for possession of Argos, just as he contested the claim over Athens with Athena, Inachus was chosen as judge. When he preferred Hera, Poseidon in anger made the region arid, so that even the Inachus, the only important river of the region and the source of its fertility, became dry part of the year.

Among the children of Inachus, who was said also to have been first king of Argos, was the beautiful maiden called Io, who served as priestess to Hera. Presently, Zeus was attracted by her beauty, and when he sought her out, Hera's jealousy was aroused. As a result the innocent young girl was transformed into a white heifer, either by Zeus to disguise her or by Hera to control her. (Io often appears in artistic representations as a young woman with small horns.) Moreover, Hera created a monstrous creature to keep watch over her and spy on Zeus, the 100-eyed Argus, which Hermes promptly killed on Zeus' orders. Not discouraged by the death of her spy, ever watchful Hera then sent a gadfly to torment Io and to prevent her from ever finding a resting place, so the unhappy, tortured girl wandered aimlessly, stung by the gadfly. She roamed through parts of Europe (it is said that the Ionian Sea was so named because she crossed it), crossed over into Asia via the Bosporus (which means, literally, Cow-Ford), and somewhere in Asia saw and was comforted by another victim of Zeus, the Titan Prometheus, chained to a rock in the Caucasus Mts. Finally she passed into Egypt, where Zeus mercifully touched her with his hand, so that she became human again. The son of Io and Zeus, named Epaphus ("Touch"), had famous grandsons, Aegyptus and Danaüs.

An early connection between Egypt and Argos is obvious, for not only did the Argive girl Io settle in Egypt, but the cow-headed Egyptian goddess Isis was very early associated with her. Moreover, one of Io's descendants, Danaüs, migrated to Argos and became king there, as the result of a dispute between Danaüs and Aegyptus over the rule of Egypt. It happened that through his many wives Danaüs had 50 daughters, while his brother Aegyptus had 50 sons, and in accordance with the Egyptian custom of inbreeding, each of the 50 daughters of Danaüs (called the Danaïds) was to be married to one of the sons of Aegyptus. Later, when Aegyptus challenged his brother for the royal power, his sons aided him, and a battle ensued between the sons of Aegyptus and the Danaïds, who were well-armed and fought like warrior women. Danaüs and his daughters were defeated and fled by ship from Egypt, landing at Argos in Greece, where he was given asylum. By coincidence, when Danaüs arrived the local king died, and though a foreigner Danaüs was chosen king — a Greek version of a common folktale theme of the elevation of a stranger to replace a dead king.

When the Danaïds fled Egypt, the sons of Aegyptus soon took ship to Argos to claim their brides. The reason for the intense aversion of Danaüs and his daughters to these marriages is not clear, although a later Greek addition held that Danaüs had received an oracle that he would be killed by a son-in-law. Another version was that he desired vengeance for having been dethroned by Aegyptus. When his 50 nephews arrived Danaüs pretended to be reconciled to the marriages, but secretly ordered his daughters to kill their new husbands on the marriage night, supplying each with a knife with which to cut off their heads. All the Danaïds obeyed their father but Hypermnestra, who, in love with her new husband Lyncaeus, wept over him as he slept, and so awoke him. Then she told him the truth, and the pair fled to Egypt. The other

49 Danaïds who did kill their husbands were eternally punished in Hades by being compelled to fill with a sieve a jar with holes in it — dramatic symbol of their own unfulfillment. Eventually Lyncaeus returned from Egypt with an army, killed Danaüs and the 49 Danaïds to avenge his brothers, and succeeded to the throne of Argos. Thereafter the people were called Danaans instead of Pelasgians as before. So, according to myth, began the Heroic Age in Argos. Imbedded in this myth are the well-known folktale motifs of the woman used to seduce and destroy an enemy, and the theme that in a collective action in which all were supposed to act uniformly "all but one" follow through.

The grandsons of Lyncaeus and Hypermnestra were the twins Acrisius and Proetus. Intense enmity existed between them beginning even in the womb, and when Proetus succeeded to the throne of Argos, Acrisius drove out his brother, who fled to Lycia in Asia Minor and married Sthenoboea, daughter of King Iobates. Eventually Proetus recaptured his kingdom with the aid of the Lycians, and later extended his rule as far as Tiryns and Corinth. He is said to have brought back from Lycia seven Cyclopes who built for him the Cyclopean walls of Tiryns.

Proetus had three daughters by Sthenoboea; Lysippe, Iphinoë, and Iphianassa. The Proetids, as they are called collectively, became famous because of their opposition to the worship of the god Dionysus, for which they were driven insane and went about mooing like cows. At this point there appeared the famous prophet of Apollo, Melampus. It is said that when he was an infant asleep his ears were licked by snakes, and when he awoke he understood the speech of animals and birds. Melampus, in Proetus' plight about his daughters, offered to cure them in return for a part of the kingdom. When Proetus rejected the offer, Melampus pursued them. After the death of Iphinoë, Proetus accepted even harsher terms, and Melampus through drugs and religious purification cured the other two daughters. Then Melampus and his brother Bias married the daughters of Proetus.

Long before all this happened Proetus' tyrannical and hated twin brother Acrisius had been troubled by his lack of a son. He had only one daughter, Danaë, and when he consulted an oracle about the possibility of having a son, he received the terrifying message that he would be killed by his grandson. To prevent the birth of a grandson, Acrisius imprisoned his daughter Danaë in a bronze underground chamber, but, despite his precautions, Zeus entered the prison of Danaë as a shower of gold, and a son was born to Danaë, the famed hero Perseus. There is an alternative version that Danaë was seduced by her uncle Proetus.

Magical means of impregnation constitute a common motif in world folklore. There were widespread beliefs that sunlight, moonlight, rain, wind, bathing in a river, could cause pregnancy, and in the case of the golden rain of Zeus we may suppose that Zeus as rain god was originally conceived of as fertilizing a mother goddess, symbolical of the earth. In the Greek humanized form, Zeus as anthropomorphic god participated in the birth of a hero.

When the birth of the child was discovered, Acrisius placed mother and child in a box and exposed them in the sea. Thus began the career of Perseus, son of a god, in a typical myth of world mythology, in which the hero and his mother are placed in a floating chest. Trial by water appears to have been widely used in Near Eastern cultures in the case of illegitimate children and women suspected of adultery. If mother and child survived the ordeal it was taken as a sign of divine protection. Such was the case of Danaë and Perseus, for they reached the tiny island of Seriphos, one of the Cyclades islands in the Aegean Sea, where the box was caught in the net of the fisherman Dictys, brother of King Polydectes of Seriphos. After this, Danaë became in the myth a colorless figure, a passive mother image that Perseus sought to defend, as when he grew to manhood and King Polydectes fell in love with Danaë and wanted to make her his queen, Perseus vigorously objected. It should be noted that Polydectes' name means "Great Host," also a name of Hades, god of the Underworld, so that in the myth of Perseus we seem to have a hero who opposed "death" successfully. Polydectes, pretending he intended to marry another woman, asked of Perseus that he bring him as a wedding gift the head of the Gorgon Medusa.

With this exploit Perseus entered upon his role as hero, one of the most popular among the Greeks. He belonged to the generation before Heracles, was honored with him all over Greece, and in some places, such as Argos, ranked even higher than the Greek national hero. His name means "Destroyer," but he was more properly a life-giver and civilizer, achieving his victories

single-handedly, not with the help of a company of other Greek heroes, as in the case of Jason and the Argonauts.

The most famous myth of Perseus is his decapitation of the Gorgon Medusa, the sight of whom turned humans into stone. In order to discover the abode of the Gorgons (they were three sisters, of whom only Medusa was mortal) Perseus visited their hag-like sisters the three Graeae. By seizing their one eye and one tooth Perseus compelled them to reveal where the Gorgons lived. Then assisted by Athena and Hermes, Perseus approached the dangerous Medusa with an arsenal of aids: a hat with wings, winged sandals, the *kibisis* (a special wallet to store the head), the helmet of Hades to make him invisible, and a sickle-shaped *harpe* from Hephaestus. As Athena held up a mirror for him, so that he would not have to gaze directly upon the Gorgon, Perseus cut off her head and stored it away in the *kibisis*. In his flight the hero was hotly pursued by the two remaining Gorgon sisters, but he made himself invisible by putting on the helmet of Hades. As Medusa lay dying there sprang from her body twin creatures fathered by Poseidon, the winged horse Pegasus and the giant Chrysaor.

The return voyage of Perseus from the home of the Gorgons was a long and complex one, and formed a cluster of myths comparable to the labors of Heracles but not as systematically integrated. Perseus voyaged to the land of the Hyperboreans in the North, then to the land of the Cyclopes, from which he brought back a number of Cyclopes who aided him in the building of the Cyclopean walls of Mycenae later when he founded that famous city. Then he went to the region in northwest Africa where Atlas stood holding the heavens on his shoulders, and irked by a dispute with Atlas, Perseus showed the Titan the head of Medusa and transformed him into stone forever after as the Atlas Mts.

Perseus' most famous stopping-off place was Ethiopia (some versions localize the well-known rescue of Andromeda in Egypt or at Joppa in Palestine). When the queen of Ethiopia, Cassiopeia, wife of King Cepheus, had boasted that she herself (or her daughter Andromeda) was more beautiful than the Nereids, Poseidon, in punishment for this *hybris*, angrily sent the monster Cetus (probably a whale) to ravage the coast. To end this menace Cassiopeia and Cepheus were ordered to offer their lovely daughter Andromeda to be devoured by Cetus, so Andromeda was chained to rocks on a cliff (sometimes she was portrayed seated on a throne) and left for Cetus. Perseus arrived in the nick of time, killed the monster and rescued Andromeda, whom he married.

The Perseus-Andromeda rescue story is based on an ancient Near Eastern tale going back many centuries, in which the sea demands tribute to a sea dragon, and a hero overcomes the dragon — a sort of victory of man over the turbulent sea. In the story of Perseus' adventures the Near Eastern dragon became more like a whale. Since it is sometimes said that Andromeda was offered to Cetus at Joppa in Palestine, one might connect this with the story of Jonah and the whale in the Old Testament, since Jonah sailed from Joppa just before he was swallowed by the whale. Also imbedded in the Perseus-Andromeda story is the folktale motif of the hero rescuing a princess from danger and marrying her. The story was popular with the Greeks for another reason: Perseus as the savior who rescued Andromeda from certain death became a symbol of the hope for immortality. Later Andromeda became the constellation sometimes known as "The Chained Woman," near the constellations Cepheus, Cassiopeia, and Cetus.

Perseus is a paradoxical hero — both savior and destroyer. At the wedding of Perseus and Andromeda in Ethiopia her uncle Phineus, to whom she had been engaged, tried to disrupt the marriage, so Perseus promptly turned Phineus and his cohorts into stone by displaying to them Medusa's head. Thus Perseus used the head of the Gorgon, originally regarded as effective in driving away dangerous animals, for a new purpose, to control human beings, an interesting example of the transformation of a primitive symbol (the *gorgoneion*, Gorgon's mask) into a device against tyrannical men in urban society. When Perseus finally returned with the head of Medusa to Seriphus and found his mother Danaë and Dictys trying to escape from the clutches of the tyrant King Polydectes, he quickly turned Polydectes and his men into stone and installed Dictys as his successor to the throne of Seriphus.

Perseus then returned with his mother and wife to his birthplace Argos. When King Acrisius heard that his grandson had come back he fled, but shortly after, Perseus, while competing in an athletic contest in the kingdom where Acrisius was living, accidentally struck his grandfather with a discus and killed him, fulfilling the prediction of the oracle that Acrisius would be killed by a grandson. The head of Medusa was given as a gift to the goddess Athena, who placed it on her aegis. Perseus then left Argos to become king of Tiryns and eventually the founder of the famed city of Mycenae.

As we have seen in the myths of Dionysus, Perseus and Dionysus came into conflict. This was a local Argive myth which probably retained the memory of an historical conflict between defenders of the Olympian religion with its emphasis on civic order, against the introduction of the worship of Dionysus with its appeal to the individual's happiness.

Perseus was the ideal austere hero of the Argives — divinely sired, wise, pious, of heroic strength and spirit, with none of the frailties of such heroes as Heracles and Theseus. As a savior hero, he fought death, while at the same time he was a destroyer of evil forces injurious to men, a civilizer and city-builder. It is strange that this favorite of the gods did not become an immortal like Heracles.

XX

HERACLES

"My heart is held by the theme of Heracles," wrote the Greek poet Pindar, echoing the universal appeal among the Greeks of their hero *par excellence*. The best known Greek mythical personage, Heracles was the only truly national hero of the Greeks, embodying their traditions and ideals. So much was in fact told of him — from the cradle to the grave — that it would almost be possible to write a full-scale biography of Heracles. Indeed Plutarch did write a life of Heracles among his famous *Parallel Lives*, but unfortunately it has not survived. Whether in origin a primitive Greek god who was in time transformed into a mythical hero, or based on an historical person of the Mycenaean Age, the figure of this early panhellenic hero attracted like a magnet a host of myths and folktales not originally connected with him but eventually constituting a great mythic cycle of stories.

At the outset the name of Heracles embodies a paradox: it means "Glory of Hera," yet it was Hera's hostility to the famous son of Zeus that dogged him with suffering throughout his life. Hera's vengeful enmity began when Heracles was still in the womb of his mother Alcmena, the last of the mortal women loved by Zeus. A granddaughter of the Argive hero Perseus, Alcmena married her cousin Amphitryon, a son of the king of Tiryns and himself a grandson of Perseus. Their marriage took place at a time of turmoil in Tiryns that resulted in the death of Alcmena's brothers and the expulsion of Amphitryon and Alcmena from their native city. Because of this tragedy Alcmena did not allow Amphitryon to consummate the marriage until he avenged the killing of her brothers by the Taphians. The banished couple fled to Thebes in Boeotia. There Amphitryon obtained the aid of the Theban king in waging a successful punitive war against the Taphians, but in Amphitryon's absence amorous Zeus, smitten by the beauty and the virtue of Alcmena, succeeded one night in obtaining her love. Disguised as Amphitryon he came to her claiming that he had just returned from a battle in which he had fulfilled his sworn duty to avenge her brothers, and that same night the victorious Amphitryon himself returned and was also united with his wife. It is told that somehow Amphitryon discovered his wife's "adultery" and proceeded to impose the penalty of burning her alive on a funeral pyre, but Zeus mercifully intervened with a rain shower that saved Alcmena, and then reconciled Amphitryon to his "glorious misfortune."

In time Alcmena gave birth to twins – Heracles, son of Zeus, and Iphicles, son of Amphitryon. When Alcmena was on the point of being delivered of her twin offspring, Zeus prophesied that a descendant of Perseus about to be born would be ruler of Mycenae. Jealous Hera, in order to prevent Heracles from obtaining the throne of Mycenae, succeeded in delaying his birth long enough to permit the prior birth of Eurystheus, a cousin of Heracles and like him a great-grandson of Perseus. Thus it was through Hera's machinations that the colorless Eurystheus inherited the royal power of Mycenae, and that Zeus' glorious son Heracles became his vassal.

As soon as Heracles was born, Zeus, in order to instill divine strength in him, ordered Hermes to bring him to Olympus and give him Hera's breast to feed from as she slept. But so violent was his nursing that Hera awoke and brushed him away in anger, causing her milk to spill across the heavens to form the Milky Way. This incident merely inflamed her anger against Zeus' illegitimate son, but she bided her time, and when the baby was about eight months old she sent two snakes to destroy him in the cradle. Iphicles awoke and cried in terror, but Heracles seized the serpents in his bare hands and calmly strangled them, thus becoming a member of the "dragon slayer" club as an infant.

Though of Argive origin, Heracles was born in Thebes, which was the first city to attempt to appropriate Heracles as its own hero. Eventually the Thebans transformed him into their national hero, not only proclaiming him a native Theban, but using his myth for political propaganda to legitimize their territorial claims, as did other Greeks, such as the Dorians and Messenians, and even foreigners like the Macedonians. Heracles was brought up by his adoptive father Amphitryon, and received the typical aristocratic training in chariot racing, wrestling, use of bow and arrows, and playing the lyre. When he was still a youth, one of his gravest failings was revealed – an impetuous and violent nature that could erupt into homicidal tendencies, the imprint of primitive savagery in his nature. For example, when his music teacher, the famed Linus, corrected his playing of the lyre, Heracles in a fit of anger struck and killed him.

Thus at the age of eighteen Heracles' troubles began in earnest. As punishment for his first homicide he was sent by the king of Thebes to do penance as a shepherd on nearby Mt. Cithaeron, and there he had the opportunity to display his valor and incredible strength. Since the savage lion of Cithaeron was terrorizing the area, Heracles decided to capture and destroy the beast to protect his own flock and rid the area of this menace to orderly life. Equipped with a great club and his bow and arrows, Heracles stalked the lion and killed him single-handedly. A neighboring king, Thespius by name, so admired the young hero's strength that he desired grandsons by him from all of his fifty daughters, a feat the young Heracles accomplished in a short time, revealing another of his traits, in which he is matched in Greek myth only by Zeus – his unrestrained sexual appetite.

We have seen in the myths of Thebes how the youthful Heracles almost single-handedly freed Thebes from payment of tribute to the Minyans under King Erginus of Orchomenus. In gratitude the king of Thebes married Heracles to his daughter Megara. Despite his violent and gross nature Heracles was capable of a happy marriage, and he had three sons by Megara and was a devoted husband and father, although his unstable nature manifested itself from time to time. One day he suddenly went berserk, driven mad by Hera, and killed his entire family. Though the homicides were involuntary (according to one version, when he recovered his reason and discovered what he had done Heracles tried to commit suicide), the hero had to do penance again to be purified of his blood-guilt, and the oracle at Delphi ordered him to serve his cousin Eurystheus for a period of twelve years as atonement.

It is an old folktale motif that an inferior ruler often wields control over a greater man than himself, but in the end must acknowledge the greater worth of his vassal. So in the myths of Heracles his cousin Eurystheus as king of Mycenae imposed upon the great Heracles, now living in Tiryns, a series of seemingly impossible tasks – the famed Labors of Heracles. In their earliest form these labors were few in number, all localized in the Argolid and other parts of the Peloponnesus, and involved the opening up of a number of regions to civilized life through the elimination of terrifying and savage animals. In time, as the myth of Heracles expanded, additional labors outside Hellas proper were added, so that Heracles thus became a prodigious traveler, going south, north, east and west to accomplish various tasks. Eventually an artificial canonical cycle of twelve labors was constructed, although the preponderant emphasis on animal adversaries is evidence of the very early origin of many of the Twelve Labors. In these glorious exploits that took him all over the world Heracles was accompanied by his faithful squire and charioteer, his nephew Iolaüs, son of his twin half-brother Iphicles. It was in his Twelve Labors that Heracles especially exhibited his valor and prowess as athlete-hero, hunting and overcoming wild animals and the forces of death, and the canon gives the labors in a specific order:

1. *Nemean Lion.* In the northeast part of the Peloponnesus, near Nemea, a ferocious lion, brother of the Sphinx, ravaged the region undeterred because he was invulnerable to weapons. Heracles succeeded in trapping the lion in its den, which had two openings. He sealed off one with a huge rock, then entered the other, and choked the lion to death with his bare hands. Then he stripped off the tough hide of the lion and wore the skin thereafter as a cloak. The lion skin, his great club and bow and arrows were his principal attributes.

2. *Lernian Hydra.* The hydra was a many-headed water serpent in the Lernian swamp in the Argolid. Such a multiple-headed serpent, indicative of the difficulty of channeling and controlling rampaging rivers, was a traditional symbol in the Near East in Mesopotamia as early as 3000 B.C. The Lernian Hydra was usually

said to have had nine heads (sometimes 50 or 100). Heracles' task was extremely arduous, because one of the hydra's heads was immortal, and the other eight would each grow into two when cut off. Furthermore, a giant crab which came to the aid of the hydra had first to be destroyed (it was then raised to the heavens by Hera and made the constellation Cancer). Aided by Iolaüs, Heracles cut off each of the eight mortal heads and cauterized it with a burning stake. He buried the ninth, immortal one under an enormous rock. Having completed this task he dipped his arrows in the blood of the hydra, which was a deadly poison. The arrows of Heracles thus became dread weapons.

3. *Erymanthian Boar*. The hunting of wild boars was a favorite sport in antiquity, a feat to which Heracles was compelled to give his attention. In the wilds of Arcadia on Mt. Erymanthus a famous boar ravaged the area. Heracles was ordered by Eurystheus to bring it back alive. Skillfully he trapped it in deep snow, caught it in a net, and brought it back to Tiryns on his shoulders. He intended merely to show it to Eurystheus before releasing it, but the king was so terrified at seeing it that he leaped into a huge bronze jar he had prepared as a place of refuge, a hiding place he used whenever he feared danger.

4. *Cerynian Hind*. Sacred to Artemis, this unique animal was remarkable for its bronze hooves and golden horns, and was extraordinarily swift. Tracking it down in its dwelling place on Mt. Ceryneia in the northern Peloponnesus, Heracles pursued it through Arcadia, wounded it slightly, and then brought it back alive to show to Eurystheus (who leaped into his bronze jar), and then released it.

5. *Stymphalian Birds*. These were voracious, man-eating birds who lived in an impenetrable forest on the shores of Lake Stymphalus in Arcadia. Heracles succeeded in frightening them out of their hiding places in the forest with the noise of a great bronze rattle, then slew them easily with his poisoned arrows.

6. *Augean Stables*. King Augeas of Elis, in the northwestern part of the Peloponnesus, possessed a vast herd of cattle, which he kept

permanently enclosed in stables. As the result of Augeas' neglect the stables became filled with animal droppings, and Heracles was assigned the task of cleaning them. He demanded and was promised one-tenth of the cattle as his fee if he cleaned the stables in one day. This he quickly accomplished by diverting the rivers Alphaeus and Peneus through the stables.

7. *Cretan Bull.* In his first labor away from Hellas Heracles was ordered to bring back alive the famed bull of Minos (perhaps the very animal which Minos did not sacrifice to Poseidon). Single-handedly Heracles caught the animal, brought it back to show to Eurystheus, and then released it. The bull wandered, coming to rest near Marathon in Attica, where it was later mastered by the Athenian counterpart of Heracles, the hero Theseus.

8. *Thracian Horses of Diomedes.* These were four mares belonging to King Diomedes of Thrace, a region northeast of Hellas. They were fed human flesh by him. Heracles caught the horses and then fed King Diomedes to them, and thus taming them, brought them back to Greece.

9. *Girdle of the Amazon Hippolyte.* Eurystheus' daughter wanted the famed girdle of the Amazon queen Hippolyte, a military token of status, symbol of the power of the Amazon ruler. Ordered to obtain this, Heracles was forced into a great battle with the Amazons at Themiscyra, their city on the Thermodon River near the Black Sea in the northeastern part of Asia Minor. In the earliest version of this myth Heracles came to the land of the Amazons alone, accompanied only by his squire Iolaüs, killed the Amazon queen Hippolyte to obtain the girdle, and fought a violent battle with the other Amazons. However, in one version we are told that the queen of the Amazons was willing to give the girdle to Heracles voluntarily, but that Hera provoked the famed Amazonomachy by instigating the other Amazons to attack Heracles. In some artistic representations of this story we find the Amazon queen willingly offering the girdle to the great hero, and, although literary sources name the queen as Hippolyte, on Greek vase paintings the favorite opponent of Heracles was the Amazon named Andromache ("Battler of Men"). Though originally

Heracles fought the Amazons alone, later other Greek heroes were associated with him in this exploit, especially Theseus, Peleus, and Telamon.

10. *Cattle of Geryon*. Heracles then turned his attention to the far West, ordered by Eurystheus to bring back the enormous herd of cattle belonging to the monster Geryon, who lived on the island of Erythia in the stream of Oceanus that flowed around the earth. In travelling to the ends of the earth to reach Oceanus, Heracles crossed North Africa, where the sun's rays were so hot that Heracles in anger threatened to shoot his poisoned arrows at the sun god. Intimidated, the god Helios offered Heracles the use of a golden cup to enable him to sail across Oceanus to Erythia. Before embarking he is said to have erected two columns on either side of the Straits of Gibraltar, one at the rock Djebel Muse at Ceuta in North Africa, one at the rock of Gibraltar, thereafter called the Pillars of Heracles. They were symbols of the end of the world, beyond which there was no further land. There was said also to be a statue of a horseman there with an inscription warning *ne plus ultra*, "nothing more beyond." When he reached his destination of Erythia he was confronted with many problems. The cattle of the three-bodied monster Geryon were guarded by an enormous monstrous dog named Orthrus and by Geryon's fierce shepherd Eurytion. With his club Heracles killed the dog and the shepherd, with his arrows the monster Geryon, and sailed back to Europe on Helios' golden cup with the cattle, landing on the Iberian peninsula.

As usual in the case of mythic heroic voyages, the return trip was complex and long. Heracles herded the cattle through the entire western part of Europe before successfully bringing them to Greece, so many regions of the West — Spain, France, Sicily, especially Italy and the city of Rome — later sought to associate the passage of Heracles through their region with their own early legends. After many adventures in his long journey to Tiryns, Heracles returned with only part of the great herd, which Eurystheus ironically sacrificed to the tormentor of Heracles, the goddess Hera.

11. *Cerberus*. Many of Heracles' exploits may be interpreted as

triumphs of a mortal hero over death, none more so than his descent to Hades to capture the three-headed watchdog of the Underworld Cerberus. Guided by Hermes, he went down into Hades to accomplish his mission. There he met the soul of Meleager, and was so moved by the story of Meleager's death that he agreed to Meleager's wish that he marry his sister Dejanira. In Hades he saw, too, Theseus and Pirithoüs, who had been captured there while still alive when they came to abduct Persephone. With Persephone's permission Heracles was allowed to free and take back with him the Athenian hero Theseus, but Pirithoüs was denied this favor, remaining eternally alive among the dead. When Heracles came before King Hades and explained his mission he was permitted to attempt to master the dog Cerberus with his bare hands, not with his customary weapons, and succeeded, carrying Cerberus back to the upper world on his shoulders to show to Eurystheus (who again leaped in terror into his bronze jar). He then brought the dog back to Hades.

12. *Apples of the Hesperides.* The last labor of Heracles involved his obtaining the golden Apples of the Hesperides, symbols of immortality, which were on the tree of life in the Garden of the Gods located in North Africa, near the spot where Atlas held the heavens on his shoulders. This tree was guarded by three daughters of Atlas, the nymphs called Hesperides, and by a 100-headed dragon named Ladon. To obtain directions to the tree, Heracles sought the aid of Nereus, the old man of the sea. He seized him, and as usual Nereus resisted, changing his shape many times, but when Heracles nevertheless held on to him he gave the desired information. It was not, however, necessary for Heracles to go to the garden of the Hesperides personally or fight the dragon Ladon, for he was told to send Atlas for the apples. To free Atlas to go for them Heracles offered to support the heavens on his shoulders in Atlas' absence. Atlas easily obtained three golden apples, which were to serve Heracles as a sort of passport to immortality on Olympus, but refused to take up his burden of the heavens again, and offered to bring the apples himself to Eurystheus. Heracles, however, tricked the guileless Atlas into holding the heavens for a moment again while the hero placed a cushion on his shoulders. When the transfer to Atlas was made Heracles seized the golden

apples and ran off. In another version Heracles himself reached the garden to obtain the apples, killed the dragon Ladon, or put it to sleep with a sop. After showing the apples to Eurystheus, Heracles gave them to Athena who then restored them to the garden of the gods.

Though he had now earned the reward of immortality, Heracles was destined to an even higher glory — to be transformed into the "thirteenth" of the Olympian gods. But before that he was involved in many other exploits and adventures that clustered around his heroic figure, some side incidents connected with his Twelve Labors, others separate deeds. When Heracles was tracking the Erymanthian Boar he visited the kindly centaur Pholus, with tragic results for both Pholus and Chiron, and on another of his long journeys, when he passed the spot where Prometheus was chained he killed with one of his arrows the eagle that daily devoured the liver of Prometheus.

When he was in North Africa in connection with his labors, he was delayed in Egypt, according to a story which arose as a late invention, when the Greeks came into contact with the Egyptians in the Seventh Century B.C. During a famine in Egypt King Busiris (his name means "House of Osiris"), a son of Poseidon, ordered the annual sacrifice of a foreigner to ensure the fertility of Egypt. Heracles was captured for this sacrifice, and, though securely tied, burst out of his chains and killed Busiris and his sons. His progress across North Africa, while he was en route to obtain the Apples of the Hesperides, was halted again for a while by the Libyan Antaeus ("Opponent"), son of Poseidon and Gaea, a giant wrestler who derived his strength from his mother Earth. So long as he kept some part of his body in contact with Earth, he could not be defeated, but Heracles in combat with him succeeded in lifting him completely off the ground with one hand and strangling him with the other. Thus Heracles not only saved his own life but performed a civilizing service by removing this menace to travel in North Africa.

Troy was the scene of a famous side adventure connected with the great labors, when Heracles stopped there on his way home from his war with the Amazons in Asia Minor, and found the kingdom in mourning. Hesione, daughter of King Laomedon of Troy, had just been exposed on the sea coast as tribute to the sea monster Cetus sent by angry Poseidon because Laomedon had cheated Apollo and Poseidon of their wages when they helped him build the fortification walls of the city. An oracle had ordered Laomedon to offer his daughter Hesione to be devoured by the sea monster, so that the city might be delivered from the anger of the gods. When Heracles arrived, Laomedon promised to pay him to rescue Hesione; he would give him the divine horses once granted by Zeus to King Tros in exchange for his son Ganymedes, whom Zeus had elevated to Olympus as his cupbearer. Heracles rescued Hesione, chained to a rock like Andromeda, from the sea monster, and in one version actually leaped inside the jaws of the whale, like Jonah, and hacked it to pieces from within. But perfidious Laomedon once more betrayed a benefactor, refusing Heracles the promised reward. Heracles left Troy in anger threatening vengeance, and, indeed, after his servitude to Omphale in Lydia, he gathered an army against Troy and captured the city. He took Hesione captive, killed Laomedon and all his other children except Hesione's brother Podarces, who became the next king of Troy under the name Priam. Heracles gave Hesione to his friend Telamon as a gift, and the Trojan princess bore Telamon the famous Teucer, who was half-brother of the great Greek hero Ajax.

There were other military expeditions which Heracles undertook. A violent brigand named Cycnus, a son of Ares, maliciously intercepted and killed travelers, declaring that he planned to build a temple of skulls in honor of his father the god Ares, and when he held up pilgrims going on religious processions to Delphi Apollo ordered Heracles to destroy Cycnus. In the combat between the son of Zeus and the son of Ares, Heracles was victorious, and when Ares tried to intervene against Heracles to save Cycnus' life, Zeus commanded Ares to desist. Fighting also in the Peloponnesus, when King Augeas refused to pay him the agreed reward for cleaning the Augean Stables, Heracles gathered an army and marched on Elis. As his champions Augeas chose his nephews the twin Molionides, Erytus and Cteatus, said in various versions to be either a normal set of twins (sons of Molione and Poseidon, or Actor) or Siamese twins, with one body but two heads and four legs. In the battle with the Molionides Heracles and his troops were for once defeated, his brother Iphicles being mortally wounded, and for the first time Heracles was compelled to retreat.

Later, however, he ambushed the Molionides and killed them, and then attacked and seized the city of Elis. In honor of his great victory Heracles established the Olympic Games in Elis. After conquering Augeas, Heracles made war on Pylos, because King Neleus had on many occasions shown outright hostility to him, and in a spectacular duel with Neleus' eldest son Periclymenus, Heracles won another glorious victory. Then he seized Pylos and killed Neleus and all his other sons, nine in number, except the youngest, Nestor, who had befriended him.

In other famous exploits, related elsewhere in this volume, Heracles helped the gods in their war against the Giants, and restored Alcestis to life after doing battle with Death itself. He is even reputed to have conquered Old Age (Geras) in combat. So popular was the ubiquitous hero that his name was connected with the great adventures of Jason and the Golden Fleece, included by later mythographers among the 50 heroes who accompanied Jason on the ship Argo. But Heracles took only a brief part in this expedition, abandoning it because of the disappearance of his beloved Hylas.

For the Greeks, as for us too, the human qualities of Heracles made him into an attractive hero. Despite his divine origin and enormous strength, success did not always come easy to him — a reminder to the Greeks through the myth of Heracles of the hazards and obstacles in life even for the greatest humans. For example, Princess Iole, daughter of King Eurytus of Oechalia, had many suitors, but Eurytus subjected each one to a contest in archery with himself, and so prevented the marriage of his daughter. None had succeeded until Heracles arrived. Though he easily won the shooting contest with Eurytus, when he was denied the hand of Iole he left in anger, returned to his home in Tiryns, and later took revenge by killing Eurytus' son Iphitus by throwing him from the walls of the city. In remorse he consulted the oracle of Apollo at Delphi to find out how he might be purified of blood-guilt, and receiving no reply, he attempted to steal the sacred tripod on which the priestess of Apollo sat when she gave prophetic answers, presumably to set up his own oracle. Apollo appeared to do battle with Heracles for possession of the tripod, but Zeus intervened with a thunderbolt in this dispute between two of his sons, and restored the tripod to its rightful owner.

For this attempt to steal a sacred object Heracles was sold to Queen Omphale of Lydia in Asia Minor, whom he served as an obedient slave for at least a year. While the notion of the subordination of the male to the female was repugnant to the Greeks, they may have viewed Heracles' enslavement to a woman in a humorous light, although actually Omphale was probably originally a prehellenic mother goddess who had a young male consort in a subordinate role joined to her in "sacred marriage." While serving Omphale, Heracles was compelled to exchange his lion skin and club for her woman's garb, and while Omphale played at being Heracles, the hero spun wool and did other household chores. Although he was obedient and humble in this enforced role, he occasionally revealed his true nature and strength. On one occasion the woodland god Pan, attracted to Queen Omphale, came to visit her at night, and mistaking the figure in woman's clothing for Omphale, Pan made amorous advances and received a beating from Heracles. And during his stay with Omphale, the Cercopes ("Ape Men") sought to capture Heracles in his subdued condition, but he quickly mastered the Cercopes, tied them by their feet to a pole and carried them about upside down, to the amusement of all.

When his servitude to Omphale was finished, he decided to marry again, remembering that when he was in Hades he had promised the dead hero Meleager that he would marry his sister Dejanira. Like Meleager, she was the child of the famed King Oeneus and Queen Althaea of Calydon and eminently suited to be Heracles' bride, for she was an athletic maiden and a vigorous personality (her name means "Hostile to Men"). Dejanira had been courted by the river god Acheloüs, but she rejected him. To win Dejanira from this suitor Heracles was compelled to engage in one of the most dangerous battles of his career, with the god of waters, Acheloüs, who transformed himself into many different shapes during the struggle with the hero. Finally Heracles destroyed his power by breaking off one of his horns when he took the shape of a bull.

The well-matched pair Heracles and Dejanira eventually had five children, of whom the oldest was their famous son Hyllus. Since Heracles was restless, Dejanira often accompanied him on his travels, and once as they came to a river Heracles quickly crossed to the other side, having arranged with a centaur named Nessus to carry Dejanira over on his back. But Nessus, true to his centaur's bestial and violent nature, attempted to abduct Dejanira for himself. Quick punishment followed. In some versions Heracles dispatched him with his club, but in the most common story he struck him from across the river with his arrows poisoned by the Lernian hydra. As Nessus lay dying he planned revenge on Heracles, confiding to Dejanira that his blood, which was in reality poison, had the efficacy of a love charm. Since Heracles was notoriously fickle, she could win back his love with the aid of Nessus' blood, so Dejanira dipped a robe in it. Somehow a well-known folktale theme of the "poisoned garment," the perfidious gift sent to an unsuspecting rival, was incorporated into the myths of Heracles.

The fate of Heracles, the victor over so many awesome dangers, evils, and opponents, even death itself, was now in the hands of a woman, his own wife. Years later he was unwittingly destroyed by Dejanira when he decided to complete some unfinished business — to punish King Eurytus for denying him the hand of Iole, whom he had won fairly in a shooting contest. Invading Oechalia, he killed Eurytus and seized Iole as his concubine. When the news that Heracles was bringing back Iole reached Dejanira, she remembered Nessus' robe, which she confidently believed would serve as a love charm, and sent it by messenger as a gift to Heracles while he was en route home. As soon as he put it on, the fatal poison began to destroy his body. Realizing with horror and remorse what a mistake she had made, Dejanira committed suicide.

Knowing that he was dying, the hero Heracles in his final agony struggled up to the summit of Mt. Oeta in Trachis in central Greece and there painstakingly built his own funeral pyre. When the pyre was erected, Heracles could at first find no one willing to put the torch to it, so great was the awe felt for the great hero. Finally the hero Philoctetes agreed to do so in exchange for the gift of Heracles' bow and arrows — weapons which were later to be declared indispensable for the capture of Troy.

The funeral pyre of Heracles on Mt. Oeta in the myth originated in an annual fire festival involving sacred bonfires held in many parts of Greece, and the remains of the sacred area on top of Mt. Oeta where the local fire festival was conducted have actually been found. It was the practice in this ancient fire ceremony to throw many offerings into the bonfire, including animals and effigies of humans, and the use of such human dummies may have been a survival of a primitive fire rite that commemorated the annual death of a god in divine fire. Out of this fire ritual developed the myth of the fire death and deification of Heracles.

Miraculous occurrences attended the immolation of Heracles. After his fire death no bones were found among the ashes, so thereafter no one ever claimed to possess relics of his body as people claimed for other heroes, and no tomb was ever erected for him. In short, Heracles was deemed to have been transformed into a god, rising to Olympus to join the immortal gods, liberated by fire from the earth and taken to Olympus in a chariot drawn by fiery horses. (The fiery chariot carrying the chosen to heaven was a Near Eastern theme, embodied in the Old Testament in the ascent of the prophet Elijah to heaven.) Thus occurred the apotheosis of the hero Heracles – the earliest instance in Greek tradition of a mortal who achieved divinity through suffering, toil, and sacrifices for humanity. This Greek myth is extraordinary, because all other heroes attained an eternal happy life in the Isles of the Blest in the Far West or in the Elysian Fields in Hades, and only Heracles among Greek heroes attained divinity on Olympus. The figure of Heracles may have originated in a primitive Hellenic divinity, but to the Greeks he merited veneration as a glorious human being who, despite his failings and errors, became a god. Accepted on Olympus, even by Hera, Heracles was married to Hebe, daughter of the king and queen of the gods.

A precursor of the Christian saints, Heracles was to become a powerful rival to Christ for the allegiance of the peoples of the ancient world, who worshipped him as savior god and divine son of Zeus. On a Greek house at Thasos there was the following inscription: "Heracles lives here; let no evil enter." The early Christians could not have failed to be impressed by many aspects of Heracles' career: the sufferings and dangers attendant on the birth of a fateful child, the mysterious birth of a child born not from the mother's husband, Heracles' deeds as wonder worker and savior, his journey to hell and heaven, his victory over death and his elevation to heaven, the absence of all relics after the ascension, the winning of immortality and divinity for his mother. Alcmena was at first said to have been taken to the Isles of the Blest, but in a later version she joined Heracles on Mt. Olympus.

The myths and worship of Heracles spread all over the known world of antiquity, both to the West, especially in Italy where the figure of Hercules, as the Romans called him, was especially important in Roman tradition, and even to the Far East. As early as 500 B.C. the figure of Heracles was mentioned in China, and in the Second Century B.C. the Chinese writer Huai-non-tze told the story of the "Deeds of the Archer I," who killed a serpent (in the Greek version this would be the Lernian hydra), battled winds (Heracles fought the Boreades), shot heavenly birds (Heracles' labor of the Stymphalian Birds), shot arrows at the sun, captured a great swine, and obtained the plant of immortality from the Queen Mother of the West (the Apples of the Hesperides).

The myths of Heracles, which may have received their initial impulse from the Babylonian hero Gilgamesh whom Heracles resembles in many ways, developed over a long period of time, reflecting the values of different ages. First known as a hero of the Mycenaean Age, pre-urban and endowed with aspects of primitive savagery, in his earliest myths he was depicted as a man of superhuman strength, achieving his triumphs not by brains or diplomacy but by brute force in victories over monsters, savage animals, giants, and in wars and conquests. His early image was that of a rather simple, even good natured man, but fallible and with grave faults and vices, such as anger, fits of violence, blundering, and excessive addiction to drinking, gluttony, and sex. In the difficult adaptation of such a primitive culture hero to Greek urban civilization, eventually Heracles acquired softer traits, and developed interests and skills, for example, in music, medicine, and prophecy. Beginning as a hero-athlete (hunter, warrior, competitor in athletic contests) performing feats of brute strength and valor, he later became a civilizing hero, the benefactor and savior of mankind. In this new aspect he confronted death in various guises and conquered it, thus enlarging man's life and achieving immortality for himself. As benefactor he not only rid the world of many evils but also conquered Geras (Old Age) and Thanatos (Death), and was even the benefactor of the gods, who needed his aid to defeat the Giants.

As civilizer and benefactor of man, he was said in some versions to have been the first hero to restore the bodies of the dead in battle for burial under the truce (the Athenians claimed this for their national hero Theseus). Yet even later when he became the suffering, much enduring hero, he retained his earlier gross qualities, closest to Zeus in sexuality, a promiscuous, prolific male "sexual athlete," with many women, numerous children, and even one male lover. With a highly charged emotional makeup, he was dangerous to thwart and homicidal, although he sometimes played the role of stupid, good-natured buffoon, relishing the grossness of his own behavior. Nevertheless, in another side to his personality that appealed to more thoughtful Greeks he was usually quick to acknowledge his own wrongdoing, genuinely felt sorrow and repented of his violence, seeking absolution and purification through atonement. In his many brushes with death he ran mortal risks and suffered for others, with saint-like dedication, an aspect of his nature illustrated in the Fifth Century B.C. by the Sophist Prodicus' famous parable of "The Choice of Heracles." When as a young man Heracles was troubled as to which path he should take as life's guide, two women appeared to him, one named Virtue, the other Pleasure. After both presented their arguments on behalf of the best path to follow, Heracles chose the path of Virtue.

Many Greek cities adopted Heracles as hero and civilizer, and established forms of worship for him. The heroes Theseus of Athens and Perseus of Argos were modelled upon his figure. In the Middle Ages he survived among the Christians as an allegory of a hero who purged the world of evils, compared with Samson, David, St. George, even Christ. He remains to this day a charismatic figure that still inspires many writers and artists.

So powerful was the image of Heracles that it had historical importance in the political affairs of the Greeks. It was particularly in the Peloponnesus that this Mycenaean hero was transformed into a Dorian hero of that region, and the history of the Peloponnesus was connected to the activities of his family and children. After Heracles' death, Alcmena and her other children were persecuted by King Eurystheus of Mycenae, but she was able to bring about Eurystheus' death, and in an outburst of hatred requested that his head be brought to her, whereupon she tore out his eyes. Heracles had numerous children – at least 70 and mostly sons – by at least 62 women, including the 50 daughters of Thespius. His sons and descendants, called the Heraclids, were also persecuted by Eurystheus, and fled to Athens for asylum. Later, seeking to regain their inheritance, they invaded the Peloponnesus and were restored, but when a plague broke out, and the Delphic oracle was consulted, the Heraclids were advised to leave the Peloponnesus and return "after the third harvest." Three years later they invaded the Peloponnesus but were defeated, and Heracles' eldest son Hyllus was killed. The oracular pronouncement was reinterpretated to mean "after the third generation," that is, 100 years later. A third attempt at reconquest of the Peloponnesus succeeded a century later, accomplishing the "Return of the Heraclids," considered by the Greeks to be the end of the Heroic Age. In this way the Dorians transformed Heracles into their national hero, and used myths as historical precedents to legitimize Dorian possession of the Peloponnesus by claiming Heracles as their ancestor. Thus in the wars between Sparta and Messenia, both sides asserted historical authority for the possession of their areas by claiming ancestry from the Heraclids.

In later ages King Philip of Macedon, though not a Greek, claimed Heracles as his ancestor to legitimize his intervention in Greece and to facilitate his acceptance by Greeks in their internal affairs. Similarly, many Hellenistic royal families traced their lineage back to the great hero Heracles, just as the Romans claimed descent from the Trojan prince Aeneas and other Trojan families. As the symbol of service to humanity and savior, Heracles was associated with themselves as a matter of policy by many later historical figures, like Alexander the Great, Julius Caesar, and the Emperor Augustus.

XXI

THE HOUSE OF ATREUS

No myth has offered so much material to writers of tragedy than the family line beginning with Tantalus and reaching its final climactic suffering three generations later in the tortured figure of Orestes. Tantalus, powerful king of Lydia in Asia Minor, was as proverbial for his wealth as the historic Lydian king Croesus. A son of Zeus, he was beloved of the gods, and among his blessings was his marriage with one of the Pleiades, Dione, by whom he had his famous children Pelops and Niobe. But all this eminence turned his head, and he committed the sin of *hybris,* becoming a "scorner of the gods." When invited to banquet with the gods on Mt. Olympus, he stole some ambrosia and nectar, which he proceeded to give to some of his mortal friends. Moreover, he had an uncontrollable tongue and revealed divine secrets to mortals. Then he stole a dog sacred to Zeus and perjured himself by glibly asserting that he had never seen it.

Finally, Tantalus committed the ultimate of crimes: he invited the gods to a banquet and to test their omniscience killed his son Pelops and fed his flesh to them, in a kind of human sacrifice. But the gods detected the human flesh and were not deceived, except that Demeter, distracted by the loss of her daughter Persephone, consumed her share, which turned out to be the shoulder of Pelops. The gods at once restored Pelops to life, fitting the dismembered parts together, and replaced the missing shoulder with an ivory one, which later became a famous sacred relic. Tantalus' punishment for his many crimes was exemplary. Originally he was said to have been punished in this world on Mt. Sipylus where he lived, a huge rock permanently suspended over his head about to fall at any moment, but in later tradition he became the most famous sinner punished in Hades, stationed in a lake in Tartarus with an eternal craving for food and water. Above his head was a fruit tree, which always eluded his grasp when he reached for the fruit, and water receded from his lips when he sought to drink.

In Greek myths scorners of the gods like Tantalus were always visited with heavy punishments, ranging from humiliation to violent death. In the most gruesome death the sinner was torn limb from limb, as in the cases of Pentheus and Lycurgus for scorning Dionysus; in other cases blindness or madness was the punishment, or a horrible sickness, like a slow wasting away to death. A common penalty, when the sinner himself escaped retribution, was the destruction of his immediate family, or a curse that pursued all his descendants to the last generation. This family curse, originating in a time when individual responsibility for crimes and wrongs did not yet exist, is especially common in Greek mythology, notably among the descendants of Tantalus.

We have already seen the pitiful fate of Tantalus' daughter Niobe, who married the Greek king Amphion of Thebes and lost all of her fourteen children. The restored Pelops rose to great heights as a king of part of Greece, but through his ambition for power committed murders that left a legacy of woe for his descendants. Pelops left his father's kingdom in Asia Minor, taking with him a group of followers and great riches, and some believe that he was an historic person, an invader of Greece from Asia Minor who conquered part of the Peloponnesus (this name means "Island of Pelops"). In any case he was a symbol of luxury of the East introduced into the Mycenaean Age.

When he cast about to make a royal match for himself in Greece he decided on beautiful Hippodamia, daughter of Oenomaüs, king of Pisa in Elis, in the northwestern part of the Peloponnesus. But there were enormous difficulties in winning her hand, for Oenomaüs was determined to prevent the marriage of lovely Hippodamia. Some sources hint that he had an incestuous passion for his own daughter, although most state that an oracle had warned him that he would be killed by a son-in-law. To prevent Hippodamia from marrying, Oenomaüs, who possessed divine horses given him by Poseidon, had established a deadly

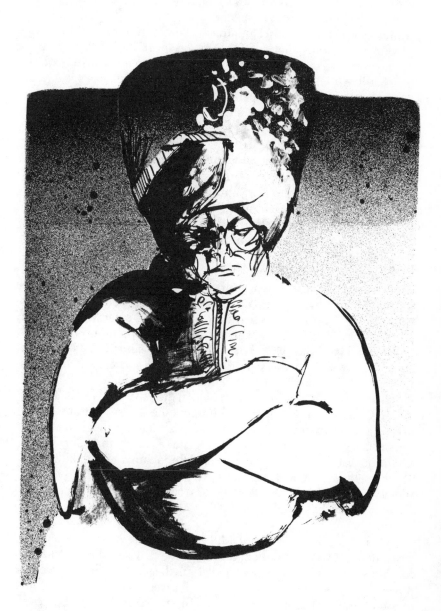

contest between himself and all suitors for her hand, a chariot race in which the suitor was given a head start in the direction of the Isthmus of Corinth toward an altar of Poseidon, then was pursued by Oenomaüs on his chariot with a magic spear.

Before Pelops arrived, there had already been a dozen or so suitors, all of whom had been killed by Oenomaüs' spear and whose heads decorated his palace conspicuously. But Hippodamia had fallen in love at first sight with this handsome, wealthy Asiatic, and, determined to save Pelops' life, enlisted the aid of Oenomaüs' charioteer, Myrtilus, a son of Hermes, who was hopelessly in love with Hippodamia. Promised favors by Hippodamia as well as half of Oenomaüs' kingdom, Myrtilus agreed to sabotage Oenomaüs' chariot, and substituted wax for the lynchpins of the axles. Oenomaüs was killed when his chariot overturned even before Pelops became his son-in-law. It is said that Pelops' victory was the origin of the contest of chariots at the Olympic Games.

Pelops and Hippodamia fled, taking the charioteer Myrtilus with them. En route, when Myrtilus tried to violate Hippodamia (or demanded his reward of half the kingdom), Pelops killed him by throwing him into the sea, thereafter called after him Myrtoan Sea. Before dying Myrtilus cursed Pelops and his family. It is said that Myrtilus, who was both sinner and sinned against, was transformed into the constellation Auriga (Charioteer). Pelops was purified of his crimes by Poseidon, became king of Elis, and conquered the Peloponnesus, to which he gave his name. Pelops and Hippodamia had many children, the most famous being Atreus and Thyestes, although Pelops also had an illegitimate son named Chrysippus, who was his favorite. Fearing that Chrysippus would succeed to the royal power, Hippodamia either killed the boy herself or egged on her sons Atreus and Thyestes to kill him, and when he discovered this, Pelops cursed his sons Atreus and Thyestes and banished them. Hippodamia fled and committed suicide.

Then King Eurystheus of Mycenae, the last of the immediate descendants of Perseus, died, and an oracle advised the inhabitants to choose as their king a son of Pelops, beginning the dispute for power between Atreus and Thyestes, between whom there already existed intense hatred and rivalry. In the struggle for the royal power of Mycenae there was much maneuvering, deception, many crimes and retaliations between the brothers, whose conflicts represent a classic example of sibling rivalry. Atreus had found what he believed to be a trump card when he discovered in his flock a golden ram, whose fleece he had kept as the embodiment of the symbol of kingship. Accordingly Atreus announced that the royal power over Mycenae would go to the one who possessed the fleece of the golden ram, and Thyestes promptly agreed, for he had already succeeded in obtaining it from Atreus' wife Aërope, whom he had seduced. Atreus countered by issuing another challenge: he would become king instead of Thyestes if the sun would reverse its usual course that day. Zeus was so angry at Thyestes' crimes that he intervened and arranged for the sun to set in the East that day. Thus Atreus became king of Mycenae, and for his own security banished Thyestes from the kingdom.

Later, after Atreus discovered the adultery of his wife with Thyestes, to get revenge he recalled Thyestes and invited him to a banquet of reconciliation. In this famous "Thyestean Banquet" Atreus fed his brother the bodies of Thyestes' three sons, whom Atreus had killed for that purpose, then showed Thyestes the heads and hands of his sons and expelled him again from the kingdom. Aërope was put to death. Thyestes harbored implacable hatred toward his brother, but could not return to Mycenae, and he had lost all his sons, one of whom might have been the tool of vengeance. Years later he heard from an oracle that he would get his revenge if he had a son by his daughter Pelopia, and undeterred by the taboo against incest, he impregnated his own daughter, who fled in shame, taking Thyestes' sword with her. Shortly after, Atreus met her, and not knowing her identity, married her. When she had a son, named Aegisthus, he assumed it was his own son and brought him up, grooming him as a tool of vengeance against his brother Thyestes.

When Aegisthus was grown Atreus sent him to kill Thyestes, but the plot came to naught when Thyestes recognized his own sword in the hands of Aegisthus. Then Aegisthus, together with Thyestes, returned to Mycenae, killed Atreus, and ruled over the kingdom. The miserable Pelopia killed herself with Thyestes' sword. Atreus' two sons, Agamemnon and Menelaüs, escaped with their lives, going to Sparta, where they were given asylum by King

Tyndareus. Menelaüs became the successful suitor for the hand of beautiful Helen and king of Sparta succeeding his father-in-law, while Agamemnon, the other grandson of Pelops, married Clytemnestra, another daughter of Tyndareus, who helped restore him to the throne of Mycenae, driving out Thyestes and Aegisthus. Thyestes died in exile; Aegisthus plotted revenge.

King Tyndareus of Sparta was married to Leda, who, after being impregnated by Zeus in the form of a swan, had, according to the usual version, two sets of twins: Helen and Polydeuces by Zeus, Clytemnestra and Castor by her husband Tyndareus. In one version Leda gave birth to two eggs out of which hatched the four children. Less traditional is the version that Helen was actually the daughter of Zeus and the goddess Nemesis, who fled the amorous attentions of Zeus and changed herself into a goose. When Zeus pursued and united with her in the form of a swan, Nemesis laid an egg, which was found by a shepherd and brought to Leda. When it hatched and Helen was born, Leda claimed the child as her own.

Because Tyndareus had no male heirs, he left the royal power of Sparta to Helen, the most beautiful woman in the world, and to her husband, Atreus' son Menelaüs. For the Greeks Helen was the pre-eminent symbol of beauty, and she has remained this ever since, perhaps because she was flawed by moral defects (adultery, theft of property, and opportunism), so that the conflict between her beauty and her morals has remained an intriguing theme throughout the pages of world literature. Originally Helen was a prehellenic fertility goddess, perhaps of the Cretan religion, somewhat like Persephone and Ariadne, for, like these prehellenic goddesses, Helen was abducted and raped in the manner reminiscent of fertility rites involving the death and return of vegetation.

Helen is indeed a true example of a faded goddess, transformed by the Mycenaeans from a vegetation divinity to a princess seized by a prince. In this rationalization of the primitive ritual Helen became the "beautiful evil" of Greek myth. Abducted twice, the first time by Theseus, as we have seen, later by the Trojan prince Paris, her elopement with Paris is a famous part of the Trojan War story. Reminiscent of the vegetation goddess origins of Helen is a version of her story that she was eventually abandoned by Menelaüs (as Theseus abandoned Ariadne), and in some parts of Greece, especially at Sparta, she remained an important divinity in the local cults. Because of her divine origins some felt it necessary to save her innocence and honor in connection with the mythic abductions, a rehabilitation which created one version of the story, that Helen never went to Troy, but that Paris took with him to Troy a phantom which Zeus created, and that the real Helen was hidden away in Egypt, completely innocent, during the entire Trojan War.

The marriage of Menelaüs and Helen was one of the celebrated marriages of mythology. Because of her extraordinary beauty Helen had a large number of suitors, of whom more than 30 are known by name. Fearful that no matter which suitor was chosen, the others, who included many of the famous Greek heroes, would later stir up trouble, Tyndareus was convinced by Odysseus, one of the suitors, to require in advance that all her suitors swear a sacred oath to protect her marriage. Tyndareus' choice was the handsome but colorless Menelaüs, and by him Helen had one daughter, Hermione.

Menelaüs' older brother Agamemnon also became Tyndareus' son-in-law, marrying Helen's half-sister Clytemnestra, but this marriage too was destined to be an unhappy one. At the very start, in order to marry Clytemnestra Agamemnon had to kill her first husband and their newborn child. Tyndareus then restored him to the throne of Mycenae and he became the most powerful king of the time. Clytemnestra and Agamemnon had four children, Iphigenia (or Iphianassa), Chrysothemis, Electra, and Orestes.

About ten years after these marriages and the assumption of royal power by both Menelaüs and Agamemnon, Helen left Menelaüs and ran off with a Trojan prince Paris. Menelaüs had previously been a guest in the palace at Troy, so that when Paris returned the visit to Sparta as a royal guest in the international protocol of the times, no one suspected that Paris had come intending to seduce Helen. Previously, Paris had been promised by Aphrodite the most beautiful woman in the world. When Menelaüs left Sparta on a visit of state to Crete, Paris and Helen ran off together, taking a large amount of Menelaüs' royal treasure with them, and began their tainted marriage, which was to bring woe to thousands, and culminate in the destruction of Troy.

When Menelaüs discovered the adultery of his wife and the loss of his property, he demanded that the oath to protect his marriage be honored. So former suitors of Helen assembled, and mobilized their contingents from among their separate peoples in Greece for an assault on Troy to win back Menelaüs' wife Helen and his treasures, and to take vengeance on all the Trojans for harboring the adulterous Helen and the sinner Paris. The Greek forces mustered at Aulis, a harbor on the east coast of Greece, and their ships — over a thousand — were readied for this great panhellenic enterprise against an Asiatic city. The commander of the entire expedition was Menelaüs' brother, King Agamemnon of Mycenae.

When the fleet was ready to sail an ominous calm suddenly fell over the sea. Since the ships could not sail, Agamemnon consulted the official prophet of the Greek forces, Calchas, who revealed that the goddess Artemis was angry and that the winds would not blow again until Agamemnon sacrificed his daughter Iphigenia to appease the goddess. Various reasons are given for this: that Agamemnon had made an imprudent vow that he would offer to the gods either his first child or the most beautiful thing born that year; or that while hunting at Aulis he had committed an impious act by killing a deer sacred to Artemis; or that he had boasted that he was a better hunter than Artemis. To bring the unsuspecting Iphigenia, the first born of his children and fairest of his daughters, to Aulis for this sacrifice, and to deceive her mother Clytemnestra about the reason, Agamemnon announced that she was to be married to Achilles before they sailed, as a reward for his joining the expedition. So Iphigenia was escorted to Aulis in her bridal gown and sacrificed on an altar by Agamemnon. Then the winds blew again. For this sacrifice of Iphigenia — the second of her children to be killed by Agamemnon — Clytemnestra never forgave her husband.

Originally the story of Iphigenia was a mixture of cult myth and folktale unconnected with Agamemnon. Indeed, Iphigenia (whose name means "she who causes the birth of strong offspring") was in origin a fertility divinity like Artemis, perhaps even a form of Artemis herself. As part of her cult maidens were consecrated, often in the form of animals dressed in girl's clothing and sacrificed, a ritual which probably preserves a survival of human sacrifice. In other cult myths the killing of a sacred animal was followed by punishment, such as plague, sent by a divinity, which could be appeased by a sacrifice made in accordance with orders of an oracle. There was still another cult practice – that of a "one for many" sacrifice of consecration for the success of an important venture, which in primitive times sometimes required the sacrifice of a relative of the leader. All these strands somehow became associated with the myth of Agamemnon and the Trojan War, and in the course of this Iphigenia was transformed from a divinity to a princess, herself the sacrificial victim.

In the case of Iphigenia, it is said that the goddess Artemis was satisfied with a substitute and that, without the knowledge of any of the participants but Iphigenia, she substituted an animal, thus signalizing the end of the cruel practice of human sacrifice. Some versions say that Artemis made Iphigenia immortal and that she later married Achilles and lived with him after the Trojan War on the blessed island of Leuce. In the usual version Iphigenia was whisked away by Artemis to the land of the Taurians (in the Crimea in South Russia), where she became priestess of their national temple, which contained a statue of Artemis to which the Taurians were accustomed to sacrifice all foreigners they caught in their land. It became Iphigenia's sworn duty to consecrate these victims for sacrifice to the goddess.

After the Greek fleet sailed from Aulis and landed on the shores of Troyland, the Greeks were away from home for ten years, tied down by the long siege of Troy. In the absence of Agamemnon from Mycenae, Aegisthus returned in secret seeking revenge, and succeeded in seducing Clytemnestra. The much sinned-against Clytemnestra was transformed through her hatred of Agamemnon into a "ruthless woman," as the Greek poet Pindar called her, the famed symbol in Greek literature of the adulteress and murderess of her husband, the epitome of evil in womanhood just as Odysseus' wife Penelope was the paragon of fidelity. Together with Aegisthus Clytemnestra plotted to murder Agamemnon and seize the kingdom, and meanwhile sent away the only son of Agamemnon and Clytemnestra to live in Phocis in central Greece with his uncle Strophius.

When Troy fell after ten years, Agamemnon returned to Mycenae as a conquering hero, bringing with him as part of his share of the war booty a princess of Troy, Cassandra, daughter of King Priam. Agamemnon taking her as his concubine served to inflame further Clytemnestra's hatred for her husband. Cassandra possessed the gift of prophecy, and as she stood before the palace she predicted that Agamemnon and herself were about to be murdered, but as always, no one believed her. Thus Agamemnon, fulsomely welcomed by his faithless and treacherous wife, confidently entering his palace as a conquering hero, shortly after was murdered while taking a bath (or at a banquet). In the usual version Clytemnestra herself wielded an axe to kill her husband, then killed the innocent Cassandra over his corpse. Aegisthus now revealed himself as Clytemnestra's accomplice, and the two seized power and ruled the kingdom tyrannically to suppress criticism of their act.

Of the children of Agamemnon who remained in Mycenae, Chrysothemis for the sake of survival and security accepted the situation, even though she was forbidden to marry, since Aegisthus feared that a grandson of Agamemnon might some day seek vengeance. But Electra, also forbidden to marry, suffered great indignities at the hands of Aegisthus and Clytemnestra because she did not disguise or keep secret her intense, almost pathological hatred of Aegisthus and Clytemnestra. Her love of her father and her hatred of her mother were central in her personality, so much so that the term "Electra Complex" has been invented in modern psychiatry to designate a sort of female Oedipus Complex. Idealizing her father, she mourned for him constantly and spewed out her hatred of her mother and Aegisthus, branding them as adulterers and murderers. Her hopes for revenge were centered on her younger absent brother Orestes, the fatherless son living far away in exile.

Seven years later, Orestes, consulting the oracle at Delphi, was ordered by the god Apollo to avenge his father by killing both his mother and Aegisthus. Though profoundly disturbed at the thought of matricide, Orestes obeyed and returned to Mycenae in disguise, accompanied by his best friend, his cousin Pylades. Together they form one of the famous pairs of friends in Greek mythology, as Achilles and Patroclus, and Theseus and Pirithoüs. By a ruse Orestes and Pylades gained entrance to the palace and succeeded in killing both Clytemnestra and Aegisthus. Some versions say that prior to this Electra and Orestes recognized each other and plotted the vengeance together, while others tell that

Orestes was reluctant to kill his mother but was steeled to the act by the urging of Pylades or Electra. At any rate, the usual version is that when he killed Clytemnestra Orestes went mad and fled from Mycenae, roaming aimlessly, pursued by the avenging Furies of his mother.

While patricide was not infrequent in Greek myths, the killing of a mother was extremely rare, the two famous instances those of Orestes and Alcmaeon. The murder of Clytemnestra by Orestes and its consequences was one of the most popular themes of Greek tragedy, and the great suffering of Orestes reflects the Greek concept that matricide was the supreme crime. The tragic figure of Orestes is the prototype of Hamlet, who like Orestes also returned from abroad, but unlike Orestes did not kill his mother, despite her adultery and complicity in his father's murder. It is noteworthy, however, that while Orestes, though full of doubts, killed his mother, Hamlet declares: "I will speak daggers to her, but use none." Efforts among psychiatrists to establish the term "Orestes Complex," to designate the desire of a son to murder his mother, have not been successful.

Orestes' revenge was followed by feelings of guilt and by madness. Pursued by the Furies, Orestes, accompanied by Pylades, sought help from the god Apollo at Delphi, who had ordered the revenge, and was instructed to seek absolution with the help of the goddess Athena in Athens. When he fled to Athens, the Furies relentlessly pursued, seeking vengeance for Clytemnestra, so the goddess Athena ordered a trial for Orestes. A jury of Athenian citizens was chosen, Athena served as judge, while Apollo was lawyer for the defense and the Furies acted as prosecutors. When the jury voted six for acquittal, six for condemnation, Athena broke the tie, absolving Orestes by a narrow margin. A more primitive version of the story tells that in his madness Orestes bit off one of his fingers, and thus regained his sanity. It was not easy for the Greeks to let Orestes off so lightly, and some stories tell that he died in Arcadia after being bitten by a snake. Indeed, his bones, preserved in Arcadia as a relic, were ultimately removed to Sparta.

The doubts about Orestes' matricide were rarely resolved in the Greek mind. In a famous version, even after the trial and acquittal in Athens some of the Furies of his mother did not

accept the verdict, and continued to pursue him, so that the madness returned, and when he sought help again from the Delphic oracle, Apollo ordered him to undergo still another trial. The god instructed him this time to travel to the faraway land of the Taurians, steal and bring back to Greece the statue of Artemis in the temple there. Accompanied by the devoted Pylades, Orestes sailed to the land of the Taurians, but captured shortly after setting foot in the strange country, as foreigners they were doomed to be sacrificed on the altar of Artemis. The priestess of the temple was actually that Iphigenia, Orestes' sister, who had taken a vow to sacrifice all strangers caught in the land, and when discovering that the two were Greeks she proposed to send one of them back to Greece with a letter for her brother. Pylades was chosen for this mission, but requested that the letter be read aloud. From the contents Orestes and his sister recognized each other, and all three plotted to steal the statue and escape to Greece. Iphigenia succeeded in deceiving King Thoas of the Taurians who trusted her, and so the escape was successful. The statue of Artemis was brought back to Attica, where it continued to be revered as a sacred relic to which symbolical human sacrifices were conducted annually.

The story is told that a rumor was spread that Iphigenia did officiate at the sacrifice of Orestes and Pylades, and that after her return to Greece, when she was at Delphi Electra came there to take vengeance on Iphigenia. She called her a murderess and was on the point of burning out her eyes when the opportune appearance of Orestes and Pylades revealed the truth. Orestes was at Delphi because of his anger at Achilles' son Neoptolemus (also called Pyrrhus), who had come there to seek satisfaction for the death of his father Achilles. Orestes had once been betrothed to Hermione, Menelaüs' and Helen's only daughter, but when Orestes was thought to be permanently mad, Menelaüs married her to Neoptolemus. The marriage was childless and, according to one version, Neoptolemus came to Delphi to consult Apollo about his childlessness in marriage. While he was consulting the oracle Orestes killed Neoptolemus inside the temple. Having brutally murdered his rival in a holy shrine Orestes then married Hermione.

Thus ended the woes of the House of Atreus. Previously Menelaüs, after the Trojan War, had been reunited with Helen.

According to the version that the real Helen had been in Egypt, not Troy, during the war, Menelaüs found her there when he was returning from Troy and was diverted by a storm, and brought her back to Sparta. After his death Menelaüs was transported to the Elysian Fields as a reward for having been the husband of Zeus' daughter Helen.

XXII

THE TROJAN WAR BEGINS

The most famous classical myth — indeed one of the most
enduring and influential myths of the world — is the story of
Troy. It has stimulated an unparalleled outpouring of works of
literature, beginning with Homer's *Iliad* and *Odyssey*, and of art
and music, and at times it has even exercised an influence on
politics. Built up layer upon layer over a period of 1500 years, it is
a mixture of many elements — an original historical kernel
embellished with Greek and Near Eastern myths and folktales.

The Trojan cycle of myths is the most comprehensive of all
classical myths, embracing many events of the Heroic Age, from
the birth of Achilles to the death of the hero Odysseus. The story
of their attack on Troy was in Greek folk memory a remembrance
of the greatest event of the Mycenaean Age, involving a vast
overseas expedition, a joint enterprise of Greeks, and a momentous siege, a tale which the Greeks retold endlessly with many
variations. So powerful a hold did this complex of myths have on
the Greek people that many of the leading personalities in the
Trojan War remained vivid figures in their traditions, and received
sacrifices and worship as heroes in later ages.

Troy (the usual Greek name for this place was Ilium) was
situated in the northwest corner of Asia Minor, about three miles
inland from the mouth of the Hellespont, the strait that separates
Europe from Asia. The founder of the royal dynasty of the
Trojans was Dardanus (his name survives in the modern name of
the Hellespont, Dardanelles). His grandson was Tros, who gave his
name to the people thereafter known as Trojans, inhabiting the
region called the Troad. Tros had three sons, Ganymedes, Ilus, and

Assaracus. As we have seen in the myths of Zeus, Ganymedes was taken up to Mt. Olympus to become Zeus' cupbearer, and as compensation Zeus gave Tros some divine horses. Prince Assaracus became famous as the ancestor of the Trojan hero Aeneas, who survived the fall and burning of Troy and resettled the remnant of the Trojan people in Italy. Ilus succeeded his father as king of the Trojans and founded the city named after him, Ilium.

In the myth of Troy the new city is said to have survived only three generations, captured and destroyed by the Greeks in the reign of King Priam, grandson of Ilus. Despite divine favor because of Ganymedes, the city acquired the reputation of being untrustworthy. This taint remained its hallmark, though there were many admirable persons among the Trojans. "Twice traitorous Ilium" began to acquire notoriety with the conduct of Priam's father King Laomedon, who, as we have seen, reneged on his agreements to pay rewards to Apollo, Poseidon, and Heracles, and lost his life when Heracles in anger destroyed the city. The only survivors of the family of Laomedon were his daughter Hesione, who became Telamon's concubine, and his youngest son Podarces, still a child at the time. When Heracles permitted Hesione to ransom one captive among the Trojan prisoners destined to be sold into slavery, she chose her brother Podarces, who was renamed Priam ("Ransomed One"), and he became king of Troy, succeeding his perfidious father Laomedon.

Priam married Hecuba, who became celebrated for her fertility when she had by Priam about twenty children, the most famous of whom were Hector, Paris, Cassandra, Creusa, Laodice, Polyxena, Troilus, Helenus, Deiphobus, and Polydorus. Of these children, Paris was to bring destruction to Troy by continuing the traitorous conduct of his grandfather Laomedon, in stealing the Greek queen Helen from her husband Menelaüs, king of Sparta, while he was a guest in his palace. When Hecuba was pregnant with Paris, she dreamed she would give birth to a burning torch, a dream interpreted to mean that the child to be born would cause the destruction of the city. To avert this fate Priam and Hecuba exposed the child on Mt. Ida in the Troad, where it was found and nursed by a bear. Soon a shepherd rescued the baby and brought it up as his own, naming him Alexander. Among the shepherds of the region Paris (Alexander) stood out for his beauty, dignity, and strength, and while living on Mt. Ida, Paris met and married the nymph Oenone, who loved her husband devotedly. Oenone, too, was a woman extraordinary in this rustic environment, for she possessed the gift of prophecy, was a fine musician, and had expert knowledge of healing drugs.

One day Paris-Alexander came down from Mt. Ida to the city of Troy for a holiday festival, participated in the contest of strength, won a prize, and was suddenly attacked by the jealous sons of Priam. Recognized and saved in the nick of time by his sister Cassandra, the prophetess, Paris then resumed his position as member of the royal family.

The prophecy that Paris would be the cause of the destruction of Troy soon began to be fulfilled. One version says that the deep-seated cause of the Trojan War was overpopulation, in that the goddess Themis, as earth goddess, complained to Zeus that the earth was excessively burdened with human beings. Zeus then developed a plan to cause a great war in order to reduce the world's population and this was approved at a council of the gods. The immediate cause, however, was Paris' abduction of Helen, promised to him by the goddess Aphrodite as reward for his decision in her favor in the famous "Judgment of Paris." In an early form of the myth, one of the most famous events in classical mythology, frequently told in literature and a favorite theme in art, three goddesses, Hera, Aphrodite, and Athena, disputed the title of "most beautiful goddess." Unwilling to be involved in a beauty contest between his wife and two of his daughters, Zeus appointed a mortal as judge, the handsome Trojan Paris. The three goddesses were then conducted in solemn procession by Hermes to Paris on Mt. Ida near Troy, and each goddess offered Paris a reward for his favorable judgment: Athena, military glory and wisdom; Hera, a vast kingdom in Asia; Aphrodite, the most beautiful woman in the world. Paris gave the decision to Aphrodite, presenting her in token of victory with an apple, an erotic symbol in antiquity, as well as of love and fertility.

In a later version this event came to be associated with the magnificent wedding of Thetis to Peleus, to which all the gods and goddesses were invited, but one, Eris, goddess of discord, sister of Ares. Angered by this slight, Eris made an appearance at the wedding in order to cause trouble, bringing with her the famous

"Apple of Discord," which was at once claimed by each of the three goddesses. Some say that she simply threw it into their midst and shouted "for the most beautiful one," others that she inscribed some such message on the apple. There are about a dozen versions of the inscription, such as, "A gift to the beautiful one," "Let the beautiful one take it," "To the most beautiful goddess."

After the judgment Paris claimed his reward. On a state visit to Sparta he enjoyed the hospitality of Menelaüs in his royal palace, where Helen and Paris fell in love, and one day, in the absence of Menelaüs on official business, the two fled to Troy taking with them the royal treasures of Menelaüs. Because of these flagrant violations of hospitality – the abduction of his wife and the stealing of his wealth – Menelaüs appealed for help to his brother Agamemnon of Mycenae, the most powerful king of Greece. Agamemnon organized and led the great Hellenic force that sailed to take vengeance upon Troy for harboring the guilty pair. The nucleus of this expeditionary force was composed of the former suitors of Helen, all of whom had sworn an oath to protect the marriage.

They were joined by the hero who became the principal warrior on the Greek side, Achilles, a prince of Thessaly in northern Greece. The marriage of his mother, the Nereid Thetis, to Peleus was an incompatible one – the immortal goddess never quite accepted her mortal husband. It is said that six children preceded the birth of Achilles, but all died soon after birth because Thetis tried to make them immortal by passing them through fire in order to burn away their mortal elements. When Achilles was born Thetis sought to give him immortality too in this way, but when Peleus surprised her during the ritual it was not accomplished, so in place of the lost immortality Thetis took Achilles to the Underworld, where she dipped him into the River Styx to make him invulnerable. But as she immersed the baby in the sacred waters she held him by one heel, which became the weak spot in Achilles' invincibility. Having bestowed this boon on her son, Thetis abandoned her husband Peleus forever, returning to her father deep in the Aegean Sea.

Abandoned by his mother, the future Greek hero Achilles was taken by Peleus to be brought up by the kindly and wise centaur

Chiron, who taught him all the knowledge and skills a prince of this warrior age needed. Like all the men of the time, he had as principal aim in life the acquisition of glory, to be won chiefly in military exploits, but when the Greek forces were being mobilized against Troy an oracle predicted that Achilles would die if he went to Troy. The choice placed before Achilles was for him a tragic dilemma: either a long inglorious life if he remained at home, or a short heroic one ending in a blaze of glory in the Trojan War.

Achilles, later to become the greatest general and military hero of the Greeks in Troy, initially tried to avoid military service, disguised as a girl and hidden among the many daughters of King Lycomedes on the island of Scyros in the Aegean. But the Greeks suspected Achilles' ruse, and sent Odysseus to discover his hiding place and bring him into the war. The shrewd Odysseus, pretending to be a travelling salesman of women's clothing, one day came in his search for Achilles to the island of Scyros, and was permitted to show his wares to the daughters of the king. Among the women's finery Odysseus placed a sword, and at one point went outside, blew a trumpet and shouted, "We are being attacked." When one of the girls seized the sword and ran to the defense, Odysseus was able to unmask Achilles, who then agreed to join the expedition against Troy of his own free will. Since he had not been a suitor of Helen nor was he a subject of Agamemnon he was under no obligation to go, but went to Troy as an independent prince in search of glory, leader of the Myrmidons of Thessaly. After Achilles left the court of Lycomedes, a son was born to Achilles from Deidamia, one of the king's daughters. Named Neoptolemus ("Young Warrior"), Achilles' son was destined to succeed his father as a military hero in the last phase of the siege of Troy.

King Odysseus of the island of Ithaca, off the western coast of Greece, had been one of the suitors of Helen, but he too had initially sought to evade military service. When the call to arms came he had only recently been married to Penelope, and was the father of a newborn son, Telemachus. When Palamedes, a cousin of Menelaüs and very zealous in his behalf, came to summon Odysseus, the Ithacan pretended to be mentally unbalanced, plowing a field and sowing it with salt. Palamedes, suspecting deception, took the baby Telemachus and put him in the path of

the plow. When Odysseus guided the plow around the baby
Palamedes declared him fit for military service, and so Odysseus
reluctantly left for the war, destined not to see his wife, son, and
aged father for twenty years.

Palamedes, son of King Nauplius of Euboea, like Achilles a
pupil of the centaur Chiron, was especially famed not as a soldier
but for his brilliance of intellect. He became, like Prometheus, a
great benefactor of mankind, the greatest mythical inventor,
famed for such inventions as the calendar, numbers, some letters
of the alphabet, money, weights and measures, the game of dice,
and military organization. One of the brains of the Greek forces at
Troy, he was an unpopular intellectual among the Greek generals
and troops. Palamedes had unmasked other "draft dodgers"
besides Odysseus, and had even ferreted out among the Greek
forces a girl named Epipole, who had disguised herself as a soldier
to be with her lover. In punishment Palamedes had her stoned to
death.

Palamedes' intellectual gifts particularly aroused the jealousy
of the "wise" Odysseus, who never forgave him for outsmarting
him in connection with his feigned madness and took a brutal
revenge upon him. During the war at Troy Odysseus forged a letter
purportedly written by King Priam offering him a bribe to betray
the Greeks, and then hid a sum of money in Palamedes' tent to
entrap him. When Odysseus produced the forged letter and the
money was found in the tent, Palamedes was charged with treason,
found guilty, and stoned to death. His tragic fate became the
subject of many (now lost) Greek plays, and was proverbial as the
symbol of unjust judgement and undeserved execution. When his
father Nauplius, seeking revenge on the Greeks for the unjust
death of his son, could get no satisfaction from Agamemnon and
Menelaüs at Troy, he went about Greece inciting the wives of the
absent warriors to be unfaithful to their husbands. Finally, after
the war he wrecked a Greek fleet by giving a false signal through
beacons along the shores, so that the ships were dashed against the
rocks.

Another famous Greek hero who went to Troy was King
Diomedes of Argos, son of the Tydeus who participated and lost
his life in the expedition of the Seven Against Thebes. Diomedes
himself took part in the subsequent successful assault of the

Epigoni against Thebes. He gained a form of immortality from Athena, whose favorite he was, and who originally intended it not for him but for his father Tydeus. Nectar for this purpose had already been given Athena by Zeus, but when she saw Tydeus eating the brains of Melanippus before Thebes, she withdrew the gift. The dying Tydeus asked that his lost immortality be given to his son Diomedes, the ideal warrior of the Greeks at Troy — brave, patriotic, chivalrous, and moderate. Though he was inferior to Achilles in military skill and daring, he represented the type of person the flawed Achilles might have been. It was Diomedes, not Achilles, who shared with Odysseus some of the most dangerous and famous exploits of the Trojan War: the slaying of Dolon and Rhesus, the entry into Troy as a spy, the stealing of the *palladium* from the city, and the bringing of Philoctetes to Troy. In fact Diomedes and Achilles seem to have been rivals, and it was Diomedes who took the place of Achilles as battle leader when Achilles' pride caused him to withdraw from the fighting in the tenth year of the war.

Several other Greeks were very close to Achilles, especially the handsome, compassionate Patroclus, his cousin and closest friend, the person most loved by Achilles. Another cousin was Ajax, son of King Telamon of Salamis. Tall and handsome, Ajax was the "bulwark of the Achaeans," as Homer calls him, tireless in battle, unflinching in his sense of duty to his fellow Greeks, and deeply religious, basically a dedicated soldier with a high sense of morality and personal integrity — although without high intelligence, diplomatic finesse, or oratorical skill — "Beef-witted Ajax" Shakespeare calls him. Equipped with huge shield, Ajax was famed for holding whatever position he chose each day on the battlefield. During the war he took as captive the Phrygian princess Tecmessa, with whom he developed a tender relationship and had a beloved son Eurysaces by her. The most famous myth of Ajax involved the competition between him and Odysseus for the divine armor of Achilles, which Thetis had presented as a prize after the death of her son. In one version the Greek generals by a secret vote awarded it to Odysseus, while in another, Trojan captives, who were to decide whether the wily Odysseus or the mighty Ajax had caused more terror to the Trojans, chose Odysseus. So infuriated was Ajax at what he regarded as unfair treatment and an affront to his dignity as the indispensable Greek fighter after the death of Achilles that he last his reason temporarily, ran berserk in the Greek camp, and tried to kill the generals he blamed most, especially Agamemnon, Menelaüs, and Odysseus, but only succeeded in slaying some cattle. When he regained his sanity, he was so humiliated by his own behavior that he committed suicide by falling on his own sword. As a traitor he was denied cremation, but later his relics in his burial place on the island of Salamis became a shrine where he was worshipped as a hero.

There was another Ajax, son of Oileus, from Locris, called Ajax the Lesser to distinguish him from the great Ajax. This Locrian Ajax, though a good warrior, was cruel, irreligious, violent, and arrogant. At the fall of Troy he raped the Trojan princess Cassandra though she was in a temple, clinging to the altar of Athena and holding a *palladium*, image of Athena. So hateful was this Ajax that the Greeks themselves wanted to stone him to death for this outrage, and the Locrians, who considered themselves his descendants, did penance for over 1000 years by annually sending a virgin to serve in the temple of Athena at Ilium as recompense for the sacrilege of the Locrian Ajax.

Famous also among the warriors on the Greek side of the Trojan War was the very aged but eternally youthful King Nestor of Pylos, wise, a counselor of moderation, compromise and restraint, but very talkative, constantly drawing in incidents from his youth and previous exploits. Two others were his son Antilochus, second only to Patroclus as beloved friend of Achilles, and Idomeneus, King of Crete, a former suitor of Helen who brought his Cretan forces to Troy.

There were two attempts to land the Greek forces at Troy. In the first expedition they sailed from Argos in the Peloponnesus across the Aegean Sea, and landed by error in Mysia far to the south, where they were met with stubborn resistance by the inhabitants, whose king was Telephus, a son of Heracles. The Greeks were so badly disorganized by this that they were compelled to return to their base in Greece. In the defense of his country King Telephus received a wound which failed to heal, and he was advised to seek out Achilles, who miraculously healed the wound by a touch of his spear.

Reorganizing their resources, the Greek forces mustered for a

second time, this time at the port of Aulis on the eastern coast of Greece. After the sacrifice of Agamemnon's daughter Iphigenia to appease the anger of the goddess Artemis, who had becalmed the Greek fleet, the winds began to blow again and the Greek fleet sailed to Troy, this time without incident. En route, however, they were forced to abandon one of their outstanding soldiers, Philoctetes, son of Poeas of Thessaly, the proud owner of the bow and arrows of Heracles, given to him as a gift for lighting the great hero's funeral pyre on Mt. Oeta. When some Greeks made a landing on the island of Tenedos, Philoctetes was bitten by a snake, because, according to one version, he had revealed the place of Heracles' funeral pyre although he had sworn not to do so. The stench from the festering wound was so repulsive that, on advice of Odysseus, it was decided to abandon the suffering Philoctetes on the island of Lemnos, where he managed to survive all alone. Treated as expendable by the Greeks, it was revealed ten years later that he was indispensable to Greek victory against the Trojans.

While the Greeks were in the process of landing on the shore near Troy the first Greek casualty occurred. Because there had been a prophecy that the first Greek to touch Trojan soil would lose his life all hesitated to be the first, but Protesilaüs of Thessaly leaped off his ship with full knowledge, and was promptly killed by the Trojan prince Hector. This "offer of the first" for success of a venture is a good example of a widespread folktale associated with the Trojan saga. Other folktale themes connected with the story of Protesilaüs, involved his devoted wife Laodamia, then a young bride. In one version she mourned so for him that the gods granted her prayers to see Protesilaüs again for a short time, but when he was brought back from the dead for three hours she was so inconsolable that she followed him to the tomb forever by committing suicide. This is the famous folktale motif of the power of the dead to draw the living with them to death. In another version Laodamia was said to have made a wax image of Protesilaüs which she worshipped almost as a god and secretly embraced. When her father Acastus, deeming this behavior unseemly, threw the image into the fire, Laodamia cast herself into the flames too and died.

The city of Troy was ruled by aged King Priam and Queen

Hecuba. Although Paris, one of their numerous children, had precipitated the Trojan War, he was not the principal defender of Troy. This responsibility fell upon his brother Hector, Priam's eldest son. Like most of the heroes of this warlike age, Hector was ambitious for fame and glory, but he was usually represented as a man with a high sense of duty to his people, tender love for his wife Andromache and their baby son Astyanax, as well as a deep sense of piety towards the gods of Troy. Prominent also on the Trojan side was Aeneas, son of Anchises by the goddess Aphrodite. Though very ambitious (indeed he was even suspected of aiming at royal power for himself and his descendants to replace Priam's line), Aeneas was second after Hector in Trojan leadership and responsibility, sometimes called "the brains of Troy." A companion of Paris on his journey to Sparta to abduct Helen, he was one of the survivors of Troy and became the hero of the most famous Roman myth.

Because of the heroic and stubborn defense of the Trojans and their numerous allies in Asia, the war was a stalemate for nine years, with much skirmishing, but nothing of importance during the long siege of the city. From their ships beached on the seashore several miles away the Greeks supported themselves by raiding and looting nearby places. Included in their booty were female captives, who were awarded to the generals as their concubines.

During these nine years few prominent persons on either side lost their lives. The most famous person killed very early in the war was a mere boy, Troilus, youngest son of Priam and Hecuba, who used to go at night, together with his lovely sister Polyxena, to fetch water outside Troy. One night Achilles waited in ambush there and slew Troilus while he was watering his horses.*

---

*The famous story of Troilus and Cressida (a corruption of the name Chryseis, who figured in the Trojan War) is not a Greek myth but a medieval romance.

XXIII

THE FALL OF TROY

In the tenth year of the war a bitter quarrel broke out between Agamemnon, commander-in-chief of the Greek forces, and the proud hero Achilles, and this crisis engulfed all the Greeks at Troy and brought them to the brink of defeat. This is the story that Homer chose to tell in the *Iliad*, limiting himself to a period of about fifty days in the tenth year of the siege. The dispute began shortly after a girl named Chryseis was taken captive in a raid by the Greeks and given to Agamemnon as concubine. She was, however, no ordinary girl but the daughter of a priest named Chryses, and when the priest came to the Greek camp to offer Agamemnon a huge ransom for his daughter, Agamemnon arrogantly rejected the offer, largely because he liked the girl. Rebuffed and saddened, the priest prayed to Apollo to punish the Greeks, and the god sent a plague at once to devastate the Greek army. When Calchas, official prophet of the Greeks at Troy, revealed that Agamemnon was to blame because of his treatment of Apollo's priest, Agamemnon, in a burst of anger showing his selfishness and arrogance, consented to give up Chryseis but demanded an immediate replacement — Achilles' concubine, the captive Briseis.

Achilles responded with his own anger, and after quarreling, the two generals were unable to bend to reach a compromise for the sake of the common enterprise. The taking of his concubine deeply offended Achilles, a proud man of high personal integrity. Regarding himself as the indispensable man in the Greek army, he withdrew from battle and appealed for aid to his mother, the Nereid Thetis, who in turn obtained from Zeus a commitment to aid the Trojans against the Greeks so that they would learn to respect Achilles. Nursing his pride and anger, Achilles sulked in his tent.

As the morale of the Achaeans, deprived of their greatest military leader, collapsed, the two sides agreed to end the war by a "winner-take-all" duel between the frivolous pleasure-seeker Paris and Helen's first husband Menelaüs. The prize was to be Helen and her wealth. When this duel proved to be inconclusive, the war was resumed, and new battle leaders arose among the Greeks to replace Achilles, especially Diomedes, who fought as Achilles would have. Sensing the Greek confusion Hector mobilized the Trojans for a massive onslaught, himself facing the mighty Greek warrior Ajax in a duel that ended in a draw. The Greeks began to build fortifications, a ditch and a wall, to protect their ships, mighty battles took place, and Zeus fulfilled his promise to Thetis by turning the tide in favor of the Trojans after all those years.

Agamemnon finally realized his mistake in offending the touchy Achilles, and sent a committee of three (Odysseus, Ajax, and the aged Phoenix, foster-father of Achilles) to offer Achilles an apology and vast quantities of wealth, together with other gifts, but the "magnificent barbarian," as Achilles has been called, rejected all efforts at reconciliation. He was simply "not for sale," remaining adamant and excessively proud.

As the Greeks fought with their backs to the wall many were seriously wounded. After Achilles allowed the gentle, compassionate Patroclus to inquire about the wounded Greek heroes, Patroclus finally persuaded Achilles to permit him to impersonate him by donning Achilles' armor and leading Achilles' men, the Myrmidons, back into battle. Reluctantly Achilles consented, but urged upon Patroclus extreme caution. The proud Achilles had begun to relent, showing some concern for his fellow Greeks, especially when the Trojans began to fire some of the Greek ships. Patroclus at the head of the Myrmidons drove the Trojans back in precipitous retreat, killing the famous hero King Sarpedon of the Lycians, a son of Zeus and a grandson of the famed hero Bellerophon. At the orders of Zeus his body was miraculously whisked away for burial in Lycia.

Sarpedon was a famed archer. When he was a child there had been an archery contest between his two uncles to determine which could shoot an arrow through a ring placed on edge on the breast of Sarpedon as he lay on the ground. This is a Greek version of the famous folktale (similar to the story of William Tell and the apple) of the skilled archer who has to demonstrate his skill at the risk of the life of a relative.

Exultantly Patroclus reached the walls of Troy, only to be killed by Hector at his moment of glory. Patroclus in the guise of Achilles had taken on not only aspects of his friend's better nature, but also his major personality flaw – excessive pride. Overwhelmed with great sorrow and a sense of personal guilt, Achilles turned his fierce anger against Hector, now ready to return to battle, fully aware that his life would be short, and that he would die soon after Hector.

Hector in his victorious mood became blind to the danger he himself now faced, though cautioned by the Trojan prophet Polydamas about excessive rashness. Having stripped Patroclus of Achilles' armor, he exulted in his trophy, although the body of Patroclus was recovered by Greek warriors. To replace his lost armor Achilles' mother Thetis appealed to the god Hephaestus, who made for Achilles a set of miraculous armor that included a famous shield decorated with scenes from war and peace in the world of the time. Achilles finally renounced his anger toward Agamemnon, was reconciled with him, and returned to battle with grim ferocity, killing many Trojans and taking captive twelve young Trojans with the intention of sacrificing them to the soul of his friend Patroclus. Then he sought out Hector, the champion of a lost cause but now blinded by the smell of victory. Yet when Achilles approached him on the battlefield, Hector fled, relentlessly pursued by the Greek hero three times around the walls of Troy. When Hector finally made a stand, deceived by the gods, he was brutally slain by Achilles, who proceeded back to his ships, dragging Hector's body in the dust behind his war chariot.

Returning with Hector's body, Achilles held funeral games for Patroclus at which famous Greek heroes competed for prizes, and sacrificed the twelve Trojan youths he had taken. And he continued to mistreat and mutilate Hector's body, dragging it about Patroclus' tomb, until, at the orders of Zeus, Thetis was sent to instruct Achilles to release Hector's body for burial. Aged King Priam risked his life to go at night to Achilles' tent to ransom his son's body. When Priam humbly knelt before his son's slayer, Achilles was moved to compassion, remembering his own father Peleus and conscious of his own coming death, and not only returned the body of Hector to Priam, but agreed to a truce to give him sufficient time for the funeral. Thus Achilles' basic heroism and innate courtesy, suppressed by his anger against Agamemnon, returned to him once he had learned the folly of excess through his own tragic suffering. On return to Troy Priam conducted a state funeral for his heroic son Hector, who was mourned by all the Trojans with a foreboding of their own imminent fate.

Besides Hector and Sarpedon other famous heroes on the Trojan side died in the course of the "wrath of Achilles," including King Rhesus, an ally of Priam from Thrace, who died on the first night of his arrival at Troy. Odysseus and Diomedes on a spying expedition raided his camp and killed Rhesus in his sleep, taking with them his famous team of white horses. Rhesus' heart-broken wife Arganthoë came to Troy, mourning his body inconsolably and embracing it until she herself died. That same night a Trojan named Dolon was sent by Hector to spy on the Greek camp, but he was taken prisoner by Odysseus and Diomedes, who promised to spare his life in exchange for military information about the Trojan army. After he gave his information Diomedes killed him anyway.

Following the death of Hector and Rhesus Priam summoned more allies of the Trojans. An army of Amazons, led by Queen Penthesileia, daughter of Ares, arrived. Shortly after, Achilles killed her in a struggle between the greatest heroine and the greatest hero of the time. Overwhelmed by her beauty, as Achilles held her dead body, he fell in love with her corpse, expressing sorrow at having killed her. When the ill-tempered Greek soldier Thersites laughed at Achilles because of this show of tenderness, Achilles killed him, arousing the anger of Thersites' relative the hero Diomedes.

In the tenth year of the war, Priam's nephew Memnon, the king of Ethiopia (son of Eos and Tithonus), came to help the Trojans, together with an army of Ethiopians. Memnon was probably an historic Near Eastern king who somehow came to be associated with the siege of Troy. Shortly after his arrival Memnon killed Nestor's beloved son Antilochus, who had replaced Patroclus as Achilles' best friend, and in a doublet of the Achilles-Hector combat, Memnon and Achilles fought a spectacular duel, which resulted in Memnon's death. At the request of Eos, Memnon was granted immortality by Zeus.

Memnon's death, however, sealed the fate of Achilles. The great hero soon met an inglorious death, struck in his vulnerable heel by a poisoned arrow shot either by Apollo or by Paris with the aid of Apollo, and after his funeral his ashes were mingled in the same funerary urn with those of his beloved Patroclus. Achilles' tomb, shown in later times in the Troad, on the shores of the Hellespont near Troy, became a famous place of pilgrimage in antiquity, and even attracted Alexander the Great for a visit to pay homage to Achilles, his ideal hero. It is said that while his body was on the funeral pyre Achilles was miraculously removed by his mother Thetis and transported either to the Isles of the Blest or to the island of Leuce, a sort of remote paradise, where he later married the beautiful Helen of Troy.

After Achilles' death Odysseus won the fateful contest for the possession of the divine armor of the great hero, and this led to the suicide of Ajax. After the fall of Troy Priam's lovely young daughter Polyxena was declared to be part of Achilles' share of the booty of the captured city, and his son Neoptolemus sacrificed her at his tomb to the ghost of his father.

This famous story of the sacrifice of Polyxena has a number of possible explanations. It may have its origin in the custom, practiced, for example, in Scythia in antiquity, of burying with a dead chief his favorite horses, dogs, and even human attendants, or it may have been associated with the story of Troy because of the liking of folktales for symmetry and balance. The Trojan war was preceded by the sacrifice of a Greek king's daughter, Iphigenia, so it was made to end with the sacrifice of the Trojan king's daughter, Polyxena. But it is also possible that Polyxena was originally an underworld goddess (her name means "Hostess to Many," just as one of Hades' bynames was Polydectes, "Host to Many"). When in time she lost her divine character and became a mortal princess, this primitive function was transformed into the romantic story that Achilles had seen Polyxena earlier, had fallen in love with her, and wanted to marry her. Because of his love for

her he even offered to betray the Greeks to the Trojans, and came
to meet her in a temple near Troy, where he was ambushed and
killed by Polyxena's brothers Paris and Deiphobus. There is
imbedded in this story of Achilles and Polyxena the folktale motif
of the dead bridegroom drawing his bride to him into the grave.

After all the fighting and dying around Troy for about ten
years, prophecies revealed that the conditions for the capture of
Troy were still unfulfilled. These prerequisites were many, some
superhuman in nature: the presence of the bow and arrows of
Heracles, who had previously captured Troy, the presence of
Achilles' son Neoptolemus, the theft of the *palladium*, protecting
talisman of the city, the bringing to Troy of a bone of the hero
Pelops, the construction of a wooden horse to break down magic
obstructions and gain entry into the city, and the death of the
sinful Paris. When all these came to pass the city would finally be
captured.

The bow and arrows of Heracles were in the possession of
Philoctetes, who had been left alone ten years before on the island
of Lemnos with his festering wound that gave off a foul odor. In
one version Odysseus and Diomedes were sent to the island and
brought him to Troy, while in another, made famous by the
Athenian dramatist Sophocles, Philoctetes, angry because he had
been abandoned by his fellow Greeks, at first refused to go to
Troy, but finally agreed to do so out of respect for Achilles' son
Neoptolemus and at the orders of the deified Heracles. At Troy
Philoctetes was cured by the army physician Machaon, who
performed surgery on his foot after putting him into a deep sleep
— the first reported instance of an operation under some form of
anaesthesia. The arrows of Philoctetes then mortally wounded
Paris, who could be cured only by his first wife, the nymph
Oenone. When Paris appealed for help from her special knowledge
of medicine she refused at first, and although she finally relented
and brought the healing drugs, she came too late. When her
beloved Paris died, she committed suicide.

Achilles' son Neoptolemus (also called Pyrrhus) was fetched
from his home on the island of Scyros by Odysseus and Phoenix.
His father's armor was given him by Odysseus, and as a "second
Achilles" he killed many Trojans.

Troy could not be captured while the *palladium* was inside the walls. This very primitive wooden image of Pallas Athena, warrior goddess of defensive warfare, fell from Olympus into Troy and became its sacred talisman, for the protection of the city depended on it. At first conceived of as life-size, it was later thought to have been small enough to carry in one's hand. There is one version that the Trojans had made a duplicate *palladium* to deceive thieves, and that the original was kept in a secret place. At any rate, Odysseus and Diomedes were sent to steal it from Troy, and Odysseus succeeded in doing so, disguised as a beggar although recognized by Helen who opportunistically did not betray him to the Trojans. Meanwhile, to satisfy another precondition for the taking of Troy, an embassy of Greeks was sent to Pisa in Elis in Greece, and they brought back the shoulder blade of the hero Pelops, himself of Near Eastern origin.

The immediate cause of the capture of Troy was the wooden horse, commonly called the Trojan Horse. Odysseus, with the aid of the goddess Athena, conceived the building of the colossal wooden horse, to be used as a deception to break down the walls and enter the city. The horse was secretly built, and its hollow interior was filled with picked Greek warriors, including Menelaüs, Odysseus, and Neoptolemus. Then it was left in the plain outside Troy, the rumor spread that the Greeks had abandoned the siege and evacuated their forces, and that the horse itself was a gift to Athena for a safe return to Greece. Actually the Greek ships merely sailed off to the nearby island of Tenedos, where they concealed themselves in readiness for a swift return once the horse was brought into the city.

The story of the capture of Troy through the ruse of the wooden horse is one of the most famous myths of the world, and resembles many traditional folktales of the captures of cities by men brought inside under cover. The improbability that a people as sophisticated as the Trojans would in fact have been taken in by such a deception has led to a great deal of speculation about the origins and interpretation of the horse motif in this story, and there are various theories. Since Troy had previously been destroyed by an earthquake, the myth involving a destructive horse may have developed from the notion that the god of horses, Poseidon, destroyed the city himself or through a magic horse sent by him. Another theory is that horse colossi were erected as sacred talismans, in this case as counter-magic against the protective devices of the magic circle of the walls of Troy and of its *palladium*. A more pragmatic theory envisions the horse as a war machine, either a huge battering ram with a horse's head as symbol, or a siege tower with a high body and an upper portion like a head projecting forward to effect entry over the walls of the city.

In the myth the colossal wooden horse filled with volunteers was left by the Greeks outside of Troy, and the Trojans poured out of the city to see the mysterious image. While the Trojans were arguing about whether it should be destroyed at once or should be brought into the city, a Greek captive was dragged before Priam. This was Odysseus' cousin Sinon, who had risked his life by volunteering to try to persuade the Trojans to drag the horse inside the city, telling them a deceitful tale that the Greeks had abandoned the war and had singled him out for human sacrifice to ensure their safe return to Greece. He managed, he said, to escape, and was now ready to reveal to the Trojans the secret of the horse: it was an offering to the goddess Athena as recompense for their theft of her *palladium*, so that she would allow their return. If the Trojans destroyed the horse, Troy would be destroyed, but if they brought it into the city, it would never be captured.

At this point Laocoön, a priest of Poseidon (or Apollo), who was a Trojan prince and prophet, warned the Trojans, "I fear the Greeks even bearing gifts," and he hurled a spear at the horse, striking its side. Suddenly to everyone's horror, two immense serpents appeared from the sea, seized Laocoön and his two young sons, killed them horribly, then glided into the city and disappeared in the temple of Athena. In other versions of the punishment, one son of, or both sons of Laocoön were crushed by the serpents, and Laocoön himself was blinded — the latter a typical punishment of scorners of the gods. The nature of the sin of Laocoön that caused this punishment took various other forms in the myths. In one version he sinned by marrying and having children though a priest, or because he had sexual relations with his wife in front of a statue of the god Apollo. In any case, at this time the Trojans interpreted his punishment as divine retribution for his sacrilege to the horse, so they dragged it into Troy and celebrated wildly over what they believed was the end of the long war.

During the night Sinon released the Greek warriors inside the horse, and a signal fire was lit to notify the Greek ships waiting at the island of Tenedos to return. The Greeks quickly joined forces, and in the destruction of the city, they looted, burned, and killed all the males they could find. Neoptolemus, the "second Achilles," cruelly killed King Priam in his own palace, in the very presence of an altar of Zeus. He beheaded the aged king and left his corpse unburied, ordered Hector's baby son Astyanax thrown from the walls of the city to his death, to prevent the rise of an avenger, and sacrificed Priam's daughter Polyxena at the tomb of Achilles. Most of the Trojans' wives and daughters were rounded up as slaves, joining the sad group of captives known as the Trojan Women, parcelled out among the Greek warriors as personal booty, to be the concubines and slaves of the victors. For example, Neoptolemus received Hector's wife Andromache, Odysseus was assigned the aged Hecuba, Agamemnon took Cassandra, daughter of Priam and Hecuba.

Cassandra was the most beautiful daughter of Priam and Hecuba. Apollo fell in love with her because of that beauty and gave her the gift of prophecy in return for the promise of her love. But once she received the gift she was determined to remain a virgin, so in anger Apollo, unable to take back the gift once given, cursed her: she was to continue to prophesy accurately but no one would believe her until after her predictions had come true. It was Cassandra who revealed the identity of Paris when he came to Troy as a shepherd, and she too had warned the Trojans about the wooden horse. During the sack of Troy Cassandra took refuge in the temple of Athena, where she was found by the Locrian Ajax, who raped her in the presence of the statue of Athena, which was sacrilegiously overturned in the struggle. As a war captive Cassandra became the concubine of Agamemnon, and her mind became unbalanced because of her own suffering and the woes of her people, but despite her fits of madness she continued to prophesy — and was never believed. On the day she was brought home by Agamemnon, for whom she had developed a measure of affection, she prophesied the coming murders of Agamemnon and herself as she stood before the palace at Mycenae. Together with

Agamemnon she was shortly after murdered by the jealous Clytemnestra, wife of the conqueror of Troy. Cassandra is a classic example of innocence, beauty, and gentleness destined to a lifetime of suffering.

Cassandra's twin brother Helenus was, like her, a prophet, and was one of the few Trojan males to survive the war. Shortly after the death of Paris he hoped to become the next husband of Helen, but she was instead married to his brother Deiphobus. Soon after, Helenus was taken prisoner by the Greeks, and either because he was fearful for his life or because of his anger at losing Helen, he aided the Greeks by predicting to them all the conditions necessary for the capture of Troy. For this help his life was spared, and he became a slave of Neoptolemus.

Helen was taken captive and brought to Menelaüs for punishment. On the night of the fall of Troy, wishing to ingratiate herself with the victors, she hid the weapons of her husband Deiphobus, who, betrayed and defenceless, was brutally killed by Menelaüs. The symbol of exquisite beauty Helen, as we have seen, was depicted in various versions of her myths as a morally flawed woman: she was unfaithful to her first husband, Menelaüs, and absconded with his wealth, helped to betray Troy to the Greeks, and sacrificed her third husband Deiphobus to save herself. In one version Achilles while once inside Troy desired her, and she became his secret lover after the death of Paris. Achilles is even said to have married her in still another version. Because of the paradox of beauty and evil in her, Goethe called her the "much admired and much reviled Helen." Yet there was a tendency in Greek myths to forgive her, partly because, as we have seen, she was probably originally a goddess, and partly because she became involved with Paris through the schemes of the gods.

When Helen was brought before Menelaüs his first impulse was to put her to death at once, but one look at her beauty melted his anger away, so he ordered her put on his ship and they were reconciled. Despite everything that had happened, Menelaüs and Helen lived happily ever after.

In the ten year siege, Troy's Queen Hecuba had lost almost all her sons. During the war Priam had sent his youngest son Polydorus to be cared for by his son-in-law, King Polymestor of Thrace, along with part of the royal treasures of Troy. When

Polymestor learned of the capture of Troy and Priam's death, he seized the treasures, killed Polydorus and threw his body into the sea. As Hecuba was about to embark on shipboard as captive of Odysseus, the body of Polydorus washed ashore at the Troad, Hecuba recognized it and decided on a macabre revenge. She secretly summoned Polymestor with a pretext that she would tell him where more of the royal treasure of Troy was hidden, and when he arrived with his two sons, Hecuba tore out his eyes, and the Trojan women killed his sons. At this time Hecuba was transformed ino a bitch, and was thus spared the indignity of slavery in Greece. This happened either when the Greeks were stoning her as punishment for blinding Polymestor, or when the attendants of Polymestor pursued her to revenge their king, or when she wailed so loudly over the body of her son Polydorus.

XXIV

THE RETURN OF THE HEROES:
Odysseus

After Troy was destroyed and the booty in treasure and humans collected, the great Greek collective expedition dispersed. As sequels to the story of the long war many stories of the experiences and adventures of the returning Greek leaders grew up, variations on one of the most popular themes of folklore — the return of the husband after many years away from home. The pattern of such stories is found in Egyptian and other Near Eastern tales: the returning husband arrives to find his wife and property in the hands of a rival, often a close relative; sometimes the husband returns just in time for the wedding of his wife and the usurper; the conflict that follows ends sometimes with the death of the husband, sometimes with his leaving and settling elsewhere, sometimes in his regaining his wife and home. Each of these variations is found in the stories of the returning Greek heroes.

On the very day of his return, Agamemnon and his concubine Cassandra were murdered together by Clytemnestra and her lover, Agamemnon's cousin Aegisthus. Agamemnon's brother Menelaüs regained his wife Helen when Troy was captured, but their return to Sparta was delayed, for while en route home the reunited couple were driven by a storm to Egypt, where they remained for eight years. Menelaüs, returning to Sparta with Helen, was blessed with a relatively uncomplicated life and, as a son-in-law of Zeus, with a happy afterlife.

Less fortunate was the experience of the hero Diomedes. In his absence from his kingdom of Argos a conspiracy against him was organized, which included his own wife, who had been unfaithful to him in his absence, and who tried to kill him on his return. Fleeing from Argos, Diomedes migrated to Southern Italy, where he became the founder of many cities and was worshipped as a hero after his death.

Idomeneus, king of Crete, had, like many of the heroes at Troy, been a suitor of Helen. At Troy he was one of the outstanding military leaders on the Greek side, heading the Cretan contingents, one of the heroes who volunteered for the dangerous mission inside the wooden horse. According to some versions his return from Troy was speedy and happy, but in another, as he was en route home his fleet was endangered by a storm, and he vowed to sacrifice to Poseidon the first person he met on landing safely in Crete. As it turned out this was one of his own children, whom he dutifully sacrificed to the sea god.

Ajax's half-brother Teucer, son of Telamon and the Trojan princess Hesione, returned in safety to his home on the island of Salamis, only to be disowned at once by his father. The two brothers, when they left for Troy, had been instructed by Telamon to protect each other in the war, and to return both alive or not at all. A famed bowman, Teucer had fought loyally at the side of Ajax all through the war, but, as we have seen, Ajax committed suicide at Troy when he lost the armor of Achilles in the contest with Odysseus. Telamon's anger against Teucer when he returned was unrelenting, he called Teucer Ajax's murderer, and accused him of not having avenged Ajax after his shabby treatment by the Greek leaders. Driven away by his father, Teucer sailed off to the island of Cyprus, where he founded a new city named Salamis.

The Locrian Ajax, violator of Cassandra at the altar of Athena, lost his life on the way home after Athena caused a storm in the Aegean Sea which destroyed his ships. Poseidon saved his life, but the incorrigible Ajax boasted that he had survived by his own efforts, so Poseidon made the rock on which he was standing disappear into the sea, and Ajax was drowned.

The Greek prophet Calchas also died on his return journey. There had been a prophecy that Calchas would die when he met a seer more skillful than himself, and when Calchas' ship landed at Colophon in Asia Minor, he met the famous prophet Mopsus, son of the prophetess Manto, grandson of the Theban seer Tiresias.

When a contest in divination involving riddle solving was held between the two prophets, Mopsus proved superior to Calchas each time, and Calchas died of mortification or committed suicide. We hear so much about Calchas as a famous prophet that he may have been a real person, and Mopsus himself was probably an historical figure, for his name appears as a ruler in Asia Minor in an inscription that puts him in the very period when the Trojan War took place.

Achilles' son Neoptolemus (also called Pyrrhus) brought home with him Hector's wife Andromache as his concubine, and had three sons by her. After returning to Greece Neoptolemus married Hermione, only daughter of Menelaüs and Helen. She had originally been the fiancée of Orestes, but because he had lost his mind after killing his mother, she was married to Neoptolemus as a reward for his services to Menelaüs at Troy. When their marriage was childless, Hermione's jealousy of Andromache's fertility led her to stir up Orestes against Neoptolemus, who was ultimately killed by him at Delphi. Before he died Neoptolemus had given Andromache to Helenus to be his wife, and after his death the pair ruled in Epirus, Helenus being eventually succeeded by Molossus, Neoptolemus' son by Andromache.

The Greek hero whose return home from Troy was delayed the longest was Odysseus, King of Ithaca, a small island off the west coast of Greece. Odysseus (from the Latin form Ulixes we know him as Ulysses) was the devoted son of Laërtes, retired king of Ithaca, and of Anticleia, whose father was the notorious Autolycus, famous for his thievery, especially of horses and cattle, even outdoing the sinner Sisyphus. Indeed Autolycus and Sisyphus became fast friends, and it was even said that Sisyphus seduced or raped Autolycus' daughter Anticleia before she married Laërtes. When a son was born to Anticleia, Laërtes accepted the child as his own and named him Odysseus. When Odysseus came of age Laërtes retired from the kingship and left the royal power to Odysseus, who married Penelope, niece of Tyndareus of Sparta. A child named Telemachus was born shortly before the Trojan War broke out. An oracle had predicted that if Odysseus participated in this war he would not return for twenty years, and when Odysseus' attempt to avoid military service was foiled by Palamedes, he sailed for the war leaving behind his young bride

Penelope and his newborn baby son Telemachus to grow up during his long absence.

After ten years of brilliant service in the Greek army, in which his distinctive qualities of intelligence, daring, and strength were always in evidence, Odysseus came out unscathed, and began his return to Ithaca with a fleet of twelve ships carrying 600 men. The tale of his experiences, as told in Homer's epic the *Odyssey*, is the most famous myth of a "Return," a story put together out of a mass of traditional folktales far older than the Trojan saga itself. Homer connected these tales with the Greek hero Odysseus, and placed them in the context of a return from an historic war, expanding the principal folktale theme of the returning husband with a mixture of sailors' yarns, travelers' stories of heroic wooing and bridal contests. Analogies may be found in the great Near Eastern literary masterpiece, the epic of Gilgamesh, in the Egyptian folk story *Tale of the Shipwrecked Sailor*, as well as in a Hittite myth of the return of a king named Girpanzah, who recovered his wife by killing her suitors with his bow and arrows. In the usual folktale the returning husband has but one ship, and Homer enlarged even this into a fleet commanded by the Greek king Odysseus.

In Homer's brilliant picture of the mythic hero we see a man of varied and extraordinary qualities – "the man of many devices" Homer called him. In addition to the physical prowess with which all the mythic heroes were endowed, Odysseus possessed high intelligence, resourcefulness, cunning, endless curiosity and love of adventure, and a capacity for endurance and suffering. He was thus "the man most likely to succeed" in overcoming all the obstacles he was to meet in the fantasy world of folktale and the real world of Ithaca, the great exemplar of the mature man – always cool, balanced, flexible, self-controlled, a superb speaker, who could be unscrupulous, crafty, and vengeful when his own interests were at stake. Though T.E. Shaw called him "a cold-blood egotist," he was capable of deep affection for those he loved. Away from his home and his model wife the faithful Penelope, he was a Don Juan whom women found irresistible, but despite the temptations he met en route in his ten-year wanderings after the fall of Troy, his ultimate goal was to reestablish his identity by regaining his power, wealth, son, wife, father. Because

of an extraordinary combination of merits Odysseus succeeded in winning his way back to his former life after twenty years' absence from Ithaca.

Since antiquity, many attempts have been made to trace Odysseus' itinerary in the Mediterranean by localizing his adventures at specific places, but such efforts are fruitless, for his trip was made up of a collection of traditional folktales. Most of his adventures seem to be placed in the Western Mediterranean, in the vicinity of Sicily and Southern Italy.

After leaving Troy Odysseus and his men turned pirates, raiding the land of the Cicones near Troy, and then, when they were fairly close to Ithaca, a storm drove them south to North Africa, possibly to the coast of Tripoli. Here some of his men ate the fruit of the lotus tree, which drugged them into a sense of euphoria, so that they forgot their past and refused to leave the place, preferring a life of indolence there. Odysseus ordered them dragged away from the enticing land of the Lotus-Eaters.

This is recognizable as a typical folktale told as a caution for sailors. The symbol of the lotus came into classical mythology from India and the Near East, where its beautiful flower had long been used as an ornamental motif in art and as a mystic concept. As an oriental symbol it represented many things: beauty, procreation, fertility, abundance, immortality, rebirth, even purity and spirituality, and its widespread application makes the lotus a forerunner of the symbolism of flowers, which was later applied to the lily, the fleur-de-lys, the rose, and others.

Next Odysseus and his men came to the land of the Cyclopes, an uncivilized tribe of cave-dwelling, one-eyed giants. Out of curiosity and the need for supplies, Odysseus and his men reconnoitered, and were exploring a cave inhabited by the Cyclops named Polyphemus, a son of Poseidon and the nymph Thoösa, when the giant came into the cave and closed the entrance with a huge rock. Discovering the Greeks he ate two of Odysseus' men that day and two more the next, locking up the rest in the cave while he went out to pasture his sheep. In Polyphemus' absence Odysseus took a huge club he found in the cave and sharpened it to a point, and when the Cyclops returned, Odysseus offered him some of the wine which the Greeks had brought with them. This was the first time the Cyclops had tasted wine, he became drunk,

and in gratitude he promised to eat Odysseus last. To mock him Odysseus told Polyphemus that his name was "Noman." Then as the Cyclops slept Odysseus heated the pointed stake and burned out the Cyclops' eye, so that when the incapacitated Cyclops removed the rock from the mouth of the cave to let out his flock, Odysseus and his men escaped by clinging to the undersides of the sheep. As the Greeks sailed away the Cyclops in his blindness hurled huge rocks aimlessly at the ships. At this point Odysseus, committing the one act of folly in his career, through a display of excessive pride could not restrain himself from taunting the Cyclops by telling him his real name. Thereupon Polyphemus prayed for vengeance to his father, the sea god Poseidon, who continued to hound Odysseus for years.

The cannibalistic Cyclopes met by Odysseus should not be confused with two other types of giants bearing the same name, the Cyclopes who were the sons of Uranus and Gaea and forged the thunderbolts, and a later tribe of giant builders who helped construct the fortification walls of such places as Mycenae and Tiryns, made up of enormous irregular blocks of stone. At a later time, during the Hellenistic period, Polyphemus was depicted as an amorous giant courting the lovely Nereid Galatea, who preferred the young Acis, whom Polyphemus killed with a huge rock in a jealous rage. In another version he serenaded Galatea so charmingly that she yielded to his love. The Cyclopes are often depicted as three-eyed rather than one-eyed, with magic power in the "third eye." Only the destruction of this third eye could overcome the magic power of its possessor. Today there are still stories about three-eyed mythical creatures on the island of Crete, and on the coasts of Sicily, Southern Italy, Corsica and Sardinia there are many caves today called "Cave of Polyphemus." The shore line near each of them is dotted with huge rocks, supposed to have been thrown by Polyphemus.

Odysseus and his men came next to the island of Aeolus, king of the winds (possibly the island of Stromboli off the northeastern coast of Sicily), from whom Odysseus received a bag of winds to help the Ithacans reach their homeland swiftly. They had just caught sight of Ithaca when Odysseus' men, consumed by curiosity and greed, opened the bag of winds, thinking it contained treasure. The ship was immediately blown far away by the raging winds, driven to the land of the Laestrygonians, giant cannibals, who ate most of Odysseus' men and destroyed eleven of his ships.

With his one surviving vessel Odysseus came to the mysterious island of Aeaea, where lived Circe, an aunt of Medea and next to her the greatest sorceress in Greek myth. Some of Odysseus' men set out to explore the island, and when they came to Circe's palace she fed them drugged food and turned them into swine. Out of duty to his men as well as great curiosity, Odysseus set out to face her, and fortunately en route met the god Hermes, who provided him with the magic herb *moly*, a charm against Circe, so the sorceress was unable to harm him. Overpowering her, he forced her to turn his men back into humans. Then she gladly became his lover. Odysseus and the entire ship's company lived in Circe's palace for a year, drinking and feasting without end, and Odysseus had a son by Circe who was named Telegonus ("Born Far Away").

After a year of pleasures on Circe's island, Odysseus was eager to be on his way, but Circe informed him that he must first go to the entrance of Hades to consult the ghost of the Theban soothsayer Tiresias about his future. As the Ithacans hastened to leave the island, young Elpenor, asleep on the roof of the palace, fell off and broke his neck, and since no one discovered his whereabouts, they sailed off without him. Odysseus and his men sailed west to the edge of the great river Oceanus encircling the earth and reached the entrance to the Underworld, where, after Odysseus offered proper sacrifices, many souls emerged to see him. This visit of a living person to the Underworld is one of the recurrent themes of world literature, with its origins in the Near East, where it was known especially from the epic of Gilgamesh.

First the soul of Elpenor came to tell Odysseus how he had died on Circe's island, and Odysseus promised him proper burial on the return voyage. Then the soul of Tiresias appeared and prophesied more suffering for Odysseus, but predicted a final happy life for him among his people on Ithaca. Odysseus also saw the soul of his mother Anticleia, who had died of a broken heart waiting for his return, and she was followed by a long procession of souls of famous women of the past.

One of the dead he saw was Agamemnon, about whose death he had not, of course, previously known, and he learned from

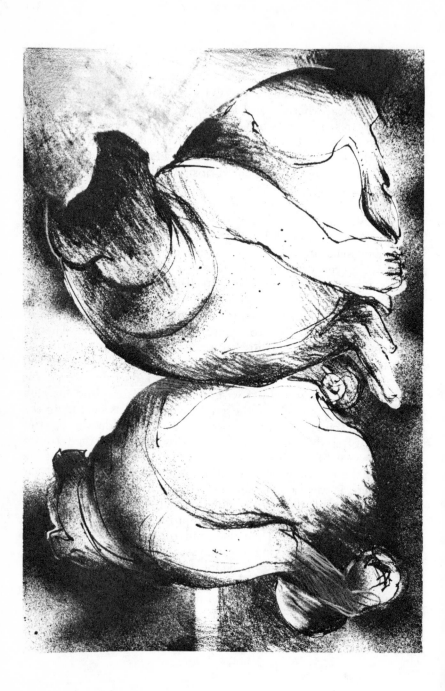

Agamemnon how he was murdered by his wife Clytemnestra and her lover Aegisthus. Then he saw Achilles' soul; the great hero sadly told Odysseus that he envied him for being alive, and that even the life of a poor farm laborer working for another man was preferable to the fame of a dead hero. The soul of Ajax appeared, but refused to talk to him, angry even in death because of his loss of the armor of Achilles to Odysseus. Finally Odysseus saw the souls of other great heroes of the past, as well as of famous sinners being punished in Hades, men like the notorious Tantalus and Sisyphus. In this journey to the land of the dead Odysseus was reassured about his future, and moreover was strengthened by knowing more than he did before about humanity. After the visit to the Underworld, he valued his own life all the more.

After returning to Circe's island to bury Elpenor's body, the Ithacans sailed toward home again. As they passed the island of the Sirens (two female temptresses who lived off the west coast of Italy), Odysseus decided to listen to their magic song. Constantly in quest of novel experiences, Odysseus wanted to hear them, for they promised to passersby all knowledge as well as exquisite erotic pleasures. Therefore he instructed his men to put wax in their ears, while he had himself lashed to the mast so that he could hear them safely, and would not suffer the usual fate of sailors, who leaped overboard toward the mysterious island and met their death in the water. It is said that after Odysseus' successful escape the Sirens themselves leaped into the sea and died.

As we have seen, Odysseus and his men passed through the twin dangers of Scylla and Charybdis, usually placed in the straits of Messina between Italy and the island of Sicily, though the straits of Gibraltar seem more appropriate. As Odysseus and his ship passed near Scylla she seized six of his men and devoured them, and rowing away from this danger the Ithacans narrowly escaped being swallowed by the monstrous whirlpool Charybdis.

The depleted Ithacans landed cautiously on the island of Sicily. They had been warned not to go there, for the cattle of Helios Hyperion, the sun god, were kept on the island. Odysseus made his men take an oath not to kill any of the sacred cattle, but after being becalmed for a month, the hungry crew killed some of the cattle for food while Odysseus slept. As a result, when they finally sailed away Zeus caused a violent storm which destroyed the ship. Only the hero Odysseus survived this disaster, by clinging to a raft he had managed to construct. After ten days on the sea he reached the island of Ogygia, which belonged to the lovely nymph Calypso, who cared for him and made him her lover. Calypso was an immortal nymph, daughter of Atlas and Pleione. Since her name means "Concealer," she may be symbolically a death goddess, and Odysseus' survival after staying with her may signify his triumph over death.

After seven years with Calypso on her beautiful island, called "the omphalos (navel) of the sea" (perhaps Malta is meant), Odysseus yearned to leave for home, and finally the gods sent the messenger Hermes and ordered Calypso to release Odysseus, who sat on the shore constantly weeping for his return home. To induce him to remain with her Calypso tempted him with an offer of immortality, but Odysseus preferred his mortal wife Penelope and the uncertainties and challenges of human life. In this way Odysseus, by opting to remain human, recovered his freedom of choice. What he yearned for was challenge, a social community, even the fragility of human life rather than the perfection of an ideal world with Calypso, and with this rejection of the temptation of Calypso Odysseus began his return to his human identity, which he had previously lost in a fantasy world in which his will was subject to a higher force.

Odysseus built a raft and set forth, but Poseidon still pursued him, causing a fierce storm. He was shipwrecked once more, this time on the island of Phaeacia (possibly Corfu), a kind of fairyland. It was ruled by the generous and lovable King Alcinoüs and Queen Arete, who had a daughter named Nausicaä, a young girl ripe for marriage. The morning after Odysseus landed, she went with her serving girls to wash clothes near the shore, where she discovered the naked Odysseus, offered him clothing and aid, and found him so handsome after a bath that she wished she might marry such a man. Soon she brought him to the fabulous palace of Alcinoüs, who ruled over a perfect society inhabited by a generous, humane people — so different from his experiences in the past and those still to come soon in Ithaca. Having finally reached an organized community, and a seafaring one at that, Odysseus began his return to real life after he had lost everything — ships, men, wealth, even his clothing.

The Phaeacians welcomed Odysseus and entertained him royally, even though they did not know his identity. Finally, after receiving many precious gifts and being entertained with banquets, music, and athletic contests, Odysseus revealed his identity and related to the Phaeacians the story of his wanderings and adventures in the ten years after he left Troy. After this the Phaeacians escorted him to Ithaca in a swift ship together with his many gifts. Poseidon took revenge on the Phaeacians for helping Odysseus by transforming the Phaeacian ship into stone when it returned to its harbor.

After twenty years of abnormal living — ten of war, ten of fantastic adventure — Odysseus came back to real life. In his home of Ithaca he slowly began to renew his humanity and resume his ties with family and enemies, the good and bad of real life, after his extraordinary experiences as a war hero and in the grandiose world of fantasy. To protect him from harm, Athena had transformed him into an ugly old filthy beggar, after hiding his gifts from Phaeacia and giving him instructions how to settle affairs in Ithaca.

Odysseus was courteously welcomed and given hospitality by his faithful swineherd Eumaeus. At this very moment Telemachus was en route home from a visit to Sparta, where he had gone to inquire from Menelaüs and Helen the whereabouts of his father. The goddess Athena, disguised as a friend of Odysseus, had urged him to assert himself, though still a youth, against the suitors of his mother Penelope. For many years now, when it appeared that Odysseus would never return, over 100 nobles of Ithaca had demanded that Penelope choose one of them as her husband and next king of Ithaca, and while waiting for her decision insolently came to the palace every day, wasting Odysseus' property in endless feasting and drinking in the great banquet hall. For four years Penelope (her name means "Unraveler of Thread") had delayed the decision by pretending she would not make her choice until she had finished weaving a garment for her aged father-in-law Laërtes, to serve as his funeral shroud. Every night she unraveled all the work she had completed during the day. But through a slave woman who was consorting with the suitors the deception was discovered, and so she was compelled to complete the robe. The decision to marry could no longer be postponed. Penelope, who became the classical symbol of fidelity in marriage, was a highly intelligent, beautiful, resourceful woman, but relatively powerless in a man's world.

So also for a long time, until Odysseus returned, was his young son. Telemachus had stood up to the suitors, but they scorned him. Crestfallen, he left for Pylos and Sparta on the mainland of Greece to seek tidings of his father, advised and guided by Athena, in the likeness of Mentor, to whom Odysseus had entrusted his household when he left for Troy. At Pylos Telemachus spoke to aged King Nestor about his father but learned little from him, then journeyed to Sparta, where he was graciously entertained by Menelaüs and Helen. From King Menelaüs he learned that the sea god Proteus had once told him that Odysseus was on the island of the nymph Calypso.

The suitors planned to ambush and kill Telemachus when he returned, but he evaded them and immediately went to Eumaeus' hut. There, alone with him, Odysseus revealed his identity, and the two planned the destruction of the suitors. Disguised as a beggar Odysseus went to the palace, where he was abused by the suitors. Amazingly, his old hunting dog Argus, whom he had not seen for twenty years, recognizing his master, died at his feet, and as Odysseus' feet were being washed by the aged serving woman of the household Eurycleia, she recognized a scar on Odysseus' leg, but in the nick of time Odysseus stifled her outcry and swore her to secrecy. Telemachus, meanwhile, had all the weapons of the suitors removed.

Penelope declared a contest for the suitors. Whichever could string the famous bow of Odysseus and shoot an arrow through the handle holes of twelve axe-heads set up in a row would marry her, and after several suitors tried but were not even able to string the great bow, Odysseus asked to handle the bow. All doors meanwhile had been bolted. Odysseus strung the bow easily, promptly shot an arrow through all the axe-heads, and then revealed his identity. In a gruesome scene the suitors were mercilessly slaughtered and, in addition, twelve serving maids who had dishonorably consorted with the suitors were hanged.

Penelope was skeptical that the stranger was indeed her husband Odysseus, for after twenty years and numerous false rumors about Odysseus, she was wary, but finally tested him by mentioning a detail about the construction of their marriage bed. His precise knowledge of it convinced her, and so after twenty years husband and wife were happily reunited.

Then Odysseus, after telling Penelope of his wanderings, went to see his aged father Laërtes in the country. An emotional reunion took place between father and son. Thus finally did Odysseus regain his identity fully, as father, husband, son, although he still had to face a challenge to his royal power. Kinsmen of the suitors mobilized to seek revenge, and marched out to attack Odysseus, Telemachus, Laërtes, and their followers, but as hostilities were about to begin in earnest, by order of the goddess Athena and a warning thunderbolt from Zeus peace was proclaimed in Ithaca, and Odysseus resumed his role as king of his people.

In a sequel to the story of his return, years later Odysseus' son by Circe, Telegonus, went in search of his father. When he arrived in Ithaca, he did not realize where he was, and began to drive off some cattle, and in a struggle with Odysseus Telegonus killed his father without recognizing him. Nevertheless, Telegonus and Telemachus were reconciled, Telemachus gave his mother Penelope in marriage to Telegonus, and Telemachus then married Circe. Finally both couples were transported to live a blessed life on the Isles of the Blest.

XXV

A MISCELLANY OF GREEK MYTHS

Sisyphus

Originally a king of Thessaly, Sisyphus founded the city of Corinth and became its first king. He is the greatest trickster of Greek mythology, the classical symbol of craftiness and deceit, notorious for thievery, duplicity, and crass opportunism. When Zeus carried off the nymph Aegina, daughter of the river god Asopus, Sisyphus, for a consideration, informed on Zeus to Asopus, who was frantically searching for his daughter, and told him where Zeus had taken the girl. Exasperated, Zeus sent Thanatos (Death) for him, but Sisyphus ambushed Thanatos and imprisoned him in chains to prevent his own death. Of course there resulted a moratorium on death everywhere until the god of war Ares liberated Thanatos. Since he had to die, Sisyphus asked his wife to die in his place and when she refused he made her promise elaborate funeral rites. After arriving in Hades, he managed to talk his way out of the Underworld by convincing Persephone he had a right to return to earth to punish his wife for neglect of his memory. When he made every effort to evade returning to Hades, Zeus killed him irrevocably, and assigned him one of the memorable punishments of sinners in Hades. Sisyphus was compelled to push a huge rock up a hill, to get it over the top, but each time he reached the summit, the rock fell down the hill, and he had to resume his eternal task.

Bellerophon

The myths of Bellerophon, national hero of Corinth, are analogous to heroic stories like those of Heracles, Perseus, and

Theseus. His story too is an amalgam of folktales, with a varying of the pattern of the hero myth, all from Hellenic perspectives. A grandson of the crafty Sisyphus and relative of the notorious sinner Salmoneus, Bellerophon began his career by committing a murder in Corinth. As a result he was exiled to Argos, where he was a guest of King Proetus, who purified him of his blood-guilt.

The name Bellerophon means "Slayer of Bellerus." It is possible that originally — in Bellerophon's connection with Lycia in Asia Minor — it meant that he was the killer of a dragon called Bellero, known from a language of that region. When the Greeks transformed him into a Greek hero prince, his name was interpreted to mean that he killed a human of that name.

At the royal court of Proetus Bellerophon unknowingly aroused the passions of the king's wife Sthenoboea (or Antaea), who tried to seduce him. When he repulsed her attentions she took revenge by accusing him of having tried to rape her, yet another version of the age-old folktale "Joseph and Potiphar's Wife." This Old Testament story has its origin in traditional stories of the ancient Near East, the earliest known being the Egyptian folktale of two brothers. The folktale has spread all over the world, retold with local coloration in medieval Europe, among the Moslems, in Zoroastrian, Persian, Buddhist, and Japanese literatures, and its most famous modern version is Thomas Mann's *Joseph Story*. In the basic formula of this tale, a handsome and chaste youth has advances made to him by his stepmother (or other married woman, usually older than himself), from motives either of love, lust, or concern for the advancement of her own children to power or wealth. The youth rejects the woman's attentions, so she accuses him falsely to her husband. As a result his life is endangered, but in almost all instances he is vindicated and the woman is punished.

To punish Bellerophon Proetus sent him to King Iobates of Lycia in Asia Minor with a sealed letter which asked the king to put the bearer to death. The "letter of death" (also called "Bellerophontic letter"), a traditional folktale theme in both Asia and Europe, had many well known victims, like Bathsheba's husband Uriah the Hittite in the Old Testament, put out of the way in this manner by David, and Rosencrantz and Guildenstern, on whom Hamlet revenged himself similarly. King Iobates of

Lycia, impressed with the youth, decided to test Bellerophon with a series of three labors, and first sent him to battle the warlike tribe called the Solymi, whom he defeated single-handedly. Then he had to undertake the defense of the area against the Amazons, against whom he won another magnificent victory. Finally he was assigned the heroic task of killing the triformed monster called the Chimaera. This creature, the strangest fantastic being in Greek mythology and of Asiatic origin, had a lion's head and a dragon's tail, with a goat's head belching flames protruding from the middle of its back. In conquering the Chimaera Bellerophon was assisted by the winged horse Pegasus, obtained from Poseidon, together with a golden bridle from Athena.

Having proved himself by his heroic deeds, Bellerophon received as reward the hand of a princess, daughter of Iobates, and was made heir to the throne. In one of his first acts after his triumph, he returned to Argos to unmask Sthenoboea and punish her, and took her up with him into the air on Pegasus and hurled her from a height into the sea. But Bellerophon's success went to his head, and when, in his pride, he tried to force his way into the company of the gods on Olympus by trying to ascend to the celestial city on Pegasus, the winged horse threw him, and he lived out his life crippled, blind, and mad, while Pegasus flew up to Olympus alone.

Salmoneus

Like Sisyphus, King Salmoneus of Elis was a scorner of the gods, and received due punishment. His arrogance consisted in calling himself Zeus, impersonating the king of the gods by having sacrifices made to himself, and creating thunder and lightning by artificial devices, so Zeus destroyed him with a thunderbolt. This myth may reflect a memory of a pre-Greek king who opposed the Olympian religion headed by Zeus.

Erysichthon

This Thessalian hero was violent and impious. Erysichthon cut down a wood sacred to the goddess Demeter, was punished by an insatiable hunger, and ate up all his wealth. So desperate was his situation that his daughter, who was able to transform herself, supported him by frequently being sold in different shapes. In the

end Erysichthon was so ravenous that he devoured himself.

We have seen that scorners of the gods, of whom there are many other instances in Greek myths, were punished with a variety of traditional penalties. This is, perhaps, why such religious skeptics as the Greek writers Euripides and Lucian were said to have lost their lives by being torn apart by dogs. The early Christians continued the concept of punishments for scorners of God. For example, St. Paul is said to have been blinded for a while for persecuting Christ, and Roman emperors who persecuted Christians were said for that reason to have met violent deaths.

Arachne

A typical tale of punishment for defying the gods is the myth of Arachne, originally a folktale. A daughter of Idmon, a weaver in Lydia, which was known for its textile art, she herself was famous as a weaver of tapestries, so much so that in her pride she boasted of her art and defied the goddess Athena to compete with her. Though indeed skilful, Arachne was humiliated by Athena, and hung herself. As a lesson Athena transformed Arachne into a spider, which is the meaning of the Greek word *arachne*.

Actaeon

Actaeon, son of Aristaeus, grandson of Cadmus, was brought up by the centaur Chiron, became a famous hunter, a favorite of Artemis, and wherever he went he was followed by his pack of fifty dogs. But his good fortune as a hunter induced him to commit *hybris*. He offended Artemis either because he boasted that he was a better hunter than the goddess, or because he threatened to violate her, or saw her bathing in the nude. Another version of his defiance of the gods was that he incurred the anger of Zeus because he too desired Semele, who was his aunt. Whatever the reason, he was transformed into a stag and promptly torn apart by his own hunting dogs. When the dogs continually lamented their master, Chiron made a statue of Actaeon to console them.

Marsyas

Athena invented the flute, but when she tried to play it, it made her look so ugly that she threw it away. The Satyr (or

Silenus) Marsyas found it and became so skilful that he challenged Apollo to a contest, the flute against the lyre, the common instrument against the aristocratic one. In the competition Marsyas lost. His punishment seems unduly severe: he was tied to a tree by Apollo and flayed alive.

The Aloades

Otus and Ephialtes were twin sons of Iphimedia by Aloeus or Poseidon. If their father was Poseidon, they constitute a set of heavenly twins like Castor and Polydeuces, sons of an early Hellenic god of thunder and horses. The twins grew very rapidly, becoming giants by the time they were nine years old. The character and behavior of these inseparable twins indicate that they belong to a very primitive layer of Greek myth, and in what is perhaps a reminiscence of a struggle between pre-Greek religion and the Olympian cult, the Aloades, as they are called, defied the Olympian gods, trying to prove themselves superior to them. They seized and imprisoned Ares for 13 months, keeping him in a bronze jar, thus incidentally putting an end to wars for that period. The "jar of punishment" is known only from one other source, the Hittites. Then Otus and Ephialtes threatened to violate Hera and Artemis, and sought to storm Olympus by piling Mt. Pelion on Mt. Ossa, a more primitive version of the Old Testament Tower of Babel. In this attempt they were either dissuaded by their father Poseidon or repulsed by the arrows of Apollo. To destroy them, Artemis led them a merry chase to the island of Naxos, and as they pursued her she suddenly substituted for herself a beautiful hind while they were separated from each other. Seeing it, they hurled their spears at it from opposite directions, but when the animal suddenly disappeared the twins killed each other simultaneously. The part played by both Artemis and Apollo in the destruction of the Aloades is a good example of a familiar folktale motif — the special magic of twins being combatted by another set of twins.

Thamyris

Thamyris of Thrace was a famed mythical musician and poet, very handsome and a superb player of the lyre and singer. He challenged the Muses to a music contest with the prize his right to sleep with all the Muses in succession. Of course he lost the contest, so as punishment the Muses blinded him (one version relates that he lost only one eye) and deprived him of his musical gifts. Humbled, he threw away his lyre.

Orion

Orion, son of Poseidon, was a giant hunter, very handsome and distinguished by both his strength and amorous propensities. After his first wife, Side, so beautiful that she committed *hybris* by daring to rival Hera, was therefore cast down by Hera into Tartarus, Orion wooed Merope, daughter of King Oenopion ("Wine Drinker") of the island of Chios. As a reward for ridding the island of wild beasts for Oenopion, he was promised Merope as his wife, but before the marriage Orion became drunk and violated Merope. For this offence Oenopion blinded him. Then Orion obtained from Hephaestus the boy Cedalion, whom he placed on his shoulders to guide him, and in this way performed the miracle of walking on the waters to the island of Lemnos. Since he walked in the direction of the sun, Orion's eyesight was restored by Helios (a folk belief that blindness can be cured by sunlight).

Later Eos, the dawn, fell in love with Orion and transported him to the island of Delos, where he offended the goddess Artemis by trying to violate one of her maidens or Artemis herself. To punish him, Artemis killed the club-bearing giant with the more advanced bow and arrows, or sent a scorpion which killed him. In one version the arrogant Orion threatened to rid the whole world of animals, and so Mother Earth sent the scorpion to kill him. (Apparently in a very primitive myth the scorpion, sent by Gaea, attacked the genitals of a male and emasculated him for a sex crime.) For punishing Orion, the scorpion was then elevated into the sky as the constellation Scorpio, and nearby in the heavens was placed Orion himself, "the mighty hunter of the skies," the most brilliant of all constellations. It is also said that the amorous Orion pursued the seven nymphs called the Pleiades, and that they too were placed in the sky near Orion to commemorate this.

Lycaon, Callisto and Arcas

King Lycaon of Arcadia had fifty sons and a reputation for piety that somehow did not ring true. Once when Zeus disguised himself as a peasant and went on a "tour of inspection" of humans, Lycaon gave him hospitality, but suspecting him to be a god decided to test his omniscience by feeding him the flesh of one of his children. To punish him for practicing human sacrifice and cannibalism, Zeus destroyed his palace with a thunderbolt, killed all but one of his sons, and transformed Lycaon into a wolf. Lycaon's impiety angered Zeus against all humanity so that he sent the great flood from which only Deucalion and Pyrrha survived.

This myth contains a variant of a local flood myth, found also in the Philemon and Baucis story and that of Lot in the Old Testament, both of which have a number of analogies to the myth of Lycaon, and there may also be imbedded in this story a pre-Greek wolf cult which was superseded by the cult of the Olympian gods. The transformation of a human into a wolf to produce a lycanthrope (half-man, half-wolf creature), with the capability of shape-shifting, is especially associated with Lycaon in classical mythology. The fear and hatred of the wolf as a baleful beast was natural in an animal breeding region such as mountainous Arcadia in Greece, although the wolf was not always a hateful animal in ancient mythology. Several stories of a female wolf as animal nurse appear in classical myths, the most famous instance the Roman myth of the suckling of the twins Romulus and Remus by a she-wolf.

Lycaon's daughter Callisto (she may have been originally a nymph of Arcadia) was devoted to the goddess of chastity Artemis, so she took a vow of virginity and lived as a huntress in the company of the companions of Artemis. Zeus however became enamored of her, and to consummate his love took the form of Artemis herself — the ultimate in his many transformations, in this case lust disguised as the very symbol of chastity. Raped by Zeus Callisto became the mother of Zeus' son Arcas, and as a result she was killed either by jealous Hera, or by Artemis, who was outraged when she discovered Callisto's pregnancy. Out of pity Zeus turned her into a bear.

The story is also told that Callisto's son Arcas (whose name is the origin of the name Arcadia) was brought up by the nymph Maia after Callisto was transformed into a bear. He too became a hunter. One day he came across the very bear that was his mother

Callisto, and was about to kill the animal when Zeus intervened and made Callisto the constellation Ursa Major (Great Bear). Then to join her with Arcas he placed his son in the sky as the nearby constellation Ursa Minor (Little Bear) or Arctophylax ("Guardian of the Bear").

Philemon and Baucis

In Phrygia in Asia Minor lived a pious peasant couple named Philemon and Baucis. Zeus and Hermes once traveled in this region disguised as humans to test man's humanity to man, and only Philemon and Baucis welcomed them and shared with them their simple food and home. In anger at the general insensitivity of the population Zeus sent a devastating flood which destroyed the area, except for the kindly couple and their home. When Zeus then gave Philemon and Baucis a wish, they asked that their hut become a temple of the gods and that they be made the temple guardians. In their old age they were transformed into trees standing before the temple, so that they continued to guard it even after they died, Philemon as an oak, Baucis as a linden tree.

This regional flood myth is an offshoot of the great Babylonian universal flood story, with analogies to the Old Testament story of Lot and the corrupt cities of Sodom and Gomorrah, and the Arcadian flood myth of Lycaon.

Adonis

Adonis came into Greek religion and mythology from the Near East, where he was a young male god of vegetation and fertility. In Babylonian myth he was called Tammuz, among the Semites on the coast of Asia Minor he was named Adon ("The Lord"), the young lover of Ishtar, goddess of love, and when the Greeks borrowed this myth from the Semitic world it developed as a hero myth, and was adapted to their own religion and mythology. Adonis' mother was said to have been Myrrha (or Smyrna), daughter of King Cinyras of Cyprus, himself of Phoenician origin, a city builder and civilizer, proverbial for both riches and handsomeness. Inspired by the goddess of love Aphrodite, Myrrha developed an incestuous love for her father, made Cinyras drunk and had sexual relations with him. When Cinyras discovered the horrible deception and tried to kill her, she fled and was transformed into a myrrh tree and in this form she gave birth to the beautiful infant Adonis.

Aphrodite took up the baby and provided for it a substitute mother, Queen Persephone of Hades, to whom she brought Adonis in a chest. In time Aphrodite came to Persephone to claim Adonis as her own, and to bring him to the upper world, but Persephone refused to part with him. The quarrel over custody of Adonis was settled by Zeus: the youth was to remain with Persephone one-third of the year, with Aphrodite one-third, and the remaining third he could choose himself.

In another version Adonis became the lover of Aphrodite, in keeping with the Near Eastern myths of the young male god as lover of the mother goddess, but because Adonis was a hunter, Artemis, goddess of hunting and chastity, was angry with him for his devotion to Aphrodite. As a result he was killed by a boar in a hunting accident, although Aphrodite's love for Adonis was so great that she won him back from Hades part of each year. One version says that anemones sprang from the blood of the dying Adonis. In his descent to Hades Adonis carried a magic branch symbolizing immortality and indicating that his stay in Hades was to be temporary. Adonis was worshipped in the ancient world as a young god symbolizing ripe fruits and the vegetation cycle of the seasons, and was venerated with very emotional ceremonies of mourning at his death, joy at his return.

The association of Adonis with a boar hunt is an interesting Greek touch. The boar is a symbol of destruction, the traditional enemy of cultivation of fields, as the wolf is of domesticated animals, and for this reason the boar hunt was in antiquity a noble occupation of heroes, just as it remains today a rich man's sport. More significant, in the myth of Adonis the original symbol of the seasonal cycle of vegetation ultimately developed into the religious concept of death and resurrection. Adonis became in ancient poetry and art a symbol of immortality.

Orpheus

Son of Oeagrus and the nymph Calliope, Orpheus was a famous musician of Thrace, preeminent in playing the lyre. In the earliest version of the myth his career was swiftly ended when, as a worshipper of Helios, he opposed the cult of Dionysus, and for this defiance was torn apart by Dionysus' Bassarids (a variant name of the Bacchantes).

In the Seventh and Sixth centuries B.C. the gentle musician was transformed into a prophet of a mystic form of the cult of Dionysus, the religion of Orphism, an early mystery religion with many adherents in the ancient world. In the myths of Dionysus Orpheus was a prophet and proselytizer of that god as key to attaining a happy immortality, so perhaps because the god Dionysus himself descended to the Underworld to bring back his mother Semele, a myth involving the restoration of the dead was also associated with Orpheus.

Originally Orpheus was unmarried and lived as an ascetic, but as founder of the Orphic religion he appeared as husband of Eurydice, and still later as a particularly loving one. In the story, Orpheus fell in love with Eurydice and they were married, but on the day of the wedding Eurydice was bitten by a poisonous snake and died. Heartbroken, Orpheus descended to Hades to win back his wife from death. He charmed everyone in the Underworld by the power of his song and the music of his lyre — even the monsters there, the sinners being punished, the dog Cerberus, and finally Persephone and Hades.

In the earliest, optimistic account of the Orpheus-Eurydice story Orpheus triumphed and succeeded in regaining his wife, but in the best known version, beginning in the Hellenistic period and told best in the *Georgics* of Vergil, there is a tragic ending. Orpheus was permitted to bring Eurydice back on the condition that he not look at her until she emerged from the lower world, but failed because he committed a ritual fault by breaking the taboo that one must not look at ghosts of the Underworld. Just as Eurydice, following her beloved husband, had reached the exit to the upper world, Orpheus could not resist the temptation to look back at her, and so lost her forever.

Because of his loss of Eurydice Orpheus was inconsolable, and after Eurydice's "second death" roamed the world in despair, became a woman hater and an ascetic, remaining celibate and preferring the company of men. This so infuriated the women of Thrace that they tore him apart. His severed head was thrown into the sea, and as it floated the lips repeated "Eurydice, Eurydice!"

Daphnis

Daphnis was a shepherd of Sicily, son of Hermes and a nymph. A young man of extraordinary beauty and charm, famous for his musical gifts, he played the shepherd's pipes and sang beautifully. He was said also to have invented pastoral (bucolic) poetry. He loved a nymph and vowed that he would always love her only, on pain of being struck blind, but once while drunk he was unfaithful with another woman, and as punishment he became blind and fell off a cliff and died (or was drawn into the water by his lover the nymph). His father Hermes raised him up to heaven.

There is another version of the Daphnis story, in which he asserted he would never fall in love. For this excess Aphrodite and Eros punished him by causing him to fall in love with a nymph, so that he was destroyed by the insoluble conflict of his resistance to love and his unsatisfied longing. Daphnis died mourned by all, including Aphrodite.

Ceyx and Halcyon

This story combines a transformation myth involving a loving couple and a folktale about the "halcyon days." Ceyx married Halcyon, in one of the most famous weddings in mythology, which many heroes, including Heracles, attended. So great was the love of this couple that they called themselves Hera and Zeus, committing the sin of *hybris,* and when Ceyx went on a sea voyage, Zeus drowned him in punishment for his excessive pride. Halcyon wept for him so inconsolably that she leaped into the sea and was also drowned. Halcyon was then transformed into a kingfisher, Ceyx into a sea-fowl.

The Halcyon Days were thought to be a period of a week before and a week after the winter solstice in the Mediterranean, when the sea was calm. This part of the story derives from Near Eastern myths of the sun as a bird, and the concept of the rebirth of the sun after the winter solstice, as the days grow longer. Actually, the halcyon was a rare bird in the Mediterranean, and the "halcyon days" are a mythical period of calm.

Daphne

Daphne (the name means "laurel"), a nymph loved by Apollo, fled from his attentions, but he pursued her relentlessly. In desperation she called on the gods for help, and was transformed into a laurel tree just as Apollo caught up with her. Today the laurel is a symbol of victory or peace, but in antiquity it was primarily a tree sacred to Apollo and used in his cult. It was said to be chewed by the Pythia, its intoxicating effect helping her speak her prophecies; as an evergreen it was also a symbol of immortality.

There is another version that Daphne was a huntress who was a favorite of Artemis and sworn to chastity. Leucippus, son of the famous King Oenomaüs, fell in love with her and she responded. To be with his beloved, Leucippus disguised himself as a girl and joined the company of Artemis' women followers. But Apollo too loved Daphne, and out of jealousy he made the other girls insist that they all bathe nude in a river, despite the objections of Leucippus, so that his sex was discovered and he was killed by the followers of Artemis. Now a confirmed devotee of Artemis, Daphne wanted no further male lovers. As Apollo pursued her she fled and was transformed into a laurel tree.

Pyramus and Thisbe

In this Near Eastern folktale which was borrowed by both the Greeks and Romans, two young Babylonians, Pyramus and Thisbe, fell in love. They were neighbors, but since their parents opposed the marriage, their only communication was through a hole in a wall separating their homes. The lovesick pair decided to elope, and agreed on a rendezvous one night at a spot outside the city. Thisbe arrived first, but while she waited for Pyramus, a lioness fresh from a kill passed by and Thisbe ran away, dropping her veil. The lioness chewed on this and left it bloody. When Pyramus arrived and saw the bloody veil he thought that Thisbe had been devoured by a wild beast and committed suicide with his sword. When Thisbe returned and saw what had happened, she too killed herself with Pyramus' sword. Their ashes were placed in the same urn, and it is said that the fruit of the mulberry tree, under which they were to meet, turned black as a result of this tragedy.

Pygmalion

Pygmalion, a king of Cyprus, had a statue of the goddess Aphrodite so beautiful that he loved it as if it were a woman.

Behind this story may be a survival of the age-old story of the great mother goddess and her young lover — the "sacred marriage" of the fertility goddess and her consort. In the famous mythical story Pygmalion was a sculptor who rejected the attentions of all women because they did not come up to his vision of ideal beauty, so he created an ivory statue of a beautiful woman, and soon fell in love with it. He prayed to Aphrodite that she transform the statue into a real woman. She granted his request, and they were married. There is no name recorded for Pygmalion's animated statue in classical mythology.

In the 18th and 19th centuries the interest in automata and the invention of automated figures led to a great interest in the myth of Pygmalion, and names were invented for the statue. The most famous of these modern names are Galatea and Elise. The concept of this love of the artist for his creation inspired such famous works as W. S. Gilbert's play *Pygmalion and Galatea* (1871), George Bernard Shaw's *Pygmalion* (1913), and the perennially popular musical comedy *My Fair Lady*.

XXVI

MORE GREEK MYTHS

Hero and Leander

This is the tragic story of lovers separated by obstacles. Hero, a priestess of Aphrodite at Sestos on the European shore of the Dardanelles (Hellespont), was forbidden by her parents to marry, and a vow of chastity was imposed upon her. With only one slave girl as attendant, she lived in isolation in a tower near the shore. One day a youth named Leander, from Abydos across the straits on the Asiatic side, came to Sestos for a festival of the goddess Aphrodite, fell in love with Hero at first sight, and declared his love for her. Because of her status as priestess he could visit her only in secret at night. She lit a lamp for him, and each night he swam across the very dangerous Hellespont, but one night in a storm the light was extinguished, and Leander drowned. When Hero found the body she leaped into the water to die with her beloved.

Cupid and Psyche

This famous story is a collection of folktales organized into a love romance made popular by the Roman author Apuleius in his novel *Metamorphoses*. The tale embodies various motifs like the supernatural unseen bridegroom, the taboo against looking at the secret lover, the jealous sisters, the cruel stepmother acting as a sort of witch, "impossible tasks" completed with miraculous aid, and animal helpers.

The myth tells of a princess named Psyche ("Soul"), the youngest and most beautiful daughter of a king. Her beauty was so exquisite that people came from all over to see her, almost to worship her, and this stirred up the enmity of Venus (the Roman name for the goddess Aphrodite). Therefore she ordered her son Cupid ("Love") to cause Psyche to fall in love with the vilest, most despicable man, but when Cupid saw Psyche he himself fell in love with her. To make her his bride, Cupid whisked Psyche away mysteriously one day to a magnificent palace of extraordinary beauty, where she was happily united with Cupid, who visited her only in the dark of night. He warned her that she was not to inquire who he was and not to try to look at him in the light, on pain of losing him forever.

Meanwhile the two sisters of Psyche were married to ordinary men. One day they visited her, and jealous of her happiness and wealth put doubts into her mind about her lover. One night as he lay asleep by her side, Psyche lit an oil lamp and discovered to her joy how handsome her lover was, but a drop of oil fell on him and he was awakened. At once Cupid rebuked her for disobeying him and disappeared. Desolated by her error, Psyche roamed all over the world searching for Cupid, and finally came to the palace of her mother-in-law Venus who vented her anger on Psyche, treating her like a slave girl and imposing upon her a series of onerous, seemingly impossible tasks, the most difficult of which was a descent to Hades to obtain a beauty charm for Venus from Persephone. But with miraculous aid, including the help of animals, Psyche managed to complete all the tasks.

Despite Psyche's great fault Cupid himself could not forget her, so great was his love, and therefore went to Olympus to ask Zeus for permission to marry a mortal. The permission was given, and Psyche became an immortal herself, so that Psyche and Venus were reconciled. Thus love conquered all in this ancient love story, and Cupid and Psyche lived happily ever after.

Narcissus

There was a mountain nymph (Oread) named Echo who agreed once to help Zeus in one of his amours, talking incessantly to Hera while Zeus managed to evade her spying. When Hera discovered Echo's part she punished her by depriving her of the power of speech, except for the ability to repeat the last word of the person talking to her. Thus far this is merely an aetiological myth to explain the origin of the echo. The notion of reflection in the sound of the echo, however, resulted in the connection of her myth with another reflection story, that of Narcissus.

Echo fell in love with the handsome youth Narcissus, but her love was unrequited, for she was unable to communicate with him because she could only repeat his last words, and Narcissus, in abnormal self-love, rejected the love of all women. Aphrodite punished him for these faults. One day out in the woods he came upon a pool of water, and as he leaned over to take a drink he saw his own reflection. He was so fascinated by the image that he was riveted to the spot, unable to move or to satisfy his longing for the insubstantial image in the water, so that he died of self-neglect, through hunger, thirst, and emotional starvation. The story ends with Narcissus' transformation into the flower that bears his name.

Naturalists tell us that the narcissus plant has an affinity to water and often grows wild at the edge of pools and springs, and that it is capable of asexual reproduction. The Narcissus story incorporates widespread folk beliefs, and the ancient superstition that it is dangerous to see one's own reflection is still alive today. This has its origin in the primitive notion that every person has a double (Doppelgänger) connected with death. To see one's double is thus dangerous. Moreover, the frustrated passion of Narcissus for the image of a male has resulted in this myth being connected with homosexuality. Indeed the term Narcissism, invented by the German psychiatrist Näcke in 1899, was adopted by Freud and his followers as the archetype of homosexual love, in which a person is incapable of transferring sex interest to the opposite sex. In modern thought Narcissus has also become the symbol of love of ideal beauty, an illusion of loveliness without substance.

Hyacinth

Another plant myth involved Hyacinth. He was originally a minor prehellenic god of the fertility cycle, a youth who died and was reborn annually, with a cult located in the southern part of the Peloponnesus. When the worship of Apollo ousted this god of vegetation the Greeks converted Hyacinth into a very handsome youth beloved by Apollo. One day when Apollo was playing at throwing the discus, he accidentally killed his young friend by striking him with it. In another version it was not Apollo who was responsible but the wind Zephyr who, jealous of Apollo, turned the discus aside so that it struck and killed Hyacinth. (Because of the homosexual theme in this myth, one story reports that it was on account of his love for the handsome Hyacinth that the musician Thamyris invented pederasty.) From the blood of Hyacinth a flower named after him grew up. On its petals this flower has markings that resemble the letters AI, the Greek word for "Alas!"

This myth is a good example of the degradation under changing conditions of a divinity — from a god to a Greek prince to a flower. In plant mythology it is usually from the blood or ashes of a dying human that flowers or trees come into being.

Endymion

Endymion, son of Aethlius and Calyce, was a handsome young hunter. The moon goddess Selene fell in love with him, and visited him at night to lie with him as he slept. Given a wish, Endymion chose to remain ageless and sleep forever, so that he enjoyed eternal youth in eternal sleep. Imbedded in this myth is the concept in folklore that the moon is evil, so that sleeping in the light of the moon was considered dangerous. Because of the eternal sleep of Endymion his story was frequently portrayed on Roman sarcophagi as a sepulchral theme, and appealed also to the early Christians as a symbol of immortality.

Idas and Marpessa

The father of the princess Marpessa compelled suitors of his daughter to compete with him in a dangerous chariot race. In this way Idas won Marpessa from her father as his wife. But Apollo too had loved Marpessa, and so he carried her off, and as a result of the quarrel which developed between Idas and Apollo, Zeus allowed Marpessa to make her own choice. She chose the human Idas because she feared a god might abandon her soon.

Idas proved to be a famous hero, who participated in the expedition of the Argonauts and in the Calydonian Boar Hunt. He and his twin brother Lynceus were the Messenian "heavenly twins," parallel to the Dioscouri, Castor and Polydeuces. Lynceus was proverbial for his uncanny eyesight, which was so extraordinary that he could see through objects, even mountains. The brothers were killed on the same day, as we have seen, quarreling over cattle or women with Castor and Polydeuces.

Aristaeus

Cyrene, daughter of a king of the Lapiths in Thessaly, was seduced by the god Apollo, who bore her off to Libya in North Africa. There she gave birth to Aristaeus, who was brought up in Thessaly by the nymphs and the centaur Chiron. Aristaeus was probably originally a god of Northern Greece who was supplanted by the Greek god Apollo, and who in Greek myth became a culture hero, a benefactor of mankind as the author of many inventions in cultivation and hunting. He was especially considered the protector of cattle, vines, fruit trees, and bees.

The most famous myth told by Aristaeus appears at the end of Vergil's *Georgics,* and is there connected with the myth of Orpheus and Eurydice. It was Aristaeus who inadvertently caused the death of Eurydice by chasing her on her wedding day, so that she stepped on a poisonous snake. As a result the sister nymphs of Eurydice destroyed Aristaeus' bees, which he was cultivating attentively. In despair he went to his mother Cyrene, who pitied him and told him to find and seize the sea god Proteus, who would instruct him on the reasons for his loss and what to do. After a long struggle he mastered Proteus, who told him that he was responsible for the death of Eurydice, and that he must atone for this sin by the sacrifice of bullocks. Aristaeus, guilt-stricken, duly performed the indicated sacrifices, and in due time a miraculous rebirth took place, as a swarm of bees emerged from the carcasses of the dead animals.

Auge

King Aleus of Tegea in Arcadia had a daughter named Auge. An oracle foretold that Auge would have a son who would kill his uncles, so Aleus forbade Auge to marry on pain of death, and made her a priestess of Athena sworn to virginity. One day Heracles passed through Tegea, was hospitably entertained by Aleus, got drunk, found Auge, and raped her. When a son named Telephus was born in the very temple of Athena, Aleus took drastic measures. The versions vary as to whether Telephus was exposed on a mountainside, or placed in a box in the sea together with his mother, but in any case both mother and child, about to

be killed, were saved by Nauplius and sold as slaves in Mysia in
Asia Minor. There King Teuthras married Auge and adopted her
son Telephus, who succeeded to the throne. Later Telephus came
to Tegea without knowing his relatives there, and mocked by some
men he killed them. They were his uncles. Thus the oracle was
fulfilled. Later, in the first, abortive invasion of Troy, the Greeks
landed in Mysia. Opposing them, Telephus was seriously wounded
by Achilles' spear, but eventually was cured by the very weapon
that had wounded him.

Admetus and Alcestis

Alcestis was the most beautiful of the daughters of Pelias, the
only one of them not duped by Medea into participating in the
killing of their father. Her marriage to King Admetus of Pherae in
Thessaly was preceded by a famous courtship, for Pelias had put
obstacles in the way of her suitors. The young man who succeeded
in yoking wild beasts to a chariot and driving it would win her
hand. Only Admetus succeeded, and in this almost insuperable
task he was aided by the god Apollo, who was at the time
Admetus' slave. The circumstances of Apollo's servitude to
Admetus, it will be remembered from the myths of Apollo, were
connected with his killing of the Cyclopes. To atone for this deed
Apollo had been banished from Olympus and assigned as a slave to
the mortal Admetus to be purified of the blood-guilt. Admetus'
piety and kindness to Apollo were so great that Apollo obtained
from the Fates the promise that when it came time for Admetus
to die — he was doomed to an early death — this could be delayed
if someone offered a life for his life.

Admetus' marriage to Alcestis was unusually happy, and they
had two children. When his destined time to die arrived, he asked
his father and mother and his other blood relatives to substitute
for him, but all declined. Thereupon Alcestis offered herself out of
love for Admetus and died. On the day of the funeral, the hero
Heracles arrived at the palace of Admetus, and following traditional rules of hospitality, Admetus welcomed Heracles despite the
sad occasion, concealing from him the fact that it was a day of
mourning for his beloved wife. As usual the lusty Heracles drank
to excess and was boisterous, but finally realizing that something
was amiss, he sobered up and discovered that his host's wife

Alcestis had just died. Without more ado he confronted the god Thanatos, battled with him for the life of Alcestis, and rescued her from death and restored her alive to her husband.

The story of the sacrifice for love was a widespread folktale, which took many forms according to local traditions. In its original form it probably concerned the son of a king who was destined to die on his wedding day, but whose death could be postponed if he could find a substitute who would freely offer to die in place of him. The substitute in the folktale might give up all or part of his life. Only the bride offered herself as a substitute, giving a life for a life out of love. The gods of the Underworld were so moved by this act of self-sacrifice that they pitied her and allowed her to return to her husband. In the Greek myth of Admetus and Alcestis, the folktale somehow became associated with a Thessalian royal family, acquiring such typical Greek motifs as the trials of courtship, the purification of a murderer, and a deed of Heracles.

Tenes

Cycnus was a Greek king who had two children, Tenes and Hemithea. When his wife died he married Philonome, who turned out to be both a wicked stepmother and another version of "Potiphar's wife." She made sexual overtures to Tenes, and when he repulsed her and she told Cycnus that he had tried to seduce her, Cycnus placed Tenes and his sister Hemithea in a chest in the sea. But they were saved, landing on Tenedos, and Tenes became king of the island, which was named after him. When Cycnus discovered the truth he killed Philonome and sought forgiveness from his son, but this Tenes irrevocably refused. Even when Cycnus tried to land at Tenedos, Tenes cut the ship's mooring with an axe, giving rise to the proverbial "Tenedian axe," signifying a hasty, drastic deed. Later when the Greeks in their war against Troy landed on Tenedos, the Tenedians opposed them. In this struggle Tenes was killed by Achilles, in one version because the Greek hero attempted to ravish Hemithea.

Demophon

By Phaedra Theseus had two sons, Acamas and Demophon. They both served in the Trojan War, and on the way home from

Troy Demophon landed in Thrace, where he fell in love with
Phyllis, daughter of the king, and married her. He decided to go
home to Athens on a visit, but swore to return. Before he left
Phyllis gave him a box, with instructions to open it only if he ever
despaired of returning. But actually Demophon soon forgot
Phyllis, who, after waiting a long time, cursed him and committed
suicide, and was transformed into an almond tree. One day when
Demophon was on his horse he opened the box given him by
Phyllis. Just then the horse stumbled, and Demophon was thrown
and impaled on his own sword.

Acontius and Cydippe

One day Acontius, a young man of Ceos, went to Delos for a
festival of Artemis. There he saw Cydippe, daughter of a wealthy
noble, and fell in love with her, but not daring to approach her, he
wrote on a quince the following inscription: "I swear by the
temple of Artemis to marry Acontius." Cydippe picked up the
quince and read the inscription aloud. Thus she became bound by
the oath. Later her father sought a husband for her, but each time
he selected one for her Cydippe became mysteriously ill with a
sickness sent by Artemis. Finally the Delphic oracle was consulted,
the matter clarified, and Acontius and Cydippe were married.

Tlepolemus and Polyxo

A son of Heracles, Tlepolemus became king of Rhodes. As one
of the suitors of Helen he was obligated to support Agamemnon
and Menelaüs against the Trojans, and left his devoted wife Polyxo
as regent when he departed with the Rhodian contingents to Troy.
Tlepolemus lost his life at the hands of Sarpedon, and Polyxo was
inconsolable. She conducted grand funeral rites for her husband in
Rhodes and harbored an intense desire for vengeance, blaming
Helen for the war and her husband's death. In the best known
version she gained her vengeance when Helen was driven from
Sparta after Menelaüs' death and came to Rhodes seeking asylum.
Pretending to be hospitable, Polyxo disguised some of her slaves as
Furies and unleashed them upon Helen while she was in her bath.
Helen was so terrified that she became insane and committed
suicide.

Byblis and Caunus

Byblis fell in love with her twin brother Caunus, who fled when he discovered this illicit passion. Byblis searched for her twin all over the world, but could not find him. Finally she tried to commit suicide and was transformed into a spring.

Canace and Macareus

Canace and Macareus, brother and sister, committed incest. When a baby was born Canace attempted to have the baby surreptitiously exposed, but their father Aeolus discovered the horrible truth. He threw the baby to dogs, and sent Canace a sword with orders to commit suicide. Macareus also killed himself.

Alastor

Clymenus of Arcadia had a daughter Harpalyce, for whom he had an incestuous passion, although she was wooed by and married Alastor, son of Neleus and brother of Nestor. When he was taking his bride home, Clymenus overtook them and seized his daughter, being unwilling to part with her. When she came home Harpalyce killed her brother, cooked him, and fed him to her father at a banquet. Then she committed suicide, and was turned into a night bird. As for the unhappy bridegroom Alastor, he was later killed when Heracles invaded his father Neleus' kingdom.

Arion

Arion of Lesbos may have been an historical person, a musician whose lyre playing and singing made him world famous. After a tour of Sicily and Southern Italy, he was returning by sea to Greece to visit the city of Corinth, when the sailors of the ship conspired to kill him and seize his great wealth. About to be thrown overboard, Arion received permission to give his last concert, dressed in his formal costume and holding his lyre. Even the dolphins listened in awe. The sailors then threw him overboard and sailed into the port of Corinth, where they reported his accidental death at sea. But a dolphin rescued Arion, took him on its back, and brought him safely to Corinth, where he then exposed the crime of the sailors, who were seized and put to death. As a reward for aiding Arion the dolphin became the constellation Dolphin, and later the famed musician himself joined it in the sky as the constellation Arion.

The dolphin was the most beloved animal in all of Greek mythology, always thought of as friendly, a savior of man, helping many in peril at sea. In fact it became a sacred animal and was never killed. There are more than a few stories in classical myths of dolphins rescuing humans or carrying them as riders on their backs, and the friendliness of dolphins to man and gods was immortalized in such stories of the dolphins' aid to Poseidon himself when he was wooing Amphitrite, and the appearance of dolphins about the ship that was carrying Dionysus when the Etruscan pirates tried to capture him. The dolphin thus became one of the most common symbols of the sea itself in ancient art. The concept of the sacredness of the dolphin and its friendliness to man influenced the early Christians, and in an early Christian legend, when St. Lucian of Antioch was martyred and thrown into the sea, a savior dolphin brought his body back to land.

Gyges

A well-known folktale tells of the rise to power of a lowly child of fortune. In this motif a lowly adventurer confronts a powerful being, a giant or a foolish king, the queen offers herself and the kingdom to the remarkable youth, he wins power and the fair lady, and they live happily ever after. Such a legend grew up around Gyges, an historical figure who was a king of Lydia in the first half of the Seventh Century B.C., founder of a dynasty and proverbial for his wealth. It is told that King Candaules once praised his wife's beauty extravagantly to his friend Gyges, and to prove his proud claim, concealed his friend behind a screen in his bedroom so that Gyges could see for himself. When the queen discovered the presence of the intruder, she gave Gyges the choice of being executed or killing Candaules and marrying her himself. In another version, Gyges was a shepherd in Lydia who one day found a ring which proved to have magic qualities. When he turned it on his finger it made him invisible, and armed with this magic he succeeded in seducing the queen, killing Candaules, and usurping the royal power.

Midas

Midas was an historical king of Phrygia in the Eighth Century

B.C., called Mita in Near Eastern records. His father was Gordius, with whom is associated the famous "Gordian Knot." In his capital was a sacred chariot attached to the yoke by a mystic knot so skilfully tied and complicated that it was not possible to see its beginning or end, apparently a symbol, analagous to the modern symbol of infinity. An oracle said that whoever could undo this knot would become ruler of all Asia. Over 400 years later when Alexander the Great visited the spot he carefully examined the complicated knot, then simply cut through it with his sword.

One day when Gordius' son Midas was king, Silenus became drunk and could not be found. Midas discovered him in his garden, returned him to Dionysus, and for this kindness was granted his wish that everything he touched become gold. This boon turned out to be a disaster, for, though he became fabulously wealthy, his food and drink also turned to gold, and since he was dying of starvation, he asked to be freed of the golden touch. He was told to bathe in the Pactolus River in Phrygia, which became gold-bearing as a result. (The Pactolus actually was a gold-bearing stream in antiquity).

Another tale about King Midas concerns a music contest between Apollo, playing the lyre, and Pan, playing the shepherd's pipes. When Midas declared Pan the winner, Apollo changed Midas' ears into asses' ears, which Midas concealed under a hat in shame and revealed only to his barber, whom he swore to secrecy on threat of execution. Eventually the barber, fearful he might reveal the secret, dug a hole in the ground and said into it, "Midas has asses' ears." Later reeds grew out of this spot, and when the wind blew through them they repeated Midas' secret. This strange story appears in many places as a folktale, in which the person with the long ears (sometimes horses' ears) is always a king, and may have arisen because in the Near East it was common for kings to wear a tall hat as symbol of their status as ruler, but which may have been taken as an attempt to conceal something. In any case, the dunce cap and the fool's cap survive as symbols.

The Phoenix

The Greeks learned of the mythical bird they called the Phoenix from the Egyptians (in Egyptian its name was *boinu* or *bennu*). This was a miraculous and unique bird, the only one of its species, distinguished by red and gold feathers, said to come to Egypt from the East once every 500 years (or 1461 years, that is, 4x365 1/4 years), and there build a nest. Eventually it died in this nest, and after both nest and bird were consumed by a spontaneous fire, the next phoenix rose miraculously out of the ashes.

This myth, which may have arisen out of the association of the sun with a bird, adapted recurring natural phemomena to human life. The phoenix has served widely as a symbol of immortality and rebirth, and continued to be used by the early Christians as a symbol of resurrection.

The Lost Continent Atlantis

In his *Timaeus* and *Critias* Plato tells in detail of a lost continent called Atlantis, a myth which he says was told to the Greeks by Egyptian priests. The myth placed the great island of Atlantis outside the pillars of Hercules (Straits of Gibraltar), in the Atlantic Ocean, and the location and historicity of Atlantis has been endlessly discussed since. The island was a favorite of the sea god Poseidon, and there he fathered by the nymph Clito five sets of male twins who became ten kings of the island, with the eldest, Atlas, as a sort of king of kings. The brothers, ruling their separate kingdoms, lived harmoniously in a kind of perfect society, a model of a utopia, which became exceedingly affluent and had many magnificent cities. But, as so often happens in ancient myths, greed and *hybris* undermined the perfect balance of the society, as Atlantis embarked on foreign conquests and ruled a vast empire. Then it tried to conquer the world, but met its first setback when it was defeated by the Athenians, the turning point in its downfall. Ultimately the island was suddenly overwhelmed by an earthquake and catalysmic flood, and it disappeared forever.

Such stories of idyllic lost lands have had a strong fascination in many parts of the world, for example, the story of Lyonesse in England (between Cornwall and the Scilly Islands), and the legend of the French land called Cockaigne. Some scholars have sought to identify the prototype of myths of lost lands with the island of Santorin (ancient Thera) which lies between Greece and Crete, a small island which was devastated by a violent volcanic eruption and earthquake about 1400 B.C. Repercussions of this catastro-

phe, through tidal waves and volcanic fallout, are claimed to have extended as far away as Crete, Asia Minor, and even Egypt, so that some scholars therefore claim that the lost continent of Atlantis is in reality the island empire of Minoan Crete, which lost its dominance about 1400 B.C. But it is not likely that there was any historical basis for Plato's highly embellished myth of Atlantis, and his famous pupil Aristotle called the myth of a lost continent pure fiction, declaring, "The man who dreamed it up made it disappear."

XXVII

ROMAN CULTURE AND MYTHOLOGY

While the Greeks preferred to live in a highly fragmented society, the Romans prided themselves on their sense of unity, order and discipline. The city of Rome on the Tiber River unified under its rule all of Italy and much of the civilized world, establishing the "Roman Peace" that afforded a measure of unprecedented stability.

During the Mycenaean Age of Greece Italy was still in a barbaric state, even though it is very fertile and could, unlike Greece, support a large population engaged in agriculture and pasturing. Yet it was for a long time sparsely settled and did not develop civilized life until relatively late, largely because of its distance from the places where civilization was born in the Near East. What eventually attracted settlers to the Italian peninsula was its fertility, and, unlike the Greeks, inhabitants of Italy depended on the land, not the sea. Although Italy too is very mountainous and has few sizable rivers (the most famous is the Tiber), there are many highly productive plains. Rome was situated in the fertile plain of Latium, about 15 miles from the seacoast. Thus for the Romans agriculture was basic, and they did not develop a seafaring civilization as the Greeks had.

As the result of upheavals and dislocations in the Aegean culture area many peoples invaded Italy, coming both by land and sea. About 1200-1000 B.C., contemporaneous with the destruction of the Mycenaean culture, Italic tribes migrated into Italy from Central Europe bringing with them the Indo-European language and customs. Among these migrants the Latins settled in the plain of Latium on the west central coast of Italy, including the site of Rome itself, on the Tiber. From Asia Minor, about 1000-900 B.C., came the Etruscans, bringing with them Near Eastern cultural traditions, and occupied the region north of Latium. The Etruscans were greatly influenced by the Greeks, adopting into their own culture many Greek myths, and their art frequently used illustrations of Greek mythological scenes. These Etruscan neighbors were to influence the Romans profoundly, transmitting to them not only Etruscan cultural achievements but borrowed aspects of Greek culture. Then, between 750 and 550 B.C., the Greeks themselves colonized Southern Italy and Sicily, becoming the neighbors of the Latins to the south, and finally in about 400 B.C. the Gauls (Celts from France) invaded Italy from the north, and settled in the Po Valley. This patchwork of many peoples, all of whom influenced the Romans, was successfully unified by the city on the Tiber.

There had been a community of villages on the seven hills of Rome from early times. But Rome bears an Etruscan name, for the Etruscans conquered Latium in the Seventh Century B.C., and transformed these hill villages into a city in about 625 B.C. (the traditional date of the founding of Rome is given as 753 B.C.). Etruscan kings of the Tarquin family ruled Rome for over 100 years, and imposed aspects of Etruscan and Greek culture upon the Romans. In the Roman tradition, Romulus founded Rome, and the city went through its first phase of history under seven successive kings. The Etruscan past was acknowledged by making the last three of these kings members of an Etruscan dynasty. The government was headed by a king, who was advised by a Senate consisting of heads of aristocratic families, along with an assembly of the people with little power. Early in this regal period the Roman feeling for order, discipline, respect for authority shows itself in the relationship between the patricians, a class of privileged families, and the rest of the Romans, called plebeians. It was customary for plebeians to seek the protection of a patron among the patricians, so that even in this early period there were already institutionalized the concepts of seniority, authority of the elders and officials, and social hierarchy.

About 500 B.C. a patriotic revolution took place, expelled the Etruscan royal family of the Tarquins, and established a republic, with the result that the notion of monarchy and the very word *rex* (king) became a hated institution among the Romans. The founding fathers of the Roman Republic, which was to last for about 500 years, established two annually elected officials, called consuls, in place of the king. Over the years additional checks were provided, but the principles of strong authority both in the government, in the senior members of society, and in the heads of families continued. Eventually a number of additional magistrates came into being with terms of office generally limited to one year.

After the expulsion of the Etruscans, the Romans in their unstable condition were menaced for about 100 years by their neighbors among the other Latins, but they survived all attacks and emergencies, each time managing to find new resources in manpower, clever diplomacy, and the patriotic spirit of her people. Then between 400 and 272 B.C. the city of Rome brought all Italy under its rule, first all of the Latins, and finally the Greeks. An almost fatal setback came in 390 B.C. when Rome was captured and almost totally destoryed by the Gauls, but within fifty years Rome recovered her military might.

In the course of her conquests Rome developed many policies for ruling the expanding territories under her control, showing generosity to people that surrendered without a struggle, invoking the tactic of "divide and rule," sending colonies into conquered territory (these did not become independent as Greek colonies were, but remained part of the Roman state), and building roads to connect Rome with her possessions. Rome brought peace to all of Italy, and established a stable union because the peoples of Italy were willing to surrender traditional local autonomy in exchange for security. As a result of her policies Rome had at its disposal the largest army in the world.

If the Greeks were remarkable for their artistic, literary, and intellectual creativity, the Roman character was marked out by a hard practicality and organizing ability. Romans were essentially an unsentimental people, highly disciplined, conservative, distrustful of change. They admired order, discipline, respect for authority, and placed the highest value on a sense of duty, called *pietas,* which involved obligations to family, gods, the state. Seriousness was drummed into them from very birth, and frivolity was considered un-Roman. With the "customs of the ancestors" venerated as sacred traditions, and ancestor worship an important part of their religion, the happiness of the individual had no place in such a society. Every Roman was disciplined to subordinate himself to his family and the state.

The head of each Roman household, called the *pater familias,* ruled like a king over all the members with almost absolute power, including life and death, while Roman women, though they had no place in political life and were subordinated to the control of males, had the highest status of all the women in the ancient world, except Egyptian women.

Early Roman religion involved animism, that is, belief in vague divine powers that governed every aspect of life, with, originally, no belief in gods in human form, like those basic to Greek religion from an early period. All Roman religious rites – prayers and sacrifices – aimed to assure the welfare and continuity of both the family and the state. But under Etruscan and Greek influence anthropomorphism came to the Romans, and statues and temples appeared in Rome, as in the cities of these earlier cultures. One of the processes of borrowing was the correlation of the older Italic spirits with specific Greek anthropomorphic gods. The Romans, like the Greeks, constantly felt the need to look into the future, and followed similar procedures, seeking omens and divine signs, and consulting prophets and oracles, including the famous Delphic oracle in Greece. The Romans also had a collection of sacred texts, the Sibylline Books, which they used for guidance to the future.

Rome's overseas conquests began shortly after it unified Italy. Its struggles with Carthage (264-241; 218-201 B.C.), a Phoenician colony on the coast of North Africa, brought Rome to the brink of extinction when the great Carthaginian general Hannibal invaded Italy, but the Romans survived by a superhuman effort and emerged victorious. Then Rome began to annex overseas provinces beginning with Sicily, Corsica, Sardinia, Spain, and then gradually extended its influence and might over the remnants of Alexander's once mighty empire, bringing under its rule and influence the entire Hellenistic world, through policies of "divide and rule," adroit diplomacy, overwhelming military might, and finally ruthless destruction of all resistance.

Rome's rise to the position of the world's superpower profoundly changed her own society of disciplined farmer-soldiers. Traditional Roman values were undermined by wealth and extravagance among the upper classes and by the importation of hordes of slaves, mostly war captives. Although the masses of the lower classes in Italy sank to the status of economically displaced persons, the all-powerful class of Senatorial families remained inflexible in the face of the urgent need for reforms, and the Roman aristocracy became accustomed to deception in international affairs, brutality to inferiors, and ambition for great personal wealth and power in the place of the traditional severe Roman moral code of the past. Individualism replaced the group-directed way of life.

Direct contact with the brilliant culture of the Greeks in the East dazzled the Roman upper classes, and this admiration for all aspects of the superior Greek civilization changed the Roman way of life. "Conquered Greece conquered the victorious Romans," acknowledged the Roman poet Horace. Hellenic influences poured into Rome in a massive flood, in art, literature, philosophy, customs, education, and the values of Roman life changed under these influences from emphasis on *pietas* and group solidarity to the priority of individual happiness. This had a disastrous effect on the traditional Roman religion, for personal yearnings led to concern for the attaining of a happy afterlife. This brought the importation of foreign cults and gods, together with the myths about them, from Asia Minor, Egypt, and Greece, to satisfy such desires.

The conflicts engendered by these changes in Roman life, together with the inability and unwillingness of the Roman ruling classes to reorder society, generated the greatest crisis in mankind's history thus far. Discontent prevailed everywhere in the world under Rome's dominion. From 133 to 30 B.C. the world was convulsed by disasters that brought the whole civilized world to the brink of chaos, with political assassinations, civil wars, blood baths, revolts, piracy, invasions of barbarians, and foreign wars combining to bring about a degree of instability unparalleled in world history. Eventually strong men like Marius, Pompey, Sulla, and Caesar came to the fore, and in the end, after the elimination of all effective competitors for power, one man, Augustus, brought under his control the whole Roman Empire.

The death of the Republic brought to absolute power in 30 B.C. the man whom the world acknowledged as the savior sent to bring peace to the world. Augustus became the first Roman emperor, and established a form of government that preserved Roman rule for hundreds of years. Hailed as the "prince of peace," Augustus brought order to the world, restored efficiency in government, reestablished confidence in Rome, and sought to reestablish the old Roman traditions of family solidarity, the concept of *pietas,* and the old Roman religion and ancestral moral code. But in the field of religion he encouraged a new movement – the wish of many to worship him in his lifetime as a god on earth.

Although the Greeks were accustomed to regarding benefactors of man as heroes and giving them divine worship and in the Hellenistic Age the worship of living kings as gods had become a widespread phenomenon, the Romans did not have such a tradition. It is true that they believed that the mythical founder of Rome, Romulus, had became a god, but it was not until after the death of Julius Caesar that a Roman was deified and granted divine honors. When Augustus, as adopted son of the deified Caesar now in heaven, thus the "son of a god," began to be honored as a god on earth in his own right, emperor worship became a part of Roman religion for the next few hundred years, until abolished by the victory of Christianity.

The Augustan Age ushered in a period of creativity in the arts and literature that make it the highpoint of Roman culture, with many traditional themes dominant. The age produced a number of works fundamental to the study of classical mythology, like the great national epic the *Aeneid,* by Vergil, the "Roman Homer," the mythological poems of the highly sophisticated Ovid, such as the *Metamorphoses,* which relate many famous Greek and Roman myths, and Livy's *History of Rome,* which tells for the early period some of the famous myths of the Romans.

After Augustus' death in 14 A.D., emperor succeeded emperor in a world that was now dependent on one man in the capital city of Rome for order and welfare. In this "one world," stretching from England across Europe and the northern coast of Africa into Asia to the Euphrates River, the bases of Greco-Roman civilization penetrated everywhere. The Greek myths adopted by the Romans, as well as their own native myths were diffused into every corner of the Roman Empire. Even with the decay of the empire and the triumph of Christianity in the Fourth Century A.D., the classical myths survived even if in altered form, in literature, art, and popular tradition.

* * *

All people in their early stages have a mythology, and the Indo-European ancestors of the Romans brought with them into Italy stories about gods and heroes of Central Europe. But, as we have seen, traces of such earlier myths are hard to find even among the Greeks, because they were crowded out by the indigenous myths of the Aegean people, by those borrowed from the Near East, and by new creations of the Greeks in their new homeland. In the field of mythology the Romans were a unique people in many ways, and compared with the enormous volume of Greek myths, and even those of such diverse peoples as the Norse, the American Indians, the Egyptians, Babylonians, Hindus, Polynesians, and Chinese, the Romans had almost no mythology.

They had no myths about the origins of man in Italy, no cosmogony, no theogony, and as for the native Roman gods, these had originally no mythology at all, no stories of their origin, birth, death and rebirth, marriage, amorous adventures or children. There are several reasons for this. The native Italic religion was animism, that is, belief in vague spirits of all kinds that affected the welfare of the people in every aspect of life, and as these divine powers were not anthropomorphic, they were not the object of stories such as the Greeks developed about their very human gods. Moreover, the religious attitude toward these spirits, large and small, was one of awe, so that humanization would have seemed disrespectful, and this discouraged the Romans from being mythmakers on a grand scale like the Greeks. Furthermore, being practical, conservative, and bound by respect for tradition, the Romans were not as imaginative and daring as the Greeks. Originally they had no statues of gods, and not thinking of them as personified, it would almost appear that the Romans originally deliberately demythologized their divine beings. To take one example, the widespread story of gods and heroes fighting dragons in many mythologies is simply not found in genuine Italian myths.

Whatever native myths the Romans possessed concerned only

humans, but even these were largely historical myths. Other than Romulus there were no semi-divine heroes and the persons who appear in Roman myths were thought of as historical individuals, not children of gods, nor capable of being deified after death. This historical emphasis is the unique characteristic of Roman myths, for the very patriotic and practical Romans thought historically, and even when they adopted common folktales or borrowed myths from other peoples, they tended to historicize them. In this process of historicization and nationalization of myths the gods had little part.

The first impulse to mythmaking among the Romans came from the Etruscans, who introduced the Romans to the concept of anthropomorphism in religion and to the making of statues and temples of the gods. However, the personification of gods which the Romans borrowed from the Etruscans did not open the floodgates to the creation of myths about their indigenous divinities. The Etruscans must have brought with them many Near Eastern myths of the kind that influenced Greek myths too at various times, and in addition, beginning in the Sixth Century B.C., they themselves absorbed Greek mythology on a vast scale. We do not know how they learned these Greek myths, but one of the distinctive characteristics of their art is the use of scenes from Greek myths on tombstone paintings and on vases and other art objects they imported from Greece or had made for them by their own artists. From the Sixth to the Fourth centuries we have an enormous array of themes borrowed from Greek myths.

The Etruscans were obsessed with death and the Underworld, and portrayed a variety of scenes from Greek myths involving death and violence, like Actaeon's death, Ajax's suicide, the sacrifice of Trojan captives on the grave of Patroclus, the deaths of Hector and Achilles, Odysseus in Hades, the king and queen of the Underworld Hades and Persephone, Agamemnon and Tiresias in Hades, the death demon called Charu, and Theseus and Pirithoüs in Hades. Other scenes from Greek myths show the cruelty and violence in the duel between Eteocles and Polynices, the battles of Heracles and Cycnus, and of Heracles and the Amazons, Apollo punishing Tityus for assaulting his mother Leto, Odysseus blinding the Cyclops, and the battle of Achilles and Memnon. In the Sixth and Fifth centuries a popular theme was the flight from Troy, in which Aeneas the Trojan hero was portrayed carrying his father Anchises on his back and leading his son Ascanius by the hand.

Direct contact between the Romans and the Greeks, particularly from the Third Century B.C. on, exposed the Romans to the whole array of Greek mythology, religion, art, and literature, although in general, the Greek myths, which were taken over as a body, did not affect to any large extent the Roman national character itself. With a number of exceptions they were not functional myths, but were used largely for decorative purposes in art and as themes and illustrations in their literature.

One important development Greek influence produced was the Roman adaptation of their own native gods to the closest equivalent in the Greek pantheon. Thus, for instance, their sky spirit Jupiter was associated with the Greek sky god Zeus, although the Roman Jupiter did not degenerate into the very human god of the Greeks with his escapades and numerous love affairs. The Roman equivalents for the Greek gods are:

Roman	*Greek*
Jupiter	Zeus
Juno	Hera
Neptune	Poseidon
Dis	Hades (Pluto)
Ceres	Demeter
Vesta	Hestia
Minerva	Athena
Diana	Artemis
Mercury	Hermes
Venus	Aphrodite
Mars	Ares
Vulcan	Hephaestus
Liber	Dionysus (Bacchus)
Cupid	Eros
Latona	Leto
Sol	Helios
Luna	Selene
Aurora	Eos
Saturn	Cronus
Tellus	Gaea

Camenae	Muses
Parcae	Moerae

There was no parallel among the Roman divinities for Apollo, so they simply imported this god lock-stock-and-barrel, just as the demigod Asclepius came unmodified to Rome from Greece in 293 B.C., after a plague, under the name Aesculapius. The Dioscouri, Castor and Polydeuces, called by the Romans Castor and Pollux, were known to them very early. The Hellenization of the Roman gods tended, it is true, to undermine the awe they previously felt toward their divine forces, but the stories they told about them under Roman names were merely a transfer of the native names to well-known Greek myths. This practice did not, however, lead to the creation of new myths by the Romans concerning their gods.

* * *

SIGNIFICANT DATES IN ROMAN CULTURE

Migration of Italic Peoples into Italy	1200-1000 B.C.
Coming of the Etruscans to Italy	1000-900 B.C.
Greek colonization of S. Italy and Sicily	750-550 B.C.
Traditional date of the founding of Rome	753 B.C.
The Etruscans transform Rome into a city	625 B.C.
The Roman Kingdom — traditional dates	753-500 B.C.
Establishment of the Roman Republic	500 B.C.
Early Roman struggle for survival	500-400 B.C.
Destruction of Rome by the Gauls	390 B.C.
Conquest and unification of Italy by Rome	400-272 B.C.
First Punic, War, against Carthage	264-241 B.C.
Second Punic War, with Hannibal	218-201 B.C.
Rome absorbs the Hellenistic World	200-30 B.C.
The Roman Revolution	133-30 B.C.
Assassination of Julius Caesar	44 B.C.
Death of Antony and Cleopatra	30 B.C.
The Augustan Age	30 B.C. — 14 A.D.
Julio-Claudian Dynasty	14-68 A.D.
Flavian Dynasty	69-96 A.D.
Good Emperors	96-181 A.D.

The Military Monarchy 181-280 A.D.
The Totalitarian State established 280 A.D.
Christianity recognized 311 A.D.
Founding of Constantinople, the Christian Rome 330 A.D.

XXVIII

ROMAN FOUNDATION MYTHS

It is characteristic of the historically minded Romans that their earliest myths were concerned with the settlement in Latium of the ancestors from whom the Romans claimed descent, and with the founding of the city of Rome. Although there were settlements at the site of Rome long before the traditional founding date of April 21, 753 B.C., and Rome was actually transformed into a city by Etruscan conquerors about 625 B.C., the classical myth of the founding of Rome singled out an eponymous hero Romulus, and wove about his figure folktale themes and typical hero stories from Greek myths.

In the Alban Mts. near Rome there was a Latin city named Alba Longa. When King Procas of Alba Longa died, he left his royal power to his eldest son Numitor, but his ambitious second son Amulius seized power and expelled his brother. Numitor had a daughter Rhea Silvia (or Ilia), whom Amulius feared because a son of hers might some day become an avenger, so he designated her one of the Vestal Virgins, priestesses of the sacred fire who took a vow to remain chaste. But the god Mars made love to her and she had twins, Romulus and Remus, and the apprehensive Amulius decided to destroy the children. At his orders they were exposed in a box on the River Tiber, but the river flooded its banks and deposited the box on the site of future Rome. There by chance a she-wolf found them and became their animal nurse. This Roman story of the wolf and the twins is probably the best known of all the animal nurse stories told in antiquity.

As we have seen, the story of "heavenly twins" is a common one, deriving probably from Indo-European traditions, and the exposure of the "dangerous child" is common in the hero myth. The story of the she-wolf as nurse may have came from the belief that the wolf was sacred to Mars. A difficulty arose in the myth because the Latin word for wolf, *lupa,* also means "prostitute," and the Romans probably disliked some elements of the story of the birth and upbringing of Romulus and Remus. Therefore a variant story grew up that a shepherd named Faustulus found the twins at the site of Rome, adopted them, and gave them to his wife Acca Larentia to nurse. It is likely that originally the she-wolf associated with Mars was a fertility spirit, for the figure Acca as nurse is a form of the early life-giving mother goddess.

In the Roman myths these two were transformed from a savage wolf and primitive divinity into the historical human nurse of Romulus and Remus with the name Acca Larentia. But, since the concept of prostitute was suggested by *lupa,* Acca Larentia gained a history which dealt with the *lupa* problem, and ultimately made her a respectable Roman matron. When Hercules was in Rome, in a gambling wager he won a meal and the favors of the most beautiful woman in the region. This turned out to be a prostitute named Acca Larentia. As a reward for her favors to him, Hercules predicted that she would marry the first man she met, who happened to be a very rich man. He married her and soon died, leaving all his wealth to her. When she died she willed her property to the entire Roman people. Thus through connection with the heroes Romulus and Remus, the myth of Acca Larentia was historicized in keeping with national pride, changing her from a lowly shepherd's wife or prostitute to a benefactor of Rome.

Romulus and Remus were devoted brothers who lived as shepherds when they grew up. One day they fell into a dispute with the shepherds of King Amulius of Alba Longa, and in the struggle, Remus was captured and brought to Alba Longa, where with the aid of Numitor or Rhea Silvia, he was somehow recognized as one of the twin sons of Rhea Silvia and Mars. Soon Romulus arrived with his fellow shepherds and rescued his brother Remus, and the two were reunited with their mother. After they had killed their great-uncle Amulius and restored their grandfather Numitor to the throne, the twin brothers decided to found their own city.

The place they chose for this was the spot where they had

been saved by the she-wolf, but before they could begin to build the city, they needed an official founder. To determine which of the twins was to have this honor they took the auspices, that is, watched for the flight of birds in the sky as omens, and Romulus took his stand on the Palatine Hill of Rome, Remus on the Aventine Hill. The first to see a few birds was Remus, but immediately after Romulus caught sight of twelve, and claiming victory on the grounds of larger numbers, promptly began to lay the foundations of the city. When Remus in anger mocked him and leaped over the first stretch of the wall, the brothers fought and Remus was killed. This story of the first historic act in Roman tradition recalls the story of Cain and Abel in the Old Testament, and it is possible that this tale reflects a struggle involving the transition from primitive pastoral times to a more stable agricultural society. Although the murder of Remus, a sort of "original sin" in Roman tradition, made it difficult to "clean up" Romulus completely, the contradiction between the myth of twins and the recollection of the strong kingship of early Rome made it necessary somehow to eliminate Remus.

Romulus was not only the founder but first king of Rome, known as the "father of his country," and tradition attributes to his reign the establishment of the fundamental political and military institutions of the Romans. Under Romulus, Rome became a place of asylum, attracting flocks of exiles, insolvent debtors, murderers, and fugitive slaves, and because of the unsavory character of the inhabitants it was difficult to attract women, so that Romulus decided on a stratagem. Proclaiming a festival commemorating the new city, he invited neighboring peoples, and the Sabines from the nearby hills came in large numbers. At a signal, Romulus and his men seized the Sabine women and drove off their men folk, an event commemorated in literature and art as "The Rape of the Sabine Women." Some time after, the women themselves, now married to Romans and the mothers of their children, declared to their Sabine fathers and former husbands that they were content to remain in Rome.

But the Sabines, led by their king Titus Tatius, attacked Rome in retaliation. The Romans were at first betrayed by one of the women, Tarpeia, a beautiful Roman maiden who fell in love with the Sabine leader and agreed to help him when he promised to marry her. In another version the Sabines agreed to a bribe she demanded — when they entered the city they were to give her the golden armbands they wore. But when they were admitte ' into the city with her help, the Sabines threw their armbands, or shields, upon her in such great numbers that Tarpeia was crushed beneath them. There was a portion of the Capitoline Hill in Rome known as the Tarpeian Rock, a place of execution, in historical times, so that the myth of Tarpeia was in part an aetiological story joined to a familiar folktale, of which there are several versions in Greek myths, especially the story of Nisus and his traitorous daughter Scylla. But the Romans characteristically transformed all of this into a political myth. The story of the treason of Tarpeia remained an embarrassment to the Romans, even though in the end Rome was saved when Romulus prayed to Jupiter and vowed to build for him a magnificent temple in Rome, and the Sabine women threw themselves between the warring forces and brought about a reconciliation and fusion of the two peoples.

Romulus' kingship did not end in a normal way. One day while he was reviewing the Roman troops, a violent windstorm and an eclipse of the sun occurred, and in the midst of the confusion Romulus disappeared forever. A Roman senator announced that in a dream he had seen Romulus ascending to heaven, so the Romans officially deified Romulus, under the name Quirinus. The apotheosis of Romulus belongs to the Greek tradition of the deification of benefactors, for the practice was not a Roman one.

Such were the earliest foundation myths of Rome. But when the Romans became the most powerful people of the Mediterranean in the Third Century B.C., they wanted a more distinguished and respectable pedigree, and so developed and accepted the famous myth that the ancestors of the Romans were a group of Trojans led to Italy by the Trojan hero Aeneas. Actually, the Etruscans first made Aeneas important for Italy, and one of the popular themes in Etruscan art, as early as the end of the Sixth Century B.C. when Rome itself was under Etruscan domination, was the "flight from Troy." On Etruscan vases and in statuettes from the Etruscan city of Veii near Rome we can find depicted the famous scene, familiar from Vergil's *Aeneid,* of Aeneas with his father Anchises on his back, accompanied by the boy Ascanius

and a female figure, presumably Aeneas' wife. The Etruscans may have developed the story that Aeneas, coming as he did from Asia Minor, was the mythical ancestor of the Etruscans.

The early Romans under Etruscan domination must have been aware of this story, but when they expelled the Etruscan overlords about 500 B.C. the theme lost popularity, connected as it had been with the hated Etruscans. When early in the Third Century they sought to establish for themselves a glorious heroic past, they revived the story, motivated particularly as they came into frequent contact with the Greeks, in whose Heroic Age were enshrined many heroes who remained revered. Roman ambitions for an heroic origin were generated not only by national pride but also for political reasons, necessity to demonstrate an heroic past equal to that of the Greeks whom they had conquered.

The choice of Aeneas as mythic ancestor was dictated not only by earlier Etruscan exploitation of the theme of Aeneas as a man of duty rescuing his family from Troy, but also by aspects of the Aeneas story in the *Iliad* of Homer. In the Greek epic, Aeneas was second after Hector as leader of the Trojan side, a member of a younger branch of the royal family, ambitious to have his line succeed to the Trojan throne. He appears as a man with an assured future, for in his duel with Achilles, Aeneas was rescued by the gods because "it is fated for him to escape . . . and the mighty Aeneas shall be king among the Trojans, and his sons' sons that shall be born in days to come."

Yet there was a difficulty in idealizing Aeneas, because of his hostility to Priam and his ambition to succeed him, so that his survival after the fall of Troy generated a tradition that Aeneas had actually betrayed Troy to the Greeks for personal advantage. But the other image of Aeneas as a pious, dutiful leader prevailed for the Romans, cleaning up the figure of the man they were to elevate into their earliest national hero. But, since they had already enshrined Romulus as the founder of Rome, they could not use Aeneas for this purpose, so he was declared the founder of another city in Italy, Lavinium, from which Rome was said to have been descended. Finally, since Aeneas was supposed to have come to Italy about 1175 B.C. and the traditional date of the founding of Rome was 753 B.C., the Romans next had to fill in the gap of about 400 years with a line of descendants from Aeneas to Romulus.

Like so many Greek heroes, Aeneas was of divine descent, his mother Venus (Roman equivalent of Aphrodite), his father Anchises, prince of Troy, descended from the line of Tros and Dardanus. One day while Anchises was on Mt. Ida near Troy, he was wooed by the goddess Venus, and their son was the hero Aeneas, illegitimate but divine in origin. Anchises was warned not to reveal his affair with the goddess, but he boasted of it, and was therefore blinded or lamed by Jupiter, mutilated by a bolt of lightning. One may assume that this is originally a version of the love of the Near Eastern mother goddess and her youthful consort, who in this case was touched by celestial fire because of his association with the awesome goddess of fertility.

Aeneas rose to high position in Troy. In one version of his story he is said to have accompanied Paris to Sparta to assist him in the abduction of Helen and so was tainted by his sin, but on the whole he was an outstanding leader, though hardly a brilliant soldier of the Trojans. He was married, in the earliest versions to a woman named Eurydica, in later versions to Priam's daughter Creusa, and had a young son, Ascanius (also called Iülus), and was a devoted son, caring for his aged and crippled father Anchises.

During the fateful events of the fall of Troy Aeneas played an important role. When the wooden horse was left outside Troy by the Greeks, he presumably did not oppose its entry into the city, and was present when the priest Laocoön cautioned the Trojans against the horse, hurled his spear into it, and was with his two sons strangled by the two serpents from the sea. He witnessed too the treachery of the Greek Sinon, "that first of Intelligence Officers," as he has been called, who by clever lies convinced the Trojans to take the horse into the city.

While the Greek invaders, including those released from the horse, were ravaging Troy, Aeneas, asleep in his own palace after the "victory" celebration, saw a vision of the dead Hector which ordered him to flee the doomed city and find a new home for the Trojan gods and people. Not convinced by this divine message, Aeneas armed himself and decided to die in the falling city, like an early Greek hero in search of personal glory, as he was not yet a Roman hero imbued with sacred obligation to his destiny, the future of his gods, family, and country. Mysteriously, a priest of

Apollo brought to him the sacred images of the gods of Troy for safekeeping, but Aeneas was still resolved to die for Troy, and fought like a madman. Then, after he rushed to the royal palace and saw the slaying of aged King Priam by Achilles' son Neoptolemus (or Pyrrhus), he decided to save his father and family, and while on the way to his home he was counseled by his mother Venus to flee the dying city.

To his dismay, the aged Anchises refused to leave the city because his infirmities would slow up Aeneas and the others. Suddenly and miraculously, a flame appeared on Ascanius' head, which he interpreted as a divine omen that the boy must be preserved for some great future, and he therefore agreed to be taken from the city. This was the famous scene of the flight from Troy — Anchises on Aeneas' shoulders holding the images of the Trojan gods, Ascanius holding on to his father's hand, and Aeneas' wife following behind the three. Soon the surviving Trojans flocked to Aeneas as their leader, but as they left the city his wife disappeared, and Aeneas returned into the doomed city to look for her, risking his life. Then, however, her ghost appeared to him and told him that she was dead, and that after a long journey he would come to Italy, settle there and marry an Italian princess.

There was an older tradition, depicted in works of art as early as the Sixth Century B.C., that Aeneas' wife did accompany him into exile from Troy, and that her name was Eurydica. But the version which remains famous, that his first wife was Creusa, a daughter of King Priam, was popularized and made standard by Vergil's *Aeneid*, and from the time of Vergil on, scenes in art portraying the flight from Troy do not show a woman accompanying Aeneas.

The Romans recognized that the choice of Troy as the place of their ancestral origin presented other difficulties, since Troy in myth was a mixture of good and evil elements, a place where the sinner Paris, with his irresponsibility, frivolity, and selfishness, lived side by side with such a hero as Hector, epitome of patriotism and sense of duty to family and country. Therefore the remnant that survived the fall of the city and left Troy for Italy was portrayed as a righteous and guiltless link with the future.

Leaving Troy, Aeneas and the Trojans began the odyssey that was to last seven years. Voyaging into an unknown future in search of a new home, their journey was not like Odysseus' return home but a quest for a new one, in which Aeneas ultimately succeeded, despite backsliding and wavering, only through trial and error and his sense of duty. In looking for a new home the Trojans who went into exile were constantly guided by a mysterious fate, and even though Italy had been intimated as the goal, they tried out other places. When they landed in Thrace, for example, the ghost of Polydorus, Priam's son who was murdered by Priam's son-in-law Polymestor for his treasures, warned Aeneas to leave that polluted spot, and they made a similar "false start" on the island of Crete when pestilence and famine struck them as they were beginning to build a city.

Then they sailed northward, and as they reached Greece they were attacked by the Harpies, who defiled their food. They drove them off, but not before the Harpies' leader had prophesied that the Trojans would not found their city until they had eaten their own tables in hunger. The Trojans then sailed north along the coast of Greece to Epirus, where they were surprised to find Priam's son Helenus and Hector's wife together ruling the region left to them by Neoptolemus, and received from Helenus a prophecy of their future and instructions to reach the destined land. Sailing west, the Trojans sighted Italy, landed briefly to make thanksgiving sacrifices, and continued their sea voyage with the intent of rounding Sicily before proceeding up the west coast of Italy. En route they discovered on the shore of Sicily one of Odysseus' men named Achaemenides, who had been captured by the Cyclops Polyphemus but had managed to escape, and compassionately took him aboard. They finally landed on the western side of Sicily, where the aged Anchises suddenly died and was buried, not destined to reach the promised land.

As the Trojan ships sailed north for Italy, Juno caused a storm that scattered the ships southward to North Africa, so that they landed at the site of Carthage, future mortal enemy of historic Rome. There Aeneas and the Trojans were welcomed by Queen Dido of Carthage. She had herself only recently arrived there from her native Phoenicia, fleeing from her cruel brother Pygmalion, who had killed her husband Sychaeus for his wealth. Dido had managed to flee, taking with her many followers, and together they built the magnificent city of Carthage, with Dido as queen.

Dido and Aeneas were immediately attracted to each other, both handsome, refugees, leaders, and both had recently lost their spouses. At a banquet arranged by Dido in honor of the Trojans, Venus substituted Cupid for Aeneas' son Ascanius, and the god inflamed Dido's love for Aeneas. She asked him to tell in detail the story of the fall of Troy and the wanderings of his people, a story so impressive that Dido fell madly in love with Aeneas.

Even though after her husband's death she had made a vow that she would never give herself to another man, her sister Anna so broke down her reserve that she not only became unfaithful to the memory of her husband but neglected her duty to her people, while Aeneas was tempted both by her beauty and charm as well as the availability of an easy way out of his own duty to find a city for his people. Absorbed in their illicit love affair, Dido and Aeneas indulged themselves in their own personal happiness, forgetful of their obligations to their peoples. In Aeneas' case he simply forgot the destiny assigned to him by the gods and fate to settle his people in Italy. In the midst of all this happiness, Jupiter's messenger Mercury suddenly appeared to Aeneas and reminded him of his destiny and obligations to Ascanius and the future, and recalled to duty by the gods, Aeneas prepared to leave Carthage and sweet Dido. No pleas of hers that he remain with her could sway him. In despair Dido cursed Aeneas and his people, praying that an avenger (Hannibal was meant) would some day arise in Carthage, and when the Trojan ships were at sea Dido mounted a funeral pyre she had ordered built and killed herself with Aeneas' sword.

The Trojans, journeying north again, stopped off in Sicily, and on the first anniversary of Anchises' death celebrated commemorative funeral games, consisting of athletic contests for prizes. In the midst of these ceremonies Juno stirred up discontent among the Trojan women, so that, tired of wandering, they set fire to the ships, determined to settle in Sicily. Almost all of the ships, however, were saved. In a dream Anchises advised Aeneas to leave most of the Trojans in Sicily and take with him to Italy only the hardiest men and women, and also told him to seek out the Sibyl at Cumae in Italy for advice. En route Aeneas' pilot Palinurus, overconfident, fell asleep at the helm, fell overboard and was drowned.

Vergil put the stopover in Sicily into the myth of Aeneas for a number of reasons. There was an old legend that the Trojans had landed in Sicily and established a settlement there on the western coast of the island, and moreover, it was in Sicily that Romans met Carthaginians in historic times, and it was there that the two peoples fought the First Punic War. Thus Vergil merged these traditions into the myth of Aeneas.

The Trojans finally reached Italy, landing at Cumae on the western coast, and Aeneas immediately went to consult the Sibyl of Cumae. There were at least ten prophetesses called Sibyls in ancient myths, the most famous one being the Cumaean Sibyl. They originated in the Near East, where prophetesses were a common phenomenon. The Cumaean Sibyl, whose name was Deiphobe, had received as a gift from Apollo the fulfillment of a wish that she live for as many years as there were grains in a handful of sand, but, in a typical version of the ill-conceived wish, she forgot to ask also for the gift of eternal youth. Thus, though she lived for thousands of years, she shrank to be so small that she was kept in a little flask, and there she still exercised her gifts of prophecy. Once she was asked what she wished for now, and her answer was "I want to die." But this happened long after Aeneas' visit.

To Aeneas the Cumaean Sibyl prophesied the perils the Trojans were to anticipate in Italy: war and the fierce opposition of the Italian prince Turnus. Aeneas asked her to guide him to the Underworld to see his father Anchises, but she told him that he must first find and pluck a golden bough in a nearby wood, an ancient folkloric symbol of immortality, accessible only to those destined, like Adonis, to return to life. This was to be his passport to the Underworld, as Aeneas joined the famous group of mythic heroes who made the descent to Hades and returned.

Unlike Odysseus, however, Aeneas actually travelled through the Underworld, led by the Sibyl, seeing all the famous sights and sinners. The ferryman Charon rowed them across the Styx, and they passed the three-headed dog Cerberus, whom the Sibyl drugged. Then Aeneas saw the soul of his pilot Palinurus, to whom he promised proper burial, and also saw the soul of Queen Dido of Carthage, to whom he tried sadly to communicate his regret. But she would not talk with him, and rejoined the soul of her husband

Sychaeus. Finally Aeneas reached the Elysian Fields, where he met the soul of Anchises, who prophesied a glorious future for the people of Aeneas, pointing out to him the souls of future descendants, culminating in Augustus, son of a god, who was destined to bring back the Golden Age to Italy. Finally, imbued with pride in his destiny, Aeneas returned to the upper world purified and "reborn," now the resolute man of destiny, unshakable in his dedication to the future, doubts and frailties gone, wholly dedicated to duty (*pietas*).

In Italy, Aeneas and the Trojans were soon to encounter hostile forces that plunged them into a devastating war. After they sailed into the mouth of the Tiber in the land of King Latinus, stopped to eat, and in their hunger ate large cakes of bread, Aeneas happily announced that this was the fated land, as prophesied in the curse of the Harpies that the Trojans would not find a resting place until they had eaten their tables. Previously, an oracle had predicted to Latinus that his daughter Lavinia, promised in marriage to Turnus, prince of the Rutulians, an indigenous Latin people, was fated to marry a foreign prince. When he heard that Aeneas was in Italy and who he was, he promptly offered him the hand of his daughter Lavinia.

But Juno decided to delay Aeneas' success by fomenting a war between the Trojans and the Latins, and poisoned the mind of Queen Amata, Latinus' wife who favored Turnus, against the marriage of her daughter to Aeneas. Turnus and Lavinia, moreover, were in love with each other. In anger Turnus mobilized his people for war, and fuel was added to the growing enmity when Ascanius, while hunting, inadvertently killed a tame stag that was the pet of the daughter of a Latin prince. In the dispute that arose between the Trojans and the Latins, Ascanius had to be rescued from a Latin mob. Two Latins were killed in the disorder, and the Latins then joined the Rutulians in declaring war on the Trojans.

Aeneas sought aid from King Evander, a Greek king ruling at Pallanteum in Latium, the site of future Rome. King Evander and his son, the youth Pallas, graciously welcomed Aeneas, agreed to a military alliance with the Trojans, and invited Aeneas to participate in ceremonies honoring Hercules for destroying the fire-breathing monster Cacus. Evander then gave Aeneas some troops commanded by his young son Pallas. Aeneas and Pallas then went to Etruria to seek further aid from an Etruscan king named Tarchon.

Meanwhile, Aeneas' mother Venus appealed to her husband Vulcan (the Roman equivalent of Hephaestus) to forge a miraculous suit of armor for Aeneas. When this was brought to Aeneas, it included a wondrous shield decorated with Roman historical and mythological scenes, culminating in the Battle of Actium where Antony and Cleopatra were defeated by Augustus. Seeing the shield Aeneas rejoiced, "lifting on his shoulders the renown and destinies of his descendants."

The "war lover" Turnus in the absence of Aeneas attacked the Trojan camp and laid siege to it. Two Trojan youths, Nisus and Euryalus, volunteered to spirit themselves out of the camp to find Aeneas, but they were, however, soon spied by a troop of the enemy, and Euryalus was captured and killed. Nisus then fought his way to the leader of the enemy, killed him and was killed in turn. Thus died two Trojan youths in the name of friendship and duty. The Rutulians then broke into the Trojan camp, and in the melee, Turnus was surrounded but managed to escape by jumping into the Tiber River. Turnus is portrayed as a kind of Homeric hero, excessively violent and eager for personal glory and war booty.

After Aeneas returned to the Trojan camp, the Rutulians under Turnus attacked again. In the battle, Turnus singled out the young gallant Pallas, the ideal youth of the story, whom he quickly killed. Then he stripped the body for booty, taking as his own trophy the youth's sword-belt, but Aeneas drove Turnus away and retrieved the body of Pallas. Then he attacked an ally of Turnus, Mezentius the Etruscan tyrant. The wounded Mezentius was rescued by his gallant son Lausus, whom Aeneas quickly slew, along with his wounded father. The Trojans and their Etruscan allies next advanced upon Laurentum, the capital of the Latins. The Italian warrior maid Camilla, a kind of Italian Amazon, was assigned the task of holding back the Trojan and Etruscan cavalry, but she was quickly killed.

It was decided to settle the war and all the issues involved by a duel between Turnus and Aeneas, but in the preparations treachery took place, and Aeneas was wounded by an arrow. Cured by his mother Venus, he promptly attacked Laurentum.

Queen Amata, believing Turnus to be dead, committed suicide. Turnus now ordered the duel between himself and Aeneas reinstated, and in the fight his sword was shattered and he fled, pursued by Aeneas. Juno now agreed to cease her intervention against Aeneas, on condition that the name Trojans be given up and the united peoples be henceforth called Latins. The wounded Turnus humbly begged Aeneas to spare his life, or at least agree to return his body to his father for burial. Aeneas was moved by pity, but suddenly catching sight of Pallas' sword-belt worn by Turnus as a trophy he was overwhelmed by fury and plunged his sword into Turnus, killing him at once.

The Roman myth does not end, as did Homer's *Iliad,* on a note of compassion — Achilles returning Hector's body for burial to his father King Priam. In the Roman story Turnus was the symbol of all that thwarted the fulfillment of destiny and the establishment of a peaceful world, so that Vergil, in telling the story in this way, implied the historic necessity to exterminate the forces of violence and internal disunity. But it is also possible that Vergil meant to imply that in their search for a better world and for peace the Romans, in using war to achieve this end, brutalized and tainted themselves by the means used.

The war over, Aeneas married Lavinia, built a new city in Latium which he named Lavinium, and deposited there the sacred images of the Trojan gods, which he had dutifully carried with him all the way from Troy. There was also a tradition that Aeneas brought with him to Italy the *palladium* that had protected Troy. Many cities of the ancient world, both in Greece and Southern Italy, claimed to have such a talisman called *palladium.* Because of the earlier story that the Greeks had spirited the *palladium* out of Troy, the difficulty was resolved by the story that the Greeks stole not the original *palladium* (which Aeneas had), but a substitute made by the Trojans (or that Diomedes had obtained the original statue which he later gave to Aeneas). In any case, the Romans later claimed that they alone possessed the true *palladium,* and kept the holy statue, supposed to have been brought by Aeneas from Troy, in the temple of Vesta in Rome. Rome's safety and empire were thought to depend on the presence of this talisman in Rome.

Aeneas was said to have had children by his Italian wife

Lavinia, but the usual version reports that Aeneas died about three years after founding Lavinium, and that he was succeeded as king by his son Ascanius (or Iülus). This son of Aeneas then founded a new city in Latium named Alba Longa, which the descendants of Aeneas ruled for hundreds of years, with a whole line of kings invented to fill the gap between the coming of Aeneas to Italy and the founding of Rome by Romulus in the traditional year 753 B.C.

This myth of the Trojan ancestry of the Romans became in time the official pedigree of the whole Roman people, and in the First Century B.C. there were many Roman families that claimed descent from specific Trojans. In particular, Julius Caesar's family claimed Ascanius, under the name Iülus, as their ancestor, and thus traced themselves back to Aeneas and the goddess Venus. This genealogy was adopted by Caesar's adopted son Augustus, so that it became the official pedigree of the imperial family, and finally the common property of all Romans.

In the Middle Ages and early modern times, royal families in Europe often sought to trace their origins back to Aeneas and the Trojans. Thus it was told that the Trojan prince Hector had a son Francus who escaped from Troy with some companions, and that his descendants settled in France in the Fourth Century A.D. and became the ancestors of the first king of France. Similarly, in England there developed the myth that a grandson of Aeneas named Brutus (Brut) was banished from Italy and migrated to England, founded a new Troy at Londinium (London), and became the founder of the British people. For this reason, the Trojans were honored in Western Europe until a few hundred years ago as the ancestors of the great European families and peoples, while the Greeks, because of their destruction of Troy, were downgraded and regarded with hostility.

XXIX

A MISCELLANY OF ROMAN MYTHS

Mars and Anna Perenna

The very few myths associated with the native Roman-Italic gods probably have their origins in Etruscan and Greek influences. Thus Jupiter, Juno, Vulcan, Vesta, Diana, etc., had no genuine native mythology. Next to Jupiter, the most important Roman god was Mars, originally an agriculture and war god, protector of lands of the community, and later associated with the Greek god of war Ares. There was another Italic war god named Quirinus, who originally was joined with Mars and Jupiter in a divine male triad worshipped as a unified group — Jupiter-Mars-Quirinus. The concept of a trinity of gods probably was Indo-European in origin. Under Etruscan influence this native trinity was replaced by a group of gods — Jupiter, his wife Juno, and his daughter Minerva — known as the Capitoline Triad, because it was worshipped in a great temple on the Capitoline Hill known later as the Capitol, center of the Roman state religion.

With Mars was associated a myth involving the Roman divinity Anna Perenna. She is probably a form of the primitive mother goddess, symbol of fertility, and in Roman religion she appears simply as a spirit of vegetation, a kindly benevolent old woman. Once in a time of famine she is said to have come to Rome disguised as an old woman, selling to the people cakes that she had baked herself. Somehow a folktale connected her with Mars, relating that when Mars once fell in love with Minerva, but was not able to win her over, he appealed to Anna Perenna to intercede for him. She told him that she had succeeded and was sending the now willing Minerva to him as a bride covered with a veil. When

Mars removed the veil the woman turned out to be old Anna Perenna herself.

Saturn and the Golden Age

Saturn was an old Italic agricultural god who had something to do with the sowing season, but who eventually became identified with the notion of plenty. When he was identified with the Greek god Cronus, father of the Olympian gods, whose reign saw the Golden Age, the story developed that Cronus, deposed from his rule, had fled to the West and settled in Italy, and that his reign in Latium was the continuation in Italy of the Golden Age. An incorruptible, benevolent god, he brought such fertility and peace to the region that later Romans looked back with nostalgia to that time and yearned for a return of this peaceful era. The principal festival in honor of Saturn was called the Saturnalia, a winter holiday that grew in length until it lasted a week, from December 17-24. It was the custom during this festive week to symbolize the condition of the Golden Age by giving thanksgiving banquets, exchanging gifts, and treating slaves with special indulgence (masters themselves served meals to their slaves). In general a carnival atmosphere prevailed during the Saturnalia.

Vertumnus and Pomona

Vertumnus was an early Italic vegetation spirit, associated with the changes in the seasons, and Pomona was a Roman spirit of fruit trees. Under Greek influence the relationship between these two was transformed into a love story, in which Vertumnus as a personified youth fell in love with Pomona, conceived of as a beautiful nymph. She rejected his affection, so the love-sick Vertumnus disguised himself as an old woman and came to Pomona as an intermediary for Vertumnus. So persuasive was Vertumnus in his disguise that Pomona consented to become the lover of Vertumnus.

Hercules and Cacus

Cacus was a minor local god in primitive Rome, whose functions we no longer know, although he may have been a kind of trickster spirit so common in primitive mythologies. Originally Hercules was unknown to the Latins, but under Etruscan and

Greek influence the famous Greek hero was incorporated into local myths about 400 B.C. To explain Hercules' presence in Italy, it was said that when he was driving the cattle of Geryon back to Greece (first through Spain, then from Southern France into Italy), he stopped with the herd at the Tiber River, where he fell asleep. Then the brigand Cacus stole some of his cattle by pulling them backwards by their tails into his cave, so that it would be difficult to track them down. It is said that Cacus was an evil thieving giant who breathed fire and ravaged the countryside. (The transformation of a local Italic god into a monster reminiscent of Typhon battled by Zeus in Greek mythology is noteworthy.) When Hercules awoke and discovered the theft he confronted Cacus and an earth-shaking struggle ensued, in which Hercules, naturally, was the victor, thus bringing to Rome also his civilizing mission and his services as benefactor of mankind. Later the deified Hercules became for the Romans a military god of victory, was called Hercules Victor, and Hercules Invictus ("The Unconquered"). Many other cities in Italy, especially Greek colonies in the southern part, had myths connected with the passage of Hercules and his cattle.

Numa and Egeria

Although most genuine myths connected with the period of the Roman kingdom deal with Romulus as founder and first king, a few involve other people and events of this time. The second king, Numa, of Sabine origin, probably an historical person, had a peaceful reign, and he established the religious institutions of the Romans, many of which lasted for over 1000 years, much as Romulus was responsible for political traditions. The story is told that when he lost his wife, a nymph named Egeria (really an early Italic spirit) fell in love with him and became his mistress. In Greek mythology the story would have been treated as an amorous adventure of a goddess with a mortal, but in the Roman myth, Egeria became Numa's adviser on religious matters.

The Horatii and Curiatii

An incident which occurred in the reign of Rome's third king, Tullus Hostilius, became famous as a symbol of some Roman values and policies. There was a war between Rome and its parent city Alba Longa, and it was decided to settle the outcome by a duel of champions from both sides. For this purpose three Roman youths from the Horatius clan — hence called Horatii — and three youths from Alba Longa, the Curiatii from the Curiatius clan, would act as champions. In the struggle two Horatii were killed, leaving one Horatius facing three Curiatii. The Roman youth pretended to flee, and when one of the Curiatii ran ahead of his fellows, Horatius took a stand and killed him. A second time he pretended to flee, and by the same method he killed a second Curiatius. Finally, in a single duel he defeated the remaining enemy. This story showed how a smaller power (such as Rome was for a long time) could defeat stronger ones by the strategy of "divide and conquer."

The sister of the victorious Horatius had been engaged to one of the Curiatii, and when she heard of the death of her fiancé, she collapsed and mourned him. Angered by her sympathy for an enemy, Horatius killed his sister. His case was referred to the entire Roman people for judgment, and though he was a murderer Horatius was exonerated. His services as a war hero and his fierce patriotism decided the issue for the Romans.

The Sibylline Books

In the reign of the Tarquins (it is not clear whether in the reign of the first of the Tarquins, Tarquinius Priscus, or the last, Tarquin the Proud), the Sibyl of Cumae came to the king with nine volumes of oracular revelations in verse. She offered them to Tarquin at a high price, but he rejected the books because he considered the cost exorbitant. Then the Sibyl burned three volumes and offered the remaining six at the same price. Again Tarquin rejected the offer, so she burned three more and offered the three left at the original cost. This time he was advised by his counselors to buy the volumes. The famous Sibylline Books were unique in ancient paganism as constituting a sort of sacred book, something unknown to the Greeks. Kept in the temple of Jupiter on the Capitoline under the supervision of state priests, they were consulted in time of crisis by order of the Senate, by opening one of the volumes and reading at random. The prophecy, usually cryptic, was then interpreted by experts.

Like the Greeks, the Romans felt the need to discover and

interpret the will of the gods at every step in their lives. Besides the Sibylline Books, which were used sparingly as a sort of last resort, the Romans observed and interpreted omens of all kinds — unusual natural phenomena, dreams, the patterns made by flights of birds, and the appearance of the vital organs of animals, especially the liver. Prophets and diviners were also consulted, and when the Romans came into contact with the Greeks they consulted the Greek oracles also, especially the oracle of Apollo at Delphi.

Horatius Cocles

The expulsion of the Etruscan kings from Rome about 500 B.C. was followed by Etruscan efforts to recapture the city, led by the Etruscan King Porsenna. When the Etruscan forces attacked, only one wooden bridge over the Tiber lay between them and the city of Rome, and as the Roman forces retreated over the bridge Horatius Cocles ("One Eyed") saved the city by taking a stand alone at the head of the bridge while the Romans cut it down behind him. When this had been completed he disengaged himself from the Etruscan attackers, jumped into the Tiber and managed to swim to safety on the other side.

Mucius Scaevola

Still another Roman patriotic myth was connected with the war of King Porsenna against the Romans at the very beginning of the Republic. Mucius Scaevola ("Left Handed") volunteered to assassinate Porsenna, and one night managed to sneak into Porsenna's tent with a concealed dagger but was caught. Taken before the king for sentencing, Scaevola demonstrated his toughness by thrusting his right hand into a glowing charcoal brazier in the tent and allowing it to be burned off. Then he announced to Porsenna that there were hundreds of other Roman volunteers ready to carry out the decision to assassinate the king. So amazed was Porsenna that he released Scaevola and escorted him back to Rome. The result of Scaevola's courageous deed was an armistice, ensuring the safety of Rome and her republican institutions.

Marcus Curtius

Another Roman myth of early Republican days is the story of

Marcus Curtius. One day a large hole opened up in the midst of the Roman Forum, the civic center of the city. A prophecy said that the hole would close only if the Romans threw into the hole what they considered most precious. Sacrificing himself, the youth Marcus Curtius mounted his horse (symbolizing the warrior youth of Rome), devoted himself by a special ceremony to the gods of the lower world, and leaped into the hole, horse and all. It promptly closed up.

Decius Mus

The self-sacrifice of Marcus Curtius was an example to be imitated by later Romans. It is said that in the fateful wars between the Romans and the Samnites, the Roman general Decius Mus devoted himself to the gods below and then charged into the enemy to certain death. The Romans won the battle.

Genucius Cipus

Cipus was originally an Italic spirit thought to protect boundaries. In the Roman myth about him — the base was a folktale — he was transformed into an historical figure, the Roman general Genucius Cipus of the time of the early Republic. Cipus, having won a military victory, was returning in triumph with his army to Rome. Outside the city he saw his own image in a stream, and was astounded to see that he had horns on his head. Now the horn was traditionally a symbol both of plenty and, because of its association with such animals as the bull, of power as well. When Cipus consulted a prophet he was informed that he would become king of Rome if he entered the city with his army to celebrate his triumph. Promptly Cipus called an assembly of the people outside the walls, revealed to them the danger of a return to monarchy, and recommended death or exile for himself as a possible enemy of the Republic. As a reward he was given as much land outside the walls of the city as he could work in a day, and he lived there for the rest of his life.

Coriolanus

During the century after the establishment of the Republic, when the city of Rome was struggling for its very existence, assailed first by the Etruscans, then by its Latin neighbors, the

Roman politician Coriolanus was exiled from the city on the grounds that he was trying to establish a tyranny at Rome. He went to live in Volscian territory, and there built up an army of Volscians under his command. He was determined to lead these traditional enemies against Rome to seize power for himself. As Coriolanus and his Volscian army reached the walls of the city and were preparing to put it under siege, the gates suddenly opened and out came two women — Veturia, Coriolanus' mother, and Volumnia, his wife. They pleaded with him, reminding him of his Roman origins. Overcome with emotion, Coriolanus withdrew and abandoned his attempt.

Caecilius Metellus

Another myth tells of patriotism, that of Caecilius Metellus. He was a very distinguished Roman of the Third Century B.C. — consul, general, *pontifex maximus* (head of the state religion). When a fire broke out in the temple of Vesta, Caecilius Metellus ran inside to save the sacred objects there, including the *palladium,* on whose safety the very existence of Rome depended. As a result he lost his eyesight, and became a high official after this event. It is not likely that the historic Caecillus Metellus was blind, although it is possible that he lost his eyesight temporarily in the fire. In any case, the story was told as a myth because of the traditional taboo that no one was permitted to see the sacred objects in the temple of Vesta.

The Rape of Lucretia

This story may have an historic base, but the form given it in Roman tradition verges on the mythic. In the reign of the last Etruscan king, Tarquin the Proud, the king's son Sextus was enamored of a Roman matron named Lucretia. During a military operation Sextus contrived to remain in the city while Lucretia's husband was on military duty. He forced his way into Lucretia's home and pleaded for her love, and when she indignantly repulsed him, he raped her and left. Lucretia then committed suicide. When her death was traced to the king's son, Lucretia's husband and other Roman aristocrats organized a national revolution against the foreign ruling house, expelled the Tarquins, and established a republic. The influence of a number of Greek myths can be found in this story, which was politicized and historicized within the context of Roman morality and patriotism.

Cincinnatus

Cincinnatus was an historical figure of the middle of the Fifth Century B.C. who was appointed dictator during a military crisis involving neighboring peoples. At the time he was living on his estate, absorbed in farming operations, and the delegation sent to announce his appointment actually found him at his plow. He completed the military assignment within sixteen days and immediately resigned the dictatorship. Then he returned to his farm to resume his plowing.

Janus

Janus was a very ancient primitive Italic spirit, uniquely Roman in concept, though myths told about him are derived from Greek sources. Janus was biform in appearance, having two heads, one that looked forward, the other backward. He may have had some connection originally with the moon, especially the new moon, since he was particularly worshipped at the time of the new moon on the first of each month, and during the month of January, which was named after him. It is possible that when Diana was identified with the Greek goddess Artemis and became the moon goddess, Janus' original function became obsolete and he lost his connection with the moon. He was also the god associated with the crossing of streams and with boundaries, especially going in and out of the city of Rome. Thus he came to be the god of all beginnings, symbolized by a gate or passageway, and protection of doorways became one of his principal functions even though he was originally not connected with them. In this regard he was associated with the beginning and ending of warfare, especially from the time of the Emperor Augustus on. In time of war the doors of the temple of Janus were left open, in time of peace they were ceremonially closed.

The association of Janus with peace may have originated in stories that he was an early king of Latium in whose reign peace prevailed. It is said that he came to the site of Rome from Greece to become king of Latium, and that it was he who welcomed Cronus when he went into exile in Italy. Cronus, the Roman god

Saturn, shared rule over Latium with Janus, and in their reign fidelity among men, abundance, and peace prevailed, as in the Golden Age. When Janus died he was deified.

During the attack of the Sabines on the Capitoline Hill when Tarpeia betrayed the city, the god Janus saved the city when he made a stream of hot water flow in front of the assailants, so that they fled. In commemoration of this miracle, the Romans decided to make his temple in Rome a symbol of war and peace. The opening of the gates of his temple facilitated the god's assistance to the Romans in wartime, and when peace reigned throughout Roman territory, the gates were closed to symbolize the fact that the god was in peace in his own home too.

XXX

STAR MYTHS

The assignment of names to the planets, stars, and clusters of stars forming constellations began in the Near East long before the Greeks, but the names by which we know them today are the mythological ones given them by the Greeks. Of the approximately 2000 stars visible on a very clear night, many were mythologized in antiquity.

An important feature of star mythology is the naming of the planets: eight of the nine planets of our solar system "wander" in the sky bearing the names of the ancient gods Venus, Mars, Neptune, Jupiter, Mercury, Saturn, Pluto, Uranus. Many stars and constellations too were associated by the Greeks with gods and heroes. Some of the best known are, for example, Orion, the seven Pleiades nearby supposedly being pursued by this "mighty hunter of the skies," the group containing Andromeda ("The Chained Woman"), Perseus, Cassiopeia, Cepheus, and Cetus, the Great Bear and the Little Bear. The galaxy we know as the Milky Way is connected with a myth of Hera, and a constellation within it is called Argo Navis from the story of the quest of the Argonauts. From the myth of Hercules come such star names as Hydra, among others. Distinctive constellations include such names as Centaur, Cerberus, Dolphin (from the myth of Orion), Pegasus, Lyra, Corona Borealis (the crown of Ariadne), Aquila (the eagle of Zeus), Cycnus (from the story of Leda and the swan), Draco (the dragon), Ophiuchus ("Serpent Bearer," supposedly Asclepius), Auriga (the charioteer Myrtilus).

There is a group of twelve major constellations which form the Zodiac, so called because the majority of them were named after mythical animals. These share the sky in twelve equal parts, along the path of the sun as it makes its annual passage in the sky. The zodiacal signs, together with their mythical associations are Aries (the ram that rescued Phrixus), Taurus (Zeus as the bull), Gemini (the twins Castor and Polydeuces), Cancer (the Crab sent to attack Heracles when he fought the Lernian Hydra), Leo (the Nemean lion killed by Heracles), Virgo (Astraea, goddess of justice who abandoned the earth in the Iron Age), Libra (the scales of Astraea), Scorpio (the destructive animal sent by Artemis or Gaea to kill Orion), Sagittarius (the centaur Chiron), Capricorn (the goat Amaltheia that suckled Zeus), Aquarius ("Water Bearer" – Zeus' cupbearer Ganymedes), Pisces (the fish into which Aphrodite and Eros transformed themselves when endangered by Typhon).

The practice of naming celestial bodies after classical mythological figures was revived on a big scale in the first half of the Nineteenth Century. When the minor planets (called asteroids or planetoids) which circulate between the orbits of Mars and Jupiter were discovered, they were named after major Greek goddesses, following the ancient usage of naming the planets themselves after the major Greek gods. In this manner, between 1801 and 1845 the names Ceres, Pallas, Juno, Vesta, and Astraea were assigned to the first five planetoids discovered. By 1891, when the first photographic method of astronomical exploration was invented, about 320 such asteroids were known – all of them named after mythological persons. When the satellites of the planet Saturn were discovered in modern times, they were given mythical names derived from the generation of the Titans, for example, Hyperion, Iapetus, Tethys, Rhea, Phoebe. Similarly, the satellites of Jupiter are called Io, Europa, Ganymedes, Callisto, and Amaltheia.

In the first decade of the Twentieth Century an interesting set of planetoids was discovered close to Jupiter. The dozen odd asteroids of this group are known collectively as the Trojans, because they are named for mythical heroes of the Trojan War, Achilles, Patroclus, Hector, Nestor, Priam, Agamemnon, Odysseus, Aeneas, Anchises, Troilus, and Ajax. The asteroid Hermes was found as recently as 1937, Icarus in 1949. The latter was so named because of all known celestial bodies in our solar system its orbital path comes closest to the sun – reminiscent of the disastrous flight of the mythical Icarus too close to the sun. Over 1700 such asteroids are known today, with the result that the original plan of naming these minor planets after mythological personages has now been abandoned in favor of a more prosaic numbering system.

Still a powerful force today is astrology, the attribution to celestial bodies of powerful influence on the lives of men, an ancient belief which arose from the association of the names of gods and heroes with planets and stars. Astrology was created by the Babylonians in the Eighth and Seventh centuries B.C. Priests, impressed by the observed regularity of the positions and movements of planets and stars named after gods and heroes, conceived the notion that there was a correspondence between movements in the sky and what happened on earth, and since they could foretell the movements of heavenly bodies, they claimed to be able through observation of the heavens to foresee human destinies and prophesy the future by casting horoscopes. What was to happen to each human was therefore thought of as being "in the stars," predestined by stellar divinities.

Though such astral cults were foreign to both Greeks and Romans in their own religion, they began to gain adherents in the Fourth Century B.C., as anthropomorphism declined among the Greeks. Under inspiration of the Near East, deification of the stars was introduced to Greek belief, though astrology itself was at first rejected as irrational. At this time the Babylonian names for the planets were translated into Greek, and the Latin equivalents of the Greek names still serve for the planets today. In the Hellenistic Age Greeks thought of the stars as divine, possessed of decisive influence on human affairs, so divination by stars became exceedingly important and was soon practiced all over the world. Each star and constellation was associated with a myth.

Astrology among the Greeks was also fostered by many myths that involved catasterism, that is, elevation of mythic heroes and heroines to the stars. Moreover, besides such genuine star myths, there developed the practice of the royal courts of the Hellenistic Age of flattering ancestors and relatives of ruling families by creating new star myths. Two famous examples are the constellation Berenice's Hair, and the comet associated with Julius Caesar shortly after his assassination.

Particular power over the destinies of men was assigned to the twelve constellations of the Zodiac and to the planets. Each planet was supposed to bestow particular qualities on humans because of traditional characteristics of the individual gods. In ancient astrology each day of the week was sacred to a different planet, a practice which accounts for the days of our week being named after ancient planetary divinities. Besides Saturday, Sunday, Monday, we know some days by early German equivalents of Greek and Roman gods. Such words and expressions as disaster, lucky star, star-crossed are survivals of the hold astrology once had.

One of the influences of astrology upon religious doctrines was the belief that the abode of the souls of great and pious humans was an eternal dwelling place in heaven. It was believed that eminent persons and ordinary people who had led eminently virtuous lives could go up into the sky, just as earlier mythical heroes had. Hence the traditional Elysian Fields were relocated somewhere in the ether among the stars, while Hades was reserved exclusively for the souls of the evil and undeserving.

XXXI

THE CONTINUITY OF CLASSICAL MYTHS

At the time of the triumph of Christianity in the Fourth Century A.D., the classical myths, both Greek and Roman, had been diffused into every corner of the Roman world. They were part of the intellectual furniture of every educated person, and the themes of myths pervaded the literature and art of the civilized world. To the early Christian apologists and the Fathers of the Church, these stories and the uses to which they were put appeared fundamentally incompatible with Christianity. They attacked them vigorously on the grounds that they exposed Christians to the influence of the pagan gods and their immoral conduct, so out of keeping with Christian standards of morality. Had the early Christian intellectual leaders succeeded in uprooting the widespread attachment to the classical myths, the literature and art of the future would have been deprived of a potent source of imaginative themes.

In practice it is not possible to eradicate completely a cultural phenomenon so pervasive as were the myths of the Greeks and Romans. Just as the early Christians eventually came to terms with Greek and Roman literature despite full scale attacks on pagan studies by leading Christians, so they allowed the classical myths to enter their culture by purifying and Christianizing them. Declaring them dangerous falsehoods in their traditional form, they subjected them to a process of selection, and reinterpreted myths to make them useful to Christian life and thought. As the result of these new perspectives and changes the myths found shelter under the wings of Christianity throughout the Middle Ages.

The most serious task was the elimination of the survival of belief in the ancient gods implicit in the myths. This the early Christian thinkers accomplished by the application of Euhemerism, an interpretation of myths invented by the Greeks themselves. Using this interpretation, early Christian writers declared that the ancient gods were, originally, outstanding historical personages of early times who were geniuses, inventors, civilizers. Because of their benefactions to man early peoples made gods of them when they died, worshipped them, and told many false stories about them. So, for example, Prometheus was said by Christian reinterpreters to have been the inventor of automated figures, Atlas a learned astrologer, Mercury a brilliant versatile genius, Apollo a physician, Chiron the inventor of medicine, Bacchus the inventor of wine making, etc. In the Middle Ages these ancient divinities were often set beside the Hebrew patriarchs and prophets as parallels, and their lives were coordinated in time with Biblical history, so that they became part of the scheme of history. By transforming myth into history the Christians sanctioned the survival of the pagan gods, and thus preserved them from oblivion.

This is one of the ways by which the pagan myths remained alive in the stories and art of the Christian Middle Ages. The classical myths of heroes and heroines were also refashioned into history, and serious efforts were made to identify mythical heroes as ancestors of European peoples and royal families. Just as the French and British long regarded themselves as descendants of the Trojans Francus and Brutus, some royal families of Europe devised family trees and portrait galleries going back as much as seventy-five generations to the time of the Trojan War. For example, the Dukes of Burgundy in France traced themselves back to Hercules, through a son of the hero and a lady named Alise whom he married in Spain while bringing back the cattle of Geryon.

A second powerful influence that led to the Christian acceptance of classical mythology was the popularity of astrology. As we have seen, the Greeks mythologized many constellations and came to regard these as celestial divinities with enormous influence in shaping human destinies. Actually, of course, a religion like Christianity, with its monotheism and concept of personal moral responsibility for salvation, ought not to have tolerated such a fatalistic belief as astrology, and indeed first attacked the concept of astrological celestial divinities as a form of polytheism and thus a view incompatible with Christianity. But astrology was so widespread in the world that it was impossible to uproot it, and there were so many Christian partisans of the occult science that the Church came to terms with it, modifying the astrological system to bring it into line with Christian doctrine.

One interesting practice which emerged in the Middle Ages for a time was the depiction in Europe of mythological figures in Arabic dress and appearance. This happened because the great popularity of astrology among the Arabs affected Europe in new ways when a wave of interest in astrology swept over Europe in the late Middle Ages. For example, Hercules can be found represented with a turban and scimitar, and Andromeda as a constellation assimilated with the dromedary. It was more common, however, to depict classical gods, heroes, and heroines dressed as medieval knights and ladies instead of in classical dress (or undress).

More important than Euhemerism and the influence of astrology in the preservation of the classical myths was the application of allegory. In this way classical mythology changed form and meaning drastically, and became a repository of profound truths embodying Christian philosophy and moral precepts. Every myth was reinterpreted as an allegory to provide edifying meanings and moral teachings. For example, various gods were reinterpreted as symbols, Minerva as Wisdom, Mars as War, Hephaestus as Fire, etc., and many Christian truths were treated as prefigured in classical myths, as these were changed in content and meaning to serve new purposes. For example, a Thirteenth Century relief in Venice depicts Hercules as a redeemer accompanied by a stag (medieval symbol of the human soul) and standing on a dragon, intended as an allegory of Hercules as savior conquering evil and redeeming souls. Thus Hercules frequently appeared as a rival of Christ who purged the world of evils and prefigured the coming of Christ. In other instances the story of Hecuba lamenting the death of Troilus was interpreted as the Virgin Mary lamenting the body of Christ, while Ceres looking for Proserpina was explained as the Church in search of strayed souls.

Early in the Fourteenth Century a long poem entitled *Ovid moralisé (Ovid Moralized)* reinterpreted the classical myths in the *Metamorphoses* of the Roman poet Ovid so thoroughly as moral lessons that it was read even by nuns for edifying moral instruction. To make them conform to Christian morality the gods and heroes were made into monks, nuns, and clergy, as, for example, the flight of Daphne from the amorous Apollo was explained: "Daphne was the daughter of a river and cold by temperament, and so represents virginity. She was changed into a laurel tree, which, like virginity, is eternally green and bears no fruit. Daphne represents the Virgin Mary, loved by Him who is the true sun. When Apollo crowns himself with laurel, he represents God putting on the body of her whom He made his mother." No wonder Martin Luther attacked this book as blasphemous!

Knowledge of the classical myths in their ancient form did not, however, disappear from the knowledge of men. An excellent example of the potency of classical mythology in its purer form is found in the creation of the famous Tristan legend by someone in Northern Britain during the Sixth Century A.D. Based on historic persons who were local heroes of the time of King Arthur, the story was compiled by adapting many aspects of Greek myths to local settings, spread from Britain all over Europe, and has become one of the great myths of the world. Tristan (originally Drust), an orphan, was the nephew of King Mark of Cornwall. King Mark (the name may mean originally "horse") had horse's ears, and to conceal this peculiarity, he had each of his barbers killed immediately after serving him. Finally one barber told the secret of the horse's ears of Mark to an inanimate object and the secret was revealed. This tale is, of course, borrowed from the myth of King Midas and the ass's ears.

The reign of King Mark became an unhappy one because the king of Ireland imposed upon Cornwall a tribute in the form of thirty young men and thirty young women. Tristan volunteered to be one of the group, and when he came to Ireland he fought and killed the giant Morholt, leaving a piece of his sword in the giant's head. Princess Isolt of Ireland retrieved the piece of the sword from the head of Morholt, who happened to be her uncle. Tristan himself had been wounded by the giant, and the wound festered and gave off such an offensive stench that Tristan was isolated in a hut near the sea. Only Isolt could cure his wound, which she did without knowing that Tristan was the one who had killed her uncle Morholt.

Tristan had earlier obtained from a bird a golden hair, and vowed that he would find its owner as a bride for his uncle King Mark. At the time, Ireland was being ravaged by a fire-breathing dragon, and the king of Ireland had offered his daughter and one-half of his kingdom to the slayer of the monster. Tristan killed the dragon, but when Isolt discovered that he had killed Morholt, and Tristan that that the golden hair belonged to Isolt, he offered her – and she accepted – the hand of his uncle Mark. Before departing for Cornwall Princess Isolt received from her mother a love charm to be drunk by Isolt and Mark, but on shipboard Tristan and Isolt inadvertently drank the love potion and fell in love at once.

After his marriage to Isolt, King Mark discovered the illicit love affair, and he imprisoned his nephew. Tristan, who escaped, was joined by Isolt in the woods, but finally, conscious-stricken because of his continued deception of his uncle, fled and became a wanderer. Later he was seriously wounded and it was revealed that only Isolt could cure him. He begged her to come to help him, giving instructions that the ship on which she was to come should fly white sails if she was on it, otherwise black ones. As a result of a mixup the ship flew black sails when it entered the harbor, and Tristan, assuming Isolt had not come, died in dispair. When Isolt reached him she was heartbroken and died. King Mark buried them side by side, and from the grave of Tristan came a vine, from Isolt's a rose.

The legend of Tristan and Isolt was obviously put together from many themes and stories borrowed from Greek myths: Hippolytus and Phaedra, the slaying of the Minotaur, dragon folktales, Theseus and Ariadne, the death of Aegeus, the "incurable wound" of Philoctetes and of Paris, the voyage of healing of Telephus to Achilles, King Midas, and Greek plant mythology.

One of the most popular of the ancient myths remained the story of Troy, which survived in Europe in unbroken continuity from the ancient world, and became the basis of the many medieval Troy romances written in France, Germany, Italy, and England. This was partly due to the tradition of the descent of the

Romans from the Trojans and the efforts of many European royal families to trace their lineage back to Trojan sources. The first printed book in the English language, Caxton's *Recuyell* published in 1474, was a version of the Troy story.

Thus the Italian Renaissance, beginning in the late Fourteenth Century, did not produce a "rebirth" of classical mythology, but rather recreated it in keeping with the new humanism, so that the myths now reappeared closer to the classical form and content, and a new love of the ancient myths was diffused among philosophers, poets, painters, sculptors. There followed a tremendous outpouring of works based on classical mythological themes, more and more liberated from the restraints of the Christian Middle Ages, as fashions and emphases changed from country to country and from time to time. For instance, in the Fifteenth Century in Italy, the principal themes selected from mythology were seductions, rapes, love, and drunken revelry. The Sixteenth Century represents the triumph of classical mythology, as the whole body of classical mythology was now explored for subjects, and mythology provided the dominant themes of the art and literature of Europe.

An important impulse to the exploitation of myths as themes came from a famous mythological handbook written by Boccaccio between 1350-1375, the *Genealogy of the Gods* commissioned by King Hugo of Cyprus, who wanted a book on the gods and heroes of classical mythology. For over 200 years Boccaccio's manual was the standard reference book on myths for artists and writers, was translated from the Latin into Italian, French, and Spanish, and served as a great storehouse of myths, systematized on a genealogical basis. But this book continued the medieval practice of allegorical interpretation of myths so as to reveal edifying lessons for Christian morality, and to make this purpose clear, Boccaccio began each of his fifteen sections of the *Genealogy of the Gods* with a prayer to Christ.

The treatment of the Orpheus myth is an instructive example of the new approach to classical myths in the Italian Renaissance. Whereas in the Middle Ages Orpheus was depicted as the redeemer triumphantly bringing back the soul of Eurydice, who in turn served as a symbol of mankind, in the Renaissance he became the very symbol of humanism – philosopher, theologian, musician, inventor of poetry and music. He was portrayed now as the exemplar of the great poet, symbol of the power of love and poetry, whose magic song enchants men, gods, nature. The Italian poet Poliziano at the end of the Fifteenth Century was so caught up by the story of Orpheus' power to charm that he called it "not a false story."

A new art form, opera, which developed in the Seventeenth Century, enthusiastically embraced the use of classical myths as plots. The first opera, written in 1594, was *Dafne*, and the first opera that is still extant is *Euridice*, written by Ottavio Renuccini, with text by Peri and Caccini, for the wedding in Florence of Maria de' Medici and Henri IV of France. In this opera Orpheus triumphantly regains Eurydice with the aid of Venus. The Orpheus theme remained one of the most popular ones in opera, and similarly, on the "lost love" theme of Hero and Leander, many operas were created during the Renaissance, as well as poems and tragedies in Germany, England, and Spain. As an example of the popularity of ancient myths, it is interesting to note that between the Sixteenth and Nineteenth centuries in Europe over 200 works were written on the minor myth of Echo.

XXXII

TWENTIETH CENTURY WRITERS
AND CLASSICAL MYTHS

The great Renaissance impulse towards a resurgence of mythical imagination and a flood of creative applications thinned to a trickle in the Eighteenth Century. The preoccupation of that age with rationalism and realism turned the attention of writers and artists to new sources of inspiration, so that the century was relatively barren of myth, but in the Nineteenth Century a second great mythological renascence occurred in Europe as the result of the Romantic Movement. As a protest against the growing dominance of technology and the development of a mechanical world, and under the influence of a revival of interest in Hellenism, many artists and writers turned again for inspiration and themes to the classical myths as a repository of the wisdom of mankind. It would take volumes to do justice to this renewal of mythological imagination and the varied influences of the classical myths on the visual arts, the poetry and drama of the Nineteenth Century. Almost all the Romantic poets reinterpreted these myths as serious commentaries on contemporary life.

After the fading of Romanticism, the Twentieth Century has seen a third vigorous rebirth of classical myths, though it is an exaggeration to say, as Michael Grant has, that " . . . the revitalizing of the classical myths can be claimed as the most significant of all the impacts that the Greco-Roman world has had upon modern thought." The reasons for this resurgence, especially in the hands of some of the great modern dramatists, among whom the French have taken the lead, are interesting. In part another form of the Nineteenth Century reaction against the technology which has diminished the grandeur of man by depersonalizing life, the repeated return to the Greek myths for plots, symbols, and themes has not been due to lack of creative imagination on the part of contemporary writers. Rather, writers and artists have wanted to illumine the present through myths of the past in order to give heightened significance to the pettiness and ugliness of contemporary life through contact with the heroic grandeur of man portrayed in many myths. In a time of world crisis the mythical heritage has represented for many modern writers eternal models by which to test and give coherence to the apparent contemporary chaos, and to provide a broader view of man transcending a specific time. The timelessness of the mythic themes and the embodiment in them of profound universal truths has made it possible to reinterpret them over and over and to adapt them to contemporary experiences and problems. As T. S. Eliot has said, the use of ancient myth today ". . . is simply a way of controlling, or ordering, of giving a shape and a significance to the immense panorama of futility and anarchy which is contemporary history . . . "

By comparing and contrasting the present with the classical element in myths, contemporary writers have also affirmed their sense of the spiritual oneness of western culture, and by associating contemporary experience with the mythic past as a model of the human condition, they have succeeded in illuminating today's dilemmas. The classic myths raise the essential questions of human life in such generalized and incisive terms that the mythic personalities have served as archetypes of human conduct. The protean malleability of the classic myths has afforded innumerable opportunities for fresh reinterpretations.

Many of these themes have a striking relevance for contemporary audiences not only because of the vitality of the symbols but also because of the horror and suffering contained in many of the classical stories. Aside from the pertinent content of the myths, modern authors have found a special artistic freedom in using them, since the plots are well known and authors can dispense with the need to create new plots, concentrating instead on manipulating old ones to provide a commentary on contemporary man. Moreover, the distance from the mythical world gives the author an additional freedom — to criticize more unrestrainedly and to test more freely political, social, psychological dilemmas of the present crisis by the universal models in the ancient myths.

Some modern dramatists have achieved different effects by transposing the basic story of a myth to a contemporary setting, with characters wearing modern dress and using modern idioms. French dramatists have frequently refused to accept an uncritical admiring attitude to the myths as eternal, glorious models, and with a deliberate irreverence many either take the myths as an ironical, cynical backdrop to today's petty life, or deliberately debunk the great mythic heroes. This deflation of the grandeur of the ancient myths has often entailed irreverent satire on the myths themselves, by bringing the grand heroes of myth down to the level of commonplace situations and types and destroying the mystery of the myths through irony, cynicism, satire. Sometimes the use of myth has even served as a convenient device to get past censors under conditions of controlled political expression.

Whether in the hands of existentialists, Marxists, or traditionalists, the classic myths in literature continue to reveal an amazing capacity for transformation to man's changing condition. At the beginning of the modern renascence of myths Goethe proclaimed, "Greek mythology is an inexhaustible mine of divine and human symbols." More recently William Butler Yeats called myths "the builders of my soul." For André Gide they were the mainspring of his creativity. "Through myths," he declared, "I contemplate Olympus and man's suffering and the smiling serenity of the gods. I learned mythology, I embraced beauty, hugging it to my eager heart."

Among the many modern writers who have creatively retold the Greek myths is the Swiss poet Carl Spitteler, who won the Nobel prize for his epic poem *Olympian Spring* (written 1900-1910), an allegorical work in which the climb of the Olympian gods to victory over Cronus is treated, only to be followed by the decay of their power and the ultimate creation of Heracles as savior to save suffering humanity. Similarly, in his *Prometheus and Epimetheus* he depicted the two Titan brothers as a study in contrast between the progress of humanity through sacrifice and suffering, and greed and acquiescence in life as it is. In order to maintain his freedom Prometheus refuses to accept power, while Epimetheus opportunistically succumbs. For profound rethinking of classical myths and glowing radiance of poetry it is hard to find an equal to this magnificent poet.

Among this century's major dramatists is another Nobel Prize winner, Gerhart Hauptmann (1862-1946), the outstanding exponent of modern German drama. In 1907, at the age of forty-five, he visited Greece, where he experienced a profound revitalization of his creative talents, and out of this new inspiration created first a tragedy about Odysseus' son Telemachus, completed in 1912 as *The Bow of Odysseus*. Though Homer had depicted Odysseus' return from the Trojan War as the triumph of justice over evil, Hauptmann transformed the story into a disillusioning drama of a homecoming after a war, in which Penelope, traditionally the model of the faithful wife, was portrayed as relishing the attentions of the many suitors who had been pursuing her in Odysseus' long absence from Ithaca. Odysseus was embittered by knowledge of this, though he returned to seek regeneration and new strength through reunion with his native soil. Hauptmann's "Hellenism" achieved its highest expression in his great epic *Till Eulenspiegel* (1927), in which, for example, there is an elaborate description of the hero's descent to the Underworld, and in his *Atrides Tetralogy,* written during the Second World War. The war itself and Nazi domination infused a hopeless fatalism into this vast dramatic cycle (the four plays are named *Agamemnon's Death, Electra, Iphigenia in Aulis,* and *Iphigenia in Delphi*). Hauptmann chose the tragic story of the House of Atreus because of the range and depth of suffering in the story, and he transformed it into a struggle between the powers of light and darkness, expressing his disillusionment with hopes for peace and the brotherhood of man. At the end of the tetralogy Hauptmann introduced a "switch" in the traditional story by having his Iphigenia sacrifice her life to end the curse and suffering of her family — symbol of a renewal of hope for reconciliation and redemption.

The Austrian dramatist Hugo von Hofmannsthal (1874-1929), who was Richard Strauss's librettist for his Hellenic operas, was constantly searching for themes from classical mythology as subjects. His first collaboration with Strauss was in the *Elektra* (1903-1909), based on the motif of fate and blood revenge and modernized with a Freudian interpretation of her conduct. More than once he turned to the theme of Oedipus, and his *Oedipus and the Sphinx* (1906/7), is the first noteworthy drama on this theme in German literature and one of Hofmannsthal's richest poetical works. The justly famous *Ariadne at Naxos* (1912), written also as libretto for a Strauss opera, employs Greek myth to explore two of Hofmannsthal's basic concepts – the problem of fidelity and the wonder of transformation. In this play Ariadne symbolizes ideal love, as opposed to pleasure, and at first finds it incompatible with her nature to transfer her affections to the god Bacchus from the hero Theseus, whom she had helped kill the Minotaur when she fell in love with him. But in the end she does transfer her love because she has become convinced that Bacchus is really the god Death, and she wants to attain fulfillment of love in death.

Another Austrian-born devotee of classical myths is the expressionist artist-playwright Oskar Kokoschka, whose tragedy *Orpheus and Eurydice* (1915-1918), made into an opera by Ernst Krenek, is a pessimistic reaction to the horrors of the First World War. Far from being a musician and poet whose song charms everything, Kokoschka's Orpheus is blind to the truth. In this treatment of the myth, Eurydice became pregnant by Hades during her stay in the Underworld, and so she returns to Hades of her own accord, not because Orpheus breaks the taboo by looking back at her ghost. Hades, thus, the god of death, has a more enduring power than that of the creative artist. In connection with the writing of this tragedy Kokoschka also executed his famous painting *Orpheus and Eurydice.* Less gloomy was the tragedy of his compatriot Franz Werfel, *The Trojan Women,* written after the Second World War, which uses the myth to underscore the futility and waste of war, and transforms Queen Hecuba into the symbol of courage and strength in disaster. Despite the horror and suffering, and the world's unreason which she has experienced, she feels it is her duty to live on, convinced that somehow goodness and justice will prevail.

It is interesting to note that even the revolutionary German dramatist Bertolt Brecht, who usually dealt quite realistically with the problems of social misery and revolution, occasionally dipped into the pool of classical mythic material for exploring contemporary themes. In 1934 he wrote a verse play *The Horatii and the Curiatii,* based on the famous Roman legend, and transformed the story into a political morality play to illustrate Marxian dialectics and tactics. In 1948 he modernized the myth of Antigone into an anti-Nazi play under the title *Antigonemodell 1948*. The prologue of this play related the events to the period just after World War II, and in Brecht's version Polynices is hanged as a deserter from the German forces, and Creon is depicted as a modern dictator.

The poetry of the German lyric poet Rainer Maria Rilke was saturated with classical myths. In 1904 he wrote the poem *Orpheus, Eurydice, Hermes,* which depicts Orpheus as a restless creative man driven by an insatiable curiosity which in the end only serves to destroy the object of his quest, Eurydice, and in his *Alcestis* (1907), Rilke totally transformed this myth of the wife who sacrificed her life for her husband into a new creation. The subject of many operas, dramas, and poems since the Renaissance, Alcestis was often treated as a noble but pathetic person, or even cast in a frivolous light, but in Rilke's poem, Alcestis must die in order to become Admetus' wife. In this way Rilke was in effect affirming that love kills the beloved and that true love is to be found only in death through a kind of rebirth, and was thus restoring Alcestis to the position of an ancient vegetation divinity. In his *Sonnets to Orpheus* (1922), Rilke uses the master artist and ideal poet Orpheus as the symbol of the creative power of poetry that helps man transcend the human condition.

In France, the leading force in the retelling of ancient myths in new forms was another Nobel Prize winner, André Gide, who very early in his career found himself attracted to myths as subject matter for his works. Often he used these to test his own feelings and experiences, for he found that a number of classical heroes, such as Narcissus, Prometheus, Oedipus, Theseus, embodied aspects of his own personality and served to clarify his own self-understanding. His early prose essay *Treatise of the Narcissus* (1891) was a treatise on symbolism, in which Narcissus represents both humanity at large and Gide himself. In his dramatic dialogue *Philoctetes* (1899), Gide made many changes in the myth of the Greek hero, seeking to define the nature of true virtue, so that Philoctetes became in Gide's hands a symbol of the rebel who maintains his freedom of action and is deified in the end. Philoctetes' wound is the symbol of Gide's own sexual abnormality as a homosexual, and in deifying Philoctetes Gide asserted his own self-assurance in his way of life. In his brief treatise

Prometheus Misbound (1899), Gide wrote an irreverent satire in which he deliberately deflated the grandeur of the myth, making Zeus "the millionaire," and creating out of Prometheus a rebel who frees himself without the aid of Zeus and makes a pet of the eagle that had devoured his liver. Still, Gide stays within the tradition long enough to stress the duty of rebellion to achieve human progress, and to make Prometheus the symbol of man's eternal unrest and concern for others.

Gide's play *King Candaules* (1901) presents a sublimely happy man who proudly displays this happiness to his best friend Gyges and thus destroys himself. In this play Candaules, besides having a beautiful wife, desires Gyges homosexually. Another Gide work, *Proserpina* (1912), was later adapted as the libretto of Stravinsky's opera *Persephone* (1934). In this version of the myth of regeneration of the fertility goddess, Persephone is not raped by Hades, but goes to him voluntarily by plucking the narcissus, to become the symbol of fertility and rebirth. And Gide's reinterpretation of the Oedipus myth for the Twentieth Century in *Oedipus* (1931), has many innovations in the story, the most important being that Oedipus blinds himself because he did not see what he should have seen, namely that happiness gives a false sense of security.

The figure of Theseus was a recurring figure in Gide's thought all his life, and his last important work, a sort of literary testament, was the short novel *Theseus* (1946). The story is treated as an autobiography of Theseus, who is presented as a modern hero — smug, cynical, ironical, a practical realist constantly maneuvering for his own interests. In his confrontation with the Minotaur, he discovers that Minos had made a drug addict out of the monster, and among other changes in the myth, Theseus cynically reveals that the reason he abandoned Ariadne on Naxos was that the thread she has given him to find his way out of the labyrinth was really a woman's device to tie him to her forever, and that he deliberately failed to change the sails to white when he returned safely from Crete in order to attain power by getting rid of his father Aegeus.

Gide's irreverent manipulation of the classical myths was continued by Jean Cocteau, his compatriot. Cocteau's first original drama was the one act tragedy *Orpheus* (1926), about "the most famous poet and musician who ever lived." When Eurydice dies of poison, Orpheus succeeds in bringing her back to earth, on the condition that he may never again look at her, but after the lovers quarrel, he does look at her and she vanishes. Soon after, Orpheus, in a competition in poetry, submits a phrase with a prophetic message: *Madame Eurydice reviendrá des enfers,* and when it is discovered that the first letters of these five words constitute an acrostic containing a French obscenity, the Bacchantes tear his body to pieces. In the end, however, the lovers separated by death are reunited in a poetic heaven. This play was later adapted by Cocteau into a highly successful film *Orpheus* (1950), the major theme of which is "the poet must die several times in order to be born." The plot and details were considerably changed in the film, which has the happy ending of the reunion of Orpheus and Eurydice on earth.

The most famous of Cocteau's reinterpretations of classical myths is *The Infernal Machine* (1934), based on the myth of Oedipus. In this powerful play the universe is Satanic, controlled by an evil intelligence, a deadly machine designed for the destruction of impotent man and timed to explode at a precise moment. Man is thus driven by forces he does not understand, and many of these are within himself — the subconscious Freudian drives. Jocasta, for example, represses the memory of her first husband Laïus when she does not listen to the warnings of his ghost against her marriage to Oedipus. Similarly, Oedipus is not affected by the efforts of Tiresias to act as moral censor of Oedipus to inhibit his ego. The sphinx becomes a lovelorn girl who, because of her sexual attraction to Oedipus, voluntarily tells him her secret. The discovery of the truth by Oedipus — that he has killed his father and married his mother — results in Jocasta's suicide and his self-blinding. By the cutting of this tie Oedipus finally becomes a man, but in the end he defies the infernal machine by submitting to his fate because that is the way the traditional myth presented the story. While incorporating into his play the deadly seriousness of the Greek tale about man's fate, Cocteau has exploited it with typical French irony and humor, and spiced it with many double meanings characteristic of French bedroom farces.

Another distinguished French dramatist whose plays are based on reworking of classic myths is Jean Giraudoux, who first won acclaim with his witty and ironic *Amphitryon 38* (1929). The title is not to be taken literally, but is intended to emphasize that the theme of Jupiter's seduction of Alcmena, mother of the hero Hercules, is a very old one, as old as Greek mythology. In this boulevard comedy, treated as a bedroom farce on the theme of the eternal triangle, there is incorporated a philosophic message that when the gods, or forces beyond human control, invade the privacy of humans, one must behave rationally and with flexibility. Alcmena in fact has greater grandeur than Jupiter because, though a human, she calmly accepts the world as it is without fear. In fact she rescues her honor by talking Jupiter into accepting her friendship instead, and thus remains the perfect wife; if "adultery" nevertheless does take place, it comes as the result of a mixup and mistaken identity of Jupiter with her husband. Through the model of Alcmena, Giraudoux advocates calm acceptance of the human condition.

His most brilliant play, *The Trojan War Will Not Take Place* (1934 – produced in England and the United States as *Tiger at the Gates*), was written shortly before the outbreak of the Second World War. In this witty, cynical drama, as Giraudoux said, "The subject . . . is not the arrival of war, but the hesitation of the world between war and peace . . . " Just before the outbreak of hostilities between Greeks and Trojans, Hector for the Trojans and Ulysses for the Greeks agree that war is hell, and that it must be prevented at all costs by negotiation and conciliation, but many Trojans want war because peace is less interesting and reduces man to the level of searching for personal happiness in the family. But Cassandra prophesies that "There will be a Trojan war." All efforts at rationality come to naught, however, when a minor incident fomented by a warmonger is blown up by propagandistic deceit. All the efforts of the statesmen are powerless against man's irrationality, and the war breaks out.

Giraudoux's *Electra* (1937), written shortly after, depicts a mythic heroine portrayed in modern psychiatric terms, driven by elemental hatred of her mother Clytemnestra without consciously knowing the reasons for her savage antagonism. Electra is a stubborn idealistic young rebel who wants vengeance no matter what the cost, in the name of absolute justice, while Aegisthus, on the other hand, is a sincere statesman who advocates acceptance of the world as it is and acquiescence in personal happiness as the goal. He seeks to impose middle class values upon Electra by marrying her off to a wealthy man, but Electra, congenital troublemaker, adhering to unwavering principles of justice and individual freedom, will not compromise. In the end Aegisthus and Clytemnestra are both killed and Electra unleashes a war against her country, in which total destruction follows, the palace is burned down and the capital of the country is overrun by the enemy. But Electra is content that justice has triumphed. Like *The Trojan War Will Not Take Place,* this play served Giraudoux as a commentary on the dilemmas of Europe just before the Second World War.

The equally famous French playwright Jean Anouilh has frequently sought doomed figures among the classical heroes and heroines to illustrate his basic theme of the insecurity of life and the corrupting influence of society and the family upon the individual. His *Eurydice* (1941), produced in English as *Point of Departure,* is based on the doomed relationship of Orpheus and Eurydice. Presented in modern setting and dress, the drama depicts the love of a wandering cafe violinist and the daughter of an actress, who has had sordid love affairs. They meet in a railway station and fall in love at once. Both renounce the ties of family and friends for love, which they consummate in a cheap hotel room, but Eurydice cannot bring herself to tell him about her past because he sees in her idealized perfection. She flees and is killed in a bus crash (symbol of modern technology's destructive power). Back in the railway station Orpheus is approached by a mysterious Monsieur Henri who offers Orpheus a second chance with Eurydice if he will not look at her until dawn. Thus he can have his love only in darkness, but because he must know the whole truth about Eurydice he looks at her and she vanishes. Then Orpheus commits suicide to join his ideal Eurydice in death. We are left with the pessimistic message that happiness and love are unattainable in life, which is corrupting and ugly. Only in death can ideal love be redeemed.

Anouilh's famous play *Antigone* (1942/3) was produced during the German occupation of France, and is full of anachronisms. Presented in modern dress, the play portrays Antigone as a congenital rebel who is in permanent revolt against the Establishment, an innocent, pure youthful idealist, who acts not out of religious or political motives but on principle and for reasons of personal conscience. Creon, on the other hand, is an intelligent, well meaning realist, who has the responsibility of maintaining tranquility in society, and pleads with Antigone to accept life as it is, with its need for expediency and compromises. But this is precisely what the nonconformist Antigone cannot accept, for she rejects personal security and happiness that entail surrender to the demands of real life, and will not accept a compromise that dooms her to life as a mediocrity in marriage and middle class society. Thus she says "No!" to life itself and goes to her death triumphantly, uncompromised and pure. Unlike Creon, who represents reason and practical experience in the trials of life, she is not prepared to model her life on the realists who capitulate to the imperatives of survival, but prefers perfection in death.

In his one-act horror play *Medea* (1946) Anouilh probes again the eternal conflict between the need for expedient accommodations to an impure world and the adherence to principle. Medea is portrayed in this play as a gypsy with a streak of savagery in her makeup. In this "battle of the sexes" we are asked to sympathize with Jason, for Medea is a monster who will not compromise with life as it is and accept peace and comfort as a goal. She must be true to her self — the evil in her nature — and so she destroys not only Jason's bride and her father, and her own sons, but also herself. In a final scene of horror she burns herself to death before Jason's eyes by setting fire to the wagon in which she had placed the bodies of her children.

It was also during the German occupation of France that the French existentialist philosopher Jean-Paul Sartre wrote his first play *The Flies* (1943). In this play Sartre succeeds in presenting both an existential reinterpretation of the myth of Orestes and Electra and a political attack on the French collaborators with the Germans. One of the reasons Sartre chose this myth for *The Flies* (a play which is, incidentally, one of the best introductions to his thought) was that his theme required a story full of horror, and the veil of myth also helped him get by the censors. Basic to Sartre's view of man is that all life is absurd, but that man is free. In this play there is no oracle of Delphi, no Apollo to impose the duty of vengeance upon Orestes, who has complete freedom, with all the choices in his own hands. Sartre changed the very meaning of the ancient myth by having Orestes kill Aegisthus and Clytemnestra not for revenge, but to validate his freedom from all authority. Originally a rootless and purposeless young man in exile, Orestes was converted to a philosophy of involvement. By the murders he reveals his social consciousness, and he commits them out of duty to the people so that they may be free. Actually, Aegisthus was from the beginning disgusted with power, guilt ridden by the deceit he must exercise. When Orestes has committed the murders he feels no remorse or fear, and denies all guilt, although the terrified Electra repudiates her part in the crimes. At the end there is no final judgment of Orestes, who simply renounces the power he has won, gives the people their freedom, and goes into exile hunted by the Furies in the form of huge flies that represent the guilt of the entire city.

Another distinguished French writer of Sartre's generation, Albert Camus, also a Nobel Prize winner, wrote a small collection of essays entitled *The Myth of Sisyphus* (1942), which proclaims the view that the life of modern man is absurd because most people are not aware that their activities and goals are hopeless. Using the myth of Sisyphus — eternally in Hades pushing uphill a rock that topples back when he reaches the top — Camus affirms that happiness is this endlessly repeated striving of man to reach some height, even if the effort is always frustrated. "The struggle itself toward the heights is enough to fill a man's heart. One must imagine Sisyphus happy." In a later essay, *Prometheus in the Underworld* (1946), Camus asks "What does Prometheus mean for the man of today?" His rebellion, says Camus, is still unfulfilled, for there are many today deprived of fire and the advances in civilization for which Prometheus suffered. But he also gave man the spirit of freedom. "In truth if Prometheus came back, men of today would act as the gods then did: they would nail him to the rock in the name of that humanism of which he is the first symbol . . . The chained hero maintains his tranquil faith in man in the face of lightning and thunder. Thus he is harder than his rock and more patient than his vulture. More than the revolt against the gods, it is this long obstinacy which has some meaning for us."

In England the adaptation of classical myth to the drama was to take a different form in the plays of T. S. Eliot. In four of his plays the dilemmas latent in the ancient stories suggested modern problems, and Eliot dealt with these using modern names and settings and introducing major revisions. The earliest of Eliot's myth-inspired plays is *The Family Reunion*, the Orestes story with divine retribution as interpreted by a Twentieth Century Christian. The play deals with the long spiritual exile of Harry Lord Monchensey, who had wished his wife dead. That unloved wife Mary died in a fall from an ocean liner, and Harry was not sure whether his guilt consisted in merely wishing her dead or in actually pushing her off, but in any case, his sin, for which he is pursued and tormented by the Furies, is finally expiated, assuring him reunion with God and redemption. In the *Cocktail Party* (1949), he tells the story of Alcestis in modern guise, introducing as an innovation the question of what happens to Alcestis when she returns from the dead. *The Confidential Clerk* (1953) is based on the myth of Ion, and *The Elder Statesman* (1958) on the old age of Oedipus.

In the 1920's the American dramatist Eugene O'Neill announced that he intended to write " . . . a modern psychological drama using one of the old legend plots of Greek tragedy . . . " In doing so he sought to domesticate Greek myth, by fusing myth, American cultural tradition and the present. In his massive modern trilogy *Mourning Becomes Electra* (1931) — the three plays are entitled *The Homecoming, The Hunted,* and *The Haunted* — O'Neill transmuted the sufferings of Agamemnon, Clytemnestra, Orestes and Electra of Greek tragedy into the ancestral woes of the New England Mannon family in the post-Civil War period. Weighed down by an ancestral curse the family moves inexorably to its doom generation after generation, as in the Greek story, and in the inevitable destruction of this once eminent family the "trapped" characters are impelled by unconscious Freudian drives that replace the concept of divine fate in the ancient myth. Uncontrollable sex, incest urges, the Oedipus complex, all have their effects as unconscious desires in sharp conflict with the conscious sham Puritan code of the community. The quarrel between Abraham and David Mannon, like that of Atreus and Thyestes, was inherited by the following generations. When General Ezra Mannon (Agamemnon) was away during the Civil War, his wife Christine (Clytemnestra) had a love affair with Adam

Brant (Aegisthus). When he returns after the war Christine causes Ezra's death. The daughter of Ezra and Christine Mannon, Lavinia (Electra), hates her mother and drives her reluctant brother Orin (Orestes) to murder Adam Brant, and Christine commits suicide. The guilt-laden Orin is haunted by the Furies — there is also an incestuous pull between him and Lavinia — and commits suicide. Alone, Lavinia locks herself up forever with her conscience inside the Mannon mansion. There is no happy ending for Orin, as there was for Orestes in the Greek source, because no divine or social justice can intervene when the family remains the ultimate source of values, inhibiting the individual, while inner compulsions in conflict with it tear him apart. Thus O'Neill substituted for the Greek perspectives Freudian determinism in conflict with Puritan tradition and the family. *Mourning Becomes Electra,* which is likely to remain a classic of the American theater, has been produced as an opera composed in 1967 by Marvin David Levy.

The same mythic material of the story of the House of Atreus was reinterpreted in a drastically different way by the American poet and dramatist Robinson Jeffers in his long dramatic poem *Tower Beyond Tragedy* (1925). This version emphasizes cruelty and violence in this doomed family, and the blood-lust and sex-lust in humans. Innovations are the incest theme between Orestes and Electra, the killing of Cassandra by Orestes in his madness, and the winning of political power at the end by Electra. Orestes finally recovers from his madness by a conversion, when he is mystically united with nature that is indifferent to man's suffering. The theme that life is inherently cruel is developed in another "play of cruelty" by Jeffers, his *At the Fall of An Age* (1933), a drama in which the revenge motive is dominant. Helen of Troy, having previously been raped by the ghost of Achilles, is murdered by Polyxo (widow of Tlepolemos, one of the men who died at Troy), who blames Helen for her suffering and seeks revenge. Jeffers' *Medea* (1946), freely adapted from Euripides' *Medea* but with emphasis on the sex-lust, cruelty and violence, was one of Judith Anderson's brilliant successes. In *The Cretan Woman* (1954), lust, violence, and brutality saturate the story of Phaedra, Hippolytus, and Theseus, with no pity in nature, no pity among humans in this play. To heighten the horror Theseus is made to kill Hippolytus in Phaedra's presence, after which she hangs herself.

A startling new reinterpretation of the Orestes story was attempted by Jack Richardson in his play *The Prodigal* (1960) which portrays Orestes as an anti-hero, a "beatnik" rebel who rejects all conventions, merely wants to have fun, has no filial devotion, no ideals, and no desire for revenge. He has been living at ease in his father's palace with full knowledge of the relationship between his mother and Aegisthus, and when Agamemnon returns he shows no respect for him as hero or father image. In fact Agamemnon allows himself to be killed because this is the only means he knows to force Orestes into action. Orestes refuses to become a part of all the killing, and is delighted to be exiled by Aegisthus to Athens with a pension. Whatever he may desire, however, after his father's murder the people want vengeance, and society finds him guilty of not avenging the murder of his father. At the end he is compelled to be true to the myth by returning home to do his duty, much against his better nature.

In *Orpheus Descending* (1957), Tennessee Williams combines Greek myth with Freudian psychology and Christian parallels. A disillusioned poet-musician, Val Xavier, has chanced upon a small bigoted Southern town named Twin Rivers, where he meets his Eurydice, Lady Torrance, who is married in a loveless union to Jabe Torrance (symbol of Hades and death). Though Val despises the town, he never emerges alive from this Hades. Lady falls in love with him, and as soon as she becomes pregnant by him she has no further need of him. After Jabe kills Lady, Val is killed by a lynch mob on Good Friday and torn apart by dogs. This Orpheus has become a sort of Christ figure who gives up his life for Eurydice.

The continued vitality and great popularity of the Orpheus myth in the Twentieth Century comes from its relevance to the modern dilemmas. Orpheus is essentially a myth-symbol of suffering and loneliness, who through the magic of song, poetry, art, transforms men from within by persuasion and charm. He reconciles opposites through love and death, not by violence and rebellion. The Prometheus myth, on the other hand, lends itself to adaptation more in a period of major societal challenges. In France alone between 1900 and 1960 the myth of Prometheus inspired

16 plays, nine essays, and three significant lyric poems. Indeed it is the Twentieth Century that has seen the figure of the Titan Prometheus elevated to a position of esteem and interest greater than at any time since the myth was invented. The myth of Prometheus, unlike that of Orpheus which concerns individual suffering, is a "collective myth" and so appeals to many authors because it symbolizes the problem of evil and suffering as well as rebellion to improve the lot of man. It is this century that has produced the term "Promethean Man" to characterize the daring and awesome advances of modern man.

The theme of the wanderer away from home in the story of Odysseus' return from Troy, and his efforts to regain his lost identity, have inspired two monumental modern masterpieces, James Joyce's great novel *Ulysses* (1922), and Nikos Kazantzakis' poem *The Odyssey: a Modern Sequel*. Through the figure of the adventurous exile of classical myth Joyce and Kazantzakis explored their own spiritual exile from their homelands, Ireland and Greece. Joyce's multi-dimensioned novel is in fact a modern prose epic of mankind that imitates Homer's *Odyssey* in many scenes and motifs, and in this way Joyce tried to give universal significance to one chaotic day in Dublin. The wanderer becomes an alienated middle-class business man, Leopold Bloom, modern man "exiled" spiritually from home, wife, children, but who finally "finds himself." The parallels Joyce constructed are numerous: the lost Leopold Bloom as a modern Odysseus who drifts through Dublin; Stephen Daedalus who represents Telemachus in search of a "father"; Mr. Deasy, a Nestor giving a lesson in history; the Library scene in which the conflict between Aristotelianism and Platonism reminds one of Scylla and Charybdis; Dignam's funeral is a Hades-like scene; the pub-barmaids patterned on the Sirens; Getrude McDowell, a kind of Nausicaä; the brothel of Bella Cohen, who is the counterpart of Circe; and Molly Bloom as a faithless Penelope. In the meeting of Bloom and Daedalus both are reborn: Daedalus to humanity and creativity, while Bloom, after a sort of mental slaying of the suitors, regains Molly and is transfigured by an affirmation of the basic goodness of life.

Nikos Kazantzakis' *Odyssey* is a vast epic poem, three times the size of Homer's, the greatest extension of the Greek mythic hero Odysseus in 3000 years. Through the figure of Odysseus Kazantzakis reconstructs his own life, his wanderings, doubts, explorations for a viable philosophy of commitment — in short, his search for identity and a spiritual homeland. Like himself, Kazantzakis' Odysseus is a driven wanderer, alienated from his home. After killing the suitors he leaves Ithaca for exile, but does not really know where he should go, and passes from the role of destroyer of civilization to the building of a utopia, only to retreat into asceticism and his inner self. Though a seeker of God, he abandons all religions and contemplates total freedom through suicide, but turns instead to Buddhism. Like the ancient Odysseus, Kazantzakis' hero has an intense love of life. At the end everything crumbles, but Odysseus retains his exultation in life, despite all the discontent and suffering. Thus through this alienated, disillusioned man, Kazantzakis tries to recreate the ancient heroic ideal in the modern world. In their efforts to test their own lives and the values of contemporary society by reinterpreting the myth of Odysseus, Joyce and Kazantzakis have created two great modern works that are likely to remain among the great classics of the world.

BIBLIOGRAPHY
For Reference and Further Study

Paperbacks are designated by an asterisk (*)

Dictionaries of Mythology

*Kirkwood, Gordon M. *A Short Guide to Classical Mythology*. New York: Holt, Rinehart & Winston, 1959.
*Oswalt, Sabine G. *Concise Encyclopedia of Greek and Roman Mythology*. Chicago: Follett, 1969.
   Generously illustrated with mythological subjects from Greek and Roman art.
Tripp, Edward. *Crowell's Handbook of Classical Mythology*. New York: Crowell, 1970.
*Van Aken, A. R. A. *The Encyclopedia of Classical Mythology*. Englewood Cliffs: Prentice-Hall, 1965.
   Randomly annotated with references to ancient and modern works of art influenced by classical myths.
*Zimmerman, John E. *Dictionary of Classical Mythology*. New York: Bantam, 1969.
   Some effort to indicate influence of myths on later Literature. To be used with caution.

Mythology Books

Fairbanks, Arthur. *The Mythology of Greece and Rome*. New York: Appleton, 1912.
Godolphin, Francis R. B. *Great Classical Myths*. New York: Modern Library, 1964.

Selections from classical literature based on mythic stories.

*Grant, Michael. *Myths of the Greeks and Romans*. New York: New American Library, 1962.

Occasional exploration of mythic themes and their influences on later literature.

*Graves, Robert. *The Greek Myths*. 2 vols. Baltimore: Penguin, 1955.

Idiosyncratic choice of aspects of classical myths to support a false theory of Greek and Roman myths.

*Hamilton, Edith. *Mythology*. New York: New American Library, 1940.

Largely a retelling of selected myths as romanticized narratives.

Kerényi, Károly. *The Gods of the Greeks*. New York: Grove, 1960.

Kerényi, Károly. *The Heroes of the Greeks*. New York: Grove, 1960.

Larousse Encyclopedia of Mythology. New York: Prometheus, 1960.

Profusely illustrated.

*Morford, Mark P. O., and Lenardon, R. J. *Classical Mythology*. New York: McKay, 1971.

Heavy emphasis on presentation of myths directly through the ancient sources.

Pinsent, J. *Greek Mythology*. London: Hamlyn, 1969.

Stunningly and profusely illustrated.

Pfister, Friedrich. *Greek Gods and Heroes*. London: Macgibbon & Kee, 1961.

*Rose, H. J. *A Handbook of Greek Mythology*. 6th Ed. New York: Dutton, 1959.

A learned work more useful for specialists and those with considerable knowledge of mythology than for the general student.

*Rose, H. J. *Gods and Heroes of the Greeks*. Cleveland: World Publishing, 1958.

A simplified smaller version of his *Handbook*.

Sabin, Frances, E. *Classical Myths That Live Today*. Rev. Ed. New York: Silver, Burdett, 1940.

*Schwab, Gustav B. *Gods and Heroes: Myths and Epics of Ancient*

Greece. New York: Fawcett, 1946.
Expanded narratives of classical myths as found in classical literature.
*Seltman, Charles T. *The Twelve Olympians*. New York: Crowell, 1962.

Near Eastern Myths

Brandon, Samuel G. F. *Creation Legends of the Ancient Near East*. London: Hodder & Stoughton, 1963.
Bratton, Fred. G. *Myths and Legends of the Ancient Near East*. New York: Crowell, 1970.
Gray, John. *Near Eastern Mythology*. London: Hamlyn, 1969.
*Hooke, Samuel H. *Middle Eastern Mythology*. Baltimore: Penguin, 1963.
Kramer, Samuel N. *Mythologies of the Ancient World*. Garden City: Doubleday, 1961.

The Nature of Myth

Barnard, Mary. *The Mythmakers*. Athens, Ohio: Ohio University Press, 1966.
*Eliade, Mircea. *Cosmos and History. The Myth of the Eternal Return*. New York: Harper & Row, 1959.
*Jung, Carl G., and Kerényi, Károly. *Essays on a Science of Mythology*. Princeton: Princeton University Press, 1949.
Murray, Henry A., ed. *Myth and Mythmaking*. Boston: Beacon, 1960.
Ohmann, Richard M., ed. *The Making of Myth*. New York: Putnam, 1962.

Special Aspects of Classical Mythology

*Allen, Richard H. *Star Names: Their Lore and Their Meanings*. Rev. Ed. New York: Dover, 1960.
*Campbell, Joseph. *The Hero With a Thousand Faces*. Cleveland: World Publishing, 1949.
*Cumont, Franz V. M. *Astrology and Religion Among the Greeks and Romans*. New York: Dover, 1960.

Galanopoulos, Angelos G., and Bacon, Edward. *Atlantis. The Truth Behind the Legend*. London: Nelson, 1969.

Kerényi, Károly. *Prometheus: Archetypal Image of Human Existence*. New York: Pantheon, 1963.

Luce, John V. *The End of Atlantis: New Light on an Old Legend*. London: Thames & Hudson, 1969.

Mavor, James W. *Voyage to Atlantis*. New York: Putnam, 1969.

*Mylonas, George E. *Eleusis and the Eleusinian Mysteries*. Princeton: Princeton University Press, 1961.

Olcott, William T. *Star Lore of All Ages*. New York: Putnam, 1911.

*Rank, Otto. *The Myth of the Birth of the Hero*. New York: Random House, 1959.

Schefold, Karl. *Myth and Legend in Early Greek Art*. New York: Abrams, 1966.

Slater, Philip E. *The Glory of Hera. Greek Mythology and the Greek Family*. Boston: Beacon, 1968.

Somerset, Fitzroy R. (Lord Raglan). *The Hero: a Study in Tradition, Myth, and Drama*. London: Watts, 1949.

*Wechsler, Herman J. *Gods and Goddesses in Art and Legend*. New York: Washington Square Press, 1961.

Influences of Classical Myths

*Agard, Walter R. *Classical Myths in Sculpture*. Madison: University of Wisconsin Press, 1951.

*Asimov, Isaac. *Words from Myths*. New York: New American Library, 1961.

Belli, Angela. *Ancient Greek Myths and Modern Drama*. New York: New York University Press, 1969.

Blake, Harriet M. *Classical Myth in the Poetic Drama of the Age of Elizabeth*. Lancaster: Steinman & Pfaetz, 1912.

*Bush, Douglas. *Mythology and the Renaissance Tradition in English Poetry*. Rev. Ed. New York: Norton: 1963.

*Bush, Douglas. *Mythology and the Romantic Tradition in English Poetry*. New York: Norton, 1963.

Bush, Douglas. *Pagan Myth and Christian Tradition in English Poetry*. Philadelphia: American Philosophical Society, 1968.

Dickinson, Hugh. *Myth on the Modern Stage*. Urbana: University of Illinois Press, 1969.

Feder, Lillian. *Ancient Myth in Modern Poetry*. Princeton: Princeton University Press, 1971.

Friedman, John B. *Orpheus in the Middle Ages*. Cambridge, Mass.: Harvard University Press, 1970.

Conradie, P. J. *The Treatment of Greek Myths in Modern French Drama*. Stellenbosch: Stellenbosch University Press, 1963.

Gayley, Charles. *The Classic Myths in English Literature and in Art*. New Ed. New York: Blaisdell, 1911.

Mayerson, Philip. *Classical Mythology in Literature, Art and Music*. New York: Ginn, 1971.

Merivale, Patricia. *Pan the Goat-God. His Myth in Modern Times*. Cambridge, Mass.: Harvard University Press, 1969.

Norton, Dan S., and Rushton, Peters. *Classical Myths in English Literature*. New York: Rinehart, 1962.

Panofsky, Dora and Erwin. *Pandora's Box: The Changing Aspects of a Mythical Symbol*. New York: Pantheon, 1956.

Root, Robert K. *Classical Mythology in Shakespeare*. New York: Gordian, 1965.

Scherer, Margaret R. *The Legends of Troy in Art and Literature*. New York: Phaedon, 1963.

Sewell, Elizabeth. *The Orphic Voice: Poetry and Natural History*. New York: Yale University Press, 1960.

*Seznec, Jean. *The Survival of the Pagan Gods. The Mythological Tradition and Its Place in Renaissance Humanism and Art*. New York: Harper & Row, 1953.

*Stanford, William B. *The Ulysses Theme: A Study in the Adaptability of a Traditional Hero*. Ann Arbor: University of Michigan Press, 1954.

Strauss, Walter A. *Descent and Return. The Orphic Theme in Modern Literature*. Cambridge, Mass.: Harvard University Press, 1971.

Vinge, Louise. *The Narcissus Theme in Western Literature*. Lund: Gleerup, 1967.

Ward, Anne G. *The Quest for Theseus*. New York: Praeger, 1970.

Watson-Williams, Helen. *André Gide and the Greek Myth*. Oxford: Clarendon Press, 1966.

Weitzmann, Kurt. *Greek Mythology in Byzantine Art*. Princeton: Princeton University Press, 1951.

White, John J. *Mythology in The Modern Novel*. Princeton: Princeton University Press, 1972.

*Yohannon, John D. *Joseph and Potiphar's Wife in World Literature*. New York: New Directions, 1968.

Young, Arthur M. *Legend Builders of the West*. Pittsburgh: Pittsburgh University Press, 1958.

Young, Arthur M. *Troy and Her Legend*. Pittsburgh: Pittsburgh University Press, 1948.

INDEX
of Recurrent Themes

GENERAL INDEX
References to works of literature, art and music are in italics
Accented syllables are followed by accent marks
See also the Note on the Pronunciation of Names — Page vi

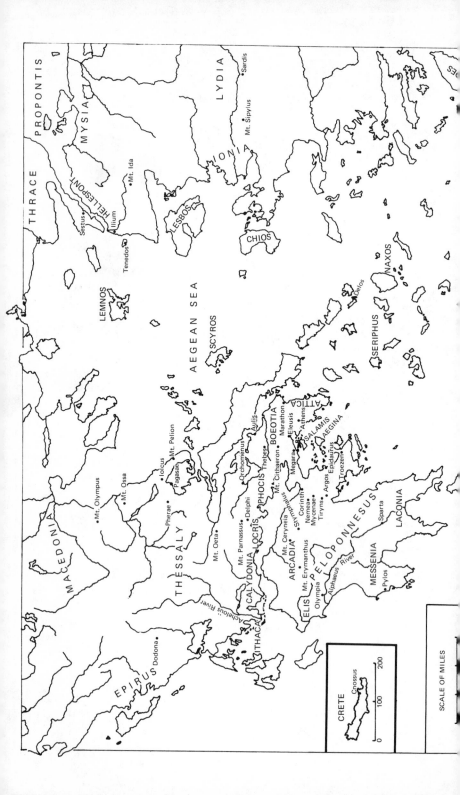

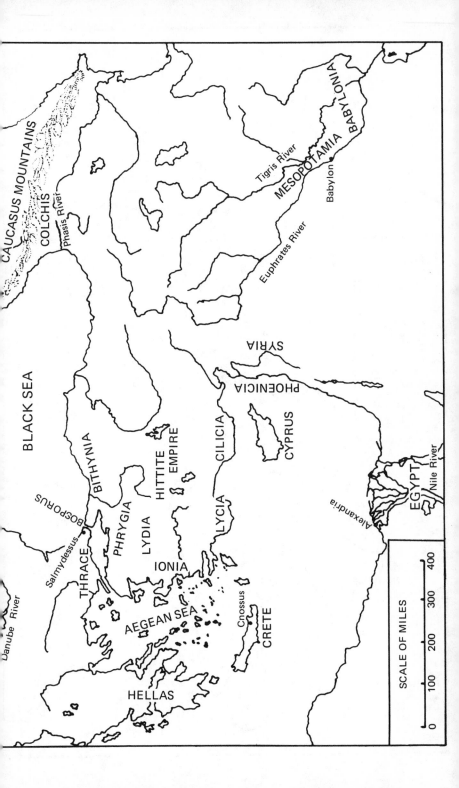

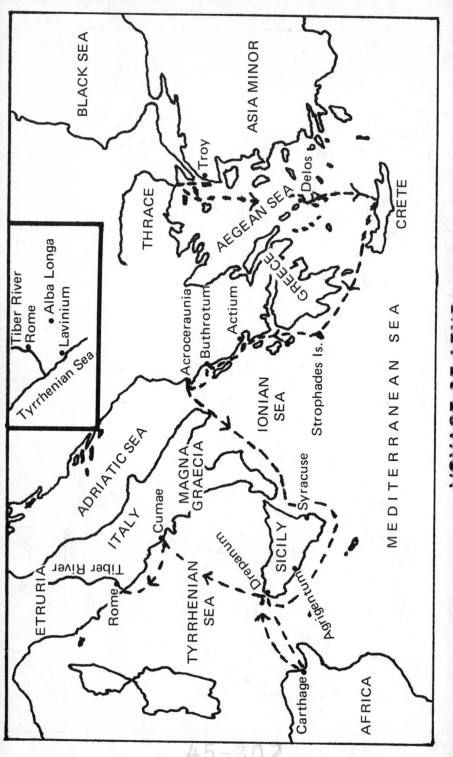

BLACK SEA

ASIA MINOR

THRACE

Troy

Delos

AEGEAN SEA

GREECE

CRETE

Tiber River
Rome
• Alba Longa
• Lavinium

Tyrrhenian Sea

Acroceraunia
Buthrotum

Actium

MEDITERRANEAN SEA

ADRIATIC SEA

IONIAN SEA

Strophades Is.

ITALY

MAGNA
GRAECIA

Cumae

Syracuse

SICILY

Drepanum

TYRRHENIAN
SEA

Tiber River

ETRURIA

Rome

Agrigentum

Carthage

AFRICA

45-302